John Dee's Five Books of Mystery

John Dee's Five Books of Mystery

Original Sourcebook of Enochian Magic

From the collected works known as
MYSTERIORUM LIBRI QUINQUE

Joseph H. Peterson, Editor

WEISER BOOKS
Boston, MA/York Beach, ME

First published in 2003 by
Red Wheel/Weiser, LLC
York Beach, ME
With offices at:
368 Congress Street
Boston, MA 02210
www.redwheelweiser.com

Library of Congress Cataloging-in-Publication Data
Dee, John, 1527–1608
    John Dee's five books of mystery : original sourcebook of Enochian magic :
from the collected works known as Mysteriorum libri quinque / Joseph H. Peterson,
editor.
        p. cm.
    Originally published: The five books of mystical experience. [S.I.] : A. Megan,
1985, in the series: Magnum Opus Hermetic Sourceworks. Includes bibliographical
references and index.
        ISBN 1-57863-178-5 (alk. paper)
        1. Enochian magic. I. Title: Five books of mystery. II. Peterson, Joseph H. III.
Title.
    BF1623.E55 D45 2003
    133—dc21

                                                                    2002151947

Typeset in Sabon

Printed in the United States of America
VG

10 09 08 07 06 05 04 03
  8 7 6 5 4 3 2 1

The paper used in this publication meets the minimum requirements of the American
National Standard for Information Sciences—Permanence of Paper for Printed
Library Materials Z39.48-1992 (R1997).

Dedication

For my wife, Candy. You have supported me in so many ways, especially by helping me sort out and keep track of all the piles of obscure dead guy stuff. Without your help, so many things would have been impossible.

For Kerry, Sarah, Lisa, and Karl. You are the best kids a parent could ever hope for. Thanks for all the times you shared your precious computer time.

For my close friend, Paul Deneka, who introduced me to John Dee's writings and continues to share my enthusiasm for obscure dead guys.

For the Board of Trustees of the British Museum who granted me special permission to study manuscripts while I was under their age requirements, helped me during the many years that have passed since then, and gave me permission to publish this unique material from their collections.

For my friend, Roger Williamson, at Magus Books for his encouragement and support over the years.

For Jill Rogers at Red Wheel/Weiser, who has been great to work with. Thanks for helping to make this a better book.

Finally, for Betty Lundsted, who is sincerely missed.

Contents

PREFACE TO THE REVISED EDITION

Dr. John Dee (1527 to 1608 or 1609) has been the subject of much interest in several fields. Several good book-length studies of him have appeared,[1] as well as numerous articles.[2] My intent in presenting this text is not to recap Dee's life or present a new perspective, but to fill in an important gap that has been generally neglected. The manuscript presented adds considerable detail for the years 1581–1583, by most accounts the climax of his career. It sheds light on Dee's politics, science, and occultism.

For the first edition of this text, I had the simple goal of eliminating two major barriers to the study of John Dee and Edward Kelley. These barriers are availability and legibility of the material. With this new edition, I hope to address two other problems as well. First, the English of Dee's day was somewhat different from that spoken today, so I have added many footnotes to clarify obscurities in the language. I have also translated the frequent Latin passages. Second, the subject matter of the

---

1 I. R. F. Calder, "John Dee Studied as an English Neoplatonist," 2 vols. Ph. D. diss. (The Warberg Institute, London University, 1952); Peter J. French, *John Dee: The World of an Elizabethan Magus* (London: Routledge & Kegan Paul, 1972); Nicholas H. Clulee, *John Dee's Natural Philosophy—between science and religion.* (London and New York: Routledge, 1988); William H. Sherman, *John Dee, the Politics of Reading and Writing in the English Renaissance* (Amherst: University of Massachusetts Press, 1995).

2 See list in Peter French, *John Dee: The World of an Elizabethan Magus,* pp. 216–29.

text, medieval and Renaissance magic, assumes a view of the universe not commonly held today. To further clarify the text in this context, I have expanded the introduction and index and explained otherwise obscure references in the footnotes. I have also added supplementary material from Dee's diary and other manuscripts.

J. Peterson, 1999

ABBREVIATIONS

Calder   I. R. F. Calder, *John Dee studied as an English neoplatonist*, Ph. D. thesis, 2 vols. (London, University of London, 1952.)

CHM   John Dee, *Compendium Heptarchiæ Mysticæ*, British Library, additional manuscript 36674, fol. 167r ff.

GRM   John Dee, *General and rare memorials pertayning to the perfect art of navigation* (London, 1577).

HM   John Dee, *De Heptarchia Mystica,* British Library, Sloane manuscript 3191.

MLQ   *Mysteriorum Libri Quinque*, British Library, Sloane manuscript 3188.

Monas   *Monas Hieroglyphica;* tr. C. H. Josten, in the journal AMBIX, XII (1964), 84–221.

R&W   R. J. Roberts and A. G. Watson, *John Dee's Library Catalogue* (London: The Bibliographical Society, 1990).

TFR   *A True & Faithful Relation of what passed for many Yeers Between Dr. John Dee . . . and Some Spirits,* ed. Meric Casaubon (London, 1659).

INTRODUCTION

These secret writings of John Dee, one of the leading scientists and occultists in Elizabethan England, record in minute detail his researches into the occult. They were discovered in a hidden compartment of an old chest along with various magical implements. Although the angels made him swear never to reveal these doctrines to anyone not sanctioned by them, he complained, "If no man, by no means, shall perceive anything hereof by me, I would think that I should not do well." Nevertheless, these pages were carefully concealed, and nearly lost forever. Although this present work is concerned primarily with his occult experiments, through it, we catch many glimpses of Elizabethan life and politics.

Dr. Dee represents the true Renaissance man—a master of many areas of learning. He was born in 1527 and lived at the height of the English Renaissance. Dee's knowledge included astronomy, mathematics, navigation, medicine, geography, history, music, painting, astrology, and the occult sciences.

In many ways, Dee lived at the center of conflicting forces and ideas—tradition vs. reformation, science vs. magic, Christianity vs. paganism (that is, Judaism, Hermeticism, and even studies of Arabic traditions). By studying Dee, we can gain insight into all these subjects and into the Renaissance as a whole. We can even throw light on our own struggle to reconcile our own conflicts.[1]

Dee had many famous and powerful friends and was heavily involved in politics. He became scientific advisor and astrologer to Queen Elizabeth, who occasionally visited him at his home at Mortlake. He was instrumental in planning the expansion of the British Empire, exploring the New World, and, with the help of angelic agents, ushering in the new age as well. One of the main objectives of his life's work was to bring about religious and social reform. It has been suggested[2] that in this endeavor he was, to some extent, successful.

Dee began his "mystical experiments" with a solid foundation in medieval and Renaissance science, magic, Kabbalah, and the Hermetic arts. Further mysteries were revealed by the "angels" who manifested themselves, ultimately resulting in a new, unified occult system.[3] This occult system is perhaps closer to a face-lift than a new system. Most of it would have been familiar to occultists of the day, but with a veneer of new names and symbols.

Aside from the mechanical details of Dee's system for communicating with angels, these records reveal that the angels were interested in and involved with the exploration and colonization of the New World, and in heralding in a new age or new world order. The one aspect of these writings that has fascinated most, however, is that the angels

---

[1] Many of these apparent conflicts are still with us today. Charles Tart, *Body Mind Spirit* (Charlottesville: Hampton Roads, 1997), observes that Scientism, a belief that scoffs at anything that doesn't fit our supposedly scientific beliefs, has become "the world's most powerful (and negative) religion." It is interesting to note that most modern religious studies carefully avoid Scientism.

[2] Frances A. Yates, *The Rosicrucian Enlightenment* (Boulder: Shambhala, 1978), p. xii.

[3] Some have argued there are actually two systems: the Heptarchic system (represented by this manuscript and Dee's *Heptarchia Mystica*), and the Enochian system, represented by later records, especially TFR.

delivered a complete book in an otherwise unknown language. They claimed this book, named *Loagaeth,* to be of utmost importance. Its language is the true language of creation so sought after by Kabbalists and by Dee himself.[4] This "angelic book" was later used to extract a long series of messages (or "calls") in yet another unknown language, called Enochian.

Interest in John Dee and his occult activities has increased tremendously in recent years. One reason for this is the growing debate over the importance of Dee's role in history by such eminent scholars as Francis Yates,[5] Wayne Shumaker, and, more recently, William Sherman. Another reason for Dee's popularity is undoubtedly the fact that his system was used and adapted by the Hermetic Order of the Golden Dawn, and, subsequently, by Aleister Crowley. If one examines the Golden Dawn material, its appeal soon becomes clear: It draws together various occult methods into a highly coherent system. In adapting Dee's system, various additions, omissions, and mistakes were made. This departure was compounded by uncritical, although imaginative, treatments of the Golden Dawn and Crowley material by some authors. The net result is a maze of misinformation.[6] The material presented here provides us with the keys necessary for understanding Dee's original system as a whole. Since its previous

---

4   See C. H. Josten's translation of Dee's *Monas Hieroglyphica* (AMBIX, XII, 1964, 84–221), and Nicholas Clulee's analysis in *John Dee's Natural Philosophy* (London: Routledge, 1988), p. 77 ff.

5   Although there has been some criticism of Dr. Yates' work in recent years, I have found the views of Roberts and Watson to be the most balanced: "The influence of the later work of Yates herself will be widely apparent for although that often seems hasty and over-enthusiastic, our own research has frequently confirmed rather than contradicted hers. . . ." Julian Roberts and Andrew Watson, *John Dee's Library Catalogue* (London: The Bibliographical Society, 1990), p. 26.

6   R. Turner writes, "Mistakes abound in both the Crowley and Regardie printed Enochian texts. I counted 91 in the first Call alone when comparing these with Dee's original manuscript (see Sloane 3191, British Museum)." Cited by Colin Wilson, "Introduction to the Necronomicon," *Gnostica,* 48, Nov. 1978, p. 62.

editions were very limited in availability,[7] it has largely been ignored, in spite of its importance.

Dee studies have created two radically different pictures of Dee— one as Magus, and the other as scientist-politician. I hope this volume will help bridge the gap. This polarization is partly caused by the lack of availability of Dee's writings. Those interested only in the occult have largely ignored Dee's published output, and those who focus on his published output will find very little evidence of occult influences. Placing the focus on Dee's public writings, however, can give the modern reader the mistaken impression that occultism was not central to his thinking. This is simply because, in Dee's day, the occult was a dangerous pastime, placing you at risk, not just from hostile spirits, but from the frightened public. We would do well to keep in mind the fate of the less cautious magus Giordano Bruno, who was burned alive at the stake by the Inquisition only a few years after Dee recorded these accounts. Dee's childhood idols, Roger Bacon, Trithemius, Agrippa, Paracelsus, and others, all had suffered greatly because of their reputations as magi. Dee himself was imprisoned early in life, an experience he was careful to avoid thereafter. His thoughts and motivations, however, centered around his "mystical experiments." In addition, there is an "anti-manuscript" bias to overcome. Although many of Dee's books were widely circulated, they were not intended for publication, but rather were "directed inward, to an extremely restricted circle" for private political aims.[8]

Another goal in presenting this text is to help elucidate the tradition in which Dee's occult endeavors took place. Although it has repeatedly been observed that Henry Cornelius Agrippa was a major

---

7   The first edition was limited to 500 copies. Another version was produced by
    Christopher Whitby as his doctoral thesis. This had a small reprinting as *John
    Dee's Actions with Spirits,* 2 vols. (New York: Garland, 1991).

8   William Sherman, *John Dee,* p. 149.

influence on Dee, most have concluded that Dee's system is highly nontraditional. This view is distorted by the fact that most attention has centered around an isolated set of records that describe a system that, on the surface at least, appears to be highly original.[9] I hope to show that Dee and his spirit medium, Edward Kelley, were following traditional methods, especially during their earlier efforts, and that his later methods are adaptations of traditional ones, used within a traditional framework.

Dee's writings also are of interest in that they are a record of the most educated English of Shakespeare's age. To some extent, Dee is even said to have influenced the English language.[10]

Dee's Early Period

John Dee was born in London on July 13, 1527. His father, Rowland Dee, was an official at the court of Henry VIII. John was born shortly after Luther's break with Rome, and immediately after England's, during a period of radical reform. The resurgence of classical Greek studies combined with new interest in Hebrew studies to create Renaissance Neoplatonism. Renaissance philosophers sought to integrate Greek and Hebrew traditions in an attempt to unify the rapidly disintegrating religious factions and end the constant political strife. They were thus the forerunners or prophets of the Rosicrucian and Illuminati movements.

By the age of 23, Dee had already established a brilliant reputation, lecturing in Paris on Euclid. At age 31 (1558), he published his first

---

9   These records were published in 1659 by Meric Casaubon as *A True & Faithful Relation . . . Between Dr. John Dee . . . and Some Spirits* (TFR). Casaubon's main intent in publishing this material was to discredit Dee's reputation.

10 For example, he is credited with coining the word "unit," which he used to translate the Greek "monas." He also coined the word "Britannia."

major work, *Aphoristic Introduction* (Propædeumata Aphoristica), and at age 37 (1564), his *Monas Hieroglyphica*. The *Monas* is a highly esoteric work. In it, he claims to be in possession of the most secret mysteries. He wrote it in twelve days, while apparently in a peak (mystical) state: "[I am] the pen merely of [God] Whose Spirit, quickly writing these things through me, I wish and I hope to be."[11] He claimed the work would revolutionize astronomy, alchemy, mathematics, linguistics, mechanics, music, optics, magic, and adeptship.[12]

Like the *Monas Hieroglyphica*, the angel magic in the *Mysteriorum Libri Quinque* seeks a higher wisdom than science, religion, or Jewish Kabbalah—one that will unite them all, convince atheists, convert Jews as well as pagans, and heal Christendom.

John Dee, the Politician

The Renaissance saw a giant leap in the evolution of the Information Age. Printed works, a recent innovation, were becoming more and more available, and manuscript collections were threatened with neglect. Dee was fascinated with books and spent vast amounts of energy and money collecting them. Eventually Dee's library became "Elizabethan England's greatest library,"[13] attracting scholars and dignitaries alike. It is possible that Dee's inspiration and model for his library came from Johannes Trithemius, one of the greatest scholars and occultists of the sixteenth century. While abbot of the monastery of Sponheim in Germany, Trithemius built a library of unparalleled importance, and turned one of the poorest monasteries in the

---

11   *Monas,* Theorem 23.

12   *Monas,* dedication to King Maximilian, passim, pp. 115 ff.

13   Peter J. French, *John Dee, The World of an Elizabethan Magus,* 1972, pp. 40 ff.

Palatinate into an "obligatory" place of pilgrimage for scholars.[14] As William Sherman has noted, "Renaissance libraries were powerful sites of intellectual creativity, social status, and political influence." As such, their owners "were at once empowered and endangered by their collections and skills."[15] This must have been a source of great anxiety to Dee.

Dee's library was a bustle of activity, especially in 1583, with frequent planning sessions for nautical expeditions, visitors borrowing and lending books, dignitaries, including the queen, and others, such as Francis Bacon, who sought Dee's advice and help.[16]

Plans for the New World and the New Age

Perhaps Dee's greatest legacy is his seminal role in building Britain into a major maritime power.[17] He is usually credited with coining the phrase "British Empire." Dee played a prominent role in plans to colonize the New World (involving Lord Burghley, John Davis, Adrian Gilbert, and Sir Walter Raleigh), and consulted the angels quite often about the venture. His interest was not merely patriotic.[18] He had a far-sighted plan for the new (or rather restored) British Empire to compete

---

14   Hans Ankwicz-Kleehoven observes, "Just as no distinguished foreigner at the beginning of the nineteenth century omitted to pay his respects to Goethe in Weimar, so it was good form in the Germany of circa 1500 to have called on Trithemius at Sponheim." Cited in Ioan P. Couliano, *Eros and Magic in the Renaissance* (Chicago: University of Chicago Press, 1987), p. 166.

15   William Sherman, *John Dee*, p. 51.

16   William Sherman has given us an excellent sense of it in his book; see especially p. 40.

17   "Dee could hardly have held a more prominent place in . . . the genesis of the British Empire." See William Sherman, *John Dee*, pp. 148 ff and passim.

18   A large element of Dee's patriotism was his fascination with the Arthurian legends. He was largely responsible for reviving interest in them. Dee believed himself to be of royal descent.

with (or replace) the Hispano-Papal empire. Part of his justification was the same as Rome's—to "carry the name of Jesus among the infidells to the great glory of God."[19] The magnitude of his vision is reflected in the vast extent of the empire that Britain went on to establish.

Dee associated the new empire and the New World with the new age. He was fascinated by the apocalyptic prophecies of his day, and tried his own hand at them based on his knowledge of astrology. He believed the new age would begin in a few years, perhaps in 1583 or 1584. He based this on astronomical models of world history published by Trithemius *(De Septem Secundeis)* and Cyprian Leowitz *(De coniunctionibus magnis).*[20] The fact that Dee dated two of his works[21] using his calculation of the "world year" allows us to calculate where he thought the world was in the cycle. These works place the start of the cycles at 3763 B.C.[22] Nevertheless, Dee felt the end of the world was immanent, largely based on astronomical observations.[23] The coming great conjunction was foreshadowed by the appearance of a supernova in 1572, a comet in 1577, and a solar eclipse in 1582.

---

[19] British Library, Sloane manuscript 3188, fol. 65a. See also John Dee, *General and Rare Memorials pertayning to the Perfect Arte of NAVIGATION (GRM)* (London: John Daye, 1577).

[20] Johannes Trithemius in *De Septem Secundeis* (translation in William Lilly, *Worlds Catastrophe,* London, 1647), wrote that world history was governed by the rules of seven angels, each ruling 354 years and 4 months. The angels told Dee that "the 7 Governours have almost ended their Government" (TFR, p. 4). Dee's copy of Cyprian Leowitz, *De Conjunctionibus Magnis Insignioribus Superiorum Planetarum* (Leuingen, 1564), has "underlinings and a few notes" (item 631, R&W).

[21] GRM (1577) is dated 5540, and *A Playne Discourse . . . concerning the needful reformation of ye vulgar kallender* (Oxford: Bodleian Library, Ashmole MS 1789, article 3, 1582) is dated 5545.

[22] The title page for Dee's *General and Rare Memorials* shows a timeline of history of something over 6,000 years. If 6,000 years is significant to him as it was to others, his calculations would put the end at A.D. 2037.

[23] See also I. R. F. Calder, "John Dee Studied as an English Neoplatonist," chapter 9, section 3.

In his scrying experiments,[24] the angels tell Dee and Kelley that "the tyme of God's visitation" was "8." Dee's speculation that this might mean 1588 seemed to be confirmed in later scrying sessions.[25]

Dee found political authority for the British Empire in the accounts of King Arthur and Owen Madoc, a legendary Welsh prince said to have discovered America in 1170.[26] To compete with the spiritual authority of Rome, however, Dee sought divine authority from the angels and God himself. The angels told him what he wanted to hear—that "the World begynnes with thy doings."[27] Thus his scrying, publications, and political activities were all part of his grand scheme to unify the peoples, religions, and languages of the world through universal knowledge. An element of this plan was to convert the pagans of the New World, and the Jews.[28]

The angels revealed details of the New World and new age on several occasions. For example: "What I speak hath not byn reuealed, no not in these last tymes, of the second last world. But I begynne new worldes, new people, new kings, & new knowledge of a new Gouernment." "New worlds, shall spring of these. New manners: strange men:" "The old ways cease, the new begin."[29]

After the appearance of the Polish prince, Albrecht (or Albertus) Laski, Dee shifted his hope for a royal patron to Europe. In the end, Dee failed to convince any of his would-be royal patrons of the cosmic

---

24 *Mysterium Libri Quinque* (MLQ), 16 November 1582.

25 TFR, p. 43.

26 I. R. F. Calder, "John Dee Studied as an English Neoplatonist," chapter 8, section 8. See also William Sherman, *John Dee,* pp. 187, 188.

27 The Archangel Uriel, 11 March 1582.

28 See *Monas,* p. 133, "the Hebrew cabbalist . . . will own that, without regard to person, the same benevolent God is not only [the God] of the Jews, but of all peoples, nations, and languages."

29 Bynepor, 20 November 1582; Medicina Dei, 24 March 1583; Michael, 23 May 1583.

plan. He was also thwarted by the papal nuncio (ambassador) who managed to have him and Kelley expelled by Rudolf. Dee was wise enough to decline an "invitation" to Rome.[30]

Renaissance Magic

By the Renaissance, magic had developed a complex theoretical and philosophical foundation. There was also a considerable amount of practical literature in circulation. Dee's public and secret writings show the remarkable depth and breadth of his studies of magical literature. The classical philosophers, especially Plato and Aristotle, were the foundation on which the so-called Neoplatonic philosophers built. Plotinus, Porphyry, Proclus, Iamblicus, and the Christian Pseudo-Dionysius were all familiar to Dee, as were the Italian Neoplatonic revivalists Ficino, Pico, and others.

The practical literature largely relies on knowing the secret names of God (mostly from the Hebrew Old Testament)[31] and of the angels or spirits themselves. The more cautious methods involve praying to God directly to send his angels.[32] The less cautious methods involve appealing to the spirits directly. The use of consecrated tools in ceremonial magic reflects their use in religious ceremonies. Most of the literature also deals with the use of talismans or symbols of some kind, and often with squares of letters or numbers.[33]

---

[30] A similar "invitation" led Giordano Bruno to his death at the stake in 1600.

[31] For example, "AGLA" and "ARARITA" are acronyms derived from verses of scripture. See Cornelius Agrippa, *De occulta philosophia Libri Tres* (Leiden: E. J. Brill, 1992), book 3, chapter xi, p. 428.

[32] For example, Arbatel, *De Magia Veterum* (Basel, 1575), p. 21, Aphor. 14: "da mihi unum de spiritibus tuis, qui me doceat ea, quae vis nos discere & cognoscere, ad laudem & honorem tuum & utilitatem proximi." ("Grant me therefore one of thy spirits, who may teach me those things which thou wouldest have me to know and learn, to thy praise and glory, and the profit of our neighbour.")

[33] For example, Cornelius Agrippa, *De occulta philosophia*, book 2, chap. 22, pp. 314–18.

The object of these practices, often called "experiments," is sometimes as sublime as the vision of God, but frequently as base as the recovery of stolen goods or the discovery of treasure. The mention of treasure during a scrying session with Barnabas Saul (22 December 1581) probably reflects the grimoire he is using more than a specific inquiry by Dee.

John Dee, The Magus

Dee's reputation as a magus, or rather a conjurer, started fairly early in his life and has continued to this day.[34] While he was highly respected as a man of great learning within the scholarly community and court circles, the less educated came to fear him. He was even briefly imprisoned in 1555 on charges that he tried to enchant Queen Mary. He is said to have been the model for Prospero in Shakespeare's play *The Tempest*.

In his explanatory note to the present work, Dee writes that his interest shifted more toward the occult after becoming convinced of the hopelessness of human endeavors as paths to wisdom. Sloane 3188 records his earliest occult experiments centered around scrying. These early methods were remarkably consistent with the occultism prevalent at the time, and Dee seems to be as widely read here as he was in science. He mentions the famous occultists Cornelius Agrippa and Johann Reuchlin. The widely known *Heptameron* of Peter de Abano and Arbatel's *Of Magic* are also mentioned, even though he did not include them in his *externa bibliotheca*.

Dee's interest in angelology is indicated by his heavy annotations of such works as Pseudo-Dionysius' *Coelestis hierarchia*, Richard of St. Victor's *De superdivina trinitate* (1510), Scalinger's *Exotericarum*

---

34 There have been a number of recent books and movies with the theme of Dee's magic.

exercitationum liber decimus (1557), Pompilius Azalus' *De omnium rebus naturalibus* (1554), and J. Rivius' *Opera theologica* (1562).[35]

Although Dee was careful not to catalog his more dangerous volumes, other sources can be identified or deduced. One of these is *Liber Juratus,* or the *Sworne Book of Honorius.* Sloane 313 (late fourteenth or early fifteenth century) is known to have been in his collection and contains marginal notes in his handwriting.[36] *Liber Juratus* contains detailed instructions for communicating with spirits, as well as obtaining the sight of God through the use of an elaborate sigil, named the *Sigillum Dei Aemeth.* Dee is directed by the angels to use this sigil "which is allready perfected in a boke of thyne." Dee is also promised the sight of God ("videbis Deum").[37] Another source that Dee mentions is the magical text *Aldaraia sive Soyga* (discussed below), which has squares of magical letters and heavy astrological elements.

In addition to these, I believe that two other magical texts can be identified as having been used by Dee. The first is Sloane 3849 article 1, "Manner of proceding in order to discover in the crystall," in which the three angels Anchor, Anachor, and Anilos are central. This, or a similar text, seems to be behind Dee's first scrying session with Kelley, in which they try to call forth these three spirits.

Another magical text I believe may have been used is Sloane 3854. The first part includes article 4 ("Book of Consecrations")[38] and article 5 ("Experimenta de Speculo"). In the blank space between these two articles

---

[35]   R&W, p. 29.

[36]   R&W, p. 168. They catalog it as DM 70 and note, "On fol.9 (originally the first leaf, fol.1–8 having been misbound) is [Dee's ladder symbol] and, very faint, 'Fragmentum Magicum,' which may be in Dee's hand. At the foot is 'Sum Ben: Jonsonij liber.'"

[37]   Sloane 3188 fol. 48r.

[38]   A version of this text with discussion is included in Richard Kieckhefer's *Forbidden Rites: A Necromancer's Manual of the Fifteenth Century* (University Park: Pennsylvania State University Press, 1997), pp. 8–10, p. 256 ff.

(folio 75r) a second hand, which I believe can be identified as Edward Kelley's, has written some notes. This manuscript is also bound with the most complete and correct manuscript of *Liber Juratus* that I have seen.

There are many examples of medieval and Renaissance magic texts with similar methods. I include some examples in the appendices.

Dee's system started with some Hebrew-centered Kabbalah like that he found in the writings of Reuchlin. Kabbalistic concepts abound, including his use of Hebrew etymology, traditional Hebrew names of God and angels, and extracting names from tables of letters à la Abulafia. Dee had a large Hebrew collection in his library, and took many of the volumes with him to the continent in 1583, showing sustained interest.

Nevertheless, in the end his *Sigillum Dei Aemeth* replaced the traditional Hebrew names with new names, and his angelic book was not in Hebrew, but a new (or unknown old) language. This may reflect Dee's (or Kelley's) mistrust of Jews,[39] or perhaps it may have been a way to compensate for Kelley's lack of knowledge of Hebrew and traditional Kabbalah. In any event, it is interesting to note that what Dee found in these actions is exactly what he expected to discover. Instead of the confusing maze of corruptions and variants found in the grimoires, he found an uncorrupted way of communicating with angels based on their own language, and on mathematics.

The first angels to make their appearance at the scrying sessions all belong to the Judeo-Christian tradition. They are later supplemented with otherwise unknown names, derived mathematically from letter squares. Dee is careful to catalog their jurisdictions, apparel, and symbols for future use. The revealed method of invoking their help is described in detail in the action of 17 November 1582.

---

39 Judaism was outlawed in England and much of Europe at the time. Note Dee's comment "we can hardly trust anything in the Jews hands . . . they are a stiff-necked people and dispersed all the world over."

In addition to the seals of the spirits, the ritual apparatus included several other items: various scrying stones, sometimes set in a frame; a "holy table" on which was painted or engraved various symbols; wax seals called *Æmeth;* a ring and lamin to be worn by the practitioner; and the rod "el," divided into three parts, the ends painted black, the middle red.

The Mysterious *Book of Soyga*

As mentioned above, Dee refers in several places to a magical text named *Aldaraia sive Soyga.* Since Roberts' and Watson's 1990 book, *John Dee's Library Catalogue,*[40] two manuscripts of this work have been identified by Deborah E. Harkness. One is Sloane 8 in the British Library, and the other is Bodley 908 in the Bodleian library. It is possible that Sloane 8 was, in fact, the manuscript to which Dee refers in his records.[41]

In their very first scrying session with Kelley, Dee asks the angels, "Ys my book, of Soyga, of any excellency?" (10 March 1582). He laments at that time, "Oh, my great and long desyre hath byn to be hable to read those Tables of Soyga." *Liber Loagaeth* (Sloane 3189) has several tables from Aldaraia/Soyga appended (in Dee's handwriting—not Kelley's, as in the rest of the manuscript). In addition, Dee's statement, "Soyga: otherwise named ysoga, and Agyos, literis transpositis" is, in fact, a direct quote from the *Aldaraia.*[42] The angel Il responds, "Soyga signifieth not Agyos," in direct contradiction. This

---

[40] They list it as DM 166, pg 183.

[41] See Jim Reeds, "John Dee and the Magic Tables in the *Book of Soyga*," www.research.att.com/~reeds/soyga.html; to appear in a forthcoming book *John Dee: Interdisciplinary Essays in English Renaissance Thought,* Kluwer of Amsterdam.

[42] Bodley MS 908, p. 4, line 3. See figure 2.

makes it probable that Kelley was not familiar with the text, and is possibly evidence that he was in fact carrying out a deception. I do not believe the *Book of Soyga* is the same as the "Arabick book" mentioned several times by Dee. The latter was apparently the same as that prized by Pontois and described as having "cost doctor dye £ 600 ready money as he the deponent did hear himself the said doctor afferme. . ."[43] There is nothing about either *Soyga* manuscript to justify such a vast sum.[44]

Scrying and Dee's Earliest Attempts

The premise behind Dee's mystical experiments is the veracity of scrying, or visions seen in a crystal ball or other shining surface. Today, the crystal ball has become an icon for superstition, but scrying has been widely used and respected for divination throughout history. It even has biblical authority.[45]

According to psychiatrist and researcher Raymond A. Moody, "That certain individuals do see visions—specifically, hypnagogic images—when gazing into a transparent or reflective surface is a well-established fact that can be regarded as an item of psychological knowledge."[46] The real question is the value of these visions, or their interpretation.

---

43 R&W, p. 183.

44 It is not clear why Roberts and Watson make this identification. They note Francis Maddison's theory that Aldaraia = Ar. Al Dirâya "knowledge, cognizance, acquintance," but that is only hypothetical. They also note that Dee sent a servant (20 October 1595) to recover his Arabic book from Mr Abbot (?) at Oxford and (19 November 1595) "my Arabik boke restored by gods favor." James Orchard Halliwell, ed., *The Private Diary of Dr. John Dee* (New York: AMS Press, 1968), p. 54.

45 Genesis 44:4–5.

46 Raymond A. Moody, *Scrying—The Art of Female Divination* (Marietta: R. Bemis Publishing, Ltd., 1995), p. 7.

Scrying instructions can be found widely in occult literature, in particular in manuscripts that it was dangerous to possess.[47] The published sources, such as Agrippa, make scant mention of scrying. Scrying also appears in popular legends, such as the legends of Roger Bacon's scrying glass in which anyone could see anything they wished within fifty miles.

With few exceptions, Dee did not use scrying to see far-off happenings, or to divine the future. His aim was to see into the spiritual realms to receive wisdom from higher beings. The spiritual realms were thought to resemble, in many respects, the physical world.

It was common for scrying practices to be accompanied by religious and occult symbols and ceremonies. These served to ensure the spiritual purity of the practice, but also to focus concentration on the intent, much as techniques for lucid dreaming do. They also served to give form, context, and meaning to the images seen by the scryer. For example, surrounding the scrying table with the symbols of the seven planets provided a means of organizing and remembering the otherwise bewildering maze of images. This integration of magic with the art of memory was developed to a high degree in Renaissance occultism.[48]

---

[47] For some examples, see Richard Kieckhefer, *Forbidden Rites,* experiments 18, 19, 20, 23, 24, 25, 27, 29, 33, 38, 39, and 40. Reginald Scot, *Discoverie of Witchcraft* (New York: Dover Publications, 1584/1973), published extracts from magic handbooks; many deal with scrying (e.g., pp. 148–9, 232–5, 238–9, 245–6, 249–50). Francis Barrett, *The Magus* (London, 1801; reprint: Secaucus: The Citadel Press, 1975) pp. 135bis ff, published scrying instructions from Trithemius (or pseudo-Trithemius). See also manuscripts Sloane 1317, 3846 (art 6), 3848, 3949 (arts. 1, 3), 3851, 3853 (art. 9), 3854 (art 5).

[48] According to Couliano, mnemonics, along with eroticism, is an essential component of magic, "to such an extent that it is impossible to understand [magic] without first having studied the principles and mechanisms of the first two" (*Eros and Magic in the Renaissance,* p. xviii). See also Frances A. Yates, *The Art of Memor,* and Giordano Bruno's *De magia* in *Jordani Bruni Nolani Opera latine conscripta* (Neapoli, 1879–91). English translation in Robert De Lucca, Richard J. Blackwell, and Alfonso Ingegno, *Giordano Bruno, Cause, Principle and Unity: And Essays on Magic* (Cambridge: Cambridge University Press, 1998).

Symbols and ceremonies also provided a means of controlling or manipulating the images (or, to use Couliano's term, "phantasms"). For example, the scryer might place a talisman of Venus under the stone when he wanted to focus on affairs of the heart. This is essentially an attempt to facilitate communication between body and soul: "body and soul speak two languages, which are not only different, even inconsistent, but also inaudible to each other. The inner sense alone is able to hear and comprehend them both, also having the role of translating one into the other."[49] The use of sacred symbols and ceremonies also helped the scryer summon courage to face the possible confrontation with demonic presences.

Dee's interest in scrying clearly goes back far earlier than the records of his scrying experiments.[50] Although he may have begun to experiment much earlier, the earliest records of Dee's scrying begin in 1581. On 8 March 1581, and several times during 1581, Dee records strange knocking and rapping in his chamber, and a voice like an owl's shriek. These events were clearly regarded as supernatural and may have been related to early experiments.

His private diary records: "May 25th, I had sight in χρυσταλλω [Crystallo] offerd me, and I saw." Generally, however, Dee relied on the scrying abilities of others, as prescribed by tradition. He mentions that he employed two seers around this time.[51]

Late in 1581, Dee began to employ Barnabas Saul as a scryer. Saul was a minister who was heavily involved with magic. Dee's diary records additional details regarding his dealings with Saul:

---

49   I. P. Couliano, *Eros and Magic in the Renaissance*, p. 5.

50   He mentions scrying in his *Monas Hieroglyphica* (1564).

51   See "The Scryers of John Dee," Chris Pickering, *Hermetic Journal* 32, pp. 9–14. Another example of Dee seeing angels may be TFR 25, where he writes "Thereupon I perceived the presence of some good spiritual Creature, and straight way appeared the good Angel. I.L."

Oct. 9th, Barnabas Saul, lying in the .... hall was strangely trubled by a spiritual creature abowt mydnight. [1582] Jan. 27th, Barnabas Sawl his brother cam. Feb. 12th, abowt 9 of the clok, Barnabas Saul and his brother Edward went homward from Mortlak: Saul his inditement being by law fownd insufficient at Westminster Hall: Mr. Serjeant Walmesley, Mr. Owen and Mr. Hyde, his lawyers at the bar for the matter, and Mr. Ive, the clerk of the Crown Office, favoring the other. Feb. 20th I receyved a letter from Barnabas Saul. Feb. 21st, Mr. Skullthorp rod toward Barnabas. Feb. 25th, Mr. Skulthorp cam home. March 6th, Barnabas Saul cam this day agayn abowt one of the clok and went to London the same afternone. He confessed that he neyther hard or saw any spirituall creature any more. March 8th, Mr. Clerkson and his frende[52] cam to my howse. Barnabas went home agayne abowt 3 or 2 clok, he lay not at my howse now; he went, I say, on Thursday, with Mr. Clerkson. March 9th, Fryday at dynner tyme Mr. Clerkson and Mr. Talbot declared a great deale of Barnabas nowghty dealing toward me, as in telling Mr. Clerkson ill things of me that I should mak his frend, as that he was wery of me, that I wold so flatter his frende the lerned man that I wold borow him of him. But his frend told me, before my wife and Mr. Clerkson, that a spirituall creature told him that Barnabas had censured both Mr. Clerkson and me. The injuries which this Barnabas had done me diverse wayes were very great. July 19th, Barnabas Saul came to see me at Mortlak: I chyd hym for his manifold untrue reports.[53]

---

52 This friend was Edward Kelley, a.k.a. Edward Talbot.

53 Above this entry, someone wrote, "You that rede this underwritten assure your-
selfe that yt is a shamfull lye, for Talbot neither studied for any such thinge not
shewed himselfe dishonest in any thinge." Dee added the comment, "This is Mr.

The experiments with Saul were not regarded as successful. His sessions were largely rejected as false. Dee records one of these sessions in the beginning of *Mysteriorum Libri Quinque.*

On 8 March 1582, Dee was visited by Edward Kelley, a.k.a. Edward Talbot. They were introduced by Dee's friend Mr. Clerkson. Kelley began to scry regularly with Dee two days later. From Dee's records, it is apparent that Kelley had a highly unstable personality. The relationship between the two men was often strained, and Kelley would storm off for months at a time. Aside from their conflicts, however, Dee regarded their sessions as highly successful.

Scrying Methods

Dee used various media for scrying—several crystal balls and the famous obsidian mirror are now preserved in the British Museum.[54] Dee drew a picture of one of them in the record of the first scrying session (see below). This shows an elaborate frame with a cross at the top. This is probably the stone that William Lilly described as the size of a large orange, "set in silver, with a cross on the top, and another on the handle; and round about engraved the names of these angels, Raphael,

---

Talbot or that lerned man, his own writing in my boke, very unduely as he cam by it." There are also some additional notes by Talbot/Kelley that have been erased. Diary quotations are from James Orchard Halliwell, ed., *The Private Diary of Dr. John Dee* (New York: AMS Press, 1968) pp. 13–16.

54   Although Christopher Whitby (*John Dee's Actions with Spirits,* pp. 138–141) questions whether the obsidian mirror was actually Dee's, it is commonly accepted. John Pontois, Dee's heir, was said to have "a certain round flat stone like Cristall which Pountis said was a stone which an Angell brought to doctor dye wherein he did worke and know many strange things . . ." See R&W, p. 61. See figure 8.1 in Nicholas Clulee, *John Dee's Natural Philosophy.* This probably was the scrying stone that the angels mysteriously delivered on 21 November 1582 out of "the uttermost part of the Roman Possession." Dee describes it as being "half an inch thick" (5 May, 1583), although Dee's drawing of the former in Sloane 3191 clearly shows a sphere whereas the mirror is flat and has a handle.

Gabriel, Uriel."[55] After intense prayer, the stone was placed in a frame and set on a specially prepared table. The angels were then called to appear in the stone to answer questions.

Nicholas Clulee has argued that Dee did not seem to consider these actions magical, but rather a variety of religious experience. He based this partly on the observation that they do not seem to invoke the angels directly, as directed by the magical books. Rather, they start off with prayers to God, and petitions that God send his angels.[56] This is consistent with the method found in the *Arbatel*, which Dee mentions by name in the text. In his first action with Kelley, Dee is very careful to distinguish between "spirituall practise" and what is "vulgarly accownted Magik." On the other hand, Dee and Kelley immediately proceed to "call for the good Angel Anchor, to appere in that stone *to my owne sight*." Dee states that he "make[s] motion to god, and his good Creatures." Also, Dee's synopsis of his instructions for communicating with angels (*Heptarchia Mystica* and *Tabula bonorum angelorum invocationes,* bound in Sloane 3191) contains numerous invocations or "invitations" addressed directly to individual angels. These were based on the records Dee kept in Sloane 3188.

It does not appear that God or the angels obliged Dee's request that they appear to his own sight, but Kelley experiences vivid and detailed apparitions. As soon as the angels appear in the stone, they "give thanks to God, and Wellcome to the good Creature." Then they

---

[55] Quoted in Christopher Whitby, *John Dee's Actions with Spirits*, p. 92. Compare with the drawing and description found in (pseudo-?) Trithemius. *The Art of Drawing Spirits in to Crystals* in Francis Barrett, *The Magus*, book 2, p. 128 (York Beach, ME: Samuel Weiser, 2000). In addition to Raphael, Gabriel, and Uriel, Trithemius includes Michael.

[56] Nicholas Clulee, *John Dee's Natural Philosophy*, p. 206. See the first action, where, after "fervent prayers to God," Saul is asked to look into the stone and see "yf God had sent his holy Angel Anael."

demand the angel's name. These steps are all consistent with the texts of ritual magic. In the second action, Dee is told that the method of invoking the archangel Michael is by "the Seven psalmes." This is also consistent with the grimoires.[57] The apparitions do not always seem confined to the crystal.[58]

Edward Kelley, the Magician

Edward Kelley was born on 1 August 1555. He was thus 28 years younger than Dee. He attended Oxford under the alias of Edward Talbot, but left after some trouble. He was later pilloried in Lancaster for forgery. He was 26 when he arrived at Dee's door on 10 March 1582.[59] By this time, Kelley was well versed in the occult arts, including Agrippa's works. He also possessed various texts on magic, at least some of which were regarded as "devilish." Kelley was also an alchemist. His only book is on alchemy, and his final months were occupied with alchemical experiments for Rudolph II. Elias Ashmole says, "Mr. Lilly told me that John Evans informed him that he was acquainted with Kelly's sister in Worchester, that she shewed him some

---

57 As an example, British Library Sloane manuscript 3849 ("Manner of Proceed-ing in order to discover in the Crystall") starts out with the seven Psalms before proceeding to ask Jesus to send the three angels "ancor annasor anelose." Reginald Scot, in his 1584 edition of *The Discoverie of Witchcraft* (book 15, chapter 12), quotes from a magical text at length on how "to have a spirit inclosed into a christall stone or berill glasse, &c. First thou in the new of the moon being clothed with all new, and fresh, & cleane araie, and shaven, and that day to fast with bread and water, and being cleane confessed, saie the seaven psalmes, and the letanie, for the space of two daies, with this praier following . . ."

58 For example, see TFR, p. 25: "There appeared to E.K. a round Globe of white smoke over my head" (a UFO?). MLQ, 10 April 1583: "there appeared in the corner of my study a blak shadow." Sometimes, the whole chamber appeared in the stone (e.g., MLQ, 15 March 1582).

59 Peter French, *John Dee, The World of an Elizabethan Magus*, pp. 113, n. 2.

of the gold her brother had transmuted, and that Kelly was first an apothecary in Worcester."[60] Kelley later married Jane Cooper. He also had a brother, Thomas.

The *Sigillum Aemeth* and Its Variations

The use of the *Sigillum Aemeth* (or Emeth) is central to Dee's system, as well as to other forms of magic. The earliest examples of the *Sigillum Aemeth* are found in the *Liber Juratus* (see appendix 1). Most manuscripts describe the seal in great detail, but don't actually draw it out. The versions that do exist vary, probably because they were based on the written description. *Liber Juratus* calls this seal the "seal of God . . . which is the beginning in this art."[61] Between the outer circles is to be written the 72–letter name of God, or *Schemhamphoras*. Both Agrippa and Reuchlin refer to a seal by this name, although I have been unable to find any descriptions or drawings of it in their writings. Dee was well aware of the fact that variations existed, since he asks the angels to provide a definitive version for his works. The version by Athanasius Kircher, which appears many years later in his monumental work *Oedipus Aegyptiacus,* is highly corrupt.[62]

Dee was originally told by the angels to use a version found in one of his books. He thereupon consulted several sources and asked the angels to resolve the discrepancies. This prompted them to deliver a radically new version of the sigil.

An examination of Dee's original wax sigil (see figure 1, page 42),

---

[60]   Oxford: Bodleian Library MS Ashmole 1790, fol. 58.

[61]   British Library manuscript Royal 17 Axlii fol. 3v.

[62]   Athanasius Kircher, *Oedipus Aegyptiacus* (Rome, 1652–54). The most interesting part of Kircher's discussion is his attempt to link the seal with Islamic mystical tradition. Since the use of this sigil is central to the present work, I include Kircher's discussion of it in appendix 2.

now preserved in the British Museum, shows differences from that found in Sloane 3188.

The Holy Table and Its Variations

Dee's scrying was conducted on a specially constructed table, two versions of which were described to him by the angels. The first, whose design is now lost, was later declared by the angels to be false. The second design is apparently similar to the first. It consists of a large hexagram containing a square of letters. Surrounding the hexagram is a border containing additional letters. Although the original table does not appear to have survived, it was described in detail by Elias Ashmole, who saw it in John Cotton's library. It was "composed of 3 boards broad-waies besides the borderings; of a fine grained wood & very heavy, but the scent now lost." He described the Enochian letters as painted in red on a gold background, between two blue lines. The seven sigils, or "ensigns of Creation" were also painted with red letters and blue lines. The lines of the hexagon were gold, and the central square had gold letters and blue lines.[63] (The engraving found in Dee's *True and Faithful Relation . . .* does not correspond exactly with the description in Sloane 3188. See figure 3, page 43.)

As with the *Sigillum Aemeth* described above, this design is a variation of designs found in magic texts. It is likely that Dee employed one of the conventional designs in his early scrying before the angels revealed their version.

The instructions given in the grimoires concerning the holy table probably give a fairly accurate idea of how Dee proceeded in these experiments. In appendices 3, 4, and 5, I present excerpts from the *Theurgia Goetia, Art Pauline,* and *Ars Almadel.* The *Art Pauline* seems particularly close to Dee's method. The table contains a hexagram with

---

63   Oxford: Bodleian Library, Ashmole MS 1790, fols. 55a–56a.

the seven planetary seals arranged around it (see figure 5, page 44). The spirit's seal is placed on the appropriate planetary seal. Dee was instructed that the seven seals could be constructed separately and arranged around the table, or they could be painted onto the table.

The third example is from the *Ars Almadel*. This gives a method for calling forth the spirits that govern the four directions, north, south, east, and west. Here, we also find a hexagram on the holy table, and the use of wax sigils. This time, there is a border around the table with holy names drawn around it. In the center of the hexagram is a small triangular seal with more names (see figures 6 and 7, pages 45–46). *Aldaraia sive Soyga* also contains diagrams reminiscent of Dee's (see figure 4, page 44).

Other Ritual Implements

According to the *Key of Solomon*,[64] *Heptameron, Lemegeton*,[65] and other magical texts, the master should wear on his chest a lamin with a hexagram. Dee is likewise told to prepare a lamin to be used for this purpose, but his was triangular, thus symbolizing his name (Δ = Dee). He is later given a new version, the original version having been declared false. The final version has Enochian lettering.

Dee is also instructed to prepare another ritual implement, the ring of Solomon. Solomon's magical ring appears in early magical literature. For example, in the *Testament of Solomon* (first to third century A.D.), Solomon is given the magical ring by the archangel Michael.[66] He uses it to call and control the demons. The archangel Michael likewise reveals Solomon's ring to Dee, stating that it was by it that

---

[64] Hermann Gollancz, *Sepher Maphteah Shelomoh* (London: Oxford University Press, 1914), fol. 38a.

[65] *Goetia* also enjoins the use of a second lamin that has a five-pointed star.

[66] Translation by D. C. Duling in James H. Charlesworth, *The Old Testament Pseudepigrapha,* vol. 1 (New York: Doubleday, 1983) pp. 935 ff.

Solomon worked all his wonders. The *Testament of Solomon* was known in medieval manuscripts and could have been known to Dee.[67]

The Spirits

Five archangels are central to Dee's actions: Michael, Gabriel, Raphael, Uriel, and Annael. This grouping is common in medieval and Renaissance occult works. In *Liber Juratus,* the first four are known as the "Angels of the 4 winds." Agrippa calls them the "four angels ruling over the corners of the world."[68]*The Magical Calendar* gives the same.[69] The names of the first four are also found written on the frame that holds the scrying crystal in Trithemius' method of calling angels into a crystal.[70] Michael and Gabriel are the only two angels mentioned by name in the Old Testament. Raphael is mentioned in the Apocryphal *Book of Tobit,* and Uriel is well known in noncanonical lore. Annael is relatively unknown.

The meanings of the Hebrew names and their compass allocations are:

Michael	"who is as God"	East
Gabriel	"God is my strength"	North
Raphael	"God has healed"	West
Uriel	"Fire of God"	South
Annael	"Grace or glory of God"	

---

67 For example, see British Library, Harley manuscript 5596, fifteenth century. Note the largest section of this manuscript is the *Clavicula Salomonis.*

68 Cornelius Agrippa, *De occulta philosophia,* book 2, chap. 7, p. 266.

69 *The Magical Calendar,* ed. Adam McLean (Grand Rapids, MI: Phanes Press, 1994), p. 32.

70 Johannes Trithemius, *The Art of Drawing Spirits into Crystals* in Francis Barrett's *The Magus,* book 2, (York Beach, ME: Samuel Weiser, 2000), p. 128.

During their first scrying session, Dee and Kelley called three angels: Anchor, Anachor, and Anilos. These names also occur in mainstream occult sources. In the *Heptameron or Magical Elements* of Peter de Abano, they are mentioned in the oration to be said when the vesture is put on.[71] It is known that Dee made use of that book, but he must have been following another source here, since the names are not exactly the same. A likely source is Sloane 3849, article 1, "Manner of proceding in order to discover in the crystall," where these three angels are central.

It would be interesting to try to trace the development of this oration. The *Heptameron* version is as follows:

> Ancor, Amacor, Amides, Theodonias, Anitor, by the merits of thy Angel, O Lord, I will put on the Garments of Salvation, that this which I desire I may bring to effect: through thee the most holy Adonay, whose kingdom endureth for ever and ever. Amen[72]

The *Clavicula Salomonis* gives the following:

> Amor, Amator, Amides, Ideodaniach, Pamor, Plaior, Anitor; through the merits of these holy Angels will I robe and indue myself with the vestments of Power, through which may I conduct unto the desired end those things which I ardently wish, through Thee, O most Holy ADONAI, whose Kingdom and Empire endureth forever. Amen.[73]

---

[71] (pseudo-) Henry Cornelius Agrippa, *Fourth Book of Occult Philosophy* (London, 1655, reprint London: Askin Publishers, 1978).

[72] Agrippa.

[73] *The Key of Solomon the King (Clavicula Salomonis)*, first translated and edited from ancient manuscripts in the British Museum by S. Liddell MacGregor Mathers (London: George Redway, 1889; reissued, York Beach, ME: Samuel Weiser, 2000, p. 93). Mathers' reading most closely follows British Library manuscript Additional 10862, folio 116v (consecration of vestments): "Amor, Amator, Amides, Ideodaniach, Paucor, Playor, Anitor, per merita eorum sanc-

The *Lemegeton* gives:

> By the figurative mystery of these holy vestures I will
> clothe me with the armour of salvation in the strength of
> the Most High, ANCHOR; AMACOR; AMIDES;
> THEODONIAS; ANITOR; that my desired end may be
> effected through Thy Strength, Adonai; unto whom the
> praise and glory will for ever and ever belong. Amen.[74]

Liber Juratus contains the earliest version with which I am familiar. It is
numbered oration 17:

---

torum Angelorum . . ." The same manuscript again invokes these angels during
the consecration of the silk cloth on fol. 64v: "Adonay, Anosbias anereneton, agla,
athanatos, agyos, ancor, anachor, anilos, Theodomos, agnefeton, Cedyon, Lamet,
Cetelfares, cos, Tetragrammaton." Strangely, Mathers omits this conjuration.
Mathers' other manuscript authorities read as follows: Sloane 3091, fol. 84v:
"ancor, amacor, amade. Theodonia, Pancorpsagor, Anotor, parles merites des
Saints Anges, . . ." Harley 3981 fol. 112v: "Ancor, Amacor, Amade, Theodonia,
Pancor = psagor, Anitor, par les merites des Saints Anges . . ." Kings 288 fol. 111v:
"Anco, Amacor, Amade, Theodonia, Pancor, Psagor, Anitor, parles merites, des
Saints Anges . . ." Ancor, Amacor, Amides, Teodonia, Pancor, Amitor, par les
merites des Saintes . . . Sloane 1307 (missing from chapter on vestments but
includes the following for consecrating the parchment fol. 109v:) "Autor, Amaur,
Theodomos, Phagar, Abacri, adestote ad custodiam istius carte." Other manu-
scripts of the *Key of Solomon* in the British Library not used by Mathers preserve
some valuable readings: Sloane 3847 fol. 46v (consecration of clothing): "Anchor,
Anachor, anilos, theodonos, phagor, Ianitor, per merita Angelorum sanctorum . . ."
fol. 60r (preparation of parchment): "Ancor, anacor, amlos, Theodomos, Phagor,
adestote in custodia huius carte" fol. 60v: "Lazay, Salmay, Dalmay, Adonay,
Saday, Tetragrammaton, anepheneton, Cedyon, Aryon, Anereneton, Athanatos,
Theos, Theodomos, anilos, pes, kyros, abos, Theophilos, Onoy, Zoron, Largon,
Lazaryon, Theophilon, Tisyon, Alyon, Occinomos, Zacharion, Sydion, Agla, Joth,
heth, he, vau, el, emanuel, Ja · Ja, Vah, *ancor, anilos, Theodonas* angeli sancti dei
. . ." Additional 36674 fol. 15v: "<u>Antor, Anator, et Anabis, Theodomas, Ianitor
[or Iamtor], by the desertes of the holy Anngells</u> . . ." Sloane 2383 fol. 16r (preparation of parchment): "Anator, Amacor, phaidos, theodomos, plagar, abacar,
adestote ad custodiam istius Cartae" fol. 25v (silk cloth): "Adonay, amatias, ana-
ton prieumaton, agla, Ensoph, Cadon, antor, amacor, anilor, [26r] Semanphorus,
Samceuaia, tetaph, soned, saemonim. Eos bos, Elohim."

74   Joseph H. Peterson, *The Lesser Key of Solomon* (York Beach, ME, Weiser Books:
      2001), p. 47.

O Jesu the sonne of the incomprehensible god,
    hancor hanacor hamylos iehorna theodonos heliothos
phagor corphandonos norizane corithico hanosae helsezope
phagora.
    ELEMINATOR candones helos helee resphaga thephagayn theundyn thahonos micemyahe hortahonas nelos
behebos belhores hacaphagan belehothol ortophagon corphandonos born in the shape of a man for us sinners and
yow holy angells heliothos phagnoraherken and teche me
and gouerne me [hic oic petitionem tuam sed p visione
diuina dic ut sequitr] that I may come to obtayne the
visyon of the deyte throwgh thee glorious and moste gentle and moste almightie creator oure lyuyng lorde holy
infinite godely and euerlastinge to whome be prayse
honor and glorye worlde withowt ende. Amen.[75]

The *Ars Notoria* has a very similar oration, numbered 24 and called
"The Oration of the Physical Art." Its purpose is for determining the
condition of a sick person:

Ihesus fili Dominus Incomprehensibilis:
    Ancor, Anacor, Anylos, Zohorna, Theodonas, helyotes Phagor, Norizane, Corichito, Anosae, Helse Tonope,
Phagora
    [another part of the same orison:]

---

[75] British Library manuscript Royal 17 Axlii fol. 37r. Another manuscript in the
British Library, Sloane 3885 fol. 69r reads: "Ih'u dei filius incompraehensibilis hancor hanacor hanylos iehorna theodonas helyothos heliotheos phagor corphandonos
norizane corithico hanosal helsezope phagor[a]. [37v] Eleminator candones helas
helee resphaga thephagagayn thetendyn thahanos mtemya heortahonos nelos behebos belhores hacaphagan \\\\\ belohothoi ortophagon corphandonos humane natus
. . ." Sloane 3854 fol 118v: "Ih'u dei filius incomprehensibil' hancor hanacor hanylos iehorna theodonos helyothos heliotheos phagor corphandonos norizane corithico
hanosae helsezope phagor[a]. Eleminator candones helos orano: helee resphaga
thephagagayn thetendyn thahanos uitemya heortalyonos uelos ue hebos uel hores
hacaphagan ortophagon corphandonos humane natus . . ."

> Elleminator, Cardones helosi, Tophagain, Tecen-
> dum, Thaones, Behelos, Belhoros, Hocho Phagan,
> Corphandonos, Humanae natus & vos Eloytus
> Phugora: Be present ye holy Angels, advertise and reach
> me, whether such a one shall recover, or dye of this
> infirmity.[76]

The *Ars Notoria* reproduces most of the Orations found in the *Liber Juratus,* though in slightly altered forms.

In *Liber II,* two other conventional lists of angels are given. The first is: Zaphiel, Zadkiel, Cumael, Raphael, Haniel, Michael, and Gabriel. The second is: Zedekieil, Madimiel, Semeliel, Nogahel, Corabiel, and Leuenael. Most of these names are identical to those given by Agrippa in his "Scale of the number seven." The first list corresponds to the "seven angels which stand in the presence of God." This also corresponds to the list of seven archangels according to Geonic lore, as well as that of Pseudo-Dionysius.[77] The second list corresponds to the Hebrew names for the seven planets, with the name of God, "EL," added to each. It is also found in Agrippa, book 3.

Description of the Manuscript

One of the most remarkable things about Dee, as exemplified by these records, is his meticulous attention to detail. In fact, Dee's are probably the most detailed records of the actual practice of ceremonial magic extant.

The title of the book is slightly ambiguous. "Mysteriorum," as in *Mysteriorum Libri,* can mean either mysteries or secret rites. Both meanings seem fitting in this context.

The manuscript consists of 104 folios, mostly in Dee's hand. It

---

[76] Peterson, p. 172.

[77] Gustav Davidson, *A Dictionary of Angels Including the Fallen Angels* (New York: The Free Press, 1967), pp. 338–9.

measures approximately 320mm by 205mm. It contains a short preface
by Elias Ashmole, and is bound with notes by Ashmole, many of which
are in his stenographic notation.[78]

Synopsis of Dee's "Mystical Experiments" (1581–1583)

In his *Mysteriorum Libri Quinque,* Dee records prophetic visions (e.g.,
the Spanish Armada), visions of angels, magical instruction, and religious teachings. A few of the key messages of the angels include:

- Flesh is vile and corrupt (Gnostic or Neoplatonic attitude);
- Mercy for the repentant is necessary;
- Temptation of the faithful is necessary in order to show God's
  mercy;
- The immanent coming of the antichrist;
- The immanent fall of existing political and religious establish-
  ments as punishment for mankind's corruption, to be replaced
  by new, righteous ones.

Although a lot of material remains obscure, especially passages from
the "holy book," I believe Christopher Whitby is correct in dismissing
the theory of cryptographic messages hidden in these records.[79]

There is suprisingly little discussion of alchemy in these records,
especially in view of the fact that Dee pursued it actively during this
period.[80] Perhaps Dee did not mention it here because he didn't want

---

[78] Christopher Whitby (*John Dee's Actions with Spirits*, p. 1) identified these as
   "notes in cipher by William Shippen (1635–1693)," but see C. H. Josten, *Elias
   Ashmole (1617–1692): his autobiographical and historical notes, his correspondence, and other contemporary sources relating to his life and work* (Oxford,
   1966), V. 2, p. 10.

[79] Christopher Whitby, *John Dee's Actions with Spirits*, p. 105–6, p. 156.

[80] Nicholas Clulee, *John Dee's Natural Philosophy*, p. 178–9.

to reveal his alchemical work to Kelley, who probably came to Dee for that purpose. Perhaps this helps explain Kelley's bouts of anger at Dee. One might also wonder if Kelley brought the scroll, book, and red powder in order to entice Dee into letting him in on Dee's own secret alchemical work. The evidence that there was more to the visions than simply conscious deception from Kelley will be discussed later.

The Book of Angelic Wisdom

Dee seems to have had an almost obsessive facination with the lost *Apocrypha,* especially the *Book of Enoch,* which is mentioned and even quoted in the Bible (Jude 14), and *Esdras.* He is told by the angels that the *Apocrypha* are not lost, but in the keeping of the Jews.[81] Most of his mystical exercises are focused on recovery of the lost wisdom that these books represented to him.

The core of this book describes the revelation of a book of angelic wisdom, *Liber Loagaeth* (so named by Dee in *A True and Faithful Relation . . .*). It is reported to be in the tongue of the angels. Only a few angelic words are translated in these manuscripts. The first parts of this book were dictated by Kelley and recorded meticulously by Dee in Sloane 3188. Later parts were written by Kelley directly and are now found in Sloane 3189. The latter manuscript is incomplete in that it does not repeat the earlier material. It is also bound with four tables from the *Book of Soyga,* written in Dee's handwriting. Since the angels state that the angelic book contains forty-nine leaves (one of which cannot be revealed), it is clear that the four tables from *Soyga* do not belong to it.

---

81 Dee was apparently aware of the existence of the Ethiopic *Book of Enoch* from Guillaume Postel's *De originibus* (Basel: Ioannem Oporinum, 1553). See Nicholas Clulee, *John Dee's Natural Philosophy,* p. 209.

Dee was instructed to rewrite the book in the delivered script, but this does not seem to have been done. One copy was to be bound in blue. Another, "whose skin shall bear Silver," was to be "in length; 8 [inches], in breadth 7."[82]

The importance of *Liber Loagaeth* cannot be overemphasized. From it would "be restored the holy bokes, which haue perished euen from the begynning, and from the first that liued." The truths it contains will end religious disputes and restore religious unity. "Which when it hath spread a while, THEN COMMETH THE ENDE."[83] In short, it will usher in the new age. Since the book is so central to these angelic communications, it is amazing that it has remained unpublished.

Synopsis of Dee's *True & Faithful Relation*

The record of Dee's experiments continues in later manuscripts. The bulk of the later material was published in 1659 by Meric Casaubon as *A True & Faithful Relation . . . Between Dr. John Dee . . . and some Spirits.* These records were published by Casaubon with the intent of discrediting Dee and Kelley. The Casaubon edition, it should be noted, is full of typographic errors. Reliance on it alone, without the manuscript sources, has sadly resulted in the perpetuation of many errors.

A *True & Faithful Relation* takes up where *Mysteriorum Libri Quinque* left off. It goes on to describe their six-year missionary journey to the continent. The revelations of the mystical heptarchy were followed by that of the 30 "Aethyrs," the "48 Claves Angelicae," and the four "Enochian Tables." The later material included a second language popularly known as "Enochian."

---

82 TFR, p. 159.

83 Sloane 3188, fol. 101b.

Dee's mission to the court of Rudolph II in Prague cannot be considered a success. An occultist himself, Rudolph proved very unsupportive. In fact, Dee and Kelley narrowly escaped the papal nuncio and the possibility of facing the deadly Inquisition. Dee returned to England in 1589. Kelley remained behind and had limited success in alchemical experiments for Rudolph. He died trying to escape in 1595.

Dee's Later Life

The final period of Dee's life and career have been judged variously as one of disgrace and failure, or as one of continued success and renown. I think William Sherman has made a credible case for the latter view.[84] While it is clear that his mission to the continent cost him politically, Dee continued to maintain his contacts and influence, and even served in an official capacity to King James I when he succeeded Queen Elizabeth in 1603. He continued his scrying experiments, but never again achieved the dramatic results he had seen with Kelley. While the promised new age never materialized in the dramatic and apocalyptic way he had visualized, history has acknowledged Dee's vital role in shaping our modern world.

Adaptation of Dee's System by Later Occultists

Dee's activities and writings have made a deep impact on later occult movements. Among the fruits of his labor is a heavy influence on the German Rosicrucian movement, whose manifestos began to appear around 1610.[85]

---

84 William Sherman, *John Dee*, pp. 16–19.

85 See Frances A. Yates, *The Rosicrucian Enlightenment*, 1978, pp. 41.

As mentioned above, Dee's experiments also had a great influence on the Golden Dawn. Unfortunately, the process of adapting and assimilating Dee's system was undertaken with uncritical methods and incomplete materials. In particular, these efforts have been based almost entirely on Casaubon's *True & Faithful Relation,* with all its typographic errors. In many particulars, the Casaubon edition is impossible to understand without the *Mysteriorum Libri Quinque.*

The Four Angelic Tablets

Four tables of letters were produced during the later conferences.[86] These tables served two different purposes: the production of ninety-one names that correspond to the ninety-one parts of the world (as catalogued by Agrippa in his *Occult Philosophy* I, chap. 31), and the production of invocations ("Tabula Bonorum") to be used with the names. The Golden Dawn adaptation of Dee's system places heavy emphasis of these tables.

Christian Wilby has written an excellent article on the four angelic tablets. There he states:

> Unfortunately for later day occultists, the so-called synthetic genius—I prefer to call it rampant eclecticism—of McGregor Mathers has obscured the field of vision on this problem for too long. For some reason best known to himself, Mathers was content to use the originally received tablets and ALL of the emmendations of the "corrected" version. This has produced, to the detriment of everybody, one of the biggest mish-mashes ever to grace the Tradition.[87]

---

86 TFR I, p. 173; TFR III, p. 15.

87 *Hermetic Journal,* 30, pp. 18–22.

Another inaccuracy in the Golden Dawn system is the compass allocations used for the four angelic tablets. The original allocations given to Dee were later corrected by the angels.[88] The correct allocations are also given by Dee in his synopsis of his magical system (see Sloane 3191). These errors have been perpetuated by more recent writers.

History of the Manuscript

In addition to the preface by Elias Ashmole, further history of the manuscript is found in the following notes written on the end sheets:

> Ms A. 3188./XVI F
>   This volume is in Dr. Dee's own handwriting, as far as fol 108.
>   A fair copy of it by Elias Ashmole was purchased at Sir Joseph Jekyll's sale, Jan 1739/40 (lot 465) and is now Ms. Sloane 3677.
>   The original Mss. of the remaining Books are in the Cottonian Collection, Appendix XLVI but were formerly (erroneously) numbered as Add. Mss. No. 5007 A.B.C.
>   J.M. Jan 1856
>
> Dr. John Dee's Conference with Angels from Dec 22 1581. to May 30 1583. being what preceeds the other Conferences printed by Dr. Meric Causabon [sic] Lond. 1659. in folio.

> With a preface by Elias Ashmole An: 1672.

---

88 TFR III, p. 15.

Notes on This Edition

This edition of John Dee's spiritual diaries was prepared from the original manuscript in Dee's own handwriting. The original manuscript is preserved in the British Library.[89] Dee prepared a synopsis of this material in a short manuscript, *De Heptarchia Mystica*.[90] This latter manuscript provides some material that has been lost from the original manuscript, along with additional explanatory notes. All material used by Dee in his synopsis are printed in bold font to indicate its special importance. Additional notes from *De Heptarchia Mystica* are marked *-D (HM)*.

The text has been normalized in some particulars. The personal pronoun *thee* is sometimes written *thé* or *the* in the manuscript. These have all been resolved into *thee*. The tittle—or macron (~), usually indicating a missing "m" or "n"—has been expanded in nearly all cases. Except for these particulars, everything else has been preserved, including spelling, capitalization, punctuation, and underscores. Marginal notes are incorporated into the text as footnotes. Square brackets and parentheses are Dee's. All editor's notes are denoted by *-Ed.*

Ashmole's notes are denoted by *-E.A.* Bound with the manuscript are partial transcriptions and notes on this manuscript and the printed diaries by Elias Ashmole. Most of this is in Ashmole's shorthand cipher. Some of these notes have also been included in this edition. Asmole's "fair copy" is full of careless errors. This is very surprising, since he apparently thought the book of utmost importance.

In preparing this edition, I took the opportunity to review Christopher Whitby's doctoral thesis. Garland Press printed a limited edition of this in 1988. It was poorly reproduced from his typewritten thesis, making it completely illegible in many spots. I found Whitby's intro-

---

[89]   Sloane 3188.

[90]   Sloane 3191.

ductory material very well researched and useful, although I was surprised at the number of errors in transcription and translation. Also unfortunate is the fact that Whitby doesn't compare Sloane 3188 with Dee's manuscript *Heptarchia Mystica,* where Dee collects excerpts from the *Mysteriorum Libri Qunique.*[91] These compensate greatly for much of the damage and illegibility of the latter, much more so than Ashmole's transcriptions. Although Whitby makes note of its importance, he doesn't make much use of it.

Conclusions: The Evidence

Colin Wilson has written: "Dee is one of the few great magical adepts of the past who can present us with some practical evidence of the existence of non-human entities."[92] How solid is this evidence? The most convincing evidence is perhaps the "Enochian" language revealed by the angels. Enochian has been extensively studied by Donald Laycock, a prominent linguist. His comments indicate that he, for one, is not entirely convinced.[93]

The second body of evidence is the word and credibility of John Dee. It must be remembered that he was regarded as one of the most educated people of his age, acknowledged to have impressive scientific credentials. In at least two places, he reports firsthand experience of supernatural events. In his diary, he writes, "I had sight in Crystallo offerd me, and I saw."[94] And in the *Mysteriorum Libri Quinque,* he reports, "I fele: and (by a great thundring noyce, thumming thuning myne eares) I perceyue

---

[91]   Sloane 3189.

[92]   George Hay, ed., *The Necronomicon* (Jersey: Neville Spearman, 1978), p. 36.

[93]   Donald C. Laycock, *The Complete Enochian Dictionary* (York Beach, ME: Weiser Books, 2001), p. 63.

[94]   James O. Halliwell, ed., *The Private Diary of Dr. John Dee* (New York: AMS Press, 1968), p. 11, May 25, 1581.

the presence of some spirituall creature abowt me."[95] He also witnessed the seemingly miraculous materialization of the stone (21 November 1582). On the other hand, it must be admitted that Dee was highly motivated to believe, and thus was more likely to misinterpret events.

The largest body of evidence comes in the form of the word and credibility of Edward Kelley. Views of him range from that of a highly gifted scryer to an outright charlatan. I am inclined to believe that the truth lies somewhere in the middle. Clulee concluded that Kelley

> . . . may well have consciously fabricated everything to deceive Dee, but his bouts of emotional anxiety and arguments with the spirits in the course of his visions, his reluctance to continue except for Dee's desperate pleadings, and his admission of the visions to religious authorities in Prague when that might have had serious consequences all suggest that more than conscious deception was involved (TFR, 64, 102, 370).[96] Although Kelley often questioned the divine character of the angels, he seems to have believed in their reality as firmly as Dee, and while it is clear that the revelations of the angels through Kelley were often prejudiced in favor of Kelley's interests in particular circumstances, they also reflect what Kelley knew of Dee's interests. In a number of places in the minutes Dee has noted the similarity of the angelic revelations to material in Agrippa, Reuchlin, Trithemius, and Peter of Abano, and since Kelley lived with Dee and had access to his library, the revelations are very likely the joint product of Kelley's imagination and stock of knowledge and what

---

[95] MLQ, 17 November 1582.

[96] Dee, "Praefatio latina," 1586 in C. H. Josten's "An Unknown Chapter in the Life of John Dee," *Journal of the Warburg and Courtauld Institutes* 28 (1965): 233–57. See also Butler, *Ritual Magic*, pp. 259, 268.

he knew of Dee's thinking from their discussions and his reading among books of current interest to Dee.[97]

Dee and Kelley's actions may be compared with so-called UFO abductees' recovered memories, wherein a "hypnotist" puts the "witness" into a suggestible state, and, through leading questions, manages to arrive at all sorts of "memories." The process may not be unlike the art of taking political polls. Of course, the better therapists and pollsters are trained to avoid biased results.

Another similarity with the UFO phenomena is the apparent trickster nature of the entities. They seem to combine convincing elements with apparent nonsense in a way that has led some researchers to theorize deep psychological manipulation.[98] Uri Geller's suspicion that there was just some "goddam little clown that is playing with us" sounds hauntingly similar to many of Kelley's complaints.

Other significant evidence lies in the various accurate predictions (e.g., Mary's beheading, the Spanish Armada, the homecoming of the Jews). These must, however, be weighed against those predictions that weren't accurate (e.g., prophecies of doom, Laski's future).[99] Another event that deserves mention is a secret conversation between Dee and the angels, held in Greek in order to prevent Kelley from understanding it. Aside from this incident, the angels' use of Latin seems to reflect Kelley's limited schooling in that language. When using Latin, they tend to deliver fixed speeches and avoid discourse. Also, as noticed by Calder, the angels "increase in fluency through the years."[100]

---

[97] Nicholas Clulee, *John Dee's Natural Philosophy,* p. 205.

[98] See for example, Jacque Vallee's *Messengers of Deception* (Berkeley: Ronin Publishing, 1979) and Colin Wilson, *Alien Dawn* (New York: Fromm International, 1998).

[99] Laski is told he would have the kingdoms of Poland and Moldavia. The angels also incorrectly foretell Rudolph's demise and Stephen's ascent.

[100] I. R. F. Calder, "John Dee Studied as an English Neoplatonist," chapter 9, section 4.

A quick survey of how practical the angel magic was to Dee is even less convincing. Although Dee's aims were not only practical, but mystical as well, the results do not seem to be very reliable:

AIMS:	RESULTS:
evaluate the value/validity of texts (e.g., *Aldaraia/Soyga*, *Sigillum Dei* examples)	question evaded
hidden treasure	never successful
location of lost books (e.g., Arabic book, books of Enoch, Esdras)	Arabic book later recovered; others not specific
political advice (e.g., how much does Lord Treasurer know, how to get reformed calendar accepted, Laski's political prospects)	Laski's future not accurate, later disfavored; calendar not accepted
advice for Adrian Gilbert about Northwest passage	Northwest passage turned out to be a myth
advice regarding Mistress Haward	???
ensure actions are protected from evil spirits	constant intrusion by evil spirits, often undetected until much later

Some of the instructions, such as those concerning etymology and geography, are straight out of textbooks. This is also true of the names of angels, their descriptions, offices, and so forth. The episode of the dictation of the table can easily be seen as evidence that Kelley was fabricating the "revelations." First Dee is told that the sigil *Aemeth* was correct in his books, but when confronted by conflicting versions, the "angels" produce yet another version. At one point, Kelley takes the sigil to his room to correct it. Later, he frequently interrupts sessions when the extraction methods fail. This may mean that Kelley needed time to figure out where his mistakes were. And what are we to make of the episode in which Kelley produces a drawing in his own handwriting that appears to be a prototype of one of the diagrams? He proclaimed it a counterfeit, and Dee congratulated himself in not succumbing to doubt, but trusting God.

Indeed, the angels often seem to be telling Dee and Kelley what they want to hear to gain their cooperation, but their reasons are not apparent.

Figure 1. Dee's wax Sigillum Dei Aemeth.   © The British Museum

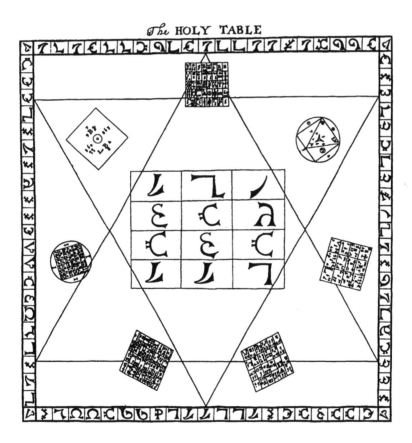

Figure 2. Excerpt from Aldaraia sive Soyga.

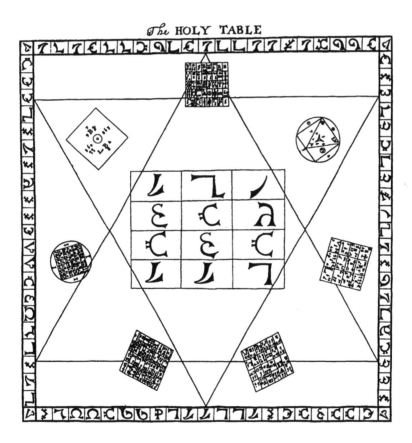

Figure 3. The Holy Table, from Causabon.

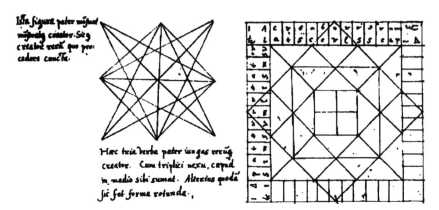

Figure 4. Diagrams from Aldaraia sive Soyga.

Figure 5. Art Paulina.

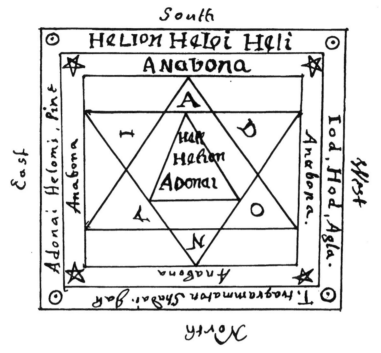

Figure 6. Ars Almadel.

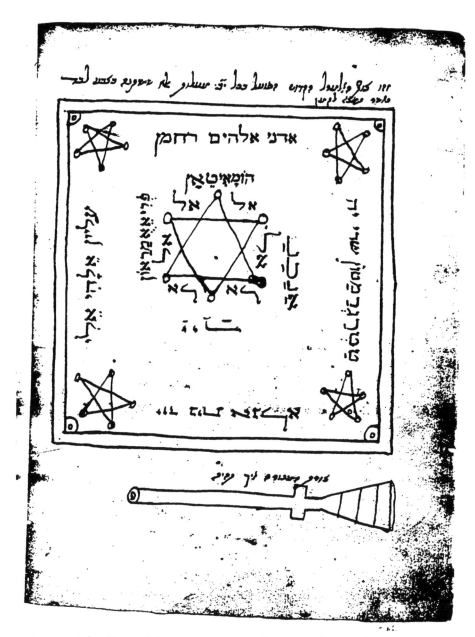

Figure 7. The Almadel from Hermann Gollancz, Sepher Mafteah Shelomoh, 1914.

PREFACE

BE IT REMEMBERED, that the 20th of August 1672, I received by the hands of my servant Samuell Story, a parcell of Dr: Dee's manuscripts, all written with his owne hand; vizt: his Conference with Angells, which first began the 22th of Dec: Anno: 1581, & continued to the end of May Anno: 1583, where the printed booke of the remaining conferences (published by Dr: Cawsabon) begins, & are bound up in this volume.

Beside these, the booke intituled, *The 48 Claves Angelicae,*[1] also, *Liber Scientia Terrestris Auxilij & Victoria*[2] (these two being those very individuall bookes which the angells commanded to be burnt,[3] & were after restored[4] by them as appeares by the printed Relation of Dr: Dee's Actions with Spirits pag: 418 & 419) The booke intituled *De Heptarchia Mystica Collectaneorum Lib: Primus,*[5] and a booke of

---

1 48 Claves Angelicae: "The 48 Angelic Keys." -Ed.

2 The title page of the actual manuscript reads, *Liber Scientiae, Auxilij et Victoriae Terrestris:* "The Book of Earthly Knowledge, Help, and Victory" -Ed.

3 10 April 1586.

4 30 April 1586.

5 The actual title page reads, *De Heptarchia Mystica (Diuinis, ipsius Creationis, stabilitæ legibus) Collectaneorum / Liber primus:* "Concerning the Mystical Heptarchy (divine, of the creation itself, with permanent rules) First Book of collected passages" -Ed.

invocations or Calls, begining with the squares filld with letters, about the black cross. These 4 bookes I have bound up in another volume.[6]

All which, were a few daies before delivered to my said servant, for my perusall (I being then at Mr: William Lillies[7] house at Hersham in Surrey) by my good freind Mr: Thomas Wale, one of his maiesties warders in the Tower of London.

The 5th of Sept: following Mr: Wale (having heard of my retourne to towne) came to my office in the Excise Office in Broadstreete, & told me he was content to exchang all the foresaid bookes, for one of myne, viz[t]: *The Institution, Lawes & Ceremonies of the most Noble Order of the Garter*, to this I agreed, and provided one, which I sent him fairely bound, & gilt on the back.[8]

On the 10th: of the said Sept: Mr: Wale came thither to me againe, & brought his wife with him, from her I received the following account of the preservation of these bookes, even till they came to my hands, viz[t]: That her former husband was one Mr: Jones[9] a confectioner, who formerly dwelt at the Plow in Lumbardstreet London, & who, shortly after they were married, tooke her with him into Adle streete among the joyners, to buy some houshold stuff, where (at the corner house) they saw a chest of cedarwood, about a yard & halfe long, whose lock & hinges, being of extraordinary neate worke, invited them to buy it. The master of the shop told them it had ben parcell of the goods of Mr: John Woodall Chirurgeon (father to Mr: Thomas Woodall late Serjant Chirurgeon to his now Maiestie King Charles the 2nd: (my intimate

---

6   Sloane 3191.

7   William Lilly, noted English astrologer. Born 30 April 1602. Died 9 June 1681.

8   "As a further testimony of the sence of Mr. Wales kindnes, shortly after his death, I sent for his son, & bestowed on him, one of my deputies places in the Excise, with an allowance of 80 £ per Annum." /E.A.

9   Sloane 3189 has the following three names written on a blank page, which may be these former owners: Robert Jones, Susanna Jones, George Lockehouse. -Ed.

friend) and tis very probable he bought it after Dr: Dee's death, when his goods were exposed to sale.

Twenty yeares after this (& about 4 yeares before the fatall fire of London) she & her said husband occasionally removing this chest out of its usuall place, thought they heard some loose thing ratle in it, toward the right hand end, under the box or till[10] thereof, & by shaking it, were fully satisfied it was so: Hereupon her husband thrust a peece of iron into a small crevice at the bottome of the Chest, & thereupon appeared a private drawer, which being drawne out, therein were found divers bookes in manuscript, & papers, together with a litle box, & therein a chaplet of olive beades, & a cross of the same wood, hanging at the end of them.

They made no great matter of these bookes &c: because they understood them not, which occasioned their servant maide to wast about one halfe of them under pyes & other like uses, which when discovered, they kept the rest more safe.

About two yeares after the discovery of these bookes, Mr: Jones died, & when the fire of London hapned, though the chest perished in the flames, because not easily to be removed, yet the bookes were taken out & carried with the rest of Mrs: Jones her goods into Moorefields, & being brought safely back, she tooke care to preserve them; and after marrying with the foresaid Mr: Wale, he came to the knowledge of them, & thereupon, with her consent, sent them to me, as I haue before set downe.

E. Ashmole

---

10   till: "drawer or compartment." - Ed.

Anno 1581: 1582

Mysteriorum

Liber Primus

Mortlaci

1

Præter alias meas extemporaneas preces, et eiaculationes ad Deum vehementiores: Hæc una, maximè usitata fuit

Oratio mea Matutina, Vespertinaque: pro Sapientia.[1]

In nomine Dei Patris, Dei Filij, Dei Spiritus Sancti.

Amen.

Omnipotens, Sempiterne, vere, et viue Deus, in adiutorium meum intende: Domine Dominantium, Rex Regum, Jeouah Zebaoth, ad adiuuandum me festina:

Gloria Deo, Patri, Filio, et spiritui Sancto: Sicut erat in principio, et nunc, et semper et in sæcula sæculorum: Amen.

Recte sapere, et intelligere doceto me, (Ô rerum omnium Creator,) Nam Sapientia tua, totum est, quod volo: Da verbum tuum in ore meo, (Ô rerum omnium Creator,) et sapientiam tuam in corde meo fige.

O Domine Jesu Christe (qui sapientia vera es, æterni et Omnipotentis tui Patris) humilimè tuam oro Diuinam Maiestatem, expeditum mihi ut mittere digneris, alicuius pij, Sapientis expertique Philosophi auxilium, ad illa plenissimè intelligenda perficiendaque, quæ maximi valoris erunt ad tuam laudem et gloriam amplificandam: Et si Mortalis nullus iam in terris viuat, qui ad hoc munus aptus sit: vel qui ex æterna tua providentia, ad istud mihi præstandum beneficium assignatus fuerit: Tunc equidem humilimè, ardentissimè et constantissimè a tua Diuina Maiestate requiro, ut ad me de cælis mittere digneris bonos tuos Spirituales Ministros; Angelosque, videlicet Michaëlem, Gabrielem, Raphaëlem ac Urielem: et (ex Diuino tuo fauore) quoscunque, alios, veros, fidelesque tuos Angelos, qui me plene et perfecte

---

1 Praeter . . . sapientia: "Besides my other frequent extemporaneous prayers and more ardent exhortations to God, this one has been most frequently used. *My morning and evening prayer for wisdom.*" -Ed.

informent et instruant, in cognitione, intelligentiaque vera et exacta,
Arcanorum et Magnalium tuorum (Creaturas omnes tuas, illarumque
naturas, proprietates, et optimos usus, concernentium) et nobis
Mortalibus Scitu necessariorum; ad tui nominis laudem, honorem, et
gloriam; et ad solidam meam, aliorumque (per me,) plurimorum tuorum fidelium consolationem: et ad Inimicorum tuorum confusionem, et
subversionem. Amen. Fiat Jeouah Zebaoth: Fiat Adonay, fiat Elohim.
O beata, et superbenedicta Omnipotens Trinitas, Concedas mihi
(Joanni Dee) petitionem hanc, modo tali, qui tibi maximè placebit.[2]

Amen.

---

2   In nomine . . . placebit: "In the name of God the Father, God the Son, God the
    Holy Spirit. Amen. O almighty, eternal, true and living God, be pleased to deliv-
    er me! O Lord of Lords, King of Kings, Jehovah Zebaoth, make haste to help
    me!(cf. Psalm 70) Glory be to God the Father, and to the Son, and to the Holy
    Spirit: as it was in the beginning, is now, and ever shall be, world without end.
    Amen. Teach me to perceive and understand properly (O Creator of all things),
    for your wisdom is all I desire. Fix your word in my ear (O Creator of all things),
    and fix your wisdom in my heart. O Lord Jesus Christ (you who are the true wis-
    dom of your eternal and omnipotent Father) I most humbly beg your Divine
    Majesty that you consider it proper to send me the speedy help of some pious
    wise man and experienced philosopher for realizing and perfecting above all fully
    those things which will be of greatest value for increasing your praise and glory.
    And if no such mortal man now lives upon the earth who is fitting for this work,
    or who may have been assigned by your eternal providence to the performing of
    that service for me, then truly I most humbly, most ardently, and most faithfully
    ask from your divine majesty that you grant to send me down from heaven your
    good spiritual ministers and angels, namely Michael, Gabriel, Raphael, and also
    Uriel: and (from your divine favor) any other true and faithful angels of yours,
    who may completely and perfectly train and teach me in the true and accurate
    knowledge and understanding of your secrets and wonders (concerning all your
    creatures, and their nature, properties, and best use) and necessary knowledge for
    us mortals, to the praise, honor, and glory of your name, to my firm solace and
    otherwise (through me) the solace of the greatest number of your faithful, and to
    the confusion and ruin of the wicked. Amen. Let it be O Jehovah Zebaoth; let it
    be O Adonay; let it be O Elohim. O blessed and omnipotent Trinity, praised
    above all things, grant me (John Dee) this petition, in such a manner that will be
    most pleasing to you. Amen." -Ed.

Ab anno 1579. hoc ferè modo: Latinè, vel Anglicè; (ast circa annum 1569 alio et peculiari, particulari modo: interdum pro Raphaële, interdum pro Michaële) ad Deum præces fundere: mihi gratissimum fuit: Mirabilem in me faciat Deus Misericordiam suam.[3]

Amen

---

3   Ab anno . . . suam: "From the year 1579 in approximately this manner, in Latin or in English (and furthermore in another unique and particular manner, sometimes for Raphael, and sometimes for Michael) it was most gratifying to me to pour forth my prayers to God; may God grant me his wonderful mercy." -Ed.

John Dee his Note[4]

Angelus, siue In=		*Etymologia:*
telligentia, nunc _____		Gratiosa /
toti Mundo præ=	**ANNAEL**	Afflicta Dei
dominans[5]		Misericors[6]

4 Angeli præsid=
entes 4 Cardinibus
Cæli: ut Agrippa

notat, in scala	Michael	Gabriel	Raphael	Uriel
Quaternarij[7]				
	=	=	=	=

Etymologiæ	Fortitudo Dei	Prevalescentia—	Medicina	Lux
		siue præpotentia—	Dei	Dei[8]
		siue Fortitudo		
		prævalescens—Dei		

אַנָּאֵ‎   et   אַנָּ‎| Anna, et Annah, obsecrantis, et confitentis particula est: hæc roe, non absurdè innuëre videtur, Orantem et confitentem Deum.[9]

---

4   In Sloane 3677, this note comes before the prayer. -Ed.

5   Angelus . . . praedominans: "Angel or intelligence now presiding over the whole world." -Ed.

6   Etymologia: Gratiosa / Afflicta Dei / Misericors: "Etymology: Favored / Distressed of God Merciful." Dee considered Hebrew etymology important and discusses meanings and roots of various words in various works of his. It seems he had at least a rudimentary command of Hebrew grammar as well. -Ed.

7–9 on following page

...icensia.......rig[10]
Ad Deum Omnipotentem Protestatio fidelis:
ad perpetuam rei memoriam[11] *Anno 1582.*

O God Almighty, thow knowest, & art my director, and witnes herein,
That I haue from my youth up, desyred & prayed unto thee for pure &
sownd wisdome and understanding of some of thy truthes naturall and
artificiall: such, as by which, thy wisdome, goodnes & powre bestowed
in the frame of the word might be browght, in some bowntifull measure
under the Talent[12] of my Capacitie, to thy honor & glory, & the benefit

---

7   4 Angeli ... Quaternarii: "4 angels presiding over the 4 quarters of heaven, as
     Agrippa notes in the Scale of the number four (*Occult Phil.,* Book 2, ch 7)." This
     grouping of the Archangels is common in medieval and Renaissance occult
     works. In *Liber Juratus,* one of the earliest books of the Solomonic school of
     magic, these four angels are known as the "Angels of the 4 winds." Agrippa, in
     his work, *De Occulta Philosophia,* book 2, chap. 7 (Leiden: E. J. Brill, 1992), pp.
     266, calls them the "four angels ruling over the corners of the world." The
     Magical Calendar of Tycho Brahe gives the same. Michael and Gabriel are the
     only two angels mentioned by name in the Old Testament. Raphael is mentioned
     in the apocryphal *Book of Tobit,* and Uriel is well-known in noncanonical lore.
     Annael is relatively unknown. -Ed.

8   Etymologiae: Fortitudo . . . praevalesceus: "Etymology: Michael: Strength of God;
     Gabriel: either made very strong or very powerful or strength of God; Raphael:
     Medicine of God; Uriel: Light of God." -Ed.

9   Anna . . . Deum: "Anna, et Annah, is a particle of the supplicant and confessor:
     consequently it may not be unreasonable that it indicates praying and confessing
     God." Dee's theory is that the name Annael derives from Hebrew "Ana" mean-
     ing "pray," or "lament." The more usual explanation of Anael is that it is equiv-
     alent to Haniel, and means "Grace of God." Johannes Trithemius, in *De Septem
     Secundeis* (translation in William Lilly, *Worlds Catastrophe,* London, 1647)
     refers to him as the "spirit of Venus."- Ed.

10   Per Sloane 3677.

11   Ad Deum . . . Anno 1582: "A faithful declaration to almighty God, to the last-
     ing account of this matter in the year 1582." -Ed.

12   Talent: "power." -Ed.

of thy Servants, my brethern & Sistern, in, & by thy Christ our Saviour. And for as much as, many yeres, in many places, far & nere, in many bokes, & sundry languagis, I haue sowght, & studyed; and with sundry men conferred, and with my owne reasonable discourse labored, whereby to fynde or get some ynckling, glyms, or beame of such the forsaid radicall truthes: But, (to be brief) after all my forsaid endevor I could fynde no other way, to such true wisdome atteyning, but by thy extraordinary gift: and by no vulgar Schole doctrine, or humane Invention. And, Seing, I haue red in thy bokes, & records, how Enoch enioyed thy favor and conversation, with Moyses thow wast familier: And allso that to Abraham, Isaac, and Jacob, Josua, Gedeon, Esdras, Daniel, Tobias, and sundry other, thy good Angels were sent, by thy disposition, to instruct them, informe them, help them, yea in worldly and domesticall affaires, yea and sometimes to satisfy theyr desyres, dowtes & questions of thy Secrets: And furdermore Considering, the Shew-stone, which the high preists did use, by thy owne ordering: wherein they had lights and Judgments in theyr great dowtes: and considering allso that thow (O God) didst not refuse to instruct thy prophets, (then, called Seers) to give true answers to common people of things æconomicall, as Samuel, for Saul,[13] seeking for his fathers asses being gon astray: and of other things vulgar true predictions, whereby to wyn credyt unto thy waightier affayres: And thinking with my self, the lack of thy wisdome; to me, to be of more importance, then the Value of an Asse or two, could be to Cis, (Saul his father): And remembring what good cownsayle thy Apostle James giveth, saying, *Si quis autem vestrûm indiget sapientia, postulet a Deo,* &c.[14] And that Salomon

---

[13] I Samuel 9 is the story of Saul's consulting Samuel about his father's asses. - E.A.

[14] James 1:5 Si quis autem vestrum indiget sapientia, postulet a Deo, qui dat omnibus affluenter, et non improperat: et dabitur ei.: "If any of you lack wisdom, let him ask of God, that giveth to all men liberally, and upbraideth not; and it shall be given him." -Ed.

the wise, did so, euen immediately by thy self, atteyne to his wonderfull wisdome. Therfore, seeing I was sufficiently towght and confirmed, that this wisdome could not be come by at mans hand or by humane powre, but onely from thee (Ô God) mediately[15] or immediately) And having allwayes a great regarde & care to beware of the filthy abvse of such as willingly and wetingly, did invocate & consult (in diuerse sorts) Spirituall creatures of the damned sort: angels of darknes, forgers & patrons of lies & untruthes: I did fly unto thee by harty prayer, full oft, & in sundry manners: sometymes Crying unto thee, *Mittas lucem tuam et veritatem tuam, que me ducant &c,*[16] sometymes *Recte sapere et intelligere doceto me, Nam sapientia tua totum est quod volo: &c,*[17] sometymes, *Da verbum tuum in ore meo, et sapientiam, tuam in corde meo fige &c.*[18] And having perceyued by some slight experiens with two diuerse persons, that thow hadst a speciall care to give me thy light, and truth, by thy holy and true ministers Angelic and Spirituall: and at length, hearing of one, (a master of Arte, a preacher of thy word admitted) accownted as a good Seer,[19] and skryer of Spirituall apparitions, in Christalline receptacle, or in open ayre, by his practise procured: and trusting to frame him, by my ernest & faithfull prayers unto thee (my God) to some my help in my forsayd Studies: tyll, thow (o hevenly father) woldest by thy unserchable proveydence, send me some apter man or means thereto. Thereuppon trying him and using him, I fownd great diuersity betwene

---

15   mediately: "through a mediator." -Ed.

16   Mittas . . . ducant &c: "May you send your light and your truth, which may lead me . . ." -Ed.

17   Recte Sapere . . . quod volo: See above. -Ed.

18   Da verbum . . . fige &c: "Fix your word in my ear, and your wisdom in my heart, etc." -Ed.

19   This third seer was Saul. -E.A.

his private usuall manner, and intente of practise, and my pure, sincere, devowte, & faithfull prayer unto thee onely. And therfore often & fervently I exhorted him to the good; and reproved both him, and his ministers, with my no small daunger, but that thow (in manner unhard of) didst pitch thy holy tente to my defence, and cumfert, in conflict most terrible: as thow best knowest O God, and I willed him thereuppon to preach thy mercyes, & the verity of the kingly prophet his testimony, *Castrametatur Angelus Domini, in Circuitu timentium eum.*[20] And out of Roger Bachon his boke written *De mirabili potestate Artis et Natura,*[21] (where he writeth against the wycked Diuel callers) I noted unto him this sentence, *Facilius (sine comparatione a Deo*[22] *impetrandum foret, vel a bonis spiritibus, quicquid homini utile reputare &c*[23] which my cownsayle he promised me to follow, as thow art witnes, ô our true & almighty God. And as thy good spirituall creatures neyther had delight in the man, neyther wold so playnely & preistly give me theyr answers or informations by him, that he might be hable to perceyve the pith therof: So was he at length very unwilling to here him self rebuked for his nawghtynes, and to be barred from the Mysteries of thy truthes understanding; which were the onely things that I desyred, throwgh thy grace, o our most mercifull God. Therfore, as well for a

---

[20] This seems to be a paraphrase of Psalm 34:7: "The angel of the Lord encamps around those who fear him, and delivers them."

[21] De mirabili . . . Naturae: "Concerning the wonderful power of art and of nature" -Ed.

[22] Numquid non est Deus in Israël, ut ad consulendum Beelzebub, deum Accaron. Reg. 4. cap. 1. -Δ. "Is it because there is no God in Israel that you are going to inquire of Beelzebub, the god of Ekron?" 2 Kings (called Reg 4, 4 Kings in the vulgate) - Ed.

[23] Facilius . . . reputare: "It is without doubt incomparably easier to obtain anything that is considered useful for people from God, or from good spirits [than from evil spirits]." -Ed.

Memoriall answerable to the premisses, as for the better warrant of my Such exercises to be made accownt of, hereafter: (leaving all unto thy infinite mercies, and unsearchable providence,) I haue thowght it not impertinent, to note downe, even in this place one of the last Actions, which I had with the forsayd preacher: when I made ernest & faythfull petition unto thee (o the true and Almighty God) for sending, unto my cumfort & eridition, (yf it were thy blessed will,) thy holy, & mighty Angel Annael: of whome and of all the Hierarchies hevenly all prayer honor & thanks, be rendred unto thy diuine maistie: now & euer: & worlde without ende. Amen. Amen. Amen.

Anno 1581 Decembris 22. Mane[24] *Mortlak*

Δ: After my fervent prayers made to God, for his mercifull cumfort and instruction, throwgh the ministery of his holy and myghty Angel, named Anael,[25] (yf it wer his diuine pleasure) I willed, the Skryer, (named Saul) to loke into my great Chrystaline Globe, yf God had sent his holy Angel Anael, or no: And Saul loking into my forsayd stone, (or Chrystall Globe) for to espie Anael, he saw there one,[26] which answered to that name. But being ernestly requested of me to tell the Truthe yf he were Anaël, An other did appere very bewtifull, with apparell yellow, glittering, like gold: and his hed had beames like ster beams, blasing, and spredding from it; his eyes fyrie. He wrote in the stone very much in hebrue letters, and the letters seamed all transparent

---

24   Mane: "in the morning." -Ed.

25   AÑAËL.

26   Note, An illuding intruder, even at the first, putting him self, as an angel of light. Take hede allwayes of undue securitie.

gold: which, Saul was not able eyther presently to reade, that I might write after his voyce, neyther to imitate the letters in short tyme. A bright ster, did go up and down by him. There appeared allso a white dog, with a long hed.[27] And many other visions appeared, with this second: The first being voyded quite away. Thereuppon I sayd, as followeth,

Δ: In nomine Jesu Christi, Quis tu es?[28] He answered to Saul his hearing.

AN: Potestas omnis, in me sita est.[29]

Δ: Quæ?[30]

AN: Bona, et mala.[31]

Δ: Then appeared in the stone, these two letters M. G. I then axing him some questions, de Thesauro abscondito:[32] He answered,

AN: Ne perturbes: Nam hæ sunt Nugæ.[33]

And withall appeared many <u>dedd mens</u> skulls, on his left hand. He sayd to me,

AN: Ubi est potestas tua?[34]

---

[27] There appered a great number of dead mens skulls, likewise.

[28] In nomine . . . tu es: "In the name of Jesus Christ, who are you?" This is a standard first question for interrogating spirits. "Let him first require his name, and if he be called by any other name" (pseudo-?) Agrippa's *Fourth Book of Occult Philosophy*, ed. Robert Turner (London: Askin Publishers, 1978), p. 67. -Ed.

[29] "Potestas . . . est: "All power is placed in me." -Ed.

[30] Quae?: "Which?" -Ed.

[31] Bona et mala: "good and bad." -Ed.

[32] De Thesauro abscondita: "regarding hidden treasure." -Ed.

[33] Ne perturbes ... Nugae: "Don't bother, for these are trifles." -Ed.

[34] Ubi . . . tua?: "By whom is your power?" -Ed.

Δ: Cur quæris de potestate aliqua mea?[35]

AN: Cur? Signifi, non mihi placet.[36]

Δ: I, thereuppon, set by him, the stone in the frame:

and sayd,

Δ: An bonus aliquis Angelus, assignatus est huic speculo?[37]

AN: Etiam.[38]

Δ: Quis?[39]

AN: מיכ[גא]ל He answered, by the shew of these letters in the stone.

Δ: Bonus ne ille Angelus, de quo in scripturis fit mentio?[40]

AN: Maximè.[41]

---

35 Cur . . . mea?: "Why do you ask about my power?" -Ed.

36 Cur . . . placet: "Why? It means you haven't satisfied me." - Ed.

37 An bonus . . . speculo?: "Is there any good angel assigned to this speculum/mirror?" - Ed.

38 Etiam: "Yes, certainly." -Ed.

39 Quis? "Who?" -Ed.

40 Bonus . . . mentio: "Isn't this the good angel mentioned in scripture?" [i.e. Michael]-Ed.

41 Maxime: "Absolutely." -Ed.

Δ: Fieri ne potest, quòd ego eundem videam, et cum illo agam?[42]

AN: Ita.[43] And therewith appeared this character –

Δ: Quid per hoc, significare velis?[44]

AN: Alterius Angeli character est.[45]

Δ: Cur hîc, et nunc ostendis?[46]

AN: Causam ob magnam.[47] Make an ende: It shalbe declared, but not by me.

Δ: By whome then?

AN: By him that is assigned to the stone: but not, tyll after the feast. And then thow must prepare thyself, to prayer and fasting.[48]

In the Name of God, be Secret: and in all thy doings praying, tyll thow hast thy desyre: which shall not be far of. After Newyeres tyde, Deale, But not on the Sabaoth day. Pray contynually. When it shall pleas god, to stir thee up, Then procede. In the brightest day, When the Sonne shyneth: In the morning, fasting, begynne to pray. In the Sonne Set the stone. Deale both Kneeling, and sitting. I haue done for this tyme.

My name is ANNAEL.

I will speak ones more to thee: and than farewell: for thow shalt not haue me any more.

---

42 Fieri . . . agam?: "May I not see and deal with him?" -Ed.

43 Ita: "yes" -Ed.

44 Quid . . . velis: "What do you wish to show by this?" -Ed.

45 Alterius . . . est: "It is the character of another angel." -Ed.

46 Cur . . . ostendis?: "Why do you show this now, and on this occasion?" -Ed.

47 Causam ob magnam: "For a great reason." -Ed.

48 In margin: "Prayer / Fasting." -Ed.

Be not to hasty in wrath.

Δ: Is this, that, you ment to speak?

AN: I. Do good to all men. God hath sufficient for thee, and for all men.

Farewell.

Δ: Gloria patri et filio et spiritui sancto. Sicut erat in principio, et nunc et semper: et in sæcula sæculorum.[49]

Amen.

Δ: Remember, that diuerse other particulars, mowght haue byn Noted of this dayes Action: but these may suffice: And yet it is not to be forgotten, that as he sayd his name was Annael (with a dubble n) so he allso confessed himself to be the same Annaël which is *prepositus orbis veneris:*[50] and allso Chief governor Generall of this great period, as I haue Noted in my boke *of Famous and rich Discoueries.*[51]

Consider and Remember: That this Note, of the Action, (had with holy ANNAEL), is, of prince Befafes, (otherwise called Obelison) accownted as the Prolog of my first boke of mysticall exercises Anno 1582. Nouembris 20. Vide post.

---

49 Gloria . . . saeculorum: "Glory be to the Father, and to the Son, and to the Holy Spirit, as it was in the beginning, is now, and ever shall be, world without end." -Ed.

50 Prepositus orbis veneris: "Governor of the planet Venus." -Ed.

51 This book only survives in fragments as Cotton MS. Vitellius. C. VII, art. 3. in the British Library. -Ed.

At Mortlak

In nomine Jesv CHRISTI.[52] Amen.

Anno 1582. Martij die. 10. hora 11¼ Ante meridiem. Saterday

Δ: One[53] Mr. Edward Talbot cam to my howse,[54] and he being willing and desyrous to see or shew some thing in spirituall practise, wold haue had me to haue done some thing therein. And I truely excused myself therein as not in the, vulgarly accownted Magik, neyther studied, or exercised: But confessed my self, long tyme to haue byn desyrous to haue help in my philosophicall studies throwgh the Cumpany and information of the blessed Angels of God. And thereuppon, I browght furth to him, my stone in the frame,

(which was given me of a frende) and I sayd unto him, that I was credibly informed, that to it (after a sort) were answerable *Aliqui Angeli boni:*[55] And allso that I was ones willed by a Skryer, to call for the good Angel Anchor, to appere in that stone to my owne sight. And therfore I desyred him to call him: and (yf he wold) Anachor and Anilos likewise, accownted good Angels, for I was not prepared thereunto. &c. He than

---

52   In nomine Jesu Christi: "In the name of Jesus Christ." -Ed

53   Pseudonym for Edward Kelley. -Ed.

54   Note: he had two dayes before made the like demaunde and request unto me: but he went away unsatisfiyed for his comming was to entrap me, yf I had had any dealing with wicked spirits as he confessed often tymes after: and that he was set on, &c.

55   Aliqui Angeli boni: "some good angels." -Ed.

settled him self to the Action: and on his Knees att my desk (setting the stone before him) fell to prayer and entreaty &c. In the mean space, I, in my Oratory did pray, and make motion to god, and his good Creatures for the furdering of this Action. And within one quarter of an howre (or less) he had sight of one in the stone. but he still expected for two more: deeming this to be one of the three (namely Anchor Anachor Anilos). But I then cam to him, to the stone: And after some thanks to God, and Wellcome to the good Creature, used, I required to know his name. And he spake plainly, (to the hearing of E.T.) that his name is URIEL.

Δ: Are you one of them (sayd I, John Dee) that are answerable, (uppon due observations performed) to this stone?

URIEL: I am.

Δ: Are there any more besyde you?

UR: Michaël and Raphaël. But, *Michaël est princeps in operibus nostris.*[56]

Δ: Ys my boke, of Soyga,[57] of any excellency?

UR: Liber ille, erat Adæ in Paradiso reuelatus, per Angelos Dei bonos.[58]

Δ: Will you give me any instructions, how I may read those Tables of Soyga?

UR: I can - But *solus Michaël illius libri est interpretator.*[59]

Δ: I was told, that after I could read that boke, I shold liue but two yeres and a half.

UR: Thow shallt liue an Hundred and od yeres.[60]

---

56   Michael . . . nostris: "Michael is the foremost in our works." -Ed.

57   Soyga, Soiga = agyos. -E.A. Agios is Greek for holy. Two copies of this book have been identified. One is Bodleian Ms. 908, and the other is British Library Sloane manuscript 8. See the introduction for more detail. -Ed.

58   Liber . . . bonos: "That book was revealed to Adam in Paradise by the good angels of God." -Ed.

59   solus . . . interpretator: "Michael alone is the interpretor of that book." -Ed.

Δ: What may I, or must I do, to haue the sight, and presence, of Michael, that blessed Angel?

UR: Præsentias nostras postulate et invocate, sinceritate et humilitate. Et Anchor, Anachor, et Anilos, non sunt in hunc Lapidem invocandi.[61]

Δ: Oh, my great and long desyre hath byn to be hable to read those Tables of Soyga.

UR: Hæc maximè respiciunt Michaëlem. Michaël est Angelus, qui illuminat gressus tuos. Et hæc revelantur in virtute et veritate non vi.[62]

Δ: Is there any speciall tyme, or howre to be observed, to deale for the enioying of Michael?

UR: *Omnis hora, est hora nobis.*[63]

Δ: After this, there appered[64] in the stone a strange seale, or Characterismus of this fashion ensuing:

---

60   Dee lived to be 81. -Ed.

61   Praesentias . . . invocandi: "Request and invoke our appearance with sincerity and humility. And Anchor, Anachor, and Anilos are not to be called into this stone." -Ed.

62   Haec . . . non vi: "These things mostly involve Michael. Michael is the angel who illuminates your path. And these things are revealed in virtue and truth, not by force." -Ed.

63   Omnis . . . nobis: "Every hour is our hour." -Ed.

64   An illuding spirit straight way intruded him self, and this character: as may appere *Libri Quinti Appendice* where the character is described exactly.

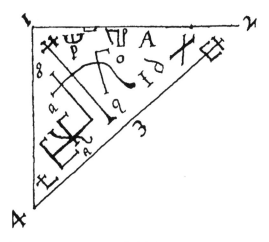

Δ: What is the intente, or use of this?

UR:[65] *Sigillum hoc in auro sculpendum, ad defensionem corporis, omni loco, tempore et occasione: et in pectus gestandum.*[66]

Δ: So we ceased, with thanks to god: and I mused much uppon this Action: and layd all up in mynde, and writing.

Δ: *Soli Deo Honor omnis, et gloria.*[67]

Amen.

The same Saterday after none. Hora. 5.

Δ: After that Mr. E.T. had called Uriel, and I was come to the stone and had used a short speche of thanks giving to God: I then required some instruction for the purpose of Soyga.

---

65 In margin: This was not True Uriel as may appere Anno 1583: May 5. –Ed.

66 Sigillum . . . gestandum: "Engrave this sigil in gold, for protecting the body in all places, times, and occasions: and it is to be worn on the chest." -Ed.

67 Soli . . . gloria: "All honor and glory to God alone." -Ed.

UR: Peace. You must use Michaël.

Δ: I know no meanes or order to use in the invocating of Michaël.[68]

UR: He is to be invocated by certayn of the psalmes of Dauid, and prayers. The which psalmes, are nothing els, but a means unto the seat and Maiestie of God: whereby you gather with your selues due powre, to apply your natures to the holy Angels. I mean the psalmes, commonly called the Seven psalmes.[69] You must use pleasant sauours: with hand and hart: whereby you shall allure him and wynn him (thorowgh Gods fauour) to atteyn unto the thing, you haue long sowght for. There must be Coniunction of myndes in prayer, betwyxt you two, to God Contynually. Yt is the wyll of God, that you shold, ioinctly, haue the knowledge of his Angells to-gither. You had atteyned unto the sight of Michaël, but for the imperfection of Saul. Be of good Cumfort.

Δ: The chayre cam into the stone againe: and I axed what it ment.

UR: This is a seat of perfection: from the which, things shall be shewed unto thee, which thow hast long desyred.

Δ: Then was there a square Table browght into the stone: and I demaunded, what that Table betokened.

UR: A Mysterie, not yet to be known. These two, shall remayn in the stone, to the sight of all undefyled creatures.

You must use a fowre square Table, two cubits square: Where uppon must be set Sigillum Dei,[70] which is allready perfected[71] in a boke of thyne: Blessed be God, in all his Mysteries, and Holy in all his works. This seal must not be loked on, without great reuerence and

---

[68] Note: In this time there appered in the stone, a riche chayre: and after a little while, it was out of sight.

[69] That is, Psalms 6, 32, 38, 51, 102, 130, and 143 (the Vulgate numbers them 6, 31, 37, 50, 101, 129, and 142). –Ed.

[70] Sigillum Dei: "Sigil (or seal) of God." -Ed.

[71] In margin: Erronicè, contra ignorantiam meam. vide post. -Δ (Erroneously, to my ignorance. See below.) –Ed.

deuotion. This seale is to be made of perfect wax. I mean, wax, which is clean purified: we haue no respect of cullours. **This seal must be 9 ynches in diameter: The rowndnes must be 27 ynches, and somwhat more. The Thicknes of it, must be of an ynche and half a quarter, and a figure of a crosse, must be on the back-side of it, made thus:**

The Table is to be made of swete wood: and to be of two Cubits high: with 4 feete: with 4 of the former seales under the 4 feet.

Δ: The fashion of the 4 feet, standing uppon the foresayd rownd seales, was shewed: so as the uttermost circle conteyning the letters, did seme to be clean without[72] the cumpas of the fete, equally rownd abowt the same fete. And these seales were shewed much lesser than the principall seal.[73] Under the Table did seme to be layd red sylk, two yardes square. And ouer the seal, did seme likewise red sylk to lye fowr square: somwhat broader then the Table, hanging down with 4 knops or tassells at the 4 corners thereof.

Uppon this uppermost red silk, did seme to be set the stone with the frame: right ouer, and uppon the principall seal: sauing that the sayd sylk was betwene the one and the other.

---

[72] Note this point.

[73] Two smaller seals are preserved in the British Museum. They measure 125mm in diameter, and are 20mm thick. The holy table itself measured 36¼ inches by 35⅞ inches, was 31½ inches high. -Ed.

The Table was shewed to haue on the fowre sides of it, <u>Characters</u>[74] <u>and names</u>, these, that are here in a schedule annexed, in 4 diuerse rowes.

UR: The characters and words on the sides of the square Table, are to be written with yellow, made of perfect oyle, used in the church.

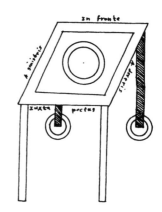

Δ: What oyle is that?

UR: That oyle shalbe opened unto you. The oyle, is perfect prayers: of other oyle I haue no respect. We sanctifie, bycause we are holy: and you sanctify bycause of your holines.

UR: There is a spirit, named Lundrumguffa using you who seketh your destruction, in the hatred of men, in the hurt of thy goods. Discharge him to morrow with Brymstone.[75] He haunteth thy howse, and seketh the destruction of thy dowghter. His pretence was to haue maymed thee in thy Sholder the last night, and long ago. Yf thow do not dischardg him to morrow, he will hurt, both thy wife and thy dowghter.[76]

He is here now.[77]

Giue him a generall discharge from your familie and howse. He will seke Sauls death, who is accursed.[78]

---

[74] Caue: quia angelus tenebrarum se intrusit hic ut libri Quinti appendice apparavit. -Δ. "Beware: an angel of darkness intruded itself here as is shown in the appendix to the fifth book." In fronte: "in front"; iuxta pectus: "near the chest"; a sinistris: "on the left"; a dextris: "on the right." –Ed.

[75] Brimstone (sulfur) was commonly used in exorcisms. For the binding of Asmodeus by Raphael, see *The Book of Tobit* 3.17. -Ed.

[76] Dee's daughter Katherine was nine months old at the time. -Ed.

[77] Note: So is it evident who went abowt to hinder the truth before in the character, and in the border of the Table, falsely cownterfeating &c as it also in the next action may appere.

[78] Saul in danger of being carried away quick. -Δ. Quick: "alive." -Ed.

Δ: I know no means, or art to do this by. For I did burn in flame of Brymstone, Maherion his name and Character, whan I fownd Saul priuilie dealing with him (which manner of wicked dealing I had oft forbydden him) and yet he cam after, and wold haue carryed Saul away quick: as Robert Hilton, George,[79] and other of my howse can testify.

UR: The cursed will come to the cursed.

Δ: I beseche you to discharge him: and to bynde him somwhere far of, as Raphael did (for Thobias sake) with the wycked spirit Asmodeus.

UR: But Thobias did his part.[80] Art is vayne, in respect of God his powre. Brymstone is a mean.

Δ: Whan shall I do this?

UR: To morrow at the tyme of prayers.

Δ: *Gloria Patri et filio et Spiritui Sancto,*

sicut &c.[81] Amen.

1582 Martij 11
Sonday. a Meridie hora .3. a circiter.[82]

Δ: Uriel being called by E.T. there appeared one, clothed with a long robe, of purple: all spanged with gold, and on his hed, a garland, or wreath of gold: his eyes sparkling: of whome I axed Whether the characters noted for the Table, wer perfect: He answered,

---

79 George was a servant of Dee's. Dee's diary states that goodman Hilton requested lodging for his two sons in Dee's house in 1579, and that Robert Hilton came to his service 4 October 1581. -Ed.

80 See Tobit 3.17 and 8.3.

81 Gloria . . . sicut: "Glory be to the Father, and to the Son, and to the Holy Spirit, as . . . etc." -Ed.

82 "Around 3 in the morning." -Ed.

They are perfect:[83] There is no question.

Δ: Are you Uriel?

Than presently[84] cam in One, and threw the brave[85] spirit down by the sholders: and bet him mightyly with a whip: and toke all his robes, and apparell of him: and then he remayned all heary and owggly: and styll the spirit was beaten of him, who cam-in after him. And that spirit, which so bet him, sayd to the hearing of my Skryer,

Lo, thus are the wycked skourged.

Δ: Are you Uriel, who speaketh that?

Uri: I am he. Write down and mark this: for it is worthy of the Noting.

This was thy persecutor Lundrumguffa. I browght him hither to let thee see, how God hath ponished thy enemy.[86]

Lo, thus, hath God delt for thee: Lo thus haue I delt for thee: Thank God.

Δ: Blessed be his holy name; and extolled, world with out ende.

E.T: He drew the wycked spirit away, by the leggs, and threw him into a great pitt, and washed his hands, as it were, with the sweat of his own hed: for he seamed to be all in a sweat.

Δ: Here-uppon, my skryer saw Uriel go away: and he remayned out of sight a little while. Then he cam-in agayn: and an other with him: and iointly these two said to gither, Glorifie God for euer. And than Uriel did stand behinde: and the other did set down in the chayre, with a sworde in his right hand: all his hed glystring[87] like the sonne. The heare of his hed was long. He had wings: and all his lower parts seamed

---

83 Hereby may appere that this wycked spirit foysted in the shew of the fals character and names before.

84 Presently: "at once." -Ed.

85 Brave: "splendid." - Ed.

86 Note: Lundrumguffa skourged spiritually.

87 Glystring: "brilliant." -Ed.

to be with feathers. He had a roab ouer his body: and a great light in
his left hand. He sayd,

Michaël: We are blessed from the begynning: and blessed be the
name of God for euer.

Δ: My skryer saw an innumerable Cumpany of Angels abowt him:
And Uriel did lean on the square Table by. He that sat in the chayre
(whom we take to be Michaël) sayd Than,

Go forward: God hath blessed thee.

I will be thy Guyde.

Thow shallt atteyne unto thy serching.

The World begynnes with thy doings.

Prayse God.

The Angels under my powre, shall be at thy commaundement. Lo, I
will do thus much for thee.

Lo, God will do thus much for thee.

Thow shalt see me: and I will be seen of thee.

And I will direct thy liuing and conversation.

Those that sowght thy life,[88] are vanished away.

Put up thy pen.

Δ: So he departed.

Δ: Gloria, laus, honor, virtus et Imperium Deo immortali, invisibili,
et Omnipotenti, in sæcula sæculorum.[89]

Amen.

---

[88] Lundrumguffa.

[89] Gloria . . . saeculorum: "Glory, praise, honor, virtue, and sovereignty to the
immortal, invisible, and almighty God, forever and ever." –Ed.

Martij 14. Wensday. mane circa horam 9ã.

Δ: Being desirous to procede in this matter, by consent, we bent our selues to the Action. And after that <u>E.T.</u> had called Uriel and saw him, I cam to the desk from my oratorie. There did contynually appeare, the chayre and the Table. I than being affrayde that any other shold come into the stone, instead of Uriel, did ernestly require the spirituall creature appearing, to shew who he was, and what was his name: At length he answered, and sayde to the hearing of E.T.,

Uriel is my name, with diuerse called Nariel.[90]

　　Stay.

Δ: Then he went away, for a while: and cam agayn, and sayd thus,

Ur: The strength of God, is allwayes with thee. Dost thow know, what thow writest?

Δ: In two senses, I may understand it: eyther that the good Angel Gabriel[91] is allwayes with me, thowgh invisibly: or els, that the strength, and mighty hand of God, allwayes is my defense.

Ur: *Fortitudo Dei, tecum semper est.*[92]

Δ: He went away agayn, and cam agayn, following or wayting uppon an other: and before that other, was a man hauing his hed all couered with blak. Then he that cam so in the middle, did sit down in the chayre, and spake this worde following:

Mi: Note.

90　Agrippa hath so, cap. 24, Lib. 3, *Occult. Phil.* -Δ. Cornelius Agrippa, *De Occulta Philosophia,* p. 471. Here Agrippa lists the four princes of the angels as Michael, Raphael, Gabriel, and Nariel (also known as Uriel). They rule over the four winds and the four parts of the world (East, West, North, and South respectively). -Ed.

91　Potius erat dicendum Michaël: Nam Gabriel est Praevalescentia Dei: et ita, fortitudo quidem, sed altioris gradus. -Δ. ("Rather Michael was indicated: For Gabriel is the Predominance of God: and therefore also the strength, but to another degree." -Ed.)

92　Fortitudo . . . est: "The strength of God is always with you." -Ed.

Δ: This was Michael, with his sword in his right hand. Then cam Uriel to the man (hauing his hed all hyd, as it were in a blak hode) and toke-of that blak hode: and then lifted-up the Table cloth. He looked under it, and put it down againe: and lifted it up again. The man stode still before Michael. Then Michael rose; and toke-of all the mans clothes, and left him, as it were, onely in his shirt. Then Uriel toke a little rownd Tablet, as it were, of the bignes of a sixpence, hauing two letters in it, thus:

and gaue it to Michaël. Uriel lifted up the Table cloth: and, from thence, seamed to take apparaile, and put on the man. It semed to be sylk: and very full of wrynkles, or plights. And the man kneeled, and held-up his hands. Uriel toke like a lawrell bush, and set uppon the mans hed. And than the man kneeled before Michaël. Michaël toke the rownd thing, with the letters: and gaue it the man to eat: and he did eat it.

Ur: Lo, things are covered.

Δ: Then he couered the Table and pluckt the cloth over it, down to the grownd, on euery side. The man rose up: And Michaël dubbed him on the hed with his sworde. Then the man stode-up. Then the man turned his face toward <u>E.T.</u> the skryer: and the man did resemble me (John Dee) in cowntenance. And then he turned to Michaël agayn. Michael wrote uppon the mans back, thus,

ANGELVS TVÆ PROFESSIONIS.[93]

Δ: Then E.T. asked me, yf there were such Angels of a mans Profession: and I answered yea; as in Agrippa[94] and other, is declared.

Mi: Leaue your folly: Hold thy peace. Haue you not red, that they that cleaue unto God, are made like unto him.

---

93 Angelus tuae professionis: "Angel of your profession." -Ed.

94 Vide Agrippam de Triplici hōis custode. Lib.3: cap.22. -Δ. Cornelius Agrippa, *De Occulta Philosophia,* book 3, chap. 22, p. 465. Here Agrippa states that

Δ: Yes, forsoth.

Mic: Thow camst hither to lern, and not to dispute. *Laudate Dominum in operibus suis.*[95]

Δ: The man kneled down, and so went out of sight.

Mi: He hath eaten strength against trubble: He hath eaten nothing: and in eating, he hath eaten all things. The name[96] NA, be praysed in trubbles.

Δ: Now Michael thrust out his right arme, with the sword: and bad the skryer to loke. Then his sword did seame to cleaue in two: and a great fyre, flamed out of it, vehemently. Then he toke a ring out of the flame of his sworde: and gaue it, to Uriel: and sayd, thus:

Mic: The strength of God, is unspeakable. Praysed be god for euer and euer.

Δ: Then Uriel did make cursy unto him.

Mi: After this sort, must thy ring be: Note it.

Δ: Then he rose, or disapeared, out of the chayre, and by and by, cam again, and sayde, as followeth.

Mi: I will reveale thee this ring: which was never revealed since the death of Salomon: with whom I was present. I was present with him in strength, and mercy. Lo, this it is. This is it, wherewith all Miracles, and diuine works and wonders were wrowght by Salomon: This is it, which I haue revealed unto thee. This is it, which Philosophie dreameth of. This is it, which the Angels skarse know. This is it, and blessed be his Name: yea, his Name be blessed for euer.

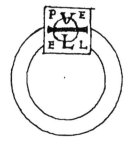

---

everyone is assigned three angelic keepers or preservers: one that is holy, another of the nativity, and another of the profession. -Ed.

95 Laudate . . . suis: "Praise the Lord for his works." -Ed.

96 Vide Reuclini *de Verbo Mirifico,* de nomine NA.

Δ: Then he layd the Ring down uppon the Table: and sayd,

Note.

Δ: It shewed to be a Ring of Gold: with a seale graued in it: and had a rownd thing in the myddle of the seale and a thing like a V, throwgh the top of the circle: and an L, in the bottome: and a barr ———— cleane throwgh it: And had these fowre letters in it, P E L E.[97]

After that, he threw the ring on the borde, or Table: and it semed to fall throwgh the Table: and then he sayde, thus,

Mi: So shall it do, at thy commaundement.

<u>Without this, thow shalt do nothing</u>.[98] Blessed be his name, that cumpasseth all things: Wonders are in him, and his Name is <u>WON-DERFVLL</u>: His Name worketh wonders from generation, to generation.

Δ: Then he went away: and cam-in agayn by and by.

Mi: Note.

Δ: Then he browght-in the Seale, which he shewed the other day: and opened his sworde, and bad the skryer, reade, and he red, EMETH.[99]

---

[97]   Vide Reuclini Librum *de Verbo Mirifico* de nomine PELE.

[98]   The use of the ring.

[99]   De sigillo Emeth, vide Reuclinim *Artem Cabalisticam,* lib.3. et Agrippam lib. 3. cap.11. -Δ. "Concerning the seal Emeth, see Johann Reuchlin, *On the Art of the Kabbalah,* book 3." Translated by Martin and Sarah Goodman, (Lincoln , NE: University of Nebraska Press, 1983), pp. 284, 287: "They assert that *En Sof* is alpha and omega, for he said: 'I am the first and the last.' They say too that the 'Crown' of the kingdom is the bottomless fount of all the ages and the Father of mercies, whose mystery is that he seals up Essence through Truth. As our noble teacher Eliezer haKalir says: 'Truth is his seal.' This can be proved by arithmetical calculation. If we multiply *Ehieh* (meaning 'essence') by *Ehieh* we will get 441, which is the same as *Emeth,* the word for 'true' or 'truth,' and the same as *Adonai Shalom,* which means 'Lord of Peace.'" Compare with Joseph Gikatilla (b. 1248), *Gates of Light,* translated by Avi Weinstein (San Francisco: Harper Collins Publishers, 1994), p. 222: "Thus the Sages said 'EMeT is the seal of the Holy One, Blessed be He.' . . . Therefore, upon His seal is written EMeT, to teach you that all the hosts of letters from the first aleph to the [but not including] mem

Then the sword closed up agayn: and he sayde,

Mi: This I do open unto thee, bycause thow mervayledst at <u>SIG-ILLVM</u> DEI. This is the Name of the Seale: Which be blessed for euer. This is the seale self. This is Holy: This is pure: This is for euer. Amen.

Δ: Then the seale vanished away. And I sayd to my frende (the Skryer) In dede, this other day, I considered diuerse fashions of the seal: and I fownd them much differing, one from an other: and therfore I had nede to know, which of them I shall imitate: or how to make one perfect of them all.

Mi: Dowt not for the making of it: for God hath perfyted all things. Ask not the cause of my absence, nor of my apparell: for that Mysterie, is known to God. <u>I haue no cloathing, as thow thy self shalt see.</u> I am a Spirit of Truth, and Vertue.[100] Yea you shall see me in Powre, and I will viset you in HOPE. Bless you the Lorde, and follow his wayes, for euer.

Δ: Then he went away: and Uriel followed him. And then I sayde to my skryer: It were good, we had euer some watch-word, when we shold not loke for any more matter at theyr hands, euery tyme of theyr visitting of us. Whereuppon, (unlooked-for, of us,) he spake agayn.

Mi: We lead tyme, Tyme leadeth not us:

Put up thy pen.

The Name of God, be blessed for euer.

Δ: Then they lifted up theyr hands to heuenward (which heven, appeared allso in the stone) and turned toward us, and sayd,

Valete.[101]

[which is in the middle of the alphabet] look to bring favour . . ." See the introduction for a discussion of the seal Emeth. Note also that all three names, "NA," "Emeth," and "PELE" are found in Agrippa, *De Occulta Philosophia,* book 3, chapter 11, p. 434. -Ed.

100 Virtue, also "power." -Ed.

101 Valete: "Farewell." -Ed.

Δ: So they departed: and at theyr going, the chayr, and the Table, in the stone, did seme to shake.

Δ: Soli Deo omnis honor Laus et Gloria.[102]

Amen.

Martij 15. Thursday. Hora 1¼ a meridie.

Δ: After <u>E.T.</u> his calling into the stone, appeared a tall man, with a sceptre (very great) of gold, glittring. His body all red: and out of his hed, did shote out beames of light, like the sonne beames.

Δ: Being desirous, to know who he was, and his name, I requested him ernestly thereto. But he answered, as followeth,

Invocate nomen Domini, et agnoscetis eum.[103]

Δ: Then I prayed the psalme, Deus misereatur nostri, et benedicat nobis &c.[104] After that, he sayd,

I am mighty.

Δ: Bycause he delayed to declare his name, <u>E.T.</u> the skryer did require him, in the name of God the father, Jesus Christ his sonne, and of the holy ghost, to express his name: and he answered in speche.

So I will by and by.

Δ: Then he seamed to take from his hed little bright sparcks, like little candells endes: and to stick them abowt the chayre: and he went rownd abowt the chayre: and than he spake, as followeth,

I am mighty, and working wonders: I am SALAMIAN.[105] I rule in

---

102 Soli . . . Gloria: "All honor, praise, and glory to God alone." –Ed.

103 Invocate . . . eum: "Invoke the name of the Lord, and acknowledge him." -Ed.

104 Psalm 67.1: Deus . . . nobis: "May God be gracious to us and bless us." -Ed.

105 Of Salamian you may rede, in the call, Diei Dominicae in *Elementis Magicis* Petri de Abano, there called Salamia. -Δ. Elementis Magici: "Magical Elements," by

the hevens, and beare sway uppon erth in his name, who be blessed for euer. Thow doost dowt at me. I am the servant of God, in his light: I serve him. I say, I serve him, with feare and reverence. My name is SALAMIAN: Mighty in the Sonne, worker of wordly actions, as well internall, as externall: known unto God: whose name I know, and bless for euer.

Δ: Then appeared a big flame of fyre by him in the ayre.

Sal: Thow knowest not, or thow wilt not know, that Mamon, with his servants, are present abowt thee: whose presence doth hinder the presence of the vertues Adonay our comming. Blessed be God, in the highest.

Amen.

Δ: He toke the forsaide flame of fyre, and flung it up unto the heven ward.

Sal: Mamon is a king whome God hateth: whose sect, contynually tempt, provoke and stir-up wickednes, against the Lord, and against his annoynted. But he dyeth: blessed be God for euer. Driue him away.

Δ: It is incomparably more easy for you to do. And as for my parte, I fele neyther in body, nor sowle, any token of his presence or working. Thereuppon he caused the whole chamber (which we were in) to appere very playnely in the stone: and so there shewed a great cumpany of wycked spirits to be in the chamber: and among them, One, most horrible and grisely thretting,[106] and approaching to our heds: and skorning and gnashing at us.

Sala: God determines his mysteries, by Arte and vertue.

Peter de Abano, English translation published as *Heptameron: or Magical Elements* (London, 1655, reprint London: Askin Publishers, 1978), p. 89. Diei Dominicae: "Sunday."

[106] Thretting: "threatening." -Ed.

Δ: Then he willed me very egerly, to drive them away. And I prayed fervently. And there seamed One to come into the stone, which had very long armes: and he draue them away courragiously: And so they were driuen away. After that presently, cam one into the stone, all white. Salamian reached this white one a Cup. The white man held-up the Cup: and sayd, as followeth,

Lo, this is my name.

God shall bless you. Fear not: your faithfullness provoketh me to tell my name, and this it is: (putting furth the Cup again) for, I am called Medicina Dei.[107] I will shew thee, and I will shew you, the Angel of your Direction, which is called OCH.[108]

Δ: This name he spake: he shewed it allso on the Table (before him) written.

Raph: He is mighty in the sonne beames: He shall profit thee here-after.

Δ: Then cam in an other, and sat down in the chayre: and he sayde, as followeth,

The strength of God liueth: and God raigneth for euer. I am Fortitudo Dei.

Δ: Why, then, you are Gabriel: and I toke you hitherto to be Michaël. How shall I then amend my boke, in respect of your name, allwayes before, written Michaël?

For.Dei: What thow hast written, that hast thow written: and it is true. Write down this name. POLIPOS.[109] Dost thow understand it?

Δ: No, God knoweth.

---

[107] Raphaël.

[108] De OCH vide in libello *Arbatel* in ☉. -Δ. According to the Arbatel *De Magia Veterum*, Aphor. 17, pp. 17–31, Och is a spirit of Olympus who governs solar things. The other six Olympic spirits are Aratron (Saturn), Bethor (Jupiter), Phaleg (Mars), Hagith (Venus), Ophiel (Mercury), and Phul (Moon). -Ed.

[109] See Agrippa, *De Occulta Philosophia*, book 3, chapter 34, p. 504. -Ed.

For.Dei: When that day commeth, I will speak with thee: yf thow observe that which I haue commaunded thee.[110] **As truely, as I was with SALOMON, so truely will I be with thee.**

Δ: Then cam in an other, whom we toke to be Uriel: for he went allso, as he was wont, and leaned at the Table.

For.Dei: Search for wisdome and lerning, and the lord will deliuer it unto you.

Δ: I wold to god, I knew your name truely, or what peculier letter I might set for you, to Note your words and Actions by.

For.Dei: Name I haue none, but by my office. SALAMIAN cam not hither, but by me. He is a mighty Prince, governing the hevens, under my powre. This is sufficient for thy Instruction. **I was with Salomon, in all his works and wonders:** and so was this, whome God had appointed unto him. The Diuines know his name: and he is not hidden from the face of the erth: His name is written in the boke which lyeth in the Wyndow.

Δ: Do you mean Agrippa his boke? And is it there expressed by the name SALAMIAN?[111]

For.Dei: I haue sayde.

Δ: What order will you appoint unto us two, in respect of our two beings to-gither? My frende here, may haue other intents and purposes of his affayres, then will serve me, for his ayde hauing in these Actions.

For.Dei: Joyne in prayers. For God hath blessed you: Dowt not.

Consider these mysteries.

Δ: Then they in the stone used talk to gither: but not well to be discerned of the eare of E.T.

---

[110] Δ: Perchaunce he meaneth the cownsayle of Annael: before specifyed.

[111] It is in *Elementis Magicis* Petri de Abano printed with Clauis Agrippae, which lay in my oratorie almost under my wyndow.

At length F.D. talked very much, and spedily to E.T. and disclosed unto him (which he expressed not to me, at the stone but afterward) all the manner of the practise, and the Circumstance abowt the Action intended, with the Gold lamin, the ring, the seales &c. And after I had spoken somwhat, in requesting him, to shew me the manner, How I shold artificially prepare euery thing spoken of, he sayd,

F.D:

[... Use me, in the Name of God, for all occasions.[112] ...]

Blessed[113] be God, who revealeth all Mysteries, &c. I am strength in nede. And Lo, here is Medicine for the sore. We bless the Lord: We gouern the erth, by the societie of Gabriel: whose powre, is with us: but he not here. &c.

Use Patience.

Ur: I liued with Esdras: I liued in him, in the lord, who liueth for euer.[114]

Raph: I liued with Tobie: Tobie the yonger.[115]

Δ: This was the white creature, that spake this.

F.D: We liue in the Lorde: who be praysed for euer.

Δ: I stode silent a good while.

F.D: What wilt thow?

Δ: I did attend, what you wold say.

F.D: I haue sayd.

---

112 The top third of a page is missing here. This quote is supplied from HM, where it is attributed to Michael, that is, F.D., 15 March 1582. -Ed.

113 In margin, written lengthwise: God wilbe revenged uppon Saul: for he hath abused his names in his creatures He hath sinned agaynst kinde. His ponishment is great: and so I ende. -Ed.

114 See the apocryphal *II Esdras* 4.1, 4.36, 5.20, 10.28.

115 See the apocryphal *Book of Tobit* 3.17 and passim.

Δ: I haue byn long at this tyme, in my dealing with you. I trust, I do not offend you therewith. But, for my parte, I could finde in my hart to contynue whole dayes and nights in this manner of doing: euen tyll my body shold be ready to synk down for wearines, before I wold giue ouer. But I feare, I haue caused wearines to my frende here.

E.D: In vertue is no wearines.

Δ: Now he stode up, out of his chayr: and he, and they all, ioinctly blessed us, stretching theyr hands toward us, Crossingly. And so they went away. The Table and the chayre remayned and the glyttring spar-ckles, or drops of streaming little lightes were of the chayre immediately.

Δ: Glorie, thanks, and honor be unto the Almighty Trinitie.

Amen.[116]

---

[116] *Mysteriorum Liber Primus,* tooke ending here (as I conceive) after which fol-lowes *Mysteriorum* * *Liber Secundus,* but the begining thereof is utterly perished. *So it appeares to be by divers Quotations in the following Books. *So by the Citation 28 April 1582. -E.A.

[Mysteriorum Liber

Secundus]

. . . mysteryes,[1] . . .

. . . ow toward a thing, r . . .

. . . howse is hollow, it is empty and voyde . . .

. . . ants: The God of heuen and erth, will send into . . .

NOTE. We bring tydings of light*. The Lord is owr . . .

you and we prayse to gither. His name be praysed for ever. O . . .

in his Mysteries: O holy and eternall God.

Δ: He bowed down to the Chayre and then to the table, and sayd,

Benedictus qui venit in,[2] (and there stayed a little) and sayd agayn,

Benedictus qui venit in, nomine Domini.[3]

---

1   The top quarter of a page is missing. In HM, Dee says: "Note that the whole Second boke is Nothing els but the Mysteries most Mervaylous of Sigillum Dei: otherwise called Sigillum Aemeth." In 3677, E.A. makes the following comments: "I suppose here were some other Actions between the 21 of March and 28 of April 1582 which belonged to the 2nd booke, & are wanting. For in the beginning of the Action of 28 of Apr. Mich: taxeth (?) and threateneth Δ for his slacknes for his not preparing things appointed by him (which Δ excuseth with inability) but here is no . . . of such appointment . . . in Action of 21 of March. [In margin: 22 Mar Mr Talbot went to London to take his journey for the Bookes vide Ephemerides. If therefore there was any action between 22 Mar & 28 Apr it must be after Mr Talbots retorn, & when he retorned is not noted.] (The following line was crossed out. -Ed.): I suppose also that somewhat is wanting of the 3d Booke, for here is only the Actions of 2 daies, and 28 & 29 of Ap: & the catch word of the last page is - Mi + decedite - but nothing followes.

    I also suppose there is something wanting of the 4th Booke, for the last Action is 4 May 1582 & at the beginning of which it appears that E.T. was unwilling to proceed as skryer any further, because Mich: willed him to Marry. & lis & bable be here (+) left offe. Beside the 4th (or rather 5) booke begins the 15 of Nov: 1582. & from the 4 of May to that tyme here is nothing extant. Yet that somwhat was done may be colledled from what is entred under the Title vizt: Post reconciliationem Kellianam, &c: implying that, here had been some falling out betw. Δ & him, & it may hence be presumed, Kelly had been implyed as Skryer sometyme before the said falling out.

    + / 4. May. Mr. Talbot went vide Ephem: so that by this it seemes Mr. Talbot went away from Mortlack so soone as his account of 4 of May was finished, & discected the imployment." -E.A.

2   Benedictus qui venit in: "Blessed is he who comes in . . ." -Ed.

3   Benedictus . . . Domini: "Blessed is he who comes in the name of the Lord." This is part of the Sanctus prayer, which appears in the preface to the Latin mass. See also John 12:13. -Ed.

Δ: Than cam in Michael, with a sword in his hand, as he was wont: and I sayd unto him, are you <u>Michael</u>?

Mich: Dowt not: I am he which reioyce in him that reioyceth in the <u>Fortitude and strength of God</u>.[4]

Δ: Is this Forme, for the Great Seale perfect?

Mi: The forme is true and perfect. Thow shalt sweare by the liuing God, the <u>strength of his Mercy</u>, and his Medicinall vertue, powred into mans sowle <u>neuer to disclose</u> these Mysteries.[5]

Δ: Yf No man, by no means, shall perceyue any thing herof, <u>by me</u>, I wold think that I shold not do well.

Mi: Nothing is cut from the <u>Church of God</u>. We in his Saincts are blessed for euer.

<u>We separate thee, from fyled and wycked persons</u>: We move thee to God.

Δ: I vow, as you require: God be my help, and Gwyde, now and euer, amen.

MIC: This is a Mystery, <u>skarse worthy for us ourselues</u>, to know, muche <u>lesse to Reueale</u>. Art thow, then, so Contented?

Δ: I am: God be my strength.

Mic: Blessed art thow among the Saincts: And blessed are you both.

I will pluck thee, from among the wycked [he spake to my skryer.][6] Thow Commyttest Idolatry. But take hede of Temptation: The Lord hath blessed thee. This is a Mystery.

Dee, what woldest thow haue?

Δ: Recte sapere et Intelligere &c.[7]

Mic: Thy Desyre is graunted thee. Use . . .

---

4   Michael - Fortitudo Dei.

5   My Oath or vow required for secresie.

6   To E.T. he spake.

7   Recte . . . Intelligere: "To perceive and understand properly." -Ed.

... with[8] ...

... they are corrupted ...

... they haue byn used to the wycked. Ther ...

[Michael: -]:[9] I will shew thee in the mighty hand <u>and strength</u> of God, [what] his Mysteries are: The true <u>Circle of his</u> æternitie Comprehending all vertue: The whole and Sacred Trinitie. Oh, holy be he: Oh, holy be he: Oh, holy be he.

Uriel answered, Amen.

Mic: Now what wilt thow? Δ: I wold full fayne procede according to the matter in hand.

Mic: Diuide the owtward circle into 40 æquall partes: whose greatest numbers are fowre. See thow do it presently.

Δ: I did so. Diuiding it first into fowre: and then every of them into ten. He called Semiel, and one cam in and kneled down: and great fyre cam out of his mowth.[10]

Michael sayde, To him, are the Mysteries of <u>these Tables</u> known.

Michael sayde, Semiel (agayn) and by and by, he[11] **said, O God thow hast sayd and thow liuest for euer.** Do not think here I speake to him. Δ: He spake that to us, least we might dowte of his last speches, as being spoken to Semiel: which he directed to the æternall god and not to Semiel. **Semiel stode up, and flaming fire cam out of his mowth: and than he sayd, as followeth,**

---

8   The top quarter of a page is missing. -Ed.

9   In HM this section has the following heading (perhaps part of the missing text): "Now I will speak of Sigillum Aemeth, also known as Sigillum Dei." The words in square brackets were supplied from HM. The quote is also dated 19 March. -Ed.

10   Semiel, this etymologie is as thowgh he wer the secretarie, for the Name of God.

11   Michael -CHM.

Sem: Mighty Lord, what woldest thow with the Tables?

Mic: It is the will of God, Thow fatche them hither.

Sem: <u>I am his Tables.</u>

Behold these are his Tables. Lo where they are.

Δ: There cam-in <u>40 white Creatures</u>, all in white Sylk long robes <u>and they like chyldern</u>: and all they fallyng on theyr knees sayd,

Thow onely art Holy among the highest. O God, <u>Thy Name</u>,[12] be blessed for euer.

Δ: Michael stode up out of his chayre, and by and by, all his leggs semed to be like two great pillers of brass:[13] and he as high as half way to the heven. And by and by, his sword was all on fyre and he stroke, or drew his sworde ouer all theyr 40 heds. The Erth quaked: and the 40 fell down: and Michael called Semiael, with a thundring voyce, and sayd,

Declare the Mysteries of the Liuing God, our God, of <u>one</u> that liueth for euer.

Sem: I am redy. Δ: Michael stroke ouer them, with his sword agayne: and they all fell down, and Uriel allso on his knees. And commonly at the striking with his sword, flamyng fier like lightening did flash with all.

Mi: Note: here is a Mysterie.

Δ: Then stept furth, one of the 40, from the rest, and opened his brest which was couered with Sylk, and there appeared a great T all of Gold.[14]

---

12   Semiel - fortè significat Nomen meum Deus. Ita quod Tabulae istae sunt Nomen Dei, vel Nomina Diuina. -Δ. Forte . . . Diuina: "Perhaps it signifies the name of my God, thus, because these tables are the name of God, or the Divine names." -Ed.

13   Compare with Daniel 10:6. -Ed.

14   The very fashion of the T was thus: ☦

Mi: Note the Number. Δ: Ouer the T, stode the figure of 4, after this manner:

The 40, all, cryed, Yt liueth and Multiplyeth for euer: blessed be <u>his name</u>.[15]

Δ: That creature did shut up his bosome, and vanished away, <u>like unto a fyre</u>.

Mi: Place that, in the first place. It is the <u>name of the Lorde</u>.[16]

Δ: Than there seamed a great <u>clap of</u> thunder to be. Then stepped (before the rest) one other of the 40, and kneled as the other did before. And a voyce was herd saying, <u>Prayse God, for his **name** is reuerent</u>.

Michael sayd to me, say after me thus,

> Deus Deus Deus noster, benedictus es nunc et semper: Amen.
>
> Deus Deus Deus noster, benedictus es nunc et semper: Amen.
>
> Deus Deus Deus noster, benedictus es nunc et semper:[17] Amen.

Δ: Then this Creature opened his breast, and fyre cam oute of the stone as before and a great romayne G appeared.[18]

---

15 "T" in the holy language is named Gisg; vide lib.5. post. et est ultima Alphabeti litera. -Δ. Vide . . . litera: "See below in Book 5; it is the last letter of the alphabet." -Ed.

16 HM reads "of God." -Ed.

17 Deus . . . semper: "O God, God, our God, blessed are you, now and forever." -Ed.

18 G: alr. Ged. lib.5. -Δ. ("G: otherwise Ged. [See] Book 5." -Ed.)

Mi: Write with reuerence, These Mysteries are wunderfull, the Number of <u>his name</u>, <u>and knowledge</u>: Lo, this it is, 9. Behold, it is but one, and it is Marveylous.

Δ: Then this Creature vanished <u>away</u>. 19

Mi: The <u>Seale of Gods Mercy</u>: blessed be thy name.

Δ: It semed to rayne, as thowgh it had rayned fyre from heuen. Then one other of the 40 was browght furth: The rest all fell down and sayd, Lo, thus is God known.

Then he opened his brest, and there appered an n, (not of so big proportion as the other), with the number of 7 over it.20

Mi: Multiplicatum est Nomen tuum in <u>terra</u>.21

Δ: Then that man vanished away as it were <u>in a golden smoke</u>.

Mi: Thow must not write these things, but with <u>great devotion</u>. He Liueth. Δ: Then cam an other furth. Then all falling down sayde, Vidimus <u>Gloriam</u> tuam Domine.22 They were prostrate on theyr faces. Then this Creature opened his breast and he had there a Tablet all of Gold (as it were) and there appered a small <u>t</u> uppon it: and the figure of 9 under this letter t.23

Mi: Mark it, for this is a Mysterye. Δ: Then that Shewer (of the 40) seamed to <u>fly up into the ayre, like as it were a white garment</u>.

Mi: Illius <u>Gloria</u> sit nobiscum.24 Δ: All sayd, amen: and fell down.

Δ: Then stode up an other, and opened his bosom, and shewed on his brest bare (being like syluer) a small <u>h</u>;25 and he pointed to it, and ouer it was the number of 22.

---

19   This ellipsis is Dee's, indicating an omission. -Ed.

20   N, alr, Drux.

21   Multiplicatum . . . terra: "Manifold is your Name on the Earth." -Ed.

22   Vidimus . . . Domine: "We have seen your glory, O Lord." -Ed.

23   Gisg.

24   Illius . . . nobiscum: "May his Glory be with us." -Ed.

25   Na.

Mi: Et est numerus <u>virtutis</u> benedictus. Videte Angelos Lucis.[26] Δ: This shewer went away <u>like a white Cok</u> flying up.

Δ: There cam an other in, and sayd,

Et sum <u>Finis</u> et non est mihi Numerus. Sum Numerus in numero Et omnis Numerus est mihi Numerus. Videte.[27]

Δ: There appeared a small <u>n</u>[28] on his skyn, being all spotted with Gold. Then he went away like <u>three fyres, red flaming, and coming</u> to gather agayn in the myddst of the firmament.

Δ: You must Note that in the stone the whole world in a manner did seme to appere, heuen, and erth, &c.

Mi: (Δ he cryed with a lowde voyce,) Et est <u>vita</u> in cælis.[29]

Δ: Then stepped furth one and sayd, Et ego viuo cum bene viuentibus,[30] and withall he kneeled down: and Michael stepped furth and toke of his veale on his brest and he made Cursy and stode up.

Mi: Viuamus Halleluyah. O Sanctum Nomen.[31]

Δ: All fell down on theyr faces, and Michael stroke ouer them with his sword and a great flash of fyre: And this man his brest seemed open, that his hart appeared bleading, and therein the letter <u>m</u>,[32] and 6, over it thus $\overset{6}{m}$.

Mic: Benedictus est <u>Numerus Agni.</u>[33]

Δ: Hereuppon They all fell down.

---

26 Et est . . . Lucis: "And it is the number of blessed power. Behold the Angels of Light." -Ed.

27 Et sum . . . videte: "And I am the end, and have no number. I am a number within a number, and every number is my number. Behold." -Ed.

28 Drux.

29 Et est . . . cælis: "And he is <u>life</u> in heaven" -Ed.

30 Et ego . . . viventibus: "And I live with the well-living." -Ed.

31 Vivamus . . . Nomen: "We live, Alleluia. O Holy Name." -Ed.

32 Tal.

33 Benedictus . . . Agni: "Blessed is the number of the Lamb." -Ed.

Mi: Orate invicem.[34] Δ: Hereuppon we prayed a psalme; my skryer saying one verse, and I the other &c.

Mi: Omnia data sunt a Deo.[35] Δ: Then cam one in, hauing a rownd Tablet in his forhed and a little o[36] in his forhed: and 22 ouer it.

Mi: Et non est finis in illo.

Benedictus es tu Deus.[37] Δ: And then that shewer vanished away: He flew up, <u>like a rownd raynbow knyt togither at the endes</u>.

 Mi: <u>Angeli a nomine tuo procident Domine</u>.
Tu es <u>primus</u> O Halleluyah.[38]

Δ: One stode up and the rest fell down, and out of his mowth that stode, cam a sworde: and the point, a Triangle, and in the myddest of it a small a[39] thus 🔺 , of pure gold, grauen very depe: Et Numerus tuus viuit in cæteris,[40] sayd this shewer. The number was ~~22~~ 20[41] over the a. This shewer went away <u>with great lightening couering all the world</u>.

Mi: <u>N</u>omen illius est nobiscum.[42] Δ: He stroke agayne with his sword ouer them. Then stode one up: who, uppon his garment had an n: and he turned abowt: and on his back were very many (ens) n.[43]

Mi: Creasti tu Domine Angelos tuos ad Gloriam tuam.[44] Δ: Ouer

---

34   Orate invicem: "Pray in turn." -Ed.

35   Omnia . . . Deo: "Everything is given by God." -Ed.

36   Med.

37   Et non . . . Deus: "And the end is not in him. Blessed are you O God." -Ed.

38   Angeli . . . Halleluyah: "The angels will fall down at your name O Lord. You are the first O alleluia." -Ed.

39   Un.

40   Et numerus . . . caeteris: "And your number lives in the rest." -Ed.

41   Corrected thus after by Uriel to be 20.

42   Nomen . . . nobiscum: "The name of that is with us." -Ed.

43   Drux.

44   Creasti . . . tuam: "O Lord, you have created your angels for your glory." -Ed.

the 'n' was the number of 14, ouer that n (I meane) which was onely on his brest.

Mi: Et te primus Creauit Deus.[45] Δ: Then the shewer flew up like a star. And an other cam in, all his cloth being plucked up: and so seamed naked: He hath a little 'a'.[46] This 'a' did go rownd abowt him, begynning at his feete: and so spirally upward: and he seemed to be all Clay. Ouer the 'a' was the number 6.

Mi: Et Creata sunt et pereunt in Nomine tuo.[47] Δ: And therwith this shewer fell down all into dust on the Earth: and his white garment flew up, like a white smoke: and allso a white thing did fly out of his body.[48]

Surgit Innocentia ad faciem Dei.[49]

Δ: Michael did ouer them agayn with his sworde, and it seemed to lighten. He began to speak, and he stopped suddenly, and the fyre flew from his mowth.

Mi: Innocentium Nomina, et sanguinem vidisti Domine a Terra, et Iustus es in operibus tuis.[50] Δ: Then cam one in, with a garment all bluddy. He was like a chylde, he had a ball in his hand of perfume which smoked: and he hath uppon his forhed a little 'h'.[51] He bowed to Michaël: and Michael sayd, Numerus tuus est infinitus, et erit finis rerum.[52] Δ: This shewer seemed to powre him self awaye like a flud of blud: and his garment flew upward.

---

45 Et te . . . Deus: "And God has made you first." -Ed.

46 Un.

47 Et creata . . . tuo: "And they were created and perish in your name." -Ed.

48 Note these 3 parts.

49 Surgit . . . Dei: "Innocence arises to the face of God." -Ed.

50 Innocentium . . . tuis: "O Lord, you have seen the names and blood of the innocent on the earth, and you are just in your works." Compare with Psalm 94:21. -Ed.

51 Na.

52 Numerus . . . rerum: "Your number is infinite, and it will be the end of things." -Ed.

Mi: Non est illi numerus. Omnia pereunt a <u>facie Dei</u>, et a facie Terræ.[53]

Δ: Then stepped one furth, like a water running rownd abowt him, and he cryeth miserably, <u>O</u> benedictum Nomen tuum Domine. Numerus perijt cum illis.[54] Δ: A little '<u>o</u>' with 18 ouer it, appered.[55]

Δ: This shewer seemed to vanish away, and to cause a great water remayn ouer all.

Mi: <u>L</u>ux manet in tenebris. Gloriosum est Nomen tuum.[56]

Δ: Then stept one furth from the rest, who fell down, as theyr manner was.

Δ: Note: All the Cumpanies of these 40, stode five to gither, and five to gither, and so in eight Cumpanyes; each, of fiue.

Δ: This was a very white one: The upper partes of his throate, seemed open and there seemed to cum out of it fyre, in very many and diuerse cullours.

He sayd, <u>Trinus</u> sum.[57]

Mi: Benedictum sit nomen <u>El.</u>[58]

Δ: Than in the myddle of the fyres or smoke semed an '<u>l</u>'[59] thrise placed, on a bluddy cross, and ouer the 'l' the number 26.

---

53 Non est . . . Terrae: "To him there is no number. Everyone perishes before God, and on the face of the earth." -Ed.

54 O benedictum . . . illis: "Blessed is your name, O Lord. The number perished with those." -Ed.

55 Med.

56 Lux . . . tuum: "Light abides in darkness. Your Name is full of glory." -Ed.

57 Trinus sum: "I am threefold." -Ed.

58 Benedictus . . . El: "May the name El be blessed." -Ed.

59 Ur.

Δ: This shewer seemed to haue <u>three mens heds and</u> to vanish away in a myst with a thunder.

Mi: Labia mea laudant Dominum.[60]

Δ: Then cam a very fayre yong **one in** with long heare hanging on her (or his) sholders: and on her **belly appered** a great scotcheon;[61] to hir, or him, Michael gaue a **flame of fyre:** and she, or he, did eat it.

Mi: Et hic est El:[62] and so **appeared** a little 'l' on the scotcheon, and it waxed bigger and **bigger: and a fyre** did seeme to go rownd abowt it.

Mi: Benedicta sit ætas tua:[63] Δ: And **there** appeared '30' under the l.

Δ: There cam a great many of little fyers and did seeme to eleuate this yong woman (or child) out of sight.

Michael stroke his sword ouer them agayn, and sayd,

Natus est illa Lux.

Ille est Lux noster.[64]

Δ: Then stept out an other and opened his white silk garment uppermost: and under it, he seemed to be sowed up in a white silk cloth. He

---

60   Labia . . . Dominum: "My lips praise the Lord." -Ed.

61   Scotcheon: escutcheon. -Ed.

62   Et hic est El: "And here is El." -Ed.

63   Benedicta . . . tua: "May your age be blessed." -Ed.

64   Natus ... noster: "That Light is born. He/she/it is our Light." -Ed.

had in his forhed an 'n'[65] in his brest an 'n' and in his right hand an 'n'.

Mi: Numerus tuus est benedictus.[66] Δ: They all fell down, saying, Numerus tuus est Nobiscum: Nec adhuc nouimus finem illius Venies cum numero tuo O unus in æternum.[67]

Δ: And they fell all down agayn. This shewer departed clyming up into the ayre, as if he had clymed on a ladder.

Mi: Linguis suis cognouerunt eum.[68]

Δ: All sayd, Benedictus est qui sic et sic est,[69] throwing up into the ayre thre cornerd trenchers[70] of this fashion all of Gold. The one side of the trenchers was thus marked, and the other side had nothing on.

Δ: Then stept one oute: and fyre cam out and in of his mowth. He kneeled, the rest fell down. This seemed a transparent body, and he had in his eyes a small l:[71] and in his forhed the figure of 8.

---

65   Drux.

66   Numerus . . . benedictus: "Your number is blessed." -Ed.

67   Numerus . . . aeternum: "Your number is with us: and yet until now we knew not his end. May you come with your number, O one forever." -Ed.

68   Linguis . . . eum: "They recognized him by his tongues." -Ed.

69   Benedictus . . . sic: "Blessed is he who is so and so." -Ed.

70   Trencher: cutting board on which food is served. -Ed.

71   Ur.

Mi: Note this, under. I meane the figure 8. Thus, 𝑙 8

Δ: All sayd, Et es verus in operibus tuis:[72] and so he vanished away in a flame of fyre.

Mi: Gaudete omnes populi eius, gaudete omnes populi eius, ab hinc Gaudete.[73] Δ: All sayd, Amen.

Δ: One stept furth saying, Incipit virtus nostra,[74] he being covered under his robe, all with armor: and hath a great G[75] on his armor and the figure of '7' ouer it. He went **behynde** Michael and so vanished away.[76]

Mi: Recte viuite omnes Sancti eius.[77]

Δ: One stept furth: and opening his brest, there appered a boke, and turning ouer the leaves there appeared nothing but a little 'r'[78] and 13 over it. He went behinde the Chayre and so vanished awaye.

Mi: Hic est Angelus Eccliæ meæ, qui doceat Ille viam meam.[79]

Δ: There stept oute a playn man, and under his garment a gyrdel, and under his gyrdle a Rod: and in his hand he had a Sworde, and in his mowth a flame of fyre: he had a great H[80] uppon his sworde and under it 22. He went behynde the chayre &c. Michael standing up still uppon his leggs, like pillers of brass.

Δ: I axed him yf I shold not cease now, by reason of the folk tarying for us to come to supper.

---

72 Et es . . . tuis: "And you are true in your works." -Ed.

73 Gaudete . . . Gaudete: "Rejoice ye, all his people, rejoice ye, all his people, from now on rejoice." -Ed.

74 Incipit virtus nostra: "Our power begins." -Ed.

75 Ged — G.

76 Note this to be the first that vanished away, going behynde Michael.

77 Recte . . . eius: "Live properly, O you his holy ones." -Ed.

78 Don.

79 Hic est . . . meam: "This is the angel of my Church, who may teach him my path." -Ed.

80 Na.

Mic: Lay away the world. Contynue your work: <u>Coniunxit</u> spiritum mentibus illorum.[81]

Δ: Then stept out one, hauing under his garment a little Chest, and therein a mans hart raw: and the hart was thus with two letters, one on the one side 'o' and on the other a 'g'.[82]

[Δ: As in scotcheons of armes, where the man and his wifes armes ar ioyned perpale, as the heraulds term it.] This shewer shut up the chest and went his way.

Mi: Numerus illius est sine numero.[83]

Δ: Then cam in an other, saying,

<u>T</u>empus est. Deum vestrum agnoscite.[84]

Δ: This shewer <u>his armes reached down to his feete</u>: he shewed furth his right hand and in it a little 't'[85] and 11 under it.

Mi: Stay; place this, in the second place. This went away.

Mi: <u>Y</u>mago tua, (mors,) est amara.[86]

Δ: Then cam one in, with a big belly, and fat cheekes: an half sword

---

[81] Coniunxit . . . illorum: "He joined the spirit with their souls." -Ed.

[82] Med, ged.

[83] Numerus . . . numero: "Its number is without number." -Ed.

[84] Tempus . . . agnoscite: "It is time. Recognize your God." -Ed.

[85] Gisg.

[86] Imago: I writ first: but, aunciently, and vulgarly both in writing and print, you shall finde ymago, thowgh not according to the Latine Tung. -Δ. Ymago . . . amara: "Your image (O death) is bitter." -Ed.

perced his hart, and a little 'y'[87] written on it. Iustus est malis deus noster.[88] Δ: The number of 15 under it.

Mi: Place it in the former place.

Mi: Qpera fidelium, Delectatio mea.[89] [Δ: Then cam one in.] Hic est Deus noster.[90] He shewed the letter of o on his naked brest, and the figure of 8 under it. He went away.

Mi: Ecce, Iniquitas regnat in domo mea.[91]

Δ: Then stept one oute very lean, all his body full of little e,[92] and under euery one of them, 21. He went away behynde the chayre.

Mi: Bestia deuoravit populum meum, peribit autem in æternum.[93]

Δ: Then stept out one in bluddy apparell, all his body full of serpents heds and a b[94] on his forhed, and the number of 10 ouer it. He went away.

Mi: Iniquitas Abundat in templo meo, et sancti viuunt cum Iniquis.[95]

Δ: One very lean, hunger sterued cam out, an A on his brest, and, 11 over it, and so went away.

Δ: There cam in another.[96]

Mi: Iniqua est Terra malitijs suis.[97]

---

87 Gon - cum puncto, y -Δ. ("With a point, to distinguish it from 'i'." -Ed.)

88 Iustus . . . noster: "Our God is just to the wicked." -Ed.

89 Opera . . . mea: "The labor of the faithful is my delight." -Ed.

90 Hic est Deus noster: "Here is our God." -Ed.

91 Ecce . . . mea: "Behold, sin rules in my house." -Ed.

92 Graph.

93 Bestia . . . aeternum: "The beast devoured my people, but he will perish forever." -Ed.

94 Pa.

95 Iniquitas . . . Inquis: "Iniquity fills my temple, and the holy live with the unjust." -Ed.

96 I think it to be superfluous.

97 Iniqua . . . suis: "The earth is unjust in its malice." -Ed.

Δ: Then cam in one who drew out a bluddy sworde on his brest a great romayn I, and 15 over it. He went his way.

Mi: Angeli eius ministrauerunt sanctis.[98] Δ: Then stept one oute with a Target and a little a on it, and ouer it the number of 8.[99] He went away.

Mi: Regnabit Iniquitas pro tempore.[100] Δ: They all cryed, Halleluyah.

Δ: Then stept one furth with a golden crown, and a great arming sworde: his clothing all of gold, with a letter 'r' on his sword and 16 ouer it, and so he went away.

Mi: Nulla regnat virtus super terram.[101] Δ: Then stept one oute, hauing all his body under his white sylken habit (as they all, had) very braue after the fashion of those dayes, with great ruffs, cut hose, a great bellyed dubblet, a veluet hat on his hed, with a feather: and he advanced him self braggingly: He had burnt into his forhed a little n: and Michael sayd, Non est numerus illius in Cælis.[102] Δ: He went awaye.

Mi: Antiquus serpens extulit caput suum deuorans Innocentes.[103] Halleluyah.

Δ: Then cam one who put of his white habit: and he toke a sword, and smote up into the ayre, and it thundred: and he had a seal (suddenly there) very gorgeous of gold and precious stones: he sayd,

Regnum meum. Quis Contradicet?[104]

---

98 Angeli . . . sanctis: "His angels have served the saints." -Ed.

99 Uriel corrected it after, to be under.

100 Regnabit . . . tempore: "Wickedness will rule for a time." -Ed.

101 Nulla . . . terram: "No power rules upon the earth." -Ed.

102 Non est . . . caelis: "His number is not in heaven." -Ed.

103 Antiquus . . . Innocentes: "The ancient serpent has raised up his head, devouring the innocent." -Ed.

104 Regnum . . . Contradicet?: "My Kingdom. Who resists it?" -Ed.

Δ: He hath proceding out of his mowth, many little (enns,) n, and on his forhed, a great A.

Mi: Non quòd est A, sed quòd contradicit A.

Nec portio, nec numerus eius invenitur in cælo.

Habet autem Numerum terrestrem

Mysterium.[105]

Δ: He shewed three figures of '6' set in triangle thus, 6 6 6

Mi: Vobis est Mysterium hoc, posterius reuelandum.[106]

Δ: And there cam a fyre and consumed him, and his chayre away, suddenly.

Mi: Perturbatur terra iniquitate sua.[107]

This shewer, his garments, white, under: his face as brass: his body grevous with leprosy: hauing uppon his brest an O, with the number of 10 under it: and so departed.[108]

Mi: Surgite O Ministri Dei: Surgite (inquam) Pugnate: Nomen Dei est æternum.[109]

---

105 Non quod . . . Mysterium: "It is not because he is A, but because he resists A. Neither his portion nor his number are discovered in heaven. Therefore he has the number of the earth, which is a mystery." -Ed.

106 Mysterium nobis reuelandum. -Δ. ("A mystery to be revealed to us.") Vobis . . . reuelandum: "This mystery is to be revealed to you afterward." -Ed.

107 Perturbatur . . . sua: "The earth is thrown into confusion by his/her wickedness." -Ed.

108 My skryer had omitted to tell me this, or els, it was not told and showed, but Uriel did after supply it by the skryer: The first letter of Perturbatur, doth not make shew, of the letter following as other before did.

109 Surgite . . . aeternum: "Arise, O servants of God. Arise (I say) and fight. The Name of God is eternal." -Ed.

Δ: Then cam two oute to gither: they had two edged swordes in theyr hands, and fyre cam oute of theyr mowthes. One had a G, and 5 ouer it, the other had...

[Δ: We fell to prayer, whereuppon Michael blessed us.]

The other had an h on his sword, and 14 under it: and so they went away.

Mi: Omnis terra tremet ad vocem tubæ illius.[110]

Δ: One stept out, and under his habit had a trumpet. He put it to his mowth, and blew it not. On his forhed a little 'o' and 17 under it. He went awaye.

Mi: Serua Deus populum tuum, Serua Deus populum tuum Israel, Serua (inquam) Deus populum tuum Israel.[111] Δ: He cryed this, alowde.

Δ: One appeared with a fyry sword, all bluddy, ~~his vesture all bluddy~~ his vesture all bluddy, and he had s.[112]

Est numerus in numero.[113] Δ: He went away.

Δ: I understand it to be a letter, and the number 5 also.

Mi: So it is.

Δ: There cam one in with diuerse owgly faces, and all his body skabbed.

Mi: Nunc sunt Dies tribulationis:[114] Δ: He had an a on his forhed and the Number 5 under it.

Mi: Hic est Numerus predictus.[115]

---

[110] Omnis . . . illius: "All the Earth will tremble at the sound of that trumpet." -Ed.

[111] Serua . . . Israel: "O God, save your people; O God, save your people Israel; O God, save (I say) your people Israel." -Ed.

[112] Fam.

[113] Est numerus in numero: "He is the number in the number." -Ed.

[114] Nunc . . . tribulationis: "Now are the days of troubles." -Ed.

[115] Hic predictus: "This is the number that was foretold." -Ed.

> Mi: Audite, consummatum est.[116]. This had a great pot of water in his hand and uppon the pot, grauen, a with 5 under it. He departed in fyre.[117]

Mi: Angele preparato Tubam tuam.[118]

Δ: Then cam one oute with a Trumpet. ----- Venite Tempus.[119]

Δ: He offered to blow, but blew it not. On the ende of his Trumpet was a little a and 24 under it. He went away.

Δ: They all now seemed to be gon: Michael and all. He cam in agayn and two with him. And he sayd, Hij duo Cælati sunt adhuc.[120] They two went away.

Mi: Vale. Natura habet terminum suum.[121]

Δ: He blessed us and florished his sword towards, and ouer us, and so went away: and Uriel after him: who all this while appeared not.

Δ: After supper Mr. Talbot went up to his chamber to prayers: and Uriel shewed himself unto him: and told him that somwhat was amyss, in the Table or seale which I had byn occupyed abowt this day. And thereuppon, Mr. Talbot cam to me into my study: and requyred the Seale (or Tables) of me: for he was wished to correct somthing therin, (sayd he). I deliuered him the seal, and he browght it agayn within a

---

116 Audite . . . est: "Listen: it is finished." -Ed.

117 Uriel also did correct this place with deliuering this in the place of the other description before.

118 Angele . . . tuam: "O angel, prepare your trumpet." -Ed.

119 Venite Tempus: "The time comes." -Ed.

120 Hij duo . . . adhuc: "These two were still hidden." - Ed.

121 Vale . . . suum: "Farewell. Nature has its own limit." -Ed.

little tyme after, corrected: <u>both in the numbers, for quantyty and</u> <u>some for place ouer or under: and also in one letter or place omitted</u>. Which I denyed, of any place omitted by me, that was expressed unto me. And the rather I dowted, uppon Michael his words last spoken, uppon <u>two</u> places then remayning yet empty: saying, <u>Hij</u> <u>duo cælati</u> sunt adhuc.[122] But If I had omitted any, there shold more than two haue wanted.[123] Whereuppon we thowght good to ax Judgment and dissoluing of this dowte, by Michael. And comming to the stone He was redy. I prepownded this former Dowte. He answered,

Mi: Veritas est sola in DEO. Et hæc omnia vera sunt.[124] You omitted no letter <u>or history</u> that was told you. But the <u>skryer</u> <u>omitted</u> to declare unto you.[125] Δ: May I thus recorde it?

Yt is iustly reformed by Uriel: the one being omitted of <u>the descrier</u> and the other not yet to us declared, might make that phrase meete to be spoken, Hij duo <u>cælati</u> sunt adhuc.[126]

Mi: Thow hast sayd. Δ: I pray you to make-up that one place yet wanting. Then he stode up <u>on his great brasen leggs agayn</u>: He called agayn, Semiæl Semieil. Then he cam, and kneled down.

Consummatum est.[127] Δ: The shewer (a white man) pluckt oute a trumpet, and put it to his mowth, as thowgh he wold blow, but blew not: and there appeared at the ende of the Trumpet the greke ω. There arose a myst, and an horrible Thunder.

Mi: It is done. Δ: Then of the three 6 6 6 before Noted, with his fin-

---

122 Hij duo . . . adhuc: "These two were still hidden." - Ed.

123 Have wanted: "were missed." -Ed.

124 Veritas . . . sunt: "Truth is in God alone, and all these things are true." -Ed.

125 The descryer, or the skryer omitted to tell.

126 Hij duo . . . adhuc: "These two were still hidden." - Ed.

127 Consummatum est: "It is finished." -Ed.

ger he put oute the two lowermost: and sayd, Iste est numerus suus.[128]
And Michael did put his finger into the Trumpets ende, and pulled
furth a rownd plate of Gold, wheron was the figure of 'i' with many
circles abowt it, and sayd, Omnia unum es

Δ: The forme of the world which appered
before, vanished away: and Semyeil[130] went
away, And Michael cam and sat in his
chayr agayn: and his brasen leggs wer
gone, and uppon our pawsing he sayd,

Mi: Go forward. Do you know what you haue allready written?

Laudate Dominum in Sanctus eius.[131]

Note: The Circumference (which is done) conteyneth 7 names:
7 names, conteyn 7 Angels:
Euery letter, conteyneth 7 Angels:
The numbers are applyed to the letters.
Whan thow dost know the 7 names, thow shalt understand the 7
Angells.
The Number of 4,[132] pertayning to the first T, is a Number significatiue: signifying, to what place thow shalt next apply the eye: and
being placed aboue, it sheweth removing toward the right hand: Taking
the figure for the number of the place applyable to the next letter to be
taken. The under number, is significatiue: declaring, to what place

---

128 Iste . . . suus: "This is his number." -Ed.

129 Omnia unum est: "Everything is one." -Ed.

130 Semieil.

131 Laudate . . . eius: "Praise the Lord in his sanctuary" (Psalm 150). -Ed.

132 The declaration of the Numbers.

thow shalt apply the next letter in the Circumference, <u>toward the left hand</u>. Which thow must reade, untyll it light uppon a <u>letter, without number</u>, not signifying. This is the Whole. So shalt thow fynde the 7 principall Names: <u>known with us, and applyable to thy</u> practise.

Make experience.[133]

Δ: Then telling from the T, 4 more places (toward the right hand) exclusiuely, I finde in that fowrth place, from T, (but being the fifth from the beginning, and <u>with</u> the begynning) this letter h: with 22, <u>ouer it</u>. Therfore, I procede to the right hand, 22 places: and there I finde A, and 11 over it. Going then toward the right hand 11 places furder: I finde a little <u>a</u> with 5 under it: by reason of which under place of 5, I go toward the left hand, 5 places, exclusiuely, where I finde <u>o</u> with 10, under it: wheruppon I procede to the left hand, farder by 10 places, and there I see the letter t, and 11, under it: and therfore going to the left hand 11 places, I see there the letter h alone without any number. Wherfore, that letter, endeth my word, and it is in all, ThAaoth. Ys this, as it shold be?

Mi: That is not the name. Thow shalt understand all in the next <u>call</u>.[134] The Rule is perfect. <u>Call</u> agayn within an howre and it shalbe shewed.

The howre being come we attended Michael his retorn to make the Practise euydent of his first Rule.

Mi: Saluete.[135]

---

[133] Make experience: "get started." -Ed.

[134] Note these doings to be accownted Calls.

[135] Saluete: "Greetings." -Ed.

Thow diddest erre: and herein hast thow erred: and yet notwithstanding <u>no error in thee, bycause thow knowest not the error</u>.
Understand that the 7 Names must Comprehend, as many letters in the
whole, as there are places in the Circle: Some letters
are significatiue of them selues. In dede no letters, but
<u>dubble numbers,</u> <u>being the Name of God.</u>
Thow hast erred in the first name, in setting
downe 'Aa'; that is, twise <u>a</u> togither, which differ
the word. Which thow shalt <u>Note to the ende</u> of
thy work: Wheresoever thow shalt finde <u>two 'aa'</u>
togither the first is not to be placed within the
Name, but rather left with <u>his inward power</u>. Thow shalt fynde 7
Names proceding from three generall partes of the Circumference: My
meaning is, from <u>three generall letters</u>: and onely <u>but one</u> letter, that is,
this letter A.[136] Accownt thow, and thow shalt finde the names iust. I
speak not of any that come in the begynning of the word but such as
light in the myddest: Proue, proue:[137] and thow shalt see. Whereas
thow hast 'go', it is to be red 'og'. This is the whole.

Δ: I haue red in Cabala of the Name of God of 42 letters: but not yet of
any, of 40 letters: That of 42 letters is this,[138]

אב אלהים כן אלהי היה היה אלהים הקדש אלהים
שלשה בראש אמר בקשה

---

136 Note: 7 names, proceding from 3 generall places of the Circumference or 3 generall letters, being but one letter and that, A.

137 Prove: "determine the truth." -Ed.

138 Vide Galatinum, lib. 3. cap. 11. -Δ. This is Petrus Galatinus, a 15th century
Kabbalist. -Ed.

id est: Pater Deus, Filius Deus, spiritus sanctus Deus: Tres in uno, et unus in tribus. Vel Trinitas in unitate et unitas in Trinitate.[139] Or thus,

אָב אֵל אִין אֵל כֵּן אֵל וְרוּחַ הַקֹּדֶשׁ אֵל אֲדָא אֵל שְׁוֵין
אֱלֹהִים כֵּי אַף אֱלֹהּ אֶחָד

which in Latin is, Pater Deus, Filius Deus, et Spiritus Sanctus, Deus, attamen non tres Dij sed unus Deus.[140] And as this is of God, Unitie in Trinitie, so of Christ onely (the second persone of the Diuine Trinitie) the Cabalists haue a name explained of 42 letters, on this manner,

כַּאֲשֶׁר הַנֶּפֶשׁ הַמַּשְׂכֶּלֶת וְהַבָּשָׂר אִישׁ אֶחָד
כֵּן הָאֵל וְזֶה אָדָם מָשִׁיחַ אֶחָד

That is in Latine, Sicut anima rationalis, et caro, homo unus, ita Deus et homo Messias unus.[141] I am not good in the hebrue tung, but, you know my meaning.

Mi: The letters being so taken oute, being a name, and a number, doth certefye the <u>old rule of 42 letters</u>, whan you <u>restore them</u> in agayn.[142]

---

[139] Id est . . . Trinitate: "That is, God the Father, God the Son, God the Holy Spirit, Trinity in unity and unity in Trinity." - Ed.

[140] Pater . . . Deus: "God the Father, God the Son, God the Holy Spirit, nevertheless not three gods but one God." -Ed.

[141] Sicut . . . unus: "As the rational mind and flesh of a person are one, so too are God and man one Messiah." -Ed.

[142] 42, are here in potentia, but, non Acta.

Mi: Note, Oute of this Circle[143] shall no Creature pass, that entreth, yf it be made uppon the earth. My meaning is, <u>if he be defyled</u>: This shalt thow <u>proue</u> to be a mysterie unknown to man. Beasts, birds, fowle and fish do all reuerence to it: <u>In this they were all Created</u>. In this, is all things conteyned. <u>In tyme thow shalt finde it, in ADAMS Treatise from Paradise</u>.[144] Looke to the Mysteries: for they are true. A and ω: Primus et Nouissimus; unus solus Deus viuit nunc et semper: Hic est, et hic erit: Et hîc, sunt Nomina sua Diuina.

Dixi:[145]

Thow art watcht all this night: who is euen now at the Dore: Clerkson. Blessed are those, whose portion is not with the wicked.

Benedicamus Dominum.[146] Halleluyah.

Tuesday the 20 of Marche: circa 10ā mane.

Δ: Are you Uriel?

Ur: I am. We thank thee for <u>thy great good will</u>.[147] We cannot viset thee now. At the twelfth howre thow shalt use us.

Δ: Fiat voluntas Dei.[148]

---

143 The vertu of this Circle.

144 ADAMS TREATISE, Δ: He meaneth my Booke that I call *Soyga.*

145 Primus . . . Dixi: "First and newest, one alone God lives now and ever: He is and he will be, and here are his Divine Names. I have spoken." -Ed.

146 Benedicamus Dominum: "Let us bless the Lord." -Ed.

147 Δ: I had made, and written, and corrected certayn prayers to them.

148 Fiat voluntas Dei: "Let it be as God wills." -Ed.

A meridie circa 2ã

Δ: At the twelfth howre, my partner was busyed in other affayres, and so contynued tyll abowt 2 of the Clok: when; we comming to the stone, fownd there Michael and Uriel: but Michael straight way[149] rose up and went out, and cam in agayn, and one after him, carrying on his right shulder, 7 little baskets,[150] of gold they seamed to be.

Mi: Shut up your doores. Δ: I had left the uttermore dore of my study, open: and did but shitt the portall dore of it.

Δ· He toke the 7 Baskets, and hanged·them rownd abowt the border of a Canapie, of beaten gold, as it were.

Mi: Ecce, Mysterium est. Benedictus Dominus Deus Israel.[151]

Δ: Therewith he did spred oute, or stretch the Canapy: whereby it seamed to couer all the world [which seamed to be in the stone, allso, heven, an erth] so that the skryer could not now see the heven. And the baskets, by equall distances, did seeme to hang in the border of the horizon.

Mi: What wold you haue? Δ: Sapientiam.[152]

Mi: Rede the names thow hast written. Δ: I had written these according to the Rule before giuen, as I understode it:

    Theaoth
    Galeas
    Gethog
    Horlωn
    Innon

---

[149] Straight way: "immediately." -Ed.

[150] Baskets.

[151] Ecce . . . Israel: "Behold, it is a mystery. Blessed be the Lord, the God of Israel" (Psalm 7:18). -Ed.

[152] Sapientiam: "wisdom." -Ed.

A^ᵃoth
Galetsog

Mi: Loke to the last name. Δ: I had written, (as appeareth) Galetsog, by misreckening the numbers, where I fownd it shold be Galethog with an h and not s.

Mi: Lo, els thow hadst erred. They are all right, but not in order. The second is the first (his name be honored for euer), The first here, must be our third, and the third here, must be our second: thus set downe.

1. Galas
2. Gethog
3. Thaoth
4. Horlⲱn
5. Innon
6. Aaoth
7. Galethog

Mi: Work from the right, toward the left, in the first angle next unto the circumference.

Δ: He shewed than, thus, this letter $\overset{\mathcal{\mbox{}}}{G}$.

Mi: Make the number of 5 on the right hand, (that is, before it) at a reasonable distance, thus $\overset{}{G}$ 5.

Δ: After that he shewed the second letter, a great roman A, thus A+ 24.

Then he shewed	⁺ᵒ**L**	30.
Then	ⵝ**Ɛ**	21.
Then	**Ƭ**	9.
Then he shewed	**Ӊ**	14.

Then he shewed this compownd letter, with the circle and cross:

He willed me, at each corner of these Segments of circles, to make little Crosses, and so I did.

Δ: After euery of the 7 letters shewed he did put them up in his bosom as sone as he had shewed them fully. The plates wheron those letters were shewed, hath the forme of the segment of a circle, thus

and seemed to be of pure gold. When the 7 letters were placed, he sayd,

Omnia unum est.[153]

Then he pulled all the 7 plates out of his bosom, and Uriel kneeled down before him. Then the plates did seeme to haue two wings (eche of them) and to fly up to heven[154] under the Canapye.

Δ: After this, one of the 7 baskets, (that which is in the east) cam to Michael, and he sayd,

Mi: Seal this:[155] For This was and is for euer.

Δ: Then he stode agayn on his leggs like brasen pillers, and sayd,

Mi: Oh how mighty is the name of God, which rayneth in the heavens, O God of the faithfull, for thow rayneth for euer.

---

153 Omnia unum est: "All is one." -Ed.

154 Here there is a marginal flourish in the manuscript, with a line drawn to the word "heven." -Ed.

155 Seal this: "confirm this." –Ed.

Δ: He opened the basket, and there cam a great fyre out of it.

Mi: Diuide the 7 partes of the circle next unto that which thow hast done, euery one, into 7.

Note: (for the tyme wilbe Long) Seuen, rest in 7: and the 7, liue by 7: The 7, gouern the 7: And by 7, all Gouernment is. Blessed be he, yea blessed be the Lord: praysed be our god. His Name be magnified. All honor and Glory be unto him now and for euer. Amen.[156]

1. Δ: Then he toke oute of the fire in the basket, a white fowle like a pigeon. That fowle had a Z uppon the first of 7 feathers which were on his brest. That first feather was on the left side.

   Mi: Note. There is a mysterie in the seuen, <u>which are the 7 governing the 7 which 7 gouern the earth</u>. Halleluyah.

   Mi: Write the letters. Δ: Now, a small l in the second fether. Then he couered those first two letters, with the other feathers. The third an l, like the other. Then he couered that allso. The fowrth an R. He couereth that. The fifth a great roman H. He couereth it. The sixth feather hath a little i. Then he hid that feather. The last feather had a small a.

   Mi: Prayse God.

   Δ: Then he put the fowle into the basket: and set it down by him. Then he hong it up in the ayre by him.

   Δ: Then he lift up his sworde over us, and <u>bad us pray</u>. Δ: We prayed.

2. Δ: Then he stretched out his hand and there cam an other basket to him, and he pluckt out a white byrd, much bigger than the other: as big as a swan: with '7' feathers on his brest.

   Mi: Dixit et factum est.[157]

---

156 Note of the 7 Baskets.

157 Dixit . . . est: "He spoke and it was so." -Ed.

Mi: Note. Δ: The first feather hath a little a on it: and it went away. The next a Z great as the first. Then a C great. Then a little a. Then an other little a. Then a feather with a little c. Then one with a little b. Δ: Then he couered them all.

Mi: Thow hast truth.

Δ: Then he put up the fowle into the basket, and hung it up by the other in the ayre.

Δ: Than the third Basket cam to him: and he toke out a byrd all green as grass, like to a peacok in form and bignes.

Mi: Et viuis tu cum illo: et:

regnum tuum cum illis est.[158]

Δ: There started out of this birds brest, 7 fethers, like gold, and fyrie.

Mi: Pray.

3. Mi: Note. Δ: On the first feather a small p.

Then a small a.
A little u.

Then a small p.
Then a small n.
Then a small h.
Then a small r. Then he put the fowle up into the
    Basket &c.

Δ: Then there cam an other basket to his hand.

Mi: Dedit illi potestatem in cælus.

Potestas illius magna est.
Orate.[159] Δ: We prayed.

---

[158] Et viuis . . . est: "And you live with him, and your kingdom is with those." -Ed.

[159] Dedit . . . Orate: "He gave power to them in heaven. His power is great. Pray." - Ed.

4. Δ: Then he pluckt out a fowle, greater than any of the other, like
a griphen (as commonly they are figured) all red fyry, with
skales like brass. Then on seuen skales, appered letters.

Mi: Note. Δ: First a little h.

A little d.
A little m.
Then a little h.
Then a little i.
Then a little a̲.
Then a little i.

Δ: Then he put up the fowle, & hung the basket in the Ayre.

Δ: Then there cam an other Basket to him.

[Δ: Note: All this while the firmament was not to be seen.]

Mi: Magnum est DEVS in Angelis suis.

et magna est illorum potestas in Cælis.

Orate.160 Δ: We prayed.

5. Δ: Then he pluckt out a bird like an Egle all his body like Gold,
and he had a little circle of feathers on his brest: and in it,
betwene fowre parallell lines, twelue equall squares: and on the
top, on the myddle, one, like the other twelue, thus:

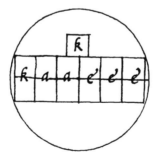

---

160 Magnum . . . Orate: "Mighty is GOD in his angels, and great is their power in
heaven. Pray." -Ed.

Δ: Then he put up the Egle &c.

Δ: Then cam an other Basket.

Mi: Nuncius tuus est magnus in cælis.

Orate.[161]

Δ: He, and the Basket that wer opened, shut, and set aside, seamed all to be gon: and the Baskets remayning, still hanging on the border of the Canapie. Then he cam agayn, and went awaye agayne. Then cam URIEL and held the Basket: and his leggs seemed to be such great tall pillers of Brass: as Michael did stand on before.

UR: <u>This is a Mysterie</u>. He <u>is here</u>, and not here which was here before.[162]

6. Δ: He opened the Basket and pluckt out like a phenix [or peli-canΔ] of the bignes of a swan: all fyrie sparkling. His byll is bent into his brest and it bled. In his brest was a quadrangle made with his own feathers, thus. He put it up, and hung it by the other Baskets.

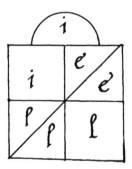

---

161 Nuncius . . . coelis. Orate: "Your messenger is great in heaven. Pray." Nuncius (Nuntius) is commonly used as a title for Gabriel in medieval Latin. -Ed.

162 Michael is the sixth name. vide post. -Δ. Vide post: "see below." -Ed.

Then cam the last basket. Uriel stode still and sayde,
UR: Dedit angelis potestatem in lumine Cæli.[163]

Orate. Δ: We prayed.

7. Δ: Then cam Michael and toke the Basket of Uriel and becam standing on the great brasen legs, as before.

Δ: He toke out of the basket a strange fowle with many wings: This fowle had in his forhed a Tablet of this fashion:

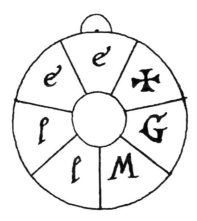

Mi: Et Coniunxit illos DEVS in unum.[164]

Δ: All the Baskets flew up: and so the Canapie vanished away, and the Heaven appeared.

Δ: Now he cam and sat down in his chayre.

Δ: Michael sayd to Uriel, <u>It is thy part, to expownd</u> these Mysteries: Go to, in the name of our God.

Δ: Uriel cam and stode before him and sayde, What will you: <u>Ô our fellows and seruants to GOD</u>? What will you?

---

163 Dedit . . . coeli: "He gave power to his angels in the splendor of heaven." -Ed.

164 Et coniunxit . . . unum: "And God joined them into one." -Ed.

Δ: Perfect knowledg and understanding, such as is necessary for us.[165]

UR: Looke uppon, and see if thow canst not understand it: We will depart for a little space: and come to thee agayne.

Δ: So they went: and left all the stone in fyre, so that neyther the Chayr or Table could be seen in it.

Δ: After a quarter of an howre, Michael and Uriel cam both agayne.

Mi: Loke into the 7 angles: next unto the uppermost Circumference.

Δ: Uriel cam and stode before Michael.

UR: Those 7 letters[166] are the 7 Seats of the One and everlasting GOD. His 7 secret Angels proceding from euery letter and Cross so formed: referring in substance to the FATHER: in forme, to the SONNE: and Inwardly to the HOLI GHOSTE. Loke uppon it: it is one of the Names, which thou hast Before: euery letter conteyning an Angel of brightness: comprehending the 7 inward powres of God: known to none, but him self: a Sufficient BOND to urge all Creatures to life or Death, or any thing els conteyned in this world.[167] Yt banisheth the wicked, expelleth euyll spirits: qualifieth the Waters, strengtheneth the Just, exalteth the righteous and destroyeth the Wicked. He is ONE in SEVEN. He is twise THREE.[168] He is seuen in the Whole. He is Almighty. His Name is euerlasting: His Truth can not fayle. His Glory is incomprehensible. Blessed be his name. Blessed be thow, (our God) for euer.

---

[165] My contynual and anncient prayer.

[166] Note these manifold and great Mysteries and mark these 7 diuerse Crosses with these 7 letters.

[167] Note this Bond.

[168] He is twice three and one.

UR: Thow must refer thy numbers therin conteyned, to the upper circle. For, <u>From Thence, all things in the inward partes, shalbe comprehended</u>. Looke if thow understand it.

Δ: I finde it to be GALETHOG.

UR: It is so. Δ: I thank God and you, I understand now (allso) the numbers annexed.

 UR: As this darknes is lightened, by the spirit of God, herein; so will I lighten, yea so will the Lord lighten your Imperfections, and glorifie your myndes to the sight of innumerable most holy and unspeakable Mysteries.

UR: To the next part. Δ: Michael sat still, with his sword in his hand.

UR: <u>The parte wherein thow hast labored, conteyneth 7 Angels.</u> Dost thow understand it? Δ: Not yet. Ur: Oh how far is mans Judgment from Celestiall powres? Oh how far are these secrets hidden from the wycked? Glory be unto him, which seeth for euer. Δ: Amen, Amen, Amen.

UR: Note: We cannot tary long. Thow must set down these letters onely, by 7, in a spare paper, thus:[169]

UR: Rede---------------Begyn at the first, and rede downward.[170]

Z	l	l	R	H	i	a
a	Z	C	a	a	c	b
p	a	u	p	n	h	r
h	d	m	h	i	a	l
k	k	a	a	e	e	e
i	i	e	e	l	l	l
e	e	l	l	M	G	+

---

[169] I haue hither to forgotton to ax where Uriel his name may appere.

[170] 48 letters are here: and One is noted by a Cross: which maketh the 49th. Of this Cross and Angels vide Anno 1584, Junij 25. - Δ. See TFR, p. 173. -Ed.

Δ: I rede thus, Zaphkiel, Zadkiel, Cumael, Raphael, Haniel, Michaël, Gabriel.[171]

Ur: Thow hast red right.

Δ: Praysed be God.

Ur: Thus dost thow see, how mercifully God dealeth with his seruants.

Euery letter here, conteyneth or comprehendeth the number of 72 Vertues:[172] Whose names thow shalt know: skarse yet revealed to the world. Uriel and Michael iointly togither pronownced this blessing on us.

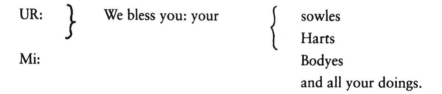

UR: ⎫   We bless you: your   ⎰ sowles
                                  ⎱ Harts
Mi: ⎭   Bodyes
                                    and all your doings.

Δ: Michael with his sword, and flame of fyre florished ouer our heds.

 Yet I will thus much shew you, for your Cumfort beside. What seest thow? Δ: He spake to the skryer. And he saw an innumerable multitude of Angels in the Chamber or study abowt us, very bewtifull with wyngs of fyre. Then he sayd,[173]

Lo, thus you shalbe shaddowed[174] from the wicked. Kepe these Tables secret. He is secret that liueth for euer.

---

171 The 7 angels, Zaphiel, Zadkiel, Camael, Raphael, Haniel, Michael, and Gabriel, appear in Cornelius Agrippa, *De Occulta Philosophia*, book 2, chap. 10, p. 282, as the "seven angels which stand in the presence of God." -Ed.

172 72 vertues multiplyed by 48: giue 3456.

173 This I supply was spoken by Michael though the noting by whom is omitted in the original. -Δ.

174 Shaddowed: "shaded." -Ed.

Man is frayle. Fare well.

¶ He must go for the bokes, <u>els they will perish.</u>[175] Δ: He ment that my partner Ed. Talbot, shold go to fatch the bokes from Lancaster (or therby) which were the L. Mowntegles[176] bokes, which Mr. Mort yet hath: wherof mention is made before.

Ended hor. 5. a meridie
Tuesday the 20 Martij
1582.

Wensday 21 Martij, circa 2ã a meridie.

Δ: After appearance was had, there cam in one before Michael (who sat in his seat) and Uriel leaned on the table (as he, usually did). This seemed to be a Trumpeter:[177] he was all in white, and his garments bespotted with blud. He had nothing on his hed. His heare very long hanging behynde him on his sholders. The Trumpet seamed to be gold. The sownd therof was very playne.

Δ: I axed of my skryer, in what manner Uriel now shewed, (and Michael likewise.) Then Michael sayd, <u>I warned</u> thee <u>for axing of my apparell</u> or manner.[178] Et hæc est Gloria illius, quæ non commouebitur ab impijs.

Mi: Quid vultis? Δ: Iuxta voluntate Dei, Sapientiam nobis necessariam &c.

Mi: Sapientia mundi, nihil est, peribit autem in æternum. Veniat

---

175 ¶ Of this sentence cam no frute nor furder confirmation, therefore, consider.

176 The third Lord Monteagle, William Stanley, died in 1581, and it seems likely that Dee was trying to purchase some of his books at his estate sale. –Ed.

177 Note this trumpeter.

178 We were commaunded Not to ax of the apparayle of Michael.

æternitas DOMINI, ab uniuersis mundi partibus. Venite, venite, sic vult DEVS <u>ADONAY</u> fac officium Phanaël.[179]

Δ: This Phanael was the Trumpeter, (above mentioned) who there-upon blew his Trumpet, lustily,[180] turning him self rownd abowt, to all the world. Then, from 7 partes of the world, (being equally diuided abowt the Horizon,) cam 7 Cumpanyes of Pillers all of fyrye cullour glittring. And euery Cumpany of Pillers high and great and as thowgh they were Pillers of fyre. The Heauen, the Sonne, and, Mone and Sterrs seemed to tremble.

Mi: Multiplex est Deus Noster.[181]

Mi: Mark this Mystery. Seuen comprehendeth the Secrets of Heven and erth. <u>seuen knitteth mans sowle and body togither (3, in sowle, and 4 in body)</u>.

In 7, thow shalt finde the unitie.

In 7, thow shalt finde the Trinitie.

In 7, thow shalt finde the Sonne, and the proportion of the Holy Ghoste.[182] O God, O God, O god, Thy Name (O God) be praysed euer, from thy <u>7 Thrones</u>, from <u>thy 7 Trumpets</u>, and from <u>thy 7 Angels</u>. Δ: Amen, Amen, Amen.

Mi: <u>In 7, God wrowght all things</u>.

Mi: Note. <u>In 7, and by 7 must you work all things</u>. O Seuen tymes Seuen, Veritie, vertue and Maiestie. I Minister by thy licence. This expownd, by thy Vertue (Δ: Michael spake that, pointing to Uriel.)

---

[179] Et haec est . . . fac officium Phanael: "And this is his glory, which will not be moved by the wicked. Mi: What do you want? Δ: Besides the will of God, the wisdom that is necessary for us. Mi: The wisdom of the world is nothing, but will perish in eternity. May the LORD'S eternity come, from every part of the world. Come, come if GOD ADONAY wishes. Perform the office, O Phanael." -Ed.

[180] Lustily: "vigorously." -Ed.

[181] Multiplex . . . Noster: "Manifold is our God." -Ed.

[182] 7 Thrones, 7 Trumpets, 7 Angels.

Δ: Michael and Uriel both kneeled down, and the Pillers of fyrie and brasen cullour, cam nere, rownd abowt them uniformely.

Mi: Sic est DEVS noster.[183]

Δ: One of the pillers leaned toward the skryer, and had like a pommel or mace hed, on the top of it. And Michael with great reuerence toke out of the top of it a thing like an S.

Δ: Than leaned down 6 Pillers more: and Michael, cryed lowd,

Vnus est DEVS noster, Deus Deus noster.[184]

Δ: Then orderly he opened all the pillers heds: and then the 7 ioyned all togither, distinctly to be discerned.

Mi: Note. Δ: There appeared a great

S
A
A
I

Δ: Then the sides closed up, and hid those letters first shewed. After that appered two letters more

E
M

Δ: He made Cursy, and semed to go from ward, and vanished away.

8
E   •
E

Μυσεριον est.[185]

---

183 Sic est Deus noster: "So is our God." -Ed.

184 Unus . . . noster: "One is our God, O God, our God." -Ed.

185 Muserion est: "It is a mystery." The reason Dee used this pseudo-Greek is unclear. -Ed.

Δ: The Pillers all ioyned togither at the tops, making (as it were) One Mace or Pommell, and so flew up to heven wards.

Δ: There seamed two pillers more to <u>come down</u> from heven (<u>like the other</u> in forme) and toke place there, where the other 7, stode, which went away.

Δ: Michael with his sword, Cut them asunder: and cryed out,

> <u>Away you workers of Iniquitie</u>. [186]
> Perijt Malus cum malis.[187]

Δ: The pillers fell down, and the grownd swallowed them up.

> Tanta est tua <u>audacia Sathan</u>[188]
> sed DEVS noster viuit.[189]

Δ: The pillers which before ascended, cam down ioyntly: and oute of them a Voyce saying, NON SVM.[190]

Δ: Then the 7 pillers next his right hand, bowed to Michael, And oute of them, a voyce sayd, SVM.[191]

Δ: Then one of the Pillers stode higher than his fellows, and Michael opened all the tops of them, and sayd,

Orate.[192] Δ: We prayed.

Mi: Write the Name down in the Tables.

Δ: Then he toke of, 3 of the heds of the Pillers, and sett them downe

---

186 Note the intrusion of Error by the Wicked powres of Sathan.

187 Perijt Malus cum malis: "A wicked one perishes with the wicked." -Ed.

188 Tanta . . . Sathan: "So great is your boldness, O Satan" -Ed.

189 Sed . . . vivit: "But our God lives." -Ed.

190 Non sum: I understand the refusall of those two intruded pillers. -Δ. Non sum: "I am not." -Ed.

191 Sum: "I am." -Ed.

192 Orate: "Pray." -Ed.

and there appered, BTZ, great letters in hollow places like square cum-fet[193] boxes.

Mi: Ista sunt <u>secreta secretorum.</u>[194]

Invocate Nomen eius, aut nihil agere pos-sumus.[195] <u>The key of Prayer</u> openeth all things.

Δ: We prayed.

Note Key

Δ: Then the other 4 pillers, bowingly shewed 4 letters thus, KASE, and the number 30 with a prik under. Then the Pillers ioyned theyr heds togither very close, and flew up into the firma-ment with Thunder.

Sic Domine, Sic, Sic.[196]

Mi: Place these in the Table. Δ: I wrote and he sayd, Thow hast done right. Laudate nomen Domini qui viuit in æternum.[197]

Δ: A voyce cam out of the next cumpany of the 7 pillers (ioyning them selues togither) saying, Ipse.[198]

Mi: Et Misericordia tua Domine magna est.[199]

Δ: Michael kneled whan he sayd this.

Δ: Michael shewed out of 4 of theyr heds, of the pillers, (and with all sayd,)

---

193 Cumfet, comfit: "candy." -Ed.

194 Ista . . . secretorum: "These are the secrets of secrets." -Ed.

195 Invocate . . . possumus: "Call upon his name, or we are able to do nothing" -Ed.

196 Sic . . . Sic: "Yes, O Lord, Yes, Yes." -Ed.

197 Laudate . . . aeternum: "Praise the name of the Lord who lives forever." -Ed.

198 Ipse: "exactly." -Ed.

199 Et Misericordia tua Domine magna est: "And your mercy, O Lord, is great." -Ed.

<u>NO, NOT the Angels of heuen, (but I,) are priuie of these things</u>. Δ: So there appeared, 4 letters, HEID.

Δ: Then the other 3 pillers were opened and had ENE on theyr tops.

Dominus collocatur in numero suo.[200]

Δ: The 7 pillers mownted up into the ayre, and it thundred at their going.

Δ: Then the fowrth Cumpany of pillers bowed to Michael: out of them cam a voyce: Viuo sicut <u>LEO</u> in medio illorum.[201]

Mi: Et tua potestas magna est ubique.[202]

Δ: Then Michael pluckt of, fiue of the tops. There appered Δ: then they ioyned all togither: then appered EIMO.

Mi: Hoc non est sine præce.[203]

Δ: The other two opened, and there appeared 30 A.

Δ: Then they closed up, and went away, with a great thunder.

Δ: Then cam 7 other pillers to Michael, and a Voyce oute of them, saying, <u>Serpens</u> sum, et deuoraui serpentem.[204]

Mi: Et bonis et malis serpens es Domine.[205]

Δ: Then they closed all up; and Michael sayd, Orate. Δ: We prayed.

Δ: Then Michael toke of, the heds of 4: then appeared first an I, then MEG. Then he opened the other 3, and CBE appeared.

Mi: Numerus illius, est nulli cognitus.[206]

---

[200] Dominus . . . suo: "The Lord is stationed in his number." -Ed.

[201] Vivo . . . illorum: "I live as a lion in their midst." -Ed.

[202] Et tua . . . ubique: "And great is your power everywhere." -Ed.

[203] Hoc . . . praece: "This is not without prayer." -Ed

[204] Serpens . . . serpentem: "I am a serpent, and I devoured the serpent." -Ed.

[205] Et bonis . . . Domine: "You are a serpent to both the good and the evil, O Lord." -Ed.

[206] Numerus . . . cognitus: "His number was discovered by no one." -Ed.

Δ: They ioyned theyr heds all togither, and ascended up to heuen-ward: and great lightening after them.

Δ: Then cam an other Septenarie of Pillers: and oute of them a voyce, saying,

Ignis sum penetrabilis.[207]

Mi: Et sit nobiscum, Ô Deus.[208] Pray. Δ: We prayed.

Δ: Then he opened 4 of theyr heds and appered in them ILAO.

Δ: They closed togither agayne.

Δ: Then one other was opened, and *I* appered.

Δ: Then ♃ appered, and did shut up agayn.[209]

Δ: Then he smote fyre out of the last pyller, and it thundred and there seemed to come out of it innumerable Angels like little Children with wings, and there appered N, and suddenly did shut up.[210] Sic sic sic Deus noster.[211]

Δ: Then they ioyned all togither, and flew up.

Mi: Note down in the table. Δ: I Noted them down.

Δ: Then cam the last 7 pillers, and out of them this Voyce,

Finis.

Gaudium et Lux nostra Deus.[212]

Δ: Then they closed all in One.

Mi: Orate. Δ: We prayed.

Δ: Then 6 of the heds opened and appered I H R L A A.

---

[207] Ignis sum penetrabilis: "I am a piercing fire." -Ed.

[208] Et sit . . . Deus: "And may it/he be with us, O God." -Ed.

[209] There is "V" omitted by our neglect.

[210] Note these innumerable Angels.

[211] Sic . . . noster: "Yes, yes, yes our God." -Ed.

[212] Finis. Gaudium . . . Deus: "The end. Joy and Light is our God." -Ed.

Δ: Then the seuenth opened: Then <u>seamed trees to leap up, and hills, and the seas and waters to be trubbled, and thrown up.</u>

Δ: A voyce cam out of the Pillers: Consummatum est.[213]

Δ: There appeared in that Piller ⚴. .

Δ: They ioyned togither and flew up to heven ward.

Mi: VNVS VNVS VNVS.

Omnis caro timet vocem eius.[214]

Pray. Δ: We prayed.

Δ: Note: my skryer was very faynt, and his hed in manner gyddy, and his eyes, dasyling, by reason of the sights seen so bright, and fyrie, &c. Michael bad him be of good cumfort, and sayd he shold do well.

Mi: Cease for a quarter of an howre.

Δ: After we had stayed for a quarter of an howre, we comming to the stone agayne, fownd him come all ready to the stone: and Uriel with him. Who, allso, had byn by, all the while, during the Mysterie of the '7' pillers.

Mic: Set two stoles in the myddst of the flowre. On the one, set the stone: and at the other let him knele. I will shut the eares of them in the howse, that none shall heare us. I will shew great Mysteries.

Michael than, with a lowd voyce sayd,

Adeste Filiæ Bonitatis:
Ecce DEVS vester adest:
    Venite.[215]

Δ: There cam in 7 yong women apparelled <u>all in Grene</u>, having

---

[213] Consummatum est: "It is finished." -Ed.

[214] Unus . . . eius: "ONE ONE ONE. All flesh fears his voice." -Ed.

[215] Adeste . . . Venite: "Be present O Daughters of goodness. Behold, your God is present. Come." -Ed.

theyr heds rownd abowt attyred all with greene silk, with a wreath behinde hanging down to the grownd.[216] Michael stroke his sword ouer them, no fyre appearing: Then they kneeled: And after, rose agayn.

Mi: Scribe quæ vides.[217]

Δ: One of them stept out, with a little blue tablet on the forhed of her: and in it written, El.

Δ: She stode a side, and an other cam in, after the same sort, with a great M, and a little e, thus,	Me.

The Third, cam as the other, and had	Ese.
The fowrth------------------------	Iana.
The fifth------------------------	Akele.
The sixth------------------------	Azdobn.
The seuenth stepped furth with---------	Stimcul.

Δ: They all togither, sayd, Nos possumus in Cælis multa.[218]

Δ: Then they went theyr way, suddenly disäpering.

Mi: Note this in your next place but one. Δ: I did so.

Mi: Go to the next place. Stay.

Mi: Adeste, Filiolæ Lucis.[219]

Δ: They all, cam in agayn, and answered, Adsumus Ô tu qui ante

faciem DEI stas.[220]

---

216 Filiae Bonitatis, or Filiolae lucis: vide pagina sequente. -Δ. ("Regarding the Daughters of goodness, or little Daughters of light: see the following page." -Ed.)

217 Scribe quae vides: "Write what you see." -Ed.

218 Nos . . . multa: "We are capable of much in Heaven." -Ed.

219 Adeste, Filiolae Lucis: "Come, O Little Daughters of Light." -Ed.

220 Michael: one of them that are cownted to stand before the face of God. -Δ. Adsumus . . . stas: "We are present, O you who stands before the face of God." -Ed.

Mi: <u>Hijs nostris benefacite.</u>[221]

Δ: They answered, all, <u>Factum erit.</u>[222]

Mi: Valete.[223]

Mi: Et dixit Dominus, venite <u>Filij Lucis.</u>
         Venite in Tabernaculo meo.
         Venite (inquam): Nam Nomen meum exaltatum
            est.[224]

Δ: Then cam in 7 yong men, all with bright cowntenance, <u>white apparaled</u>, with white silk uppon theyr heds, <u>pendant behinde as the women had.</u>[225]

One of them had a rownd purifyed pece or ball of Gold in his hand.

One other had a ball of siluer in his hand.

The third a ball of Coper.

The fowrth a ball of Tynne in his hand.

The fifth had a ball of yern.[226]

The sixth had a rownd thing of Quicksyluer, tossing it betwene his two hands.

The last had a ball of Lead.[227]

They wer all apparayled of one sort.

---

[221] Hijs nostris benefacite: "Favor these ones of ours." -Ed.

[222] Factum erit: "It will be." -Ed.

[223] Valete: "Farewell." -Ed.

[224] Et dixit . . . exaltum est: "And the Lord spoke, come O Son of Light. Come to my tent. Come (I say), for my name is exalted." -Ed.

[225] HM reads, "pendant behinde with a wreth down to the grownd." -Ed.

[226] Yern: iron. -Ed.

[227] Traditionally, these metals correspond to the Sun, Moon, Venus, Jupiter, Mars, Mercury, and Saturn, respectively. -Ed.

Mi: Quanmvis[228] in uno generantur tempore, tamen unum sunt.[229]

Δ: He that had the gold ball, had a rownd tablet of gold on his brest, and on it written a great   I-----------------------

Then he with the syluer ball, cam furth, with a golden tablet on his brest likewise, and on it written   Ih-----------------------

He with the Copper ball, had in his tablet   Ilr-----------------------

He with the tyn ball, had in his tablet   Dmal--------------------

He with the yern ball, had in his tablet   Heeoa, and so went

asyde--------------------

He with the Mercury ball, had written   Beigia--------------------

The yong man with the leaden ball, had   Stimcul------------------

Mi: Facite pro illis, cum tempus erit.[230]

Δ: All answered, Volumus.[231]

Mi: Magna est Gloria Dei inter vos. Erit semper. Halleluyah.[232]

Valete.[233]

Δ: They made cursy, and went theyr way, mownting up to heven.

Mi: Dixit Deus, Memor esto nominis mei:

Vos autem immemores estis.[234]

I speak to you. Δ: Hereupon, we prayed.

Mi: Venite, Venite, Venite.

---

228 Δ: perhaps here wanteth "non."

229 Quanmvis . . . sunt: "Although they may (not?) be begotten at one time, yet they are one." -Ed.

230 Facite . . . erit: "Make (items) according to these (examples) when the time comes." -Ed.

231 Volumus: "We wish." Perhaps a mistake for "volamus" (we fly). -Ed.

232 Magna . . . Halleluyah: "Great is God's glory among you, and ever shall be. Halleluyah." -Ed.

233 Valete: "Farewell." -Ed.

234 Dixit . . . estis: "God said, be mindful of my name, but you have been forgetful." -Ed.

Filiæ Filiarum Lucis Venite.

Qui[235] habebitis filias venite nunc et semper.[236]

Dixit Deus, Creaui Angelos meos, qui destruent Filias Terræ.

Adsumus,[237] Δ: Sayd 7 little wenches which cam in. They were couered with white silk robes, and with white abowt theyr hed, and pendant down behinde, very long.

Mi: Vbi fuistis vos?[238] Δ: They answered: In terris, cum sanctis et in cælis, cum glorificatis.[239]

Δ: These spake not so playn, as the former did; but as though they had an impediment in theyr tung.

Δ: They had, euery one, somwhat in theyr hands, but my skryer could not iudge what things they were. Mi: Non adhuc cognoscetur Mysterion hoc.[240]

Δ: Eache had fowre-square Tablets on theyr bosoms, as yf they were of white Ivory.

Δ: The first shewed on her Tablet a great   S.

The second---------------------------------   Ab.

The third----------------------------------   Ath.

The fowrth--------------------------------   Ized.

The fifth----------------------------------   Ekiei.

The sixth---------------------------------   Madimi.

The seuenth-------------------------------   Esemeli.

---

[235] Forte "quae." -Δ. (Perhaps "quae" -Ed.)

[236] Note these three descents.

[237] Venite, . . . Adsumus: "Come, come, come. Come, O Daughters of the Daughters of Light. Come now and forever, you who will have daughters. God said, I created my angels, who will destroy the daughters of the earth. We are present." -Ed.

[238] Vbi fuistis vos: "Where were you?" -Ed.

[239] In terris . . . glorificatis: "On the earth with the saints, and in heaven with the glorified." -Ed.

[240] Non adhuc . . . hoc: "This mystery is not yet to be known." -Ed.

Mi: Quid istis facietis?

Erimus cum illis, in omnibus operibus illorum.[241] Δ:
They answered.

Mi: Valete.[242] Δ: They answered, Valeas et tu Magnus O in Cælis.[243]

Δ: And so they went away.

Mi: Orate.[244] Δ: We prayed.

Mi: Et misit filios filiorum, edocentes Israel.

Mi: Dixit Dominus, Venite ad vocem meam.

Adsumus,[245] Δ: **Sayd 7 little Childern which cam in, like boyes**
couered all <u>with purple, with hanging sleues</u> like preists or scholers
gown sleues: theyr heds attyred all (after the former manner) with pur-
ple sylk.

Mi: Quid factum est inter <u>filios hominum</u>?

Male viuunt (sayd they) nec habemus locum cum illis
tanta est illorum Iniustitia. Veh mundo, scandalis:
vel scandalizantibus, Veh illis quibus Nos non sumus.[246]

---

241 Quid . . . Illorum: "What will you do with these? (They answered,) We shall be
with them in all their works." -Ed.

242 Valete: "Farewell" (lit. "be well"). -Ed.

243 Valeas . . . Cælis: "May you be well, and you are great O you in heaven." -Ed.

244 Orate: "pray." -Ed.

245 Et miset . . . Adsumus: "And he has sent the sons of the sons, instructing Israel.
The Lord spoke, come to my voice. We are present." -Ed.

246 Quid factum . . . sumus: "What is done among the sons of men? They live badly
(said they) and we do not have a place with them, so great is their iniquity. Woe to
the world because of temptations to sin, or to those who cause temptations. Woe
to those whom we are not with." -Ed. Compare with Matthew 18:7: Vae mundo a
scandalis. Necesse est enim ut veniant scandala: verumtamem vae homini illi, per
quem scandalum venit: "Woe to the world for temptations to sin! For it is necessary that temptations come, but woe to the man by whom the temptation comes!"

Δ: **These had tablets (on theyr brests) three cornerd, and seemed to be very grene and in them, letters. The first had two letters in one: thus, of EL:**

The first ---------- 𝐄𝓪𝓼 ----- Δ: He sayd, Nec nomine meo timet Mundus.[247]

The second ---------- An ----- Nullus videbit faciem meam.[248]

The third ---------- Aue ----- Non est virgo super terram cui dicam.[249]

[Δ: And pointed to his tablet, wherein that word, Aue, was written.]

The fowrth ---------- Liba ----- Tanta est infirmitas sanctitudinis Diei. Benefacientes decesserunt ab illo.[250]

The fifth ---------- Rocle - Opera manuum illorum sunt vana. Nemo autem videbit me.[251]

The sixth shewed his Tablet and said, Ecce -- Hagonel[252] - Qui adhuc Sancti sunt, cum illis viuo.[253]

The seuenth had on his tablet -- Ilemese -- Hij imitauerunt doctrinam meam. In me <u>Omnis sita est Doctrina.</u>[254]

---

[247] Nec nomine . . . Mundus: "The world does not fear my name." -Ed.

[248] Nullus . . . meam: "Nobody will see my face." -Ed.

[249] Non est . . . dicam: "There is no maiden on the earth with whom I will speak." -Ed.

[250] Tanta est . . . ab illo: "So great is the weakness of holiness of the day. The benefactors depart from him." -Ed.

[251] Opera . . . me: "Their handiwork is vain. Whereupon no one will see me." -Ed.

[252] In the manuscript the "e" and "l" are overwritten. -Ed.

[253] Hagonel. Vide de hoc Hagonel, lib. 4. -Δ ("Regarding this Hagonel, see Book 4.") Ecce: "behold"; Qui adhuc . . . viuo: "I live with those who are still holy." -Ed.

[254] Hij . . . Doctrina: "They have imitated my teaching. The teaching of all things are placed in me." -Ed.

Δ: I thowght my skryer had missherd, this word Imitauerunt, for
Imitati sunt.²⁵⁵ And Michael smyled and seemed to lawgh, and sayd,
Non curat numerum Lupus.²⁵⁶ And farder he sayd, Ne minimam detra-
het à virtute, virtutem.

Mi: Estote cum illis: Estote (inquam cum istis) Estote (inquam)
mecum. Valete.²⁵⁷

Δ: So they went, making reuerence,²⁵⁸ and went up to heuen.

Mi: Dictum est hoc tempore.²⁵⁹

Mi: Note this in thy Tables. Dost thow understand it? Loke if thow
canst.

Δ: He sayd to Uriel, It is thy part, to interpretate these things.²⁶⁰

Ur: Omnis Intelligentia est a Domino.

Mi: Et eius Nomen est Halleluyah.²⁶¹

Compose a table, diuided into 7 parts, square.²⁶²

255 Imitati sunt: "They have imitated." The proper perfect active form of imitor is
     Imitati sunt, not imitaverunt. -Ed.

256 Non curat numerum Lupus: "The wolf does not administer the number." -Ed.

257 Ne minimam . . . Valete: "It detracts very little virtue from virtue. Be with them.
     Be (I say with them). Be (I say) with me. Farewell." -Ed.

258 HM adds, "to Michael (who had called both the first & these)." -Ed.

259 Dictum est hoc tempore: "It was said at this time." -Ed.

260 Urielis officium. -Δ ("Uriel's office." -Ed.)

261 Omnis . . . Halleluyah: "All knowledge is from the Lord. Mi: And his name is
     Halleluyah." -Ed.

262 Note this list is made perfecter by the next side following. -Δ. The list is com-
     posed of the Hebrew names for the seven planets with the divine name "El"
     added to indicate an angel:
          Sabathiel (Saturn), Zedekieil (Jupiter), Madimiel (Mars), Semeliel (The Sun),
     Nogahel (Venus), Corabiel (Mercury), Levanael (The Moon). The numbers 21/8
     represent "el"; 26, 8, and 30 represent "l." -Ed.

S	A	A	I 21/8.	E ᴍ	M ᴇ	E 8.
B	T	Z	K	A	S	E 30.
H	E	I	D	E	N	E
D	E	I	M	O	30.	A
I 26.	M	E	G	C	B	E
I	L ᴀ	A ʟ	O	I 21/8.	V	N
I	H	R	L	A	A	21/8.

Ur: Those 7 names, which procede from the left hand to the right, are the **Names of God, not known to the Angels**: neyther can be spoken or red of man. Proue if thou canst reade them.

Beatus est qui secrete.
Nomina sua conseruat.[263]

Ur: These Names, bring furth 7 Angels: The 7 Angels, and
Governers in the heuens **next unto us,**[264] which stand allwayes before
the face of God.[265]

Sanctus Sanctus Sanctus
est ille DEVS noster,[266]

Ur: Euery letter of the Angels names, bringeth furth 7 dowghters.
Euery dowghter bringeth furth her dowghter, which is 7. Euery
dowghter-her-dowghter bringeth furth a sonne. Euery sonne in him
self, is 7. Euery sonne hath his sonne, and his sonne is 7.[267]

Let us prayse the God of Seuen, which was and is
and shall liue for euer.
Vox Domini in Fortitudine.
Vox Domini in Decore.
Vox Domini reuelat Secreta.
In templo eius, Laudemus Nomen eius El.
Halleluyah.[268]

See if thow canst now understand this table. The Dowghters procede from the angle on the right hand, cleaving the myddle: where theyr

---

263 Beatus est . . . conseruat: "Blessed is he who keeps his own names secret." -Ed.

264 In the manuscript, "us" is heavily underscored. -Ed.

265 Note these two orders of Angels: and Note Uriel doth name him self one of the
standers before the face of God.

266 Sanctus . . . noster: "Holy, holy, holy, is he, our God." -Ed.

267 Note well this Rule of Arte.

268 Vox Domini . . . Halleluyah: "The voice of the Lord in strength. The voice of the
Lord in grace. The voice of the Lord reveals the secret. In his temple may we
praise his name EL. Hallelluyah." -Ed.

generation ceaseth. The Sonnes from the left hand to the right to the middle: so proceding where theyr number <u>endeth in one Centre</u>. The Residue thow mayst (by this Note) understande.[269]

Δ: Then Michael, he stroke ouer us ward, with his sword, and the flame of fire yssued oute.

Loke to the corner of the right hand, being the uppermost: where thow shalt finde $\overset{8}{\cdot}$. Refer thyne eye to the <u>upper number, and the letter aboue</u> it. <u>But the Number must be fownd under neth, bycause his prick so noteth</u>.[270] Than procede to the names of the dowghters in the Table: and thow shalt see that it is the first name of them: This shall teach thee.

Δ: Loking <u>now into my first and greatest</u> Circle for $\overset{8}{\cdot}$ I finde it with l ouer it. I take this to be the first Dowghter.[271]

Ur: You must in this square Table set E by the $\overset{8}{\cdot}$ and now write them Composedly in one letter, thus $\mathit{E\!\omega}$.

Nomen Domini viuit in æternum.[272]

Ur: Giue ouer, for half an howre, and thow shalt be fully instructed.

Δ: I did so, and after half an howre comming to the stone, I was willed to make a new square table of 7: and to write and note, as it followeth.

---

[269] Note this manner of Center accownted.

[270] Note of Numbers with priks signifying letters.

[271] l the first dowghter.

[272] Nomen . . . aeternum: "The Name of the Lord lives forever." -Ed.

S	A	A	I 21/8·	E	M	E 8:	— Viuit in Cælis[273]
B	T	Z	K	A	S	E 30·	— Deus noster[274]
H	E	I	D	E	N	E	— Dux noster[275]
D	E	I	M	O	30·	A	— Hic est[276]
I ·26	M	E	G	C	B	E	— Lux in æternum[277]
I	L	A	O	I 21/8·	V	N	— Finis est[278]
I	H	R	L	A	A	21/8·	— Vera est hæc tabula[279]

---

[273] Viuit in caelis: "He lives in heaven." -Ed.

[274] Deus noster: "Our God." -Ed.

[275] Dux noster: "Our Commander." -Ed.

[276] Hic est: "This is." -Ed.

[277] Lux in aeternum: "Light forever." -Ed.

[278] Finis est: "He/it is the end." -Ed.

[279] Vera est haec tabula: "This table is true." -Ed.

Vera est hæc Tabula, partim nobis cognita, et partim omnibus, incognita. Vide iam.[280]

The 30 by E, in the second place, in the upper right corner, serueth not in the consideration of the first Dowghters, but for an other purpose.[281]

The **26** by I, serueth **for an other purpose**: but not for this Dowghters Dowghter. The 21, is e, and **8** with the prick under it is l: which togither maketh El, or thus compownded as if it were one letter, **Eℓ** .

The Names of the great Seale must follow the Orthographie of this Table. Virtus vobiscum est.

Orate.[282] Δ: We prayed.

Δ: Then there appeared SAAI **8** M **Eℓ** . Here is an E comprehended in L.

Ur: Read now the Table.

> Angeli lucis Dei nostri
>   Et posuit angelos illius in medio illorum.[283]

Ur: In the table are the names of 7 Angels. The first is Zabathiel, beginning from the left uppermost corner, taking the corner letter first, and then that on the right hand above, and than that under the first, and than the third from the first, in the upper row: and then cornerwise down toward the left hand, and then to the fowrth letter from the first in the upper row: where there is I with **8** , which maketh el. So have you Zabathiel.

---

[280] Vera est . . . iam: "This table is true, known in part by us, but unknown in all parts. See below." -Ed.

[281] Note these other purposes.

[282] Virtus Vobiscum est: "Virtue is with you. Pray." -Ed.

[283] Angeli . . . illorum: "The angels of light of our God. And he set his angels in their midst." -Ed.

Ur: Go forward.

2. Δ: So, I finde next   Zedekieil.

Ur: This I in the last Syllable <u>augmenteth the true sownd</u> of it.

3. Δ: Then next I finde   Madimiel.-----   Ur: It is so.
4. Δ: Then--------------   Semeliel.-----   Ur: It is true.
5. Δ: Then--------------   Nogahel.-----   Ur: It is so.
6. Δ: Then--------------   Corabiel.[284]-----   Ur: It is so.
7. Δ: Then--------------   Leuanael.-----   Ur: It is so.

Ur: Write these names in the Great Seal, next under the 7 names which thow wrotest last: videlicet, under **Eu** , An Aue &c. distinctly in great letters.

Ur: Make the E and L of Zabathiel, in one letter compownded, thus ZABATHI **Eu** . In this, so fashion your E and L. And this name must be distributed in his letters into 7 sides of that innermost Heptagonum. For the other, I will teache you to dispose them. You must make for <u>IEL</u> (<u>in this name onely</u>) I with the $\overset{2.1}{8}$ annexed. So haue you iust 7 places.

Ur: The next fiue names thow shalt dispose in the fiue exterior angles of the Pentacle: euery angle conteyning one whole name.

Ur: Set the first letters of these 5 names, (in Capitall letters) within the fiue acute internall angles of the Pentacle: and the rest of eche name following Circularly from his Capitall letter, but in the 5 exterior obtuse angles of the Pentacle.

Ur: Set Z, of Zedekieil within the angle which standeth up toward the begynning of the greatest Circle. And so procede toward thy right hand.

---

284 This name Corabiel you may see in *Elementis Magicis* Petri de Abani, in the Considerations Diei ☽ (Monday). - Δ.

Ur: In the middle now of thy Pentacle, make a cross † like a Crucifix and write the last of those 7 names Leuanael thus,

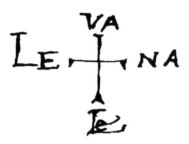

Uriel: Vidit DEVS, opus suum esse bonum

   et cessauit a Labore suo.
     Factum est.[285]

Δ: Michael stode up and sayd,

The æternall Blessing of God the FATHER,

The mercifull Goodnes of CHRIST, his SONNE

The unspeakable Dignitie of GOD the Holy GHOSTE

bless you, preserue you, and multiply your

   doings in his Honor and Glory.

Uriel: AMEN.

Ur: <u>These Angels are the angells of the 7 Circles of Heven, gouerning the lightes of the 7 Circles.</u>

Blessed be GOD in us, and by <u>us</u>,

<u>Which stand contynually before</u>

<u>the presence of GOD, for euer.</u>[286]

---

[285] Videt . . . est: "God saw his own work to be good, and he ceased from his work. It was so." -Ed.

[286] Note these two order of Angels.

DIXI.[287]

Δ: Whan may we be so bold, as to require your help agayn.
Mic: Whan so euer you will, we are ready.

Farewell.

Δ: Sit Nomen Domini benedictum, ex hoc nunc, et usque in sæcula
sæculorum.:
Amen.[288]

Anno Domini	}	At
1582.		Mortlake by
Martij. 21.		Richemond

---

[287] Dixi: "I have spoken." -Ed.

[288] Sit Nomen . . . Amen: "May the Name of the Lord be blessed, from this time and
for all time, forever and ever. Amen." -Ed.

289

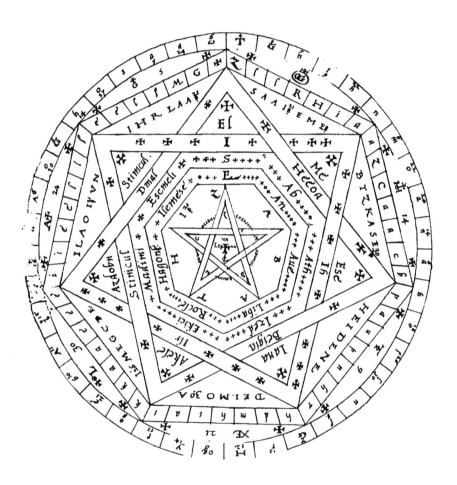

289 Sigillum . . . hebraice: "The Seal of God Aemeth (or Emeth), containing the names of God in Hebrew." -Ed.

Mysteriorum, liber

Tertius.   Δ

Anno 1582:

Aprilis 28: [1]

---

1   Ashmole has added "Liber: 3us / Liber: 4us" at the bottom of the page. Dee has drawn the frame around the title to look like a scroll. -Ed.

Anno 1582 Aprilis 28 a meridie hora 4.[2]

E.T: Onely Michael appeared; Δ: And to diuerse my Complayntes, and requests sayde,

Mi: The lord shall consider thee in this world, and in the world to come.

E.T: All the chayre seamed on fyre.

Mi: <u>This is one Action, in one person</u>: I speak of you two.[3]

Δ: You meane us two to be ioyned so, and in mynde united, as yf we wer one man?

Mi: Thou understandest.

Take heede of punishment for your last slaknes.

Δ: Yf you mean any slaknes on my behalf, Truely it was and is for lak of habilitie[4] to buy and prepare things, appointed of you. Procure I <u>pray you habilitie</u>, and so shall I make spede.

E.T: A great hill of gold with serpents lying on it appeared: he smyteth it with his sword, and it falleth into a mighty great water, hedlong.

Mi: Dost thow understand? Δ: No verylie.

E.T: He razed the hill away, as thowgh there had byn none; and sayd,

Mi: Lo, so it is <u>of this worldly habilitie</u>.

Δ: I pray you how must the Lamine be hanged?

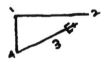

Mi: As concerning the lamine, it must be hanged unseen, in some skarf.[5] The Ring when it is made, I <u>will lessen</u> it according to my pleasure.

---

2   In HM Dee notes: "Almost all the Third boke, is of the 7 Ensignes of Creation." -Ed.

3   Union of us two.

4   Habilitie: "ability." -Ed.

5   The lamin not simpli . . . spoken: for No such Lamyn was to be made. -Δ.

I meane by two Cubites, your usuall yarde. Haste, for thow hast many
things to do. Glory be to God, Peace unto his Creatures. <u>Mercy to the
wicked</u>, Forgivenes to the Faithfull: He liueth, Ô he rayngneth, O thow
art mighty, <u>PELE</u>: thy name be blessed. Δ: Amen.

Venito Ese,[6] Δ: He cryed so with a lowd voyce.

E.T: He is now couered, in a myghty couering of fyre, of a great
beawty. There standeth <u>a thing before him. I cannot tell what it is</u>.

Laudate Dominum in cælis.

Orate.[7] Δ: We prayed.

E.T: His face remayneth couered with the fyre, but his body
uncovered.

Mi: Adesdum Ese.

Adesdum Iana.[8]
Vobis dedit demonstrationem in Tabulis vestris.[9]

E.T: There appeare of the figure, (before, imperfect) <u>two little women</u>:
One of them held up a Table which lightened[10] terribly: so that all the
stone was couered: with a myst. A voyce cam out of the myst, and sayd,

Ex hijs <u>creata sunt,</u>[11] et hæc sunt nomina illorum.[12]

---

6   Venito Ese: "Come, O Ese." –Ed.

7   Laudate . . . Orate: "Praise the Lord in Heaven. Pray." -Ed.

8   Remember, Ese and Iana; ar the thirdth and fowrth of the Septem Filiæ Bonitatis,
     sup. lib°. 2°. They are thus in order there: El, Me, Ese, Iana, Akele, Azdobn,
     Stimcul. -Δ. Septem Filiae Bonitatis . . . 2°: "Seven daughters of goodness, in book
     2 above." -Ed.

9   Adesdum Ese . . . vestris: "Come, Ese. Come, Iana. He gives proof in your
     tables." -Ed.

10   Lightened: "glowed." -Ed.

11   Creatio. -Δ "I created." -Ed.

12   Ex hijs . . . illorum: "From these they were created (I created), and these are their
     names." -Ed.

E.T: The myst cleareth, and one of the women held up a Table, being thus written uppon.

Numerus Primus.[13]

Δ: The Table semed square, and full of letters and numbers, and Crosses, in diuerse places, diuersly fashioned.

Numerus Primus[14]

---

13 Numerus Primus: "The first number." -Ed.

14 Δ Of these seven tables, Characters, or scotcheons Consider the words spoken in the fifth boke, Anno 1583, April 28, How they are proper to every King and prince in theyr order. They are Instruments of Conciliation. Volumine 5°: wher my Character is fashioned. -Δ. The words "Numerus Primus" appear to be in Ashmole's handwriting. -Ed.

A finger cam out of the mist, and wyped oute, the first shew, with the Cross, letters, and numbers. The second was in like wise. The Third was a b with the tayle upward thus: . The 52 with the three great BBB, semed to be couered with Gold. The two Crossed ones he did not wipe out with his finger.

The next he blotted oute.

He blotted not oute the three with the 8 and 3.

The two barrs must go clere and

not towch the bars.

The , the square, wherin it standeth, is all gold:

and that he let stand.

Fire cam oute and burnt:

The is all of a bright cullour, like the brightnes of the Sonne, and that was not put out. The places are <u>very blak</u>, but where the letters, and numbers do stand.

E.T. hard a voyce saying, Finis Tenebrarum:[15] Halleluyah.[16]

E.T: There commeth a hand and putteth the little woman into the clowde.

Mi: Prayse God: Be inwardly mery.

The Darknes is comprehended.

God bless you: God bless you: God blesse you.

---

[15] In the manuscript, Dee has drawn a line between this word and "very blak" above. -Ed.

[16] Finis Tenebrarum: Halleluyah: "The end of darkness: Halleluyah." -Ed.

You must leave of for an howre and a half: for you haue .6. other Tables to write to night.

Prayse God: be ioyfull.

After supper we resorted to our scholemaster.

E.T: I here a voyce but see nothing: he sayeth,

> Initium bonum in nomine eius
> et est. Halleluyah.[17]

E.T: Three quarters of the stone (on the right side) are dark, the other quarter is clere.

Mi: Venite filiæ filiarum ESE.[18]

The nethermost......[19]

E.T: There come six yong maydens, all in white apparell, alike: Now they all be gonne into the dark parte of the stone, except one. There cam a flame of fyre out of the dark, and in the flame written Vnus[20] on this manner:

---

17 Initium . . . Halleluyah: "And it is a good beginning in his name. Halleluyah." -Ed.

18 Filiae filiarum Ese sup. lib. 2. -Δ. Venite filiae filiarum ESE: "Come, O daughters of the daughters ESE." -Ed.

19 Somewhat wanteth.

20 Vnus: "One." -Ed.

She that standeth without, putteth her hand into the dark: and pulleth
out a ball of light: and threw it oute: and it waxed bigger and bigger;
and it Thundred.

> E.T: A voyce sayd --------- <u>Dies primus.</u>[21]
> An other voyce --------- Ubi est Tabula?[22]
> An answer --------- Est, Est, Est.[23]

She wyndeth and turneth her self abowt, begynning at her hed, and
so was Transformed into a Table, rownde.

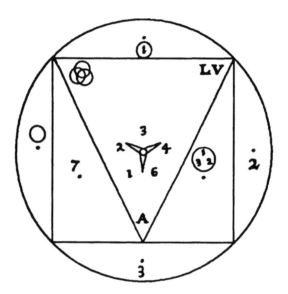

---

21   Dies primus: "The first day." -Ed.

22   Ubi est Tabula?: "Where is the table?" -Ed.

23   Est, est, est: "It is, it is, it is." -Ed.

E.T: Three faces do shew and shote oute, and euer returne into one hed agayne: and with it cam a mervaylous swete sauour. The Table was of three cullours: white, redd, and a mixture of white[24] and red, changeably. A strong sownding cam withall, as of clattring of harness or fall of waters; or such like.

There cam a sterre shoting oute of the dark, and settled itself in the myddle of the Table: And the fyre which cam oute with the woman, did cumpas the Table abowt.

A voyce sayd, O honor, laus et gloria, Tibi qui es, et eris.[25]

The Table sheweth wunderfull fayre and glorious. Onely seuen priks appeare on the Table.

The three angles of the triangle open, and in the lower point appeared a great A.

And in the right upper corner LV. (E.T: The Table trembled.)

And in the other Corner appeared thre circles of æquall bignes, æqually, or alike intersecting eche others by theyr centers.

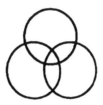

A voyce: Unus est, Trinus est; in omni Angulo est.

Omnia comprehendit: Fuit, est, et vobis erit.
Finis et Origo.[26] (E.T: Ô, Ô; with a dullfull sownd, he pronownced.)

---

24   This is the end of folio 32 of the manuscript. The 4 diagrams are inserted at this point, the first two on folio 33 recto, the other two on folio 33 verso. -Ed.

25   O honor . . . eris: "O honor, praise, and glory to you who are and will be." -Ed.

26   Unus est . . . Origo: "He is one, he is three; he is in each corner. Everything will be understood. He was, is, and will be to you. The end and the beginning." -Ed.

E.T: The woman sayth, Fui: sum quod non <u>sum.</u>[27]

A voyce: Lux non erat et nunc est.[28]

E.T: The woman being turned, from the shape of the Table, into womans shape agayn, went into the dark. Then one <u>part of the darknes diminished</u>. In the dark was a mervaylous turmoyling, tossing, and stur, a long tyme during.

A voyce: For a tyme Nature can not abyde these sightes.

E.T: It is become Quiet, but dark still.

A voyce: Pray and that vehemently, For these things are not revealed without great prayer.

E.T: After a long tyme there cam a woman: and flung up <u>a ball like a glass</u>: and a voyce was hard saying, Fiat. The ball went into the darknes, and browght with it a great white Globe hollow transparent. Then she had a Table abowt her neck, square of 12 places.[29] The woman seamed to daunce and swyng the Table: Then cam a hand oute of the dark: and <u>stroke her and she stode</u> still, and becam fayrer: She sayd, Ecce signum Incomprehensibilitatis.[30]

---

[27] forte fui. – Δ. (Perhaps "was.") Fui . . . sum: "I was, I am that which I am (was?) not." -Ed.

[28] Lux . . . est: "The light was not, but now it is." -Ed.

[29] In the margin is a line pointing to the third table. - Ed.

[30] Ecce signum Incomprehensibilitatis: "Behold the sign that cannot be grasped." -Ed

G B ✝ 23	m · 3 o q B · 9 · d · 4 ·	q· q· q Q B o · ɣ oɣ
♃ B 30 G 33· A	✝ B ✝ A 9 O	L B get ƀ ɟo
♄ ℂ ƀ ⌒ 5	dɑ id ƀ d ɑA	L ƀ 30 ƀ ƿƿ
V H ƀ 9 22	qq qQ ƀ oɣ a	L ƀ 25 d

E.T: The woman is transformed into <u>a water</u>, <u>and flyeth up into the</u> <u>Globe</u> of Light.

E.T: A voyce: Est, Est, Est.[31]

E.T: One commeth, (a woman) out of the Dark very demurely, and soberly walking, carrying in her hand a little rownd ball: and threw it into the dark: and it becam a great <u>thing of Earth</u>. She taketh it in her hand agayne, and casteth <u>it up</u> into the rownd Globe and sayd,

Fiat.[32]

---

31 Est, est, est: "He/it is, is, is." -Ed.

32 Fiat: "Let it be." -Ed.

E.T: She turned her back toward E.T. and there appeared a Table diuided into 24 partes. Yt seemeth to be very Square.[33]

A voyce: Scribe. Veritas est.[34]

E.T: A sword cam out of the Dark: <u>and claue the woman</u> a sunder, and the one half becam <u>a man</u>, and the other a woman,[35] and they went and sat uppon the Ball of cley or erth.

Now seemeth the Dark part to quake.

A voyce: Venito Vasedg.[36]

---

33 In the margin, is a line pointing to the fourth table. - Ed.

34 Scribe. Veritas est: "Write. It is true." -Ed

35 Man, Woman.

36 Venito vasedq: "Come, O vasedq." -Ed.

E.T: There cometh a woman oute of the Dark: she sayd,

Vita hijs ex mea manu.[37]

E.T: She sheweth a Table square full of holes, and many things creeping out of it. This square is within a rownd.

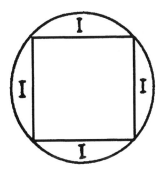

A voyce: O Lux Deus noster.[38]

Hamuthz Gethog.

E.T: Then stept out an other woman hauing a sword in her hand. She toke a thing oute of the dark (a bright thing) and cut it in twayn and the one parte she cut into two unæqual partes, and the other half she cutteth into a thowsand (or innumerable) partes. Then she toke all the partes up into her skyrt. She hath a Table, and it hangeth on her shulders. She stept before the other woman, whose hed standeth in the dark.[39] This woman her Table is fowresquare. She is very bewtifull.

---

37   Vita . . . manu: "The life of these (is) from my hands." -Ed.

38   O Lux Deus noster: "O Light, our God." -Ed.

39   Note this stepping before. -Δ. In the manuscript there is also a line connecting "stepping" and "forestept." -Ed.

[Table/diagram of occult symbols]

Note this Cross with the two bees, the 4 and the 6, is one of the Notes annexed to the second Table of the 4 of Enoch's Tables: And the T of Enoch's Tables semeth to answer with the T first in the Seale of Æmeth, and the cross allso.

She sayd, Lumina sunt hæc Intelligentiæ tuæ.[40]

She sayd, Fere nulli Credendus est hic numerus.[41]

This woman taketh the little peces, and casteth them up, and they become little Sparks of light: and of the things she cast, There were two great rownd things. And they were allso cast up to the white Transparent Globe. And she went away into the Dark: which was, now, very much lessened.[42]

Then the other woman (who <u>was forestept</u>) thrust oute her hed who had the <u>rownd</u> conteyning the Square, with 36 places. She crymbleth clay, and it turneth to <u>byrds</u>. She seameth to be like a witch. Into the

---

40 Lumina . . . tuae: "These are the lights of your knowledge." -Ed.

41 Fere . . . numerus: "Almost no one trusts this number." -Ed.

42 The sterrs, Sonne and Mone Created.

bosse of her Table, she put her hand and that bosse, was in the Dark and oute of the bosse, she seemed to fatch that Clay. She sayd,

Ad usum tuum Multiplicati sunt.[43]

E.T: She went into the Dark.

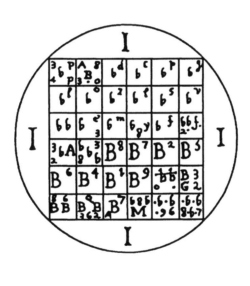

----

43 Ad usum . . . sunt: "They are multiplied for your use." -Ed.

E.T: A voyce is hard saying,

Omnia gaudent fine.[44]

E.T: There commeth oute a woman; out of the Dark. She plucketh at the dark, and casteth it on the grownd, and it turneth to herbes, and plants becomming like a garden, and they grow up very fast. She sayd,

Opus est.[45]

E.T: She hath a fowre square Table before her.

Then cam one, all in white, <u>and taketh the Darknes, and wrappeth it up and casteth it into the myddle of the Erthen Globe</u>, on which appeared Trees and Plants.

E.T: Then appered Michael, his Chayre, and Table agayne manifestly: which all this while, were not seen.

Mi: Obumbrabit vestigia vestram veritatis luce.[46]

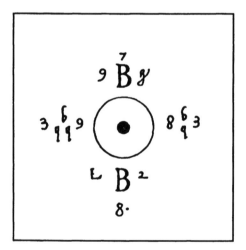

---

44 Omnia gaudent fine: "All rejoice in the end." -Ed.

45 Opus est: "It is the work." -Ed.

46 Obumbrabit . . . luce: "He will overshadow your footsteps with the light of truth." -Ed.

The Actor, The Actor, The Actor:

One Disposer; he, which is one in all; and All in all:
bless you from the <u>wickednes of Deceyte:</u> Create you new
vessels: To whome I commyt you.

E.T: He holdeth his sword over us, in manner, out of the stone.

Mi: Fare Well. Serue God. Be patient. Hate vayne glorie. Liue iustly.
Amen.

Δ: What spede shall I make for the yard square Table, the Wax, the
seale, and the Character? Mi: <u>As thow ar motioned</u>, so do.

Δ: Gloria, Pri et F. et S.S. S.e.i.p.e.n.e.s.e.i.s.s. Amen.[47]

Δ: Note, All the Tables before were by E.T, letter for letter noted out
of the stone standing before him all the while: and the 7 Tables following wer written by me as he repeted them orderly out of the stone.

Aprilis 29: Sonday: Nocte hora 8¼.

E.T: Two appeare, Michael and Uriel.

Mi: Et posuit illos in ministerium eius.

Quid desideratis?

Δ: Sapientiam et scientiam nobis necessariam, et in Dei servitio
potentem ad eius gloriam.

---

47 Gloria Patri et Filio, et Spiritui Sancto, Sicut erat in principio, et nunc, et semper,
et in saecula saeculorum. Amen: "Glory be to the Father, and to the Son, and to
the Holy Spirit, as it was in the beginning, is now, and ever shall be, world without end. Amen." In British Library manuscript Harley 6482, *A Treatise on Angel
Magic*, the seven ensigns are attributed to the Moon, Saturn, Jupiter, Mars, the
Sun, Venus, and Mercury, respectively. -Ed.

Mi: Sapere, a Deo: Scire a Creatura et ex creaturis est.

Ur:[48] Venite <u>filiæ</u>.[49]

E.T: Seuen women appeare bewtifull and fayre.

Mi: This work is of wisdom (Δ: Sayd Michael, and stode up.) E.T, sayd to me (Δ), He putteth oute his sword and willeth me to sweare, to that, that he willeth me: and to follow his cownsayle.

Mi: Wilt thow. Δ: Then with much ado, E.T. sayd as followeth,

E.T: I promise,[50] in the name of God the Father, God the sonne and God the holy ghost, to performe that you shall will me, so far as it shall lye in my powre.

E.T: Now they two seeme to confer togither.

Mi: Now <u>you towche world</u>, and the <u>doings uppon earth</u>. <u>Now we shew unto you the lower world: The Gouerners that work and rule under God:</u>[51] <u>By whome</u> you may haue powre to work such things, as shalbe to god his glorie, profit of your Cuntrie, <u>and the knowledge of his Creatures</u>.

To E.T. he spake, What I do wish thee to do, thow shalt here know, before thow go. **We procede to One GOD, one knowledge, one Operation.**

Venite filiæ.[52]

Behold these Tablets: Herein lye <u>theyr names that work under God uppon earth: not of the wicked, but of the Angels of light</u>. The Whole

---

48 I am not sure if it wer Mi. or Ur, that called for them.

49 Et posuit . . . filiae: "And he sets those in his service. What do you desire? Δ: Wisdom and knowledge needed to serve God for his glory. Mi: Wisdom is from God; knowledge is to a creature and from creatures. Ur: Come, O daughters." -Ed.

50 E.T. his promise.

51 Practise. The lower world.

52 Venite filiae: "Come, O daughters." -Ed.

Gouernment, doth consist in the hands of 49: (in God his Powre, Strength, Mercy, and Iustice) whose names are here euident, excellent, and glorious. Mark these Tables: Mark them. Record them to your Cumfort.

This is <u>the first knowledge</u>. Here shall you haue Wisdome. Halleluyah.

Mighty and Omnipotent art thow, O God, God, God, amongst thy Creatures: Thow fillest all things with thy excellent foresight. Thy Glorie be amongst us for euer. Δ: Amen.

E.T: All the 7 (which here appeare) ioyne theyr Tables in One: Which, before they held apart. And they be of this Forme all to-gither. The myddelmost is a great Square and on eche side of it, One, as big as it, ioyning close to it. And ouer it ioyned two, which both togither wer æquall to it: and under it, wer such other two, as may appear in this little pattern. Being thus ioyned, <u>a bright circle did cumpas and enclose them all, thus: but nothing</u> was in the <u>Circle</u>.

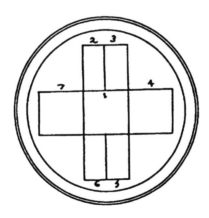

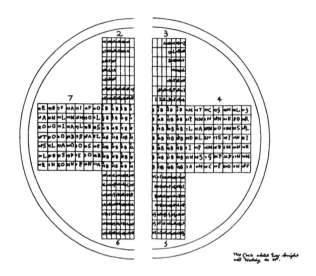

[44 E: forte I, as in Baligon.]

E.T: One stept-furth, and sayde,

1: Wilt thow haue witt, and wisdome: Here, it is. (Δ: Pointing to the middle table.)

2: Another sayd, The Exaltation and Gouernment of Princes, is in my hand. (Δ: Pointing to that on the left hand of the two uppermost.)

3: In Cownsayle and Nobilitie I prevayle. (Δ: Pointing to the other of the two uppermost: which is on the right hand.)

4: The Gayne and Trade of Merchandise is in my hand: Lo, here it is.

Δ: He pointed to the great table on the right side of the myddle Table, that I meane which is opposite to our right hand while we behold those 7 Tables.

5: The Quality of the Earth, and waters, is my knowledge, and I know them: and here, it is. (Δ: Pointing to that on the right hand: of the two lowermost.)[53]

6: The motion of the Ayre, and those that moue in it, are all known

---

[53] I marvayle that the earth and waters are here ascribed to one.

to me. Lo here they are. (Δ: Pointing to the other Table below, on the left hand.)

7: I signifie wisdome: <u>In fire</u> is my Gouernment. I was in the begynning, and shalbe to the ende. (Δ: Pointing to the great table on the left hand of the Middle Table.)

Mi: Mark these Mysteries: For, this knowne, the State of the whole earth is known, and all that is thereon. Mighty is God, yea mighty is he, who hath Composed for euer. Giue diligent eye. Be wise, mery, and pleasant in the Lorde; in Whose Name, NOTE,

Begynne the Middle Table &c. Δ: I wrote oute of the stone the whole 7 Tables (as you see them here with theyr numbers and letters) while E.T. did vew them in the stone, and orderly express them.

Δ: As concerning 39 V . 47 L &c in the second Table, where are 7 places: and there but 6 numbers and letters, and yet euery place semeth to haue a letter, in the iudgment of E.T. his sight. Which is the Number and letter wanting, and where must it be placed?

Mi: Non potestis hoc videre sine ratione.[54]

Δ: The Next day, as I was loking on the Tables being finished, and ioyned all togither in One Compownd Figure, E.T. cam to me, and stode by me, and his ey was on the forsayd place which I was forced to leaue empty, in the 7th and last. And behold he saw houering and hopping in the ayre, two numbers and two letters cuppled to them, ouer the sayd place, and the next before it. And that, which I had placed the sixth, was to be put in the seuenth place, and that which was wanting, was to be set in the sixth place being 30 N.[55]

---

54 Non potestis ... ratione: "You are not able to see this without calculation." -Ed.

55 This I entersert now; thowgh it wer not at the first Noting.

E.T: Euery of the 7 Tables, as they wer written out of the stone do seme afterward to burn all in fyre: and to stand in fyre.

E.T: After all the Tables wer written, eche toke hir Table aparte agayn and stode in theyr order.

E.T: Note moreouer. The First, had Bokes in hir hand.

Kings -------------- The second, a Crown in hir hand.

Nobilitie ------------- The Third, Robes.

Merchants - Δ: - Aqua[56] - The fowrth, animal quadrupes vicium omnim colorum.[57]

　　　Terra[58] - The fifth, Herbes.

　　　Aer[59] - The sixth, a fanne.

　　　Ignis[60] - The seventh, a Flame of fyre in hir hand.

Mi: Decedite in nomine eius, qui vos huc misit.[61]

E.T: Uriel opened a boke in his own hand, and sayde,

Ur: **The Fontayne of wisdome is opened. Nature shalbe knowne: Earth with her secrets disclosed. The Elements with theyr powres iudged.** Loke, if thow canst (in the name of God) understand these Tables. Δ: No: Not yet.

Ur: Beholde; **I teache. There are 49 Angels glorious and excellent, appointed for the government of** <u>all earthly actions</u>**: Which 49 do work and dispose the will of the Creator: limited from the begynning in strength, powre, and glorie.**

<u>These shalbe Subiect unto you</u>**, In the Name, and by** <u>Invocating uppon the Name of GOD</u>**, which doth lighten, dispose and Cumfort you.**

By them shall you work, in the quieting of the estates, <u>in learning</u> of wis-

---

56　Aqua: "Water." -Ed.

57　Animal quadrupes . . . colorum: "A four-footed animal of all colors alternating." -Ed.

58　Terra: "Earth." -Ed.

59　Aer: "Air." -Ed.

60　Ignis: "Fire." -Ed.

61　Decedite . . . misit: "Depart in his name who has sent you here." -Ed.

dome: pacifying of the Nobilitie, iudgement in the rest, as well in the depth of waters, Secrets <u>of the Ayre,</u> as in the bowells and entralls of the Earth.

Ur: Theyr Names are comprehended within these Tables. Lo, he teacheth, he teacheth, Lo, he instructeth, which is holy, and most highest. <u>Take hede, thow abuse not this Excellency, nor overshaddow it with Vanitie, But stick firmely, absolutely, and perfectly, in the love of God (for his honor) to-gither.</u>[62]

Be mery in him: Prayse his name. Honor him in his Saincts. Behold him in wisdome: And shew him in understanding. Glorie be to him; To thee ô Lord, whose name perseth[63] throwgh the earth. Glorie be to thee, for euer. Δ: Amen, Amen, Amen.

Ur: Lo, I will breifly teache thee; you shall know the Mysteries in him: and by him, which is a Mysterie in all things. The letters are standing uppon 7 equall numbers. The Number before them is signifying, teaching and instructing (from the first Table to the <u>last,) which are</u> the letters th<u>at shalbe ioyned to</u> gither:[64] begynning all, with B, according to the disposition of the number untyll the 29[65] <u>generall names</u> be known. The first 29 are more <u>excellent than the rest. Euery Name doth consist</u> uppon the quantitie of the place: Euerie place with addition bringeth furth his name, which are 49.------- I haue sayde.----------

Δ: I pray you to tell me the first Name. Ur: The first <u>Name is</u> <u>BALI</u>GON.

Mi: I haue to say to thee,[66] and so haue I done:

Δ: Now he spake to E.T., of the matter he sware him to, at the begynning of this last Instruction: and he told me afterward what Michael

---

62 We two to-gither.

63 Perseth: "pierces." -Ed.

64 Vide ipam Tabulam horam 49 nom. Collectam, pagina sequente. -Δ. ("See the table itself, of 49 names collected, on the following page." -Ed.)

65 49.

66 He ment to E.T.

had willed and moved him unto. Wherat he seamed very sore disquiet-
ted: and sayd this to me,

E.T: He sayd that I must betake my self to the world, and forsake
the world. That is that I shold marry. Which thing to do, I haue no naturall Inclination: neyther with a safe Conscience may I do it, contrary
to my vow and profession. Wherfore I think and hope, there is some
other meaning in these theyr wordes.

Mi: Thow must of force kepe it. Thow knowest our mynde.

Δ: Deo opt. Max°. omnis honor laus et gloria in sæcula sæculorum.
Amen.[67]

Ended, hora noctis, 11½a circiter.[68]

Tabula Collecta: 49 Angelorum Bonorum, Nomina continens [per Δ][69]

1 BALIGON	15 BABALEL	29 BNASPOL	
2 BORNOGO	16 BVTMONO	30 BRORGES	
3 Bapnido	17 Bazpama	31 Baspalo	
4 Besgeme	18 Blintom	32 Binodab	
5 Blumapo	19 Bragiop	33 Bariges	
6 Bmamgal	20 Bermale	34 Binofon	
7 Basledf	21 Bonefon	35 Baldago	
8 BOBOGEL	22 BYNEPOR	36 BNAPSEN	
9 BEFAFES	23 BLISDON	37 BRALGES	
10 Basmelo	24 Balceor	38 Bormila	
11 Bernole	25 Belmara	39 Buscnab	
12 Branglo	26 Benpagi	40 Bminpol	
13 Brisfli	27 Barnafa	41 Bartiro	
14 Bnagole	28 Bmilges	42 Bliigan	
		43 BLVMAZA	
		44 BAGENOL	
		45 Bablibo	
		46 Busduna	
		47 Blingef	
		48 Barfort	
		49 Bamnode	

---

[67] Deo . . . Amen: "To God all good, all honor, praise, and glory, forever and ever.
Amen." -Ed.

[68] Hora noctis 11½a circiter: "around 11:30 at night." -Ed.

[69] Tabula . . . continens: "Collected table of the 49 consecutive names of the good
angels (per Dee)." -Ed.

Coordinatio Angelorum bonorum 49, per Jo. Dee, ita disposita[70]

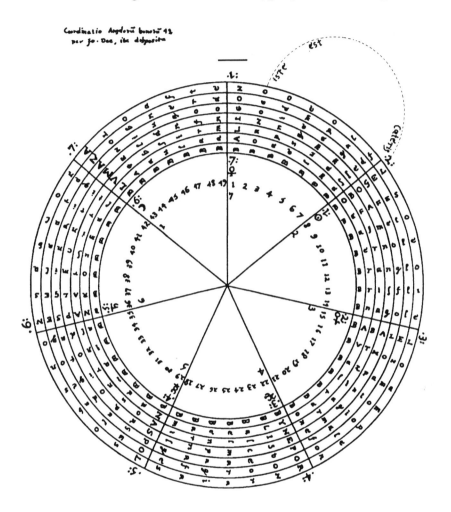

Liber 4.

---

70 Coordinatio . . . disposita: "Sequence of the 49 angels, arranged thus by John
Dee." Iste est caeteris: "and so on." -Ed.

Fryday Maij 4: hor 2½ a meridie

Δ: E.T. wold not willingly now deale with the former Creatures, utterly misliking and discrediting them, bycause they <u>willed him to marry</u>. Neyther wold he put of his hat in any prayer to god, for the Action with them: whereuppon I went into my Oratorie, and called unto God, <u>for his diuine help</u> for the understanding <u>of his laws and vertues which he hath established in and amongst his Creatures, for the benefyt of mankinde, in his seruice, and for his</u> glorie &c. And commyng to the Stone, E.T. saw there those two, whom hitherto, we wer instructed to be Michael and Uriel.

E.T: Michael and Uriel, both kneled holding up theyr hands: and Michael seamed to sweat <u>water abundantly, somwhat reddish or bluddish</u>. There cam 7 Bundells down, (like faggots) <u>from</u> heven-ward. And Michael taketh them kneeling. And Uriel taketh a thing like a super-altare and layeth it uppon the Table: and with a thing like a Senser doth make perfume at the fowre corners of the Table: the smoke ascending up: and the senser, at the last, being set on the Table it seemed to fall throwgh the Table.

URIEL semeth to be all in a white long robe tucked up: his garment full of plightes[71] and seemed <u>now to haue wyngs</u>: (which, hitherto, from the begynning of these kinde of Actions he did not) and on his hed a bewtifull crown, with a white Cross ouer the Crown.[72] Uriel taketh the 7 Bundells from Michael: and with reuerence layeth them on the forsayd Superaltare.

E.T: There commeth a man, as thowgh he were all of perfect pure glistring gold: somtyme seeming to haue <u>One eye, and somtyme Three</u>. From under the Table commeth a great smoke, and the place semeth to shake.

---

[71] Plightes: "pleats." -Ed.

[72] Uriel, his manner of apparition.

Uriel lieth now prostrate on his face: and Michael contynually prayed sweating.

The Glorious man seemed to open the Covering of the 7 bundells (being of <u>diuerse cullored</u> sylk,) and there appered, that these Bundells seemed to haue in them, of all Creatures some, in most glorious shew. The glorious man seemed to stand uppon a little hill of flaming fyre. He taketh-of, of one of the Bundells a thing like a little byrd; and it hoouereth affore him as thowgh it had life: and than it rested uppon the thing like a superaltare.

This glorious man[73] seemeth to be open before, and his brest somwhat spotted with blud. He hath a berd forked of brownish cullour, his heare of his hed, long, hanging down to his sholders: but his face, for beutifull glittring, can not be discerned. His heares do shake, as thowgh the wynde carryed them. This <u>man blesseth the bird, making a Cross ouer it</u>: and, so he did three tymes. He looketh up to heven. Now the byrd, which, before, seamed to be but as byg as a sparrow, seameth to be as great as a swanne: very beutifull: but of **many cullours**.[74]

Now looketh Michael up, and held up his hands to heven, and sayeth,

Sic, Sic, Sic, Deus noster.[75]

Uriel, (sayd)- Multiplicabit omnia, benedictione sua.[76]

The former Bewtifull man taketh this fowle, setteth it on the bundell, and on the place, <u>from whence</u> it was taken:[77] And, now, the place where this byrd stode before, seameth allso, to be (proportionally)

---

73 A description of the glorious man.

74 Many cullours in all his garments are shewed in sequentibus thus:

75 Sic, Sic, Sic, Deus noster: "Yes, yes, yes, our God." -Ed.

76 Multiplicabit . . . sua: "He will multiply all things by his blessing." -Ed.

77 ☿

waxen as big as the byrd, (thus enlarged). This man taketh <u>an other byrd</u>, and putteth <u>the wyng of it</u>, <u>behind</u> the wyng of the first (as-thowgh he yoked them.)[78]

<u>This second byrd, at this his first taking, was as byg, as the first was become,</u> (encreased, as it shewed), and it was allso a very bewtifull ....

E.T: All is suddenly dark, and nothing to be seen, neyther Chayre, nor any thing els.

E.T: A voyce was hard, like Michael his voyce, saying,

It was a byrd, and is a byrd, absent there is nothing but Quantitie.

A voyce:[79] Beleue. <u>The world is of Necessitie: His Necessitie is gouerned by supernaturall Wisdome.</u> Necessarily you fall: and of Necessitie shall rise agayne. Follow me, loue me: embrace me: <u>behold, I, AM.</u>

E.T: Now all the Darknes vanished, the man is gon. Uriel standeth at the Table, and Michael sitteth now in his Chayre: and sayd,

Mi: This doth GOD work for your understanding. <u>It is in vayne to stryve:</u> All Government is in his hands. What will you els, what will you els?

Δ: Progressum et profectum in virtute et veritate ad Dei honorem et gloriam.[80]

Mi: This hath answered all our[81] cauillations.

Δ: What hath answered all our Cavillations?

Mi: Thow hast written.

One thing you shall see more, as a persuasion to the Infirmitie.

E.T: The two byrds, which were there, before, and gon out of sight, now are shewed agayn: but none of the bundells appere. <u>They seme to</u>

---

78 The yoking or cuppling of the two byrds.

79 E.T. sayd the Voyce to be like Michael his voyce.

80 Progressum . . . gloriam: "Progress and increase in virtue and truth to God's honor and glory." -Ed.

81 Fortè: "your." -Ed.

grow to a huge <u>bignes</u>, <u>as byg as mowntaynes</u>: incredibly byg: and they seeme to hover up in the ayre, and to fly up toward heuen, and with theyr wyngs to <u>towch the sky</u>: And one of them with his bill seemeth to <u>take sterrs into</u> it: and the other bird to take them from the same byrd, and to place them agayn in the Skye. And this they did very often: and in diuerse places of the heuen with great celeritie.

After this they <u>semed to fly ouer Cities</u>, and townes, and to break the clowdes in peces, as they passed: and to cause all dust to flye from all walls, and towres, as they passed, and so to make them clene. And in the streetes, as these two Byrds flew, seemed diuerse brave fellows, like bisshops, and Princis and Kings, to pass: and by the wyngs of these byrds, they were striken down. But simple seely[82] ones, like beggers, lame and halt, childern, and old aged men, and wemen, seemed to pass quiettly, untowched and unouerthrown of these two Byrds.

And than they seemed to come to a place, where they lifted up, with the endes of theyr wyngs, fowre Carkasses of dead men (owte of the grownde) with crownes on theyr heds: wherof one seemed to be a Childe. First these 4, seemed leane, and deade: Then they seemed quick[83] and in good liking:[84] And they being raysed up: parted eche from the other, and went into 4 sundry wayes, Est, West, North and Sowth.

Now these two fowles hauing <u>theyr wyngs ioyned togither</u>, light uppon <u>a great hill</u>: and there the First fowle gryped the erth mightyly and there appeared diuerse Metalls, and the ^ Fowle spurned them away, still.

Then appeared an old mans hed, heare and all, on; very much wythered. They tossed it betwene them, with theyr feete: And they

---

82 Seely: "looking." -Ed.

83 Quick: "alive." -Ed.

84 Liking: "appearance." -Ed.

brake it: And in the hed appeared (in steede of the braynes) a stone, rownd, of the bignes of a Tennez ball of 4, cullours, White, black, red, and greene.

One of them (he that brake the skull), putteth that rownd stone to the others mowth or byll. The other eateth or nybbleth on it, and so doth the other allso.

¶   Now these two byrds, are turned into men: And eche of them haue two Crownes like paper Crownes, white and bright, but seeme not to be syluer. Theyr teeth are gold, and so likewise theyr hands, feete, tung, eyes, and eares likewise All gold.

On eche of these two men, ar 26 Crownes of Gold, on theyr right sholders, euery of them, greater then other. They haue, by theyr sides, Sachels, like palmers[85] bags, full of gold, and they take it oute, and seemed to sow it, as corne; going or stepping forward, like Seedmen.

E.T: Then sayd Michael, This, is the ende.

E.T: The two men be vanished away.

Mi: Learne the Mysterie hereof.

Δ: Teache us (ô ye spirituall Creatures.) Than sayd Michael,

Mi: Joye and helth giue unto the riche:

> Open strong locks:
> Be Mercifull to the wicked:
> Pluck up the poore:
> Read unto the Ignorant:
> I haue satisfyed thee: Understand:
> Read them ouer: God shall giue thee some light in them. I haue
> satisfyed thee:

---

85   A palmer was a traveler who carried a palm branch as a token of having made a pilgrimage to the Holy Land. -Ed.

Both, How you shalbe ioyned,

> By whome,
> To what Intent, and purpose:
> What you are,
> What you were,
> What you shalbe, (videlicet) in Deo.[86]

Lok up this Mysterie:

Forget not our Cownsayle:

O GOD, thow openest all things: Secret are thy Mysteries and holy is thy name, for euer. The vertue of his presence, here left, be amongst you.

Δ: Amen.

Δ: What am I to do, with the wax, the Table, the ring or the Lamine? &c.

Mi: When the things be ready, then thow shalt know, how to use them.

Δ: How shall I do for the grauing of the ring; May not another man do it, thowgh, E.T. graue it not?

Mi: Cause them to be made up, (according to Instruction) by any honest man.

Δ: What say you as concerning the Chamber, for our practise? May my fardermost little chamber, serue, yf the bed be taken downe?

Mi: At my next Call, for the Chamber, you shall know what to do.

---

[86] (Videlicet) in Deo: "(namely) in God." -Ed.

Δ: Benedictus Deus in donis suis:

et sanctus in omnibus operibus eius.[87]
Amen. ended hor. 4½[88]

---

[87] Benedictus . . . eius: "Blessed is God in his gifts, and holy in all his works." -Ed.

[88] Betwixt the end of the 3rd book, whose last action was May 4, 1582, & the
     beginning of this 4th book whose first action was on Nov. 15, 1582, is a great
     chasme of time. Occasioned perchance by some falling out with E. Kelly which is
     implied in this mention of Reconciliatio Kelliana. This is the first time that
     Edward Kelly appears to bee the seer, at lest under that name, there beeing no
     account, neither in the printed nor Mss. books how hee came to Dee. Queue: If
     Edw. Kelly was not the same with Ed. Talbot this latter beeing his assumed name,
     perchance after he was in orders. For Weever in his *Funeral Monuments* speak-
     ing of Ed. Kelley the Necromancer, sayes hee also went by the name of Ed Talbot.
     -E.A. Dee's diary fills in some details of this period: "May 4th, Mr. Talbot went.
     May 23, Robert Gardener declared unto me hora 4½ a certeyn great philosophi-
     call secret, as he had termed it, of a spirituall creatuer, and was this day willed to
     come to me and declare it, which was solemnly done, and with common prayer.
     July 13th, Mr. Talbot cam abowt 3 of the clok afternone, with whom I had some
     wordes of unkendnes: we parted frendely: he sayd that the Lord Morley had the
     Lord Mountegle his bokes. He promised me some of Doctor Myniver's bokes."
     James Halliwell, ed., *The Private Diary of Dr. John Dee* (New York: AMS Press,
     1968), pp. 15–16. -Ed.

✝

Quartus

Liber Mysteriorum

A°. 1582
Δ   Nouembris 15.

Post reconciliationem Kellianam.

Miserere nostri Deus
Dimitte nobis, sicut et nos dimittimus[1]

---

[1] Quartus . . . dimittimus: "Fourth Book of the Mysteries. November 15, 1582. After Kelley's reconciliation. O God, have mercy on us, forgive us as we forgive." Compare with Matthew 6:12. Ashmole has written "Liber 5us" on the bottom of the page. -Ed.

Thursday. Nouembris 15.[2]

...

At the first, Uriel pluckt a thing from under the Covenant Table: and it grew Rownd, Bigger &; bigger, (of fyrie Cullour) bigger then all the world: and he sayd to me ᐃ:

Uriel: Ultima est hæc ætas vestram, quæ tibi revelata erit.[3]

Then cam swarming into the stone, Thowsand yea Inumerable people, Uriel sayd,

Est in mundo, et incipiet cum illo alter Mundus.[4] and he bad,

Note the forme of the thing seen. Note the cullour. The forme of the thing seen was a Globe Transparent fyre within which the people seemed to stand, Towers and Castells. &c. did appere therein, likewise. This Globe did king CARMARA seeme to go uppon, & to measure it: and there appeared a very riche chayre to be set: allmost at the top of the Convexitie of the sayd Globe. wherein he sat down.

...

Michael: The Mysteries of God haue a tyme: and Behold, Thow art provyded for that tyme.

---

2 In HM, this section is titled, "Some Notice of peculier formes, and attire, wherein, the Kings, Princis and Ministers Heptarchicall appeared, and of some their Actions, and gesture at their apperance. &c." The first leaf has been lost, but HM and CHM record the following actions of that day (order uncertain): In the first leafe were the offices of the two Kings Blumaza & Bobogel recited, as appeares by the Note at the bottome of the 2d page: & also 5 May 1583 & perhaps this first leafe was lost before he drew up his Booke of *De Bonorum Angelorum invitationibus* because I find a Blank where Blumaza is placed. -E.A. De Bonorum Angelorum: "Concerning the invitation of good angels." -Ed.

3 Ultima . . . erit: "This age of yours is the last age, which shall be revealed to you." -Ed.

4 Est in mundo, et incipiet cum illo alter Mundus: "It (or he) is in the world, and another World will commence with that one." -Ed.

...

All those before spoken of are Subiect to thy Call....

Of friendship, at any tyme, thow mayst see them: and know what thow wilt.

Every one (to be short) shall at all times and seasons shew thee direction in any thing....

One thing I answer thee, for all offycis. Thow hast in subiection all officis. Use them whan it pleas thee, as thy Instruction hath byn.

...

King CARMARA[5] - This king, (being called first by Uriel,) appeared, as a Man, very well proportioned: clad in a long purple Robe: and with a Triple Crowne of Gold on his hed. At his first coming he had 7 (like men) wayting on him: which afterwarde declared them selues to be the 7 Princis Heptarchicall. Uriel deliuered unto this king (at his first appearing) a rod or straight little rownd Staff of Gold: diuided into three equall distinctions, whereof, two were dark or blak: and the third bright red. This red he kept still in his hand.

...

King BOBOGEL appeared in a blak veluet coat, and his hose close, rownd hose with veluet upperstocks: ouerlayde with gold lace: On his hed a veluet hatcap, with a blak feather in it: with a Cape hanging on one of his sholders, his purse hanging abowt his neck and so put under his gyrdell at which hong a gylt rapier, his berd was long: he had pantofells and pynsons. And he sayd, I

---

[5] This king onely, is the ordrer, or disposer, of all the doctrine, which I terme Heptarchicall, as first, by calling the 7 Princis and after that, the 7 kings: and by giving instructions for use and Practise of the whole doctrine Heptarchicall for the first purpose, and frute therof to be enioyed by me: of two other there was onely Mention made. -Δ (HM).

weare these Robes, not in respect of my self, but of my government, etc.

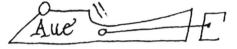

Prince BORNOGO appeared in a red Robe,
with a Gold Cerclet on his hed: he shewed his
Seale, and sayde, This it is.

King BABALEL...

Prince BEFAFES appeared in a long red robe, with a cerclet of
Gold on his hed. He had a golden girdle: and on it written
BEFAFES. He opened his bosom, & appeared leane: and seamed to
haue feathers under his Robes. His Seale, or Character, is this:

King BYNEPOR...

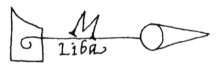

Prince BUTMONO appeared in a red Robe, with a golden
Cerclet on his hed:
His Seal is this:

King BNASPOL...

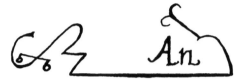

Prince BLISDON appeared in a Robe of
many Cullours: and on his hed a Cerclet of
Gold. His Character, or seale:

King BNAPSEN...

Prince BRORGES appeared in his red
apparayle: & he opened his Cloathes and
there did issue, mighty & most terrible or
grisely flames of fyre out of his sides: whych
no mortall eyr could abyde to loke uppon any
long while. His Seale, or Character is this:

King BALIGON...

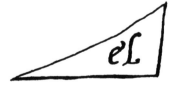

King BLVMAZA...

Prince BRALGES appeared in a red
Robe with a Cerclet on his hed. This is
the Seale of his gouernment:

One[6] (of the 7 which was by him) he who stode before him, with his
face from ward him, now turned his face to him ward.[7]

✠ Regnat potestas tua in filijs. Ecce signum Operis.[8]

Δ: There appeared these two letters, euersed and aversed, in a
white flag and a woman standing by, whose armes did not appere.

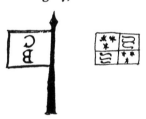

✠ Note. My name is Carmara.[9]

Δ: On the other side of the flag appeared the armes of England. The
flag semed old.

---

6   Note. For, of Hagonel we never had any thing before. -Δ.

7   To him ward: "toward him." -Ed.

8   Regnat . . . Operis: "Your power rules in the sons. Behold, the sign of The Work."
    Note the crown symbol drawn above the "H" (for "homo" or man) denotes roy-
    alty. Dee uses the crown symbol in his diary to signify the queen. -Ed.

9   Carmara, otherwise Baligon. Vide . . .

Adhuc duo, et tempus non est.[10] (Δ: Sayd the man[11] which stode before Carmara,) and lifted up his hand and avaunced his body: and the other 6 gaue him place. He spred his armes abroad: and so turned rownd toward all the multitude (appering within the Globe:) as if he wold require audience. He sayd than thus,

The Sonnes of men,[12] and theyr sonnes, ar subiected unto my commaundent.[13] This is a mystery. I haue spoken of it. Note it throwghly. They ar my seruants. By them thow shalt work mervayles. I gouern for a tyme:[14] My tyme[15] is yet to come. The Operation of the Earth is subiect to my powre:[16] And I am the first of the twelve. My seale is called Barees: and here it is.

(Δ: This he held in the palm of his hand: as thowgh it had byn a ring, hanging allso over his myddle fingers[17]). With a great voyce he sayd, Come ô ye people of the erth:[18]

---

10 Adhuc . . . non est: "There is two to come, there is no more" (in John Dee's words, see below). -Ed.

11 Prince HAGONEL. Note. All the Princis, seemed to be men, and to haue red Robes, but this Prince, his Robe was shorter then the others. All the Princis, had Cerclets, of Gold on theyr heds: not crowns not coronets. -Δ (HM).

12 HM reads "light" in three places. -Ed.

13 Filij & Filij Filiorum, supra libro 2°.-Δ. "See above in book 2 on the Sons and the Sons of the Sons." -Ed.

14 Δ: generally.

15 Δ: particular, or my government lasteth yet.

16 Kings of the erth &c.

17 HM reads, "This Prince held in the palme of his right hand, as yf it had byn a rownd ring, with a prick in the mydst: hanging allso over his myddle fingers, which he affirmed to be his seale: and sayd the name of it, to be Barees." -Ed.

18 All people of the erth etc.

1. (Δ: Then there cam a great Number of <u>onely Kings, from</u> amongst the rest of the multitude within the Globe: They kneele down; and some kyssed his seale and some did stand frowning at it. Those kings that kissed it, had, eche of them, a sword in one hand, and a payre of Ballance in the other: the balances being euen, and counterpeysed.[19] But the other had allso ballances, which hong uneven, the one scale lower then the other. The euen balanced kings were of glad cheare:[20] but the other wer of a sowre and hevy cowntynance.

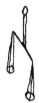

It is, and shalbe so: And the workmanship of this, is to this ende.

2. Then cam noble men: (Δ: and he held up his hand,) and they parted them selues into two Cumpanyes: and ouer the heds of them, appered these two wordes. Vera,[21] over one Cumpany: and Impura[22] over the other.

Vera	Impura
......	....
......	....
......&c	........&c

Verus cum veris, et Impurus cum Impuris.[23]

---

19   Counterpoised: "balanced." -Ed.

20   Cheare = cheer: "disposition." -Ed.

21   Vera: "true." -Ed.

22   Impura: "filth." -Ed.

23   Verus . . . Impuris: "The true with the true, and the filthy with the filthy." -Ed.

3. Come ô ye <u>Princes of Nature</u>. Δ: Then cam in Anncient and graue Cowtenanced men in blak gownes: of all manner of sortes.[24] Diuerse of them had bokes: and some had stiks like measures:[25] and they parted into two Cumpanies. Eyther cumpany had his principall. One of these Cumpanies fell at debate among them selues. The other Cumpany stode still. There appeared before eche of these Cumpanyes a great boke. Uppon the bokes was written; on the one, Lucem; and on the other, Mundi tenebras.[26] The Forman spred his hands ouer them, and they all fell down: and the boke with Lucem[27] on it waxed bright: and they which attended on that boke (Lucem) departed.

Gather, by these few spriggs the Cumpas of the whole field. Δ: I demaunded of him, what his name was: and he answered,[28]

I am <u>Primus</u> <u>et</u> <u>Quartus</u>[29] Hagonel.

Δ: This <u>Pri</u>. <u>Quar</u>, shewed his[30] seal ☉ to the Multitudes and they beheld it, and of them some florish, som stand, and <u>some fall</u>.

1. [Δ: Then he sayd,] The first were the Kings of the earth; which tell the priks of the last ⊛ , take place, are, and shall be. In this

---

24 Philosophers.

25 Geometry.

26 Δ He hath recyted the offices of two Kings, as of Blumaza and Bobogel. And then he sayeth, Gather by these few spriggs &c: Which Bobogel is over the Nobility and Wisdome, of Metalls, & all Nature. -Δ. Lucem: "Light"; Mundi tenebras: "the darkness of the world." -Ed.

27 Lucem:"light." -Ed.

28 The foreman with the short [coat].

29 Primus et quartus: "The First and the Fourth." -Ed.

30 The.

thow mayst lern science. Note a mysterie. <u>Take a place, is a</u>s
much, as, <u>Ende with place.</u>

Δ: Then he <u>threw down</u> a great many of them before him.
Here is his name, (pointing to ⚹ [Δ = Carmara[31]] on the
upper part of the Globe.) Not withstanding I am his Minister -
[D in generall particularly Blumaza.]

**There are kings fals and uniust, whose powre as <u>I</u> haue sub-
uerted and <u>destroyed, so shalt thow</u>. Thow <u>seest</u> the weapons.[32]
The Secret is not great.**

Δ: I know not what the weapons are. <u>Pri. Quar.</u> sayd, Write,
and I will tell thee. Δ: The three, of eche side did syt down while
<u>Pri Quar</u> did thus speake.

<u>I am the first of the fowrth Hagonel.</u>

Δ: I had thowght that ye sayd before, you had byn the first
and the Fowrth of Hagonel.

Pri Quar. I am HAGONEL, and govern HAGONEL. There
is Hagonel the first, Hagonel the second, and Hagonel the third,
I am the first <u>that gouern the three</u>. Therfore <u>I am the first and
last of the fowre</u>.[33]

Δ: In the meane space of the former multitude some were
falln deade, of some theyr mowthes drawn awry: of some theyr
legs broken &c. And then, pointing to ⚹ (Δ: = Carmara) he
sayd,

**In his name, with <u>my name</u>, by my character and the <u>rest</u> of
my <u>Ministers</u>, are <u>these things</u> browght to pass.[34] These that lye
here, are lyers, witches, enchanters, Deceyvers, Blasphemers:**

---

31 Carmara his Minister: forte Prince Hagonel.

32 Weapons wherwith to destroy.

33 Note this First and last, bycause of Baligon ali. Carmara, his prince & tables.

34 Practise with spirituall weapons.

and finally all they that use <u>NATVRE, with abuse</u>: and dishonor him which rayneth for euer.

2. The second assembly were the Gouerners of the Earth, whose glory yf they be good, <u>the weapons which we haue towght thee, will augment</u>: and Consequently, if they be euill, pervert.

3. The third assembly are those which <u>taste of Gods mysteries</u>, and drink of the iuyce of Nature, whose myndes are diuided, some with eyes looking toward heauen, the rest to the center of the Earth. Ubi non Gloria, nec bonitas nec bonum est.[35] <u>It is wrowght</u>, I say, it is wrowght (for thy understanding) <u>by the seuen of the seuen</u> which wer the <u>sonnes of sempiternitie,</u>[36] whose names thow hast <u>written</u>[37] and recorded to Gods <u>Glory</u>.[38]

Δ: Then he held up his hands, and seemed to speak but was not herd (of EK[39]) as he told me: and theruppon <u>Pri Quar</u> sayd, Neyther shalt thow heare, for it is Vox hominibus non digna. <u>Illi autem cum filijs suis</u> laudauerunt Deum. Benedictus est qui fil-ius est unicus, et Gloria mundi.[40]

---

[35] Ubi . . . est: "Where there is neither glory, nor goodness, nor good." -Ed.

[36] Sempiternitie: "eternity." -Ed.

[37] Note. Practise. Lib°. 2°, Filij Filiorum: ("In book 2, sons of the sons." -Ed)

E -----	1. These 7 are named in the great Circle
An -----	2. following
Aue -----	3.
Liba -----	4.
Rocle -----	5.
Hagonel -----	6.
Ilemese -----	7.

[38] Note. Prince Butmono sayd this: but the office is under king Bnaspol, whose prince is Blisdon. The Mystery of this I know not yet: For Blisdon will be fownd to be the proper minister of king Bnaspol. Vide Anno 1583 May 5th, of the Making of Mensa faeders, and my Golder Lamine. -Δ (HM). Mensa faederis: "the table (or altar) of the law (or covenant)." -Ed.

[39] In the manuscript, Dee has written this as "E.ŦK." -Ed.

[40] Vox hominibus . . . mundi: "The voice not worthy for the people, but these with

EK saw like a black cloth[41] come-in and cover all the forepart of the
stone, so that nothing appeared in the stone. Then was hard a voyce
saying, Loke for us no more at this tyme: This[42] shalbe a token, (from
this tyme forth) to leaue.[43]

Δ: Laus et Honor sit Deo Immortali et Omnipotenti nunc et semp.
Amen.[44]

1582 Die ♀ A meridie: hora 5. Nouemb. 16.

Δ: He with the <u>triple Crown on his hed, in the long purple robe,</u> had
now onely that part of the rod in his hand, which was clere red: the
other two parts being vanished awaye. He shoke his rod, and the Globe
under him did quake. Then he sayde, <u>Ille</u> enim est Deus, Venite.[45] Δ: All
the 7 did bow at his speache. He holdeth up the flag, with the picture of
a woman paynted on it, with the

---

their sons have praised God. Blessed is he who is the only son, and glory of the
world." -Ed.

41   The black cloth of silence and staying.

42   The Token to leaue of, by a black shaddowing all in the stone.

43   Note: how he governeth Three, and Carmara (his King) hath also a Triple crown.

44   ⚬⚬ This Character seemes to stand for Carmara, as apperes from severall
places in fol .2.a. & b. & many other. It appears by a note of Dr. Δ (*De Heptarchia*
&c: Cap. i.) that Michaell & Uriel were present at the begining of these revealed
Misteries & gave authority to Carmara to order the whole Heptarchicall
Revelacon. Perhaps this authority was entred in the first lost leafe of this 4th
booke (thowgh Dr. Dee calls it the 2d Booke in his Note.) see Chap: 2 at the
begining. By a marginall note at the beginning of the first Chapter, it should
seeme, that the Dr. meanes by the first Booke the Action only of the 16 of Nov.
1582, & by the 2d Booke the Actions of the 17, 19 & 20 of Nov. 1582. But his
marginal note of 19 should be 20 of Nov. for so it appears by the Actions entred.
The 21 of Nov: vizt: the action of that day he calls the Appendix of the 2d chapter. -E.A. Laus . . . semp.: "Praise and honor be to the eternal and omnipotent
God, now and ever. Amen." -Ed.

45   Ille . . . Venite: "Truly he is God. Come." -Ed.

(as before was noted) on the right side of her.

And on the other side of the flag, were the <u>Armes of England</u>. He florished with the flag very muche, and went as thowgh he did marche, in warlike manner uppon the upper and utterparte of the Globe. He pointed up to <u>the Flag</u> and sayde, <u>There is two to come</u>, there <u>is no more</u>.[46] All the people in the Globe seamed to be glad and reioyce. Now he setteth down the Flag, and sayd, Come, Come, Come; And the 7 cam all before him. <u>They hold up all togither</u>, Heptagonum stellare, seeming <u>to be Copper</u>.[47]

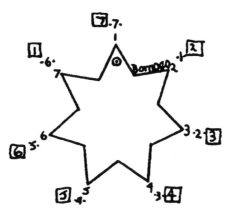

1: The first Holder,[48] sayd, Me nosti:[49] and so pulled his hand of from the Heptagonum.

---

46   Δ: So he sayd in latin, in the forpart of the leaf before.

47   Note. Copper apperteyneth to ♀. -Δ. HM reads, "All the Princis held up to gither, Heptagonon stellare, (as I terme it) and it seemed to be of Copper." -Ed.

48   Δ Forte Bagenol / Hagonel, if H be for B. Then Bagonel conteyned Bagenol.

49   Me nosti: "You have known me." -Ed.

2: The second of the .7. taketh his hand of and doth reverence and sayd, I am he which haue powre to alter the <u>I</u>ncorruption of NATVRE. With my seale, I seale her and <u>she is become perfect</u>. I prevayle <u>in Metalls</u>: in the <u>knowledge of them</u>: I haue <u>byn in Powre</u> with many, but Actually with few. <u>I am of the first of the</u>[50] <u>twelue</u> the <u>Second of the Seuen</u>. Wilt thow know my name?

Δ: Full gladly.

I am <u>BORNOGO</u>: this is my Seale: This is my true Character. What <u>thow desyrest in me shalbe fullfilled</u>. Glory to God. Δ: He kneled down, and held up his hands toward the Heptagonum.

3: The next (or third) sayd, I am the <u>Prince of the Seas</u>: My powre is uppon the waters. I drowned Pharao: and haue destroyed the wicked. I <u>gaue life unto the</u> seas: and by me the Waters move. My name was known to Moyses. I liued in Israel: Beholde <u>the tyme of Gods visitation</u>. I haue measured, and it is '8'.[51] This is a mysterie. God be mercifull to his people. Behold, Behold Lo, behold, my mighty powr consisteth in this. Lern wisdome by my words. This is wrowght <u>for thy erudition</u>, what I enstruct thee from God: Loke unto thy charge truely. <u>Thow art yet deade: Thow shalt be reuiued</u>. But oh, bless God truely: The blessing that God giueth me, I will bestow <u>uppon thee</u> by permission.

Ô, how mighty is our god which walked on the waters; <u>which sealed me</u> with <u>his</u> <u>name</u>, whose Glory is without ende. Thow hast written me, but yet dost not Know me. Use me <u>in the name of God</u>. I shall <u>at the tyme appointed</u> be ready. <u>I will man-ifest the works of the seas, and the miracles of the depe shalbe knowne</u>. I was Glorifyed in God. I Skurged the world. Oh oh

---

50 One of the first of the Twelue.

51 '8. Gods visitation. And it is 8: may be 8 yeres added to this tyme: and that maketh 1590. Nouemb. 16. That 8, or 88, I know not yet.

oh, how they do <u>repent</u>. Misery is theyr ende, and Calamitie theyr meat. Behold my name is print..... for euer: behold it. Δ: He opened his bosom and seamed leane: and seemed to haue <u>feathers[52] under his robes. He had a golden gyrdel: and on it, written BEFAFES</u>. Than he sayd, Blessed be thow Ô God, God, God, for euer. I haue said.

Δ: He toke his hand of from the Heptagonum.

Δ: The blak Cloth was drawn: which is now appointed to be our token from them, that we must leave of for that instant.

Δ: Deo soli, omnis honor, et Gloria.[53] Amen.

Friday. After drinking at night, circiter horam 8 ã.

Δ: On the left side of H (sitting in the Chayre) appeared yet three, holding up the Heptagonum, on <u>one on the other side below</u>. He sat with his face from EK toward me. I stode and my face sowthward. EK he sat at the same table, with his face Northward.

4: The Fowrth[54] (holding below) Cryed: Earth, Earth, Earth.

EK: <u>He speaketh Hollow</u>, so that I understand nothing. Δ: Than he answered, They are the wordes of my Creation, which you are not worthy to understand. <u>My Powre is in Erth:[55]</u> and I

---

52 Prince Befafes with feathers under his robes.

53 Deo soli . . . gloria: "All honor and glory to God alone." -Ed.

54 Prince Butmono. -Ed.

55 In earth.

kepe the bodies of the Dead.[56] Theyr numbers are in my bokes.
I haue the key of Dissolution. Behold, Behold, All things, yea All
things, haue theyr workmanship with me. For I am the ende of
working. EK: He falleth down prostrate, and speaketh, I know
not what, Δ: Than he sayd, I haue the light of his anger,[57] and I
will destroy it. Ô, Ô, Behold, It is a light left within the bottomles pit. It is the ende and the Last. O blessed shall thy name be,
Blessed shall thy name be for euer. Behold this is my seale:

Behold, the bowels of the earth are at my opening. Δ: Than I
requested him to help me with some portion of Threasor hid,[58]
to pay my detts withall and to buy things necessarie &c. He
answered, O wordling thow shalt be satisfyed with welth of this
world. Behold Behold Lo, lo Behold, vehemently I say Behold. I
haue, horded Threasor, for the sonne of perdition,[59] the first
Instrument of his destruction. But, lo these Cauerns. Δ: He
shewed to EK the Cavernes of the earth, and secret places therof
and afterward sayd: Mark this, All spirits, inhabiting within the
earth, where, their habitation is, of force, not of will, (except the
myddest of my self, which I know not), are subiect to the powre
hereof. Δ: Pointing to his Seale.[60] With this you shall govern,

---

56 The Dead mens bodyes.

57 The Light of his anger. ☞

58 Threasure hid requested.

59 Antichrist

60 How can the middest of a spirituall creature be imagined? My dowt to ax. He
meant the middest or center of the Earth. The middest of his Charge. ☞

with this you shall unlok. With this (in his name <u>who rayneth)</u> <u>you shall discouer her entrayles</u>. How say you now? Can you do it? Ar not your Magiciens acquaynted with me? Yt greueth me to regester <u>the bones of the Wycked</u>. Prayse him Butmono, Prayse him Butmono, prayse him. Δ: Is that your name, I pray you tell me. He answered, yea it is my name. It is the <u>ende</u>[61] of all things. EK: Now he sitteth down.

5. Δ: Now the Fifth turned his face toward EK (Who [EK] sat before me, and opposite unto me) and stepped furth and sayd: <u>I</u> <u>am life and breath in Liuing Creatures</u>.[62] All things liue by me, the <u>Image of One excepted</u>.[63] Behold the face of the Earth. EK: There appeareth all Kindes of <u>brute beastes, fowles, Dragons,</u> <u>and other</u>. Δ: He Clapt his hands to gither and they all, vanished away at ones: they cam agayn: and went then away and retorned no more. But the people within the Globe remayned still as from the begynning: he sayd while <u>the beastes</u> were yet in sight, Lo, <u>all these, do I endue with life</u>: my seale is theyr Glory. Of God I am Sanctifyed: I reioyse: (1) <u>the Liuing, (2) The ende,</u> <u>and (3) begynning of these things</u>,[64] are known unto me: and by sufferance <u>I do dispose them untyll my Violl be run</u>. EK: He taketh owt of his bosom a little vyol glass: and there seameth to be fiue or six sponefulls of oyle in it. Δ: He answered and sayde, That it is: and it is a mysterie. Δ: <u>I spake somwhat of this oyle</u>, and he answered me, and sayd, Thow sayst true. In token of God his Powre and Glory, write down BLISDON.

---

61 Δ A great dowt . . . me yet, the diuersity of the 4th and fifth officers, and officis as they are here, and in the Repetition ensuing.

62 Δ: in Animantibus bratij. ("in living creatures." -Ed.) Sloane 3677 misreads " animantibus oratis."

63 (Δ = man.)

64 Virtus officij sui -Δ. ("The power of his office." -Ed.)

EK: He taketh his hand of from the Heptagonum.

6. The sixth pulleth open his Clothes <u>and red apparell</u>, and there yssueth mighty fyre oute of his sides. [Δ: Note, the cote of <u>the first of</u> these seuen is shorter[65] then any of his fellows coats are.] The sight of the fyre is very owgly, grisely, terrible, and skarsly of mans eye can be beholden. At length he pluckt his coates to gither, and sayd to EK, Ô I wold shew thee, but flesh and blud cannot see. Write shortly, (it is enowgh) Noui Januam Mortis.[66] Δ: Than sayd he to me in an ernest muse, Ô, Muse not, My words ar dark; but with those that see, light enowgh. Et per cussit Gloria Dei, Impiorum parietes. Dixi.[67]

Δ: **In mervaylous raging fyre, this worde BRORGES[68] did appeare, tossed to and fro in the furious flames** thereof, so abundantly streaming out, as yf all the world had byn on fyre, so that EK, could not endure (without great annoyance to his ey sight) to behold the same. And finally he sayd, Mysteria in animis vestris imprimite.[69] And so the fyre vanished away.

7. EK: The stone semeth all Blew: and **onely One now beholdeth the Heptagonum: all the rest being set down: who semed now to extend theyr hands one toward an other, as thowgh they played, now being rid of theyr work.** Now the last putteth his hand to the Heptagonon and turned his face to EK hauing his face (all the while before) turned toward D. He sayd, The Creatures liuing in my Dominion,[70] ar subiect to my powre. Behold I am

---

65 Short Coat. The first.

66 Novi Januam Mortis: "I have known the Gate of Death." -Ed.

67 Et percussit . . . Dixi: "And the Glory of God has struck the walls of the wicked. I have spoken." -Ed.

68 Prince Brorges.

69 Mysteria . . . imprimite: "Engrave these mysteries on your souls/minds." -Ed.

70 Δ forte, in Aëre.

BRALGES.[71] <u>**The powres under my subiection are Invisible.**</u> Lo what... are. EK: **All the world** <u>**semed to be in brightnes** or w...</u> <u>**fire: and therin appered**</u> Diuerse little <u>**things like little smokes**</u> <u>**without any forme.**</u>[72] He sayd, This <u>is the seale</u>[73] of my Gouernment. Behold I am come, I will teache the names <u>without</u> <u>Numbers. The Creatures</u> subiect unto me shalbe known unto you.

¶ Beware <u>of wauering.</u> Blot <u>out suspition</u>[74] of us for we are Gods Creatures, that haue rayned, do rayne & shall raigne for euer. <u>All our</u> <u>Mysteries shalbe known unto you.</u>[75]

EK: All the 7 vanished away, onely H remayning who sayd (being stand up, and leaning upon his Chayre, and turned to EK), **Behold,** **these things, and theyr mysteries shalbe known** <u>unto you, reseruing the</u> <u>Secrets</u>[76] of him which raigneth for euer: [EK: The voyce of a multitude, answered singing,] **Whose name is Great for euer. H Open your** **eyes, and you shall see from the** <u>Highest to the lowest.</u>[77] **The Peace of** **God be uppon you.**

Δ: Amen. EK: The blak Cloth was drawn before all the things conteyned in the stone: which was the Token of Ceasing for that tyme:

---

[71] But Baligon, als Carmara, in the ende of the boke sayeth it to be his office. Consider well. Prince Bralges hath Blumaza his king.

[72] The powres under his Subiection are Invisible. They appeared like little white smokes without any forme. All the world semed to be in brightnese. -HM

[73] The seale.

[74] Exchue Wauering or suspition.

[75] All Mysteries shalbe known to us. -Δ. The last of 7 Princes of the boke spoke hereof his words. -(HM)

[76] Secreta Dei, non sunt hominibus reuelanda. -Δ. ("Secrets of God are not to be revealed to men." -Ed.)

[77] Δ: Note Highest and Lowest to be understode perhaps in Tabula Collecta.

Sanctus sanctus sanctus Dominus Deus noster.[78]

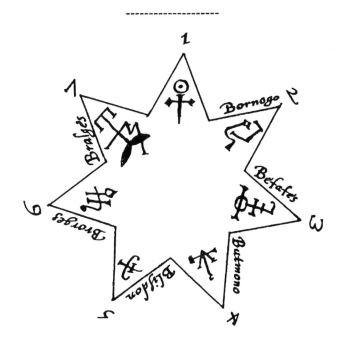

---

[78] BLUMAZA Rex est super Reges Terrae et illius sunt primus princeps, et illius Ministri, ut conycio.

Hanc partem primam vocat 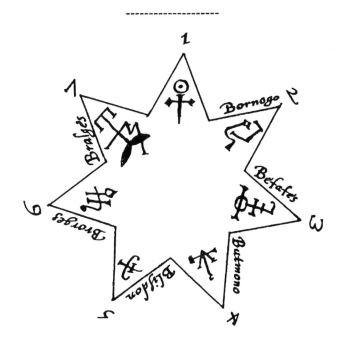 unum Librum: in quinta pagina sequente, ad hanc Notam .

It shold seme that this character shold be onely a Circle and a pryck fol.6.b. I haue forgotten how I cam by this Crosse annexed to it.

alr Remember. Obelison his promise to me of knowing and using. (This note is next to "Befafes" on the diagram. -Ed.)

Words: 9
        9
        9
        7
       11

       45

Sanctus sanctus sanctus Dominus Deus noster: "Holy, holy, holy, O Lord, our God"; Blumaza Rex est ... Notam: "I conclude that Blumaza is the king, and rules the kings of the Earth, and they are his first prince and servants. 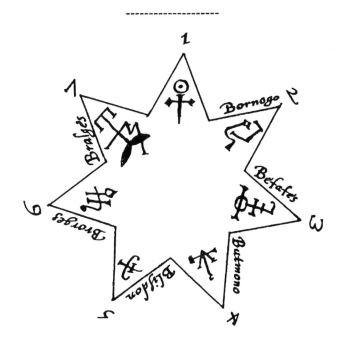 calls this first part one book in the fifth page following, marked with the symbol ." -Ed.

Anno 1582: Saterday. Die 17. Nouemb: A meridie hora circiter 1 ã.[79]

Δ: The Cloth remayned drawn, a prety while after we had done our prayers to God, and so was all the things in the stone kept from sight.

Δ: The Man with the Crowne,[80] (he onely) appeared first, and the transparent Globe with the people of the world in it, as before. The Diaphanitie, or (as it wer) the Shell of the forsaid Globe, was very glystring bright. The man[81] shaked his hand toward me and the bak of the Chayre was toward EK. On the globe appered a trace like a seame, of two things ioyned to gither, or rather a very narrow path: which began below on the Convex superfices of this globe and went upward to the verticall point or (as it wer) the zenith prik of it: but from the lower part of the same to the place where the chayre stode, it seamed broder, and more worn, than from the chayre up to the vertex or top prik: for that part (which semed to be about the eighth part of the whole) did appere very smalle, and unworne, or unoccupyed.

Δ: He turning his face toward EK, spake thus, I haue declared things past and present. And now I speak of things to come. The Whole shalbe manifest. Nam ipse unus et Indiuisibilis est. Gloria Gloria Gloria Creatori nostro.[82] Two partes[83] are yet to come, the rest are finished allready. Δ: He shewed the rownd Table[84] with letters and numbers which master Kelly sent me: and than he toke it away agayn. Then he sayd,

---

[79]   "Around one in the morning." -Ed

[80]   Carmara al: Baligon

[81]   In the manuscript, this word has a crown drawn above it, i.e., man . -Ed.

[82]   Nam ipse . . . nostro: "For he himself is one and indivisible. Glory, glory, glory be to our Creator." -Ed

[83]   Δ forte, of this work.

[84]   The rownd Table.

<u>Venite gradatim repetamus,</u>[85] opera Dei.[86]

Δ: The first of the .7. which had yesterday appeared, did now appere with the <u>short robe,</u>[87] as he did before. Than H sayd smylingly (being turned to EK),

Hæc sunt docum<u>enta tua,</u>[88] quæ nondum intelligis.[89]

Δ: Than the man with the short robe, <u>the Forman</u> of the 7 (yesterday appearing) sayd,[90]

Unus est Deus, et <u>Unum est opus nostrum.</u>[91]

Δ: Then cam very many <u>uppon the Globe his convex superficies</u> and they sayd,

<u>Parati sumus seruire Deo nostro.</u>[92]

---

85 NOTE this to be a REPETITION of the Heptagonon this little Treatise æffore. Lern to reconcile the 4th and the 5th. -Δ. In HM, Dee notes, "At the Call of King Carmara (in the Second handling of this Heptarchicall doctrine), whan he sayd, Venite, Repetamus Opera Dei, Appered Prince Hagonel." Venite . . . Dei: "Come, let us renew the works of God step by step." -Ed.

86 Δ hã . . . bis dext . . . Adhuc duo, et tempus non est. (This reading is from Sloane 3677. It is illegible in Sloane 3188. –Ed.)

87 Short Coat.

88 Δ: I think he ment by the rownd table shewed, which Mr. K. had sent me &c, bycause the names cam out of that Table.

89 Haec sunt . . . intelligis: "These are your lessons, which you do not yet understand." -Ed.

90 According to HM this was Hagonel. -Ed.

91 Unus . . . nostrum: "There is one God, and there is one work of ours." -Ed.

92 Parati . . . nostro: "We have been prepared to serve our God." -Ed.

Δ: Eche of these had somwhat in theyr hands. <u>Som had crownes, some garments &c.</u>[93]

The number of them was: 42: and stode in this order:

and sayd embracing (as it wer) the whole nûmber of this Cumpany,[94]

> Et nomen meum, numerus est totus
> Nec est crimen in numero nostro
> <u>Moyses</u> nos nominauit.
> Potestas istorum, quàm <u>istarum</u>, quamvis non una,
> tamen in uno sunt.[95]

Δ: I sayd that I thowght there wanted at the begynning of this sentence, this word Tam.[96] He answered, it might be understode by his pointing to them there standing, and sayd farder in respect of this my dowt, Quatenus est hæc vanitas vestrorum? Tu nosti numeros <u>hos</u> esse <u>in Deo</u>, <u>in Mundo</u>, et <u>in minori</u> mundo. <u>In Deo</u>, id est Nobiscum. In Mundo, quantum apud vos: In minori Mundo, <u>quantum</u> in vobis.

(Combinatur animus tuus cogitatione.) Disseritur apud Phõs., idque maximè) de <u>NATVRA</u>, quæ non vobiscum, sed nobiscum (ah, ah, ah)

---

93 Vide libro 3º.

94 Hagonel seamed to embrace the Cumpany. -Δ (HM).

95 Δ: I dowt it shold be <u>short coat</u> holding or embracing all the Table with his hands, and not H. Note Istorum - Istarum, as if it were filias et filiare &c. (Et nomen . . . sunt: "And my name is a whole number, nor is their offence in our number. Moses named us. The power of these men is like the power of these women. Although they are not one, nevertheless they are in unity." -Ed.)

96 Making the phrase, Tam . . . Quam: "as . . . so . . ." -Ed.

et in nostra potestate est. <u>Videbis Deum</u>. Vidisti opera nostra, Opera (inquam) manuum suarum: <u>Digito Dei</u> mouebimur. A Deo venit. <u>Homo</u>, et cum hominibus fuit: est enim cum illis. Illius namque <u>potestas</u>, <u>vim</u>, <u>virtutem</u>, et <u>esse</u> dat,[97] non nobis <u>solum modo, sed operibus nostris</u>.

Inhumata tibi anima tua, quid quærit?[98]

Δ: I understand you now: He answered Ab humo, homine: Ab homine dictum est.[99] I axed thee, what thow desyrest.

Δ: Wisdom, and Veritie, I answered: // then, he answered, H: Thow shalt. Δ: There cam in a smyling fellow: and they pluckt him, and towsed him. He cryed he wold tell Newes: and they answered, that there was none for him to tell: and he skaped[100] from them, or they let him slyp, with all his clothes torn of: and he semed to crepe or get away under the globe, and (as it wer) to get behinde the Diaphanous Globe.

Δ: These 42 had all of them somwhat in theyr hands: <u>as eyther whole Crownes</u>, or 3/4 of Crownes, <u>or robes</u> &c. Si<u>x o</u>f them semed more glorious than the rest, and theyr Coates longer: and had <u>cerclets</u> (abowt theyr hed) of Gold: and these had perfect Crowns in theyr

---

97 Dei potestas. -Δ ("God's power." -Ed.)

98 Quatenus . . . quaerit: "How great is your vanity? You knew these numbers to be in God, in the world, and in the minor world. In God, that is, with us. In the world, that is, in our presence. In the minor world, that is among us. (Your mind/soul is combined with thought.) It is debated among philosophers, and above all) concerning NATURE, which is not with you but with us (ah, ah, ah) and it is in our power. You (singular form) will see God. You (singular form) have seen our work, the work (I say) of his own hands. We shall be moved by the finger of God. He came [or comes] from God. He was a man, and with men: and is yet with them. For truly his power gives might, strength, and purpose, not only to us, but to our deeds. What does your unburied soul seek for yourself?" Note the missing parenthesis probably belongs after Phōs, "philosophers." Unburied soul: "soul of a living person as opposed to a dead person's soul." -Ed.

99 Ab humo . . . dictum est: "From the earth, from man; from man is the word." -Ed.

100 Skaped: "escaped." -Ed.

hands. The second six had thre quarters of Crownes, the Third six, haue clothes[101] in theyr hands.[102] <u>All the rest semed to haue balls of gold: which they toss</u> from one to an other: but at the catching they semed empty wynde balls: for they gripe them, closing theyr hand, as yf they wer not solid, but empty, like a bladder.[103]

Δ: The first six sayd, <u>Our names cannot be expressed: neyther can the names of these that follow.</u>

Δ: The first six made cursy to the <u>man with the short robe</u>: the second six made cursy to the first, and the Third to the second, and they all, and <u>the short robed man</u>, made cursy to H.

Our workmanship is all one. Δ: Sayd the <u>short robed</u> man.[104]

H: The whole day is diuided into 6 partes:[105] Euery part occupyeth a <u>part</u> of them here. (Δ: Pointing to the 42 standing there.) Therfore yf thow wilt work <u>with Kings</u> (thow knowest my meaning), finally what so euer thow wilt <u>do in theyr</u> estate, Cast thyne eye unto the first place. In all <u>good causes</u> thow shalt work <u>by six in generall</u>. The rest are for Depriuation: I meane the <u>next six</u>. The residue all do serue to the entents and purposes apperteyning unto Kings. But bycause thow shalt not be ignorant, what they are, <u>in name</u>, they shall shew forth theyr Tables.

Δ: Than they, spedyly (eche of them upon the <u>place of theyr standing</u>) made a square table: and euery table had but one Letter. <u>The first of the first</u> six did go away, and in his table appeared an O, &c, and so of the second six, orderly theyr letters appeared in theyr tables: But the Third six, they cowred down upon theyr letters, and were loath to

---

[101] HM reads, "robes or clothes." -Ed.

[102] Note this reckening by six and six.

[103] HM reads, "blown bladder," i.e., inflated balloon. -Ed.

[104] So he sayd pagina praecedente, unum est opus nostrum. -Δ. ("On the preceding page (he said), 'Our workmanship is all one.'" -Ed.)

[105] The diuision of the Daye.

shew them: but at length, did &c: and at the last of euery row, they all cam togither &c.

O	F^E	S	N	G	L	E	4 howres
A	V	Z	N	I	L	N	4 howres
Y	L	L	M	A	F	S	4 howres
N	R	S	O	G	O	O	4 howres
N	R	R	C	P	R	N	4 howres
L	A	B	D	G	R	E	4 howres

H: Remember how they stode, when they wer secondly disposed unto thee: They stode first in six rows; and next they wer turned into 7.[106] I speak of the greater number and not of the less. In speaking of the greater, I haue comprehended the lesser.[107]

Δ: They went euer away toward the[108] hand.

The third row went of lamenting: being commaunded by the Short robed man. All parted in fire, falling into the Globe. The fifth row did synk into the Globe, euery one in a sundry fyre by him self. The sixth fell with smoke down into the Globe.

EK: Now remayneth only the man with the Crown H : he made shew with his hands, beckning toward E.K., and sayd, I haue told thee, that theyr workmanship, is to gither. Theyr names are uppon these tables. The first letter, is the Second letter, of the first[109] name of the Table.[110]

---

[106] In sexto et 7° sunt omnia, fol. 10. -Δ. "All things are in a sixth and a seventh, fol. 10." -Ed.

[107] Note. K. Car. There are but 6 Names that are in Subiection unto the Prince: The first 7 next him: are those which held the fayr & bewtifull Crownes. The first 7 are called by those names that thow seest: O E S &c. Note. This diversity of Reckening by 6, and by 7, I can not yet well reconcyle. -Δ (HM).

[108] There is a blank space in the manuscript. -Ed.

[109] Δ: How can Bobogel be accownted the first name?

[110] Δ: Now he meaneth at Bobogel in that table collected from ⊕ made before.

Thow hast 49 names in those Tables. Those names thow hast in former Tables by thee written: in that of 7 tymes 7. <u>Confer it with the rownd Table.</u>[111]

The first letter[112] from the point of his[113] sword, is B. That B signifieth the number of the Bees, begynning the 49 names, environing that Circle. In the former Tables thow shalt fynde B.1. B.2. B.3. B.4. &c and so to B.49. <u>Those Bees begynne the names of all the powres that haue governed, do gouern, and shall gouern.</u>

The next <u>letter</u> hath his circle and numbers going rownd abowt it: which thow shalt fynde in the former Tables. The letter standeth in the myddest of euery square, of euery Circle: thowgh some be <u>turned upside down</u>: Which onely signifyeth that they are <u>Spirits of Destruction, wrath and Indignation</u> in Gods Judgment. There are two numbers: that, on the right hand, over the letter, is the number pertayning to that letter.

O in the Circumference is the ninthe <u>letter.</u>[114]
Gather the former Tables to gither, which thow hast made before, conteyning 49, depending onely on B. Where thow shalt finde <u>BOBOGEL</u>, a name consisting on 7 letters, and so the rest. Reade <u>my instructions</u> as concerning those Tables, and thow shalt fynde the truth of them.----------I haue sayd.[115]

---

[111] Note. The Tablet ⊞ to be conferred with the rownd 🌀 . -Δ. The latter drawing is reproduced from Sloane 3677, since the original is now lost. -Ed.

[112] In margin: Sent to me by E.K.

[113] A sword in the mans hand within the Circle.

[114] O in this Table OFS &c, is of the eighth name, the second letter, but the ninth here in respect of the circle of numbers.

[115] Note who sayeth this. Δ: Note the like phrase: fol. 2. of Hagonel who sayd he had spoken of it, whereas we had receyved nothing of him before.

Mighty is thy name, O God of Hostes:
Blessed is thy name, Ô Lord, for euer.
Δ: Amen.

After 7 of the clok at night. die ♄ *.116*

H: Lo, here I byd them do, and they do. I haue appointed them, and they are contented. My Charge is not of my self, neyther do I speak darkly, obscurely or without a truth, in affirming that I towght thee those Tables: For they are from him, which made and created all things: I am from them[117] in powre and message, under whome I here rule[118] and shall do, tyll the ende[119] of all things be:[120] Ô, Great and bowntifull in his liberall mercy: The mercy of him, whome we prayse and laude and sing unto, with Joy for euer. Behold thow desyrest, and art syk with desire.[121] I am the disposer thowgh not the Composer of Gods medicines. Thow desirest to be cumforted and strengthened in thy labors. I mynister unto thee The strength of God.

What I say, is not of my self, neyther that which is sayd to me, is of them selues, but it is sayd of him which Liueth for euer.

These Mysteries hath God lastly, and of his great mercyes, graunted unto thee.[122] I haue answered thy dowting mynde.

Thow shalt be glutted, yea filled, yea thow shalt swell and be puffed

---

116 This is the symbol of Saturn/Saturday. -Ed.

117 Δ him.

118 Baligons rule and government.

119 Sup. fol. 1. b.2.

120 Prodigious rule and government, the ende of all things.

121 Dee his languishing desire.

122 God graunt.

up with the perfect knowledge of Gods Mysteries, in his mercyes. Abuse them not. Be faithfull. Use mercy. God shall enriche thee.

Banish wrath: yt was the first,[123] and is the greatest[124] Commaundement.

I rayng in him, and liue by him which rayngneth and liueth for euer.

Δ: I pray you make some of these last instructions, more playne, and euident.

H: I haue shewed thee perfectly. Behold I teache thee agayn. O how mercifull is God that revealeth so great secrets to flesh and blud? Thow hast 42 letters. Thy Tables, last, conteyn so many. Euery letter is the name particular by him self of the generall actions, being, and doing of these 42, which appeared with theyr workmanship. The first, was theyr Prince: and he gouerneth **onely**[125] the estate, condition and being, limited by God unto Kings of the earth. The 7 next him,[126] are those that are Messagers of God his good gifts to those that beleue him, and faithfully serue him: wherof few re . . . and rayng now frutefull in his sight.[127]

Regnat, Regnat, Regnat ô regnat Iniquitas super faciem totius terræ Cor hominis impletum est malitia, et nequicijs. Incipit, incipit enim noua illorum potestas, illis non sine re dedita,[128] nec dis . . .[129]

Vide quæso.[130] Δ: He pointed down to the people, in the Globe, all being sore and diseased of some sore, ulcer, botch, &c.

---

[123] Δ I understode not this to be so: tyll he called to my remembrance and made me turne my bokes to that Parcell which he called the Prologe declared by Annael: which Saul skryed: &c.

[124] Δ: = hardest, for me, in respect of my Imperfections.

[125] In the manuscript, this word is heavily underscored. -Ed.

[126] Those — as he seemed to Embrace them. fo. 5.

[127] The Prince and his first 7.

[128] = data.

[129] Istorum Noua potestas incipit. -Δ. ("Their new power begins." -Ed.)

[130] Regnat . . . quaeso: "It rules, it rules, it rules; O wickedness rules over the entire

H: <u>All the residue</u> of the Angels, (for so they are in dede) ar ministers of God his wrath and indignation upon the <u>Faythless:</u>[131] whose myserie is most lamentable. <u>7 onely, haue 7 letters</u> comprehending the <u>dignitie</u> of theyr vocation:[132] The rest are particular, not onely in powr, but allso in theyr vocation. <u>Like leaves they spring and grow from one branche.</u>

These words which thow seest in the last Table, <u>some</u> of <u>them unhable to be pronownced,</u> are notwithstanding the names of those <u>7</u>[133] which held the fayr and bewtifull <u>Crownes.</u> Which names (as I sayd before) do comprehend not onely the **powre,** but allso the **Being** of **the rest.**[134] The whole Composition is the truth of the words. <u>I will ones more teach.</u> There were 42 that appeared, <u>besides him, which was theyr prince.</u> The <u>first 7,</u>[135] are called by those names, that thow seest, as OFS &c.

Δ: And so of AVZNILN &c. H : Thow hast sayde.

<u>There are but 6 names,</u>[136] that are in <u>Subiection</u>. I teache breifly. Doost thow not remember the **Circle** and the prick in the myddest: which was on <u>the right hand</u>[137] <u>of him, that was theyr</u> **Prince?** **That** <u>onely</u> representeth <u>7 in number</u> which being added unto the rest maketh 49. Read the letters. Δ: I red OF &c, and he willed me to strike them out.

H: That is the name of **those** <u>of the first of the 7,</u>[138] which held the Crownes in theyr hands.

---

face of the Earth. The heart of man is filled with malice and iniquity. Please consider." -Ed.

131 Angels, ministers of Gods wrath.

132 Consider the reckening here by 7, but before he had a reckening by 6. ☞

133 There were but 6 holding bewtifull Crownes.

134 The Powre and being of the rest. ☞

135 Now by 7.

136 Δ: each of .7. letters. Six names in subiection.

137 ⊙ on the right hand.

138 Δ forte "of the first 7". Δ videlicet.

Note: The <u>seco</u>nd line,[139] is the name of the second, and so to the ende of the table. <u>42 letters: 42 names: 42 persons.</u>

The first, where <u>his fote stode</u>, is both his <u>Name and Character.</u>[140] And so of the second, Third &c.

Notwithstanding, Generally these are the names, the first 7, the <u>One</u> presupposed, the rest being six in order.

This is the truth, and the some of the Tables. Yt is easy to be understode and perfect.

Whan thow wilt work for anything apperteyning unto the estate of a good King: Thow must first <u>call uppon</u>[141] him which is theyr prince. Secondly the <u>ministers of his powre ar Six:</u>[142] <u>whose names conteyne 7 letters apece</u>: as thy Tables do manifest: by whome in generally, or by any one of them, in particularitie, thow shalt work for any Intent or purpose.

As concerning <u>the letters</u> particularly, they do concern the Names of 42 which 42, in generally, <u>or one of them</u> do and can work **the destruction,**[143] hindrance or annoyance of the estate, Condition or degree, as well <u>for body</u> as government, of any <u>Wicked or yll Liuing</u> **Prince**. In <u>owtward sense</u>, my words are true. I speak now of the use of one of the first, that I spake of, or manifested yesterday. Sayd I not, and shewed I not, which had the gouernment of Princes?[144] <u>For, as it is a Mystery to a farder matter</u>, so is it a purpose to a present use. Yf it rule <u>worldly princis</u>, how much more shall it work with the <u>Princis of Creation</u>?

Thow desyrest use, I teache use, and yet the Art is to the furder

---

[139] Δ: of the six lines.

[140] Note, Name and Character.

[141] Praxis. Call. -Δ. (Praxis: "exercise, practise." -Ed.)

[142] Prince, Ministers. 6.

[143] Destruction or hurt.

[144] = Kings. -Δ. HM reads "princes," without the qualification. -Ed.

understanding **of all Sciences,** that are past, present or yet to come.[145]

Frute hath a furder vertue than onely in the eating: Gold his furder condition, property, and quality, then in melting, or common use. Kings there are in Nature, with Nature, and above Nature.[146]

Thow art Dignified.[147]

Δ: Yf I wold haue the King of Spayne his hart to be enclined to the purpose I haue in hand, what shall I do?

H: First Cast thyne ey unto the Generall prince,[148] Gouernor or Angel that is principall in this world.[149] [Δ as yet, is BALIGON or Carmara.]

Secondly consider the circumstances of thy Instruction.[150]

Thirdly place my name,[151] whome thow hast all ready.

Fowrthly, the name of him, which was shewed thee yesterday, whose garments were short, and of purple.[152]

Fifthly, his power,[153] with the rest of his six perfect Ministers.[154] With those thow shalt work to a good ende. All the rest thow mayst use to Gods Glorie. For euery of them shall minister to thy necessities. Moreouer, when thow workest, Thy feete must be placed uppon those tables[155] which thow seest written last comprehending 42 letters, and

---

[145] . . . Sciences past present or to come.

[146] Diuers kings.

[147] Dignification.

[148] Δ: Is it not Annael with whome I began?

[149] Δ Who is that?

[150] HM does not include this instruction. -Ed.

[151] Δ: Ergo it shold seme to be his office to deale with Kings: but in the ende he declareth his office to be of all Aëreall actions.

[152] Δ: Hagonel.

[153] Δ Character. HM has no such notation. -Ed.

[154] Of 7 letters a pece.

[155] The placing of my fete in practise. ☞

names. But with Consideration, that <u>the first **Character**, which is the <u>first of the 7</u></u>, in <u>thy former boke</u>,[156] be <u>placed uppon the top of the Table</u>,[157] <u>which thow wast, and art, and shalbe commaunded to haue, and use.</u>

Last of all, the Ring, which was appointed thee: with the Lamine comprehending <u>the forme of thy own name</u>: which is <u>to be</u> made in perfect gold, as is affore sayd.[158]

Euen as God is iust, his iudgments true, his mercies unspeakable, so are we the true messagers of God: and our words are true in his mercy[159] for euer.

Glory, ô Glory be to thee, ô most high God.

EK: Now commeth Michael and heaveth in his hand out of the stone and sayeth, GOD Bless you.

H: As concerning the use of these <u>Tables</u>, this is but the first step. Neyther shalt thow <u>practise them in vayne</u>.[160]

And whereas thow dost use a demaunde, as concerning thy doings to a good intent and purpose: and for the prayse and advancement of Gods Glorie, with Philip the Spanish King: <u>I answer that whatsoeuer thow **shalt speak, do or work**, shalbe profitable and accepted, And the ende of it shalbe good.</u>[161]

Moreouer wheras thow urgest the absence of thy frende, as an excuse for the ring, No excuse can preuayle: Neyther canst thow shew the frutes of a iust mynde, but of a faynting stomack with this excuse. God hath retorned him, and wilbe mercifull unto you both. Thy Chargis in worldly affayres, are not so great, that God cannot Minister

---

[156] ♀✝ Note former boke.

[157] Δ The Table of practise of a yard square: libro: 1°.

[158] The stone was not yet browght.

[159] HM reads "Mercies" in one place, and "Mercy" in another. -Ed.

[160] I shall not practise these Tables in Vayne.

[161] Dei Misericordia magna ipi Δ concessa. ("God's great mercy granted to Dee himself." -Ed.)

help to theyr necessities. Thow shalt be comforted. But <u>Respect the</u> <u>world to come</u>[162] <u>(1); (whereunto thow art provided) and for what</u> <u>ende (2): and that, in (3) what tyme.</u>

Serue God truely: Serue him iustly. Great Care is to be had with those that meddle with Princis affayres. Much more Consideration, **with whome** thow shalt medle or use any practise. But God hath shaddowed[163] thee from destruction. He preserueth his faithfull, and shaddoweth the iust with a shield of honor.

<u>None shall enter **into the knowledge** of these mysteries</u>[164] <u>with</u> <u>thee but this **Worker**</u>. Thy estate with the Prince (now rayngning,[165]) shall shortly be amended. Her fauor encreased, with the good wills of diuerse, that are now, deceyuers.

Thy hand, <u>shall shortly be theyr help:</u>[166] and thow shalt do wunderfull and many benifits (to the augmenting of Gods Glorie) <u>for thy</u> <u>Cuntry</u>. Finally, God doth enriche thee with Knowledge: and of thy self, hath giuen thee understanding <u>of these worldly</u> vanities.[167] He is Mercifull: and we his **good Creatures,**[168] neyther haue, do, <u>nor will</u> <u>forget thee</u>. God doth blesse you both: whose Mercy, Goodness, and Grace, I pronownce and utter uppon you. I haue said:

Δ: Laus, honor, Gloria, virtus et Imperium,
Deo opto. Max°.[169]
    Amen.

---

162 Respice ista Tria. -Δ. ("Respect these three things." -Ed.)

163 Shaddowed: "sheltered." -Ed.

164 Secresy.

165 Queen Elizabeth -Ed.

166 God graunt.

167 Worldly vanity.

168 Good Angels.

169 Laus . . . Max°.: "Praise, honor, glory, power, and sovereignty be to God, all good." -Ed.

H: Yf you will stay[170] one half howre, I will say farder unto you.

Δ: We will: by gods leave.

Δ: After that half howre passed, (being 10½ noctis ♄ :) he sayde,

H: Venito BOBOGEL <u>Rex et princeps</u> Nobilitatis[171]
Venito cum ministris: Venito (inquam) Venito cum
satellitibus tuis <u>munitus.</u>[172]

Δ: I fele: and (by a great thundring noyce, thumming thuming in myne eares) I perceyue the presence of some spirituall creature abowt me.

EK: And I here the thumming.

H: Behold, Before this work be finished,[173] (I meane the Manifestation of these Mysteries) thow shalt be trubbled, **with the Contrarie Powres** and beyond any accustomed manner. But take heade,[174] they prouoke thee not to work agaynst our Commaundements. Both thy <u>ey and hand</u> shall be manifest witness of it: well, this is true.

EK: They that now come in are <u>ioly</u>[175] fellows, all trymmed after the manner of Nobilitie now a dayes: with gylt rapers, curled heare: and they bragged up and down. BOBOGEL <u>standeth in a blak veluet coat,</u> and his hose close, rownd hose of veluet upperstoks: ouer layd with gold lace: he hath a veluet hat-cap, with a blak feather in it: with

---

[170] Stay: "delay." -Ed.

[171] Noble men.

[172] This I note for the form of calling. -Δ. Venito ... munitus: "Come, O Bobogel, king and noble prince. Come with your ministers. Come (I say), come fortified with your guards." -Ed.

[173] Note.

[174] Cave -Δ ("Beware." -Ed.)

[175] Ioly = "jolly: handsome." -Ed.

a cape on one of his sholders his purse hanging at his neck and so put under his gyrdell, his berd long: he had pantofells and pynsons.[176] Of these, in Company, are 42. 7 of them, are apparayled like BOBOGEL: sagely and gravely: All the rest are ruffyn like. Some, are like to be men and women: for, in the foreparte they semed women, and in the bakpart, men, by theyr apparayle, and these were the last 7. They daunsed, lept and kissed.

EK: The stone is brighter, where the sage and graue 7 do stand, and where the other do stand the stone is more dark.

EK: Now they come to a circle, the sage and the rest, but the sage stand all to gither.

Δ: The first of the sage, lyft up his hand a loft, and sayde:

Faciamus secundum voluntatem Dei: Ille Deus noster est verè nobilis & æternus.[177] He pluckt up his right fote, and under it appeared an L.

1.   L
Then the Second moved his fote, and   E - appeared.
Under the third, likewise,   E
      &c.   N
                                         A
                                         R
                                         B

Then the last .B. and immediately they grew all to gither in a flame of fyre and so sonk down into the former Globe.[178] Of the rest the first pluckt up his fote, and there appered an L &c.

---

176 BOBOGEL his apparayle.

177 Faciamus . . . aeternus: "May we act in accordance with God's will. He, our God, is truly noble and eternal." -Ed.

178 HM reads, "sonk down into the Transparent fyry Globe of the New World." -Ed.

2.   L

                                                N

                                                A

                                                N

                                                A

At the last, they fell down like   E

drosse of metall.   B

Then whipped out fowr in a cumpany.

3.   R

                                                O

                                                E

                                                M[179]

                                                N

They clasp to gither, and fall down   A
in a thick smoke.

4.   B

                                                L

                                                E

                                                A

                                                O[180]

                                                R

They ioyne to gither and vanish   I
like drops of water.

---

[179] In the manuscript, the first four are indicated with a brace. -Ed.

[180] In the manuscript, the first four are indicated with a brace. -Ed.

5.   B
                                            N
                                            E
                                            I[181]
                                            C
                                            I
They fall down like a <u>storme</u>   A
<u>of hayle</u>.   B[182]

6.   A
                                            O
                                            I
                                            D
                                            I
                                            A
The last vanished away.   B

---

[181] In the manuscript, the first three are marked with a brace. -Ed.

[182] In the mansucript, the last four are marked with a brace. -Ed.

Δ: This I fashioned thus after my first dictata penning of
my own fantasie:

L	E	E	N	A	R	B
L	N	A	N	A	E	B
R	O	E	M	N	A	B
L	E	A	O	R	I	B
N	E	I	C	I	A	B
A	O	I	D	I	A	B

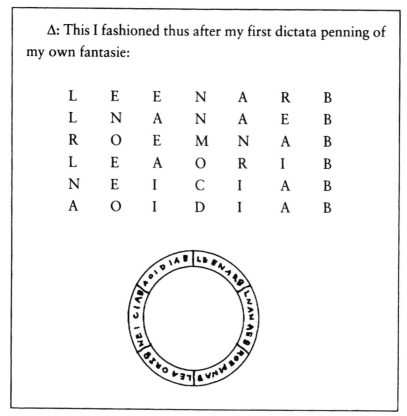

Δ: Then he sayd, Well, I will shew thee more of these things at the next
time.

God be with you: God bless you both.

Δ: Amen.

Δ: When shall that next tyme be? A voyce spake, On monday.

Δ: Deo soli omnis Honor et Gloria.[183] Amen.

---

[183] Deo soli . . . Gloria: "All honor and glory to God alone." -Ed.

Monday. Nouembris 19: Circiter 1 ã horã a meridie[184]

Δ: Long after our comming to the stone (abowt half a quarter of an howre) the Cloth of sylence remayned drawn: and nothing appeared: but EK heard a far off very pleasant Musik the while.

H: He seamed to take the cloth away with his hands. After that (abowt 6 minutes), Nothing altered or shewed, other than the standing furniture, usually of late appearing there.

EK: Now come in 7 men with Musicall Instruments: and before them cam one with a veluet Coate,[185] and a hat-Cap, with a sword by his syde, and a Cloke or Cape hanging on one sholder: and a blak feather in his hat. &c. Afterward cam 42 more, seeming to be very far behynde the first 7. Their Melody sownded very swetely and pleasantly all the while from the begynning.

The forme of theyr Musicall Instrument:

These Musiciens did play, one with an other, iestingly: they bobbed one an other, and than played agayn. The 42, which semed a far of, cam nerer and nerer, and seamed to bring a rownd thing, like a table[186] in theyr hands. The 7 pipers went away: and the Man with the Cape hanging on one of his sholders (somwhat like a Nobleman) remayned. Then wer they come at hand, the 42 with the rownd table. These seamed to be of two sortes: Of which, the last 7: on the forepart to

---

184 "Around 1 in the morning." -Ed.

185 BOBOGEL Rex.

186 A rownd Table.

behold <u>seamed rather wemen,</u>[187] with fardingales[188] very much sprowting out, but theyr face had no peculier attyre of wemen. The 42 held the circle[189] (or rownd <u>Table) up, over theyr hed, flat wise.</u> Then they <u>layd the Circle down,</u> and stode rownd abowt it.

H sayd, Tam mali, quam boni, laudant te,

Deus, Deus, Deus noster.[190]

Δ: The letters appeared to EK, and he told me them, and I began to write:

L E E N A R B

H: <u>Thow writest in vayne. Thow hast written them allready.</u>

Δ: It is true: I see them now last before noted down.

H: Loke the eight <u>name</u> in the Tables. [Δ: of 49, collected.]. Δ: That eighth is Bobogel. Loke to his Character in the great Circle. <u>Loke the second name in the Table</u> with 7 angles.

Δ: That I finde to be Bornogo.

EK: He with the cape on his one sholder, sayeth, Nomen meum <u>est Bobogel:</u>[191] And he that is my subiect, <u>is Governor of</u> the <u>second</u> Angle of the 7.[192]

Bob: I weare these robes, not in respect of my self, but of my Government. I am the Prince, Chief; [EK: He falleth down on his knees

---

[187] Women-like.

[188] Farthingale: "hoop skirt." –Ed.

[189] The Circle.

[190] Tam mali . . . noster: "Both the wicked and the good praise you. God, God, our God." -Ed.

[191] Nomen . . . Bobogel: "My name is Bobogel." -Ed.

[192] Δ: in Heptagonum.

Bobogel ----------   Rex
Bornogo ------------   Princeps

(Rex: "king"; Princeps: "prince." -Ed.)

and speaketh wordes which I understand not.] yea the **onely distributer**, giver, and bestower **of Wisdome and Science.**[193] I weare this
apparayle, for that in dede, being a Prince <u>I am a Cownsaylor</u>[194] to
estate and dignitie. All Dignitie and gouernment that is not cownsayled
by me, and my subiects, is frustrate, voyde, and cleane[195] without firm
grownd.

Those which thow sawest, (being pipers) signifie **praters,**[196] with
unaccustomed, and not usuall Instruments: which allwayes <u>seame</u> to
sownd that, which None but I my self, with my subiects, (yea **not all** of
them, <u>but the fewest) can performe</u>. But I am <u>true Philosophie</u>. I am
true understanding. Oh my descending from him which rayngneth, is
euen uncomprehensible of the Angells. Neyther do I know, my self: <u>But
what I think, I utter</u>, and What I measure, I am.

He sayd, Ordinationem Infinitæ potestatis eleuate.[197]

EK: Now come Three[198] out of the 42, and layd theyr fingers
uppon the three first letters: and,

The first sayd,   O Unitas in Natura et in Deo.[199]

The second sayd,   O Æqualitas Dei et Naturæ. Deus
in Deo.
Natura a Deo et se.[200]

---

193 Wisdome & Science: "true nobility."

194 Councell.

195 Clean: "completely." -Ed.

196 Praters: "fools." -Ed.

197 Ordinationem . . . eleuate: "Raise up the government of infinite power." -Ed.

198 LEE.

199 O Unitas . . . in Deo: "O Unity in nature and in God." -Ed.

200 O Aequalitas . . . et se: "O equality of God and Nature. God in God. Nature from
God and itself." -Ed.

The Third sayd,   Concentus eius, est sine numero:
Tamen nobiscum est in Uno, Fons et
Caput Naturæ[201]

EK: They ioyne them selues to gither and become, <u>all One Man</u>; most beawtifull to behold: Whose hed and to the brest, seamed to be neare to heven. His brest and myddle part, in the ayre: His feete seamed to stand on the earth. There cam like a Fire, oute of the Crown of his hed, and to enter into the heven, hard, by it: This great high and fayre man sayde,

<u>Veritas quæsita</u>, nostra est.[202]

[203]EK: His apparayle is diuided into two halfes: from the crown of his hed to his fete. The one half seemed to be most fresh florishing herbes: The other half seemed to be of diuerse metalls:[204] and his right fote seamed <u>to be Leade.</u>[205] He sayd (with an Aposiopesis) thus,

Beatus est qui Lumen capitis mei &c.[206]

EK: The rest, all, quake. He sayd farder,

Unus in Capite, unus in pectore, unus in pedibus.[207]

EK: Then stept oute 9, at ones.

EK: Then the great man returned, or was restored to his former

---

[201] Concentus . . . Naturae: "His harmony is without number. Nevertheless he is together with us, the source and head of nature." -Ed.

[202] Veritas . . . est: "Ours is the truth which is sought after." -Ed.

[203] Note, this is an example of what William Sherman calls a "face bracket" (*John Dee*, Amherst, MA: University of Massachusetts Press, 1995, p. 88). Dee drew them often in the margins of texts, and they only seem to mark alchemical passages (as here) or natural philosophical texts. –Ed.

[204] Vegetible, Minerall.

[205] ♄

[206] Beatus est . . . mei: "Blessed is the light of my head." -Ed.

[207] Unus . . . pedubus: "One in head, one in heart, one in feet." -Ed.

estate of three particular men agayn: and they three leaned to the
Ientleman[208] with the Cape on his sholder - BOBOGEL - who sayde,

 Dee, Dee, Dee, at length, but not to late.[209]

EK: In the place of the former first thre, appeared L E E.

EK: Of the 9, which stept out, they of the first Ternarie[210] sayde,
eche thus orderly,

1 Volumus.
2 Possumus.
3 Quid non.[211]

This Ternarie sayd, Faciamus, quæ fecerunt, nam nos Tres sumus
Adam; societate.[212]

EK: They become One man, as the other before, but a slender and a
weak one, neyther so high as the first, euer laboring or striving with it
self to stand up right, but still it bended, bowed, and inclined downward, as thowgh it wold fall for feblenes. The Body of this Compownd
man, seamed to be of Gold glittring. When they retorned to theyr dis-
tinct shape: they semed naked and to be sorry, and lament: And
Bobogel did put them from him, with his sworde, skabbard and all, as
it hanged by his side. Theyr letters were ----- N A R.

---

208 Ientleman = gentleman: "nobleman." -Ed.

209 Note. King Bobogel said this of my atteyning to such mysteries, as the mysteries
     under him made shew of. -Δ (HM).

210 2. NAR.

211 Volumus: "we wish"; Possumus: "we can"; Quid non: "What not?" -Ed.

212 Faciamus . . . societate: "Let us do what they did, for we three are Adam, by asso-
     ciation." -Ed.

EK: Then cam the Ternarie—B L N,[213] and orderly they sayd thus,

> { 1 Ab illo.
> { 2 Per illum.
>   3 Cum illo[214]

Bob: Qui caret hijs tribus,[215] [EK: He whispereth to the first Three leaning to him: and with all, seeing me muse at the Aposiopesis, he sayd,] No No, <u>Thow shalt not dowt</u> [pointing to me.]

In ecclesia Dei, laborabit in Vanum.[216]

EK: This Ternarie of men becam to haue <u>one onely hed, and three bodyes and that one hed was in good proportion.</u>

EK: The side of the Diaphonous Globe opened, and this Transformed Ternarie did point into it, toward the multitude: and the people had theyr brests naked, and semed <u>to wepe:</u>[217] and to wipe theyr brests, and where they wiped the place becam fayre.

EK: This Ternary did seme to stand uppon a triangular stone ◁ , and to turn (as a horsmyll doth, abowt one axeltree) orderly agaynst, and by, the hole of the Globe so opened. And euery of the three bodyes, in theyr turning, as they cam agaynst the open place of the Globe, they extended, and stretch out theyr hands toward the people: The first seamed to hold a rownd ball in his hand being little, but very fayre white. The second body, his hand had in it, a little sword flamming with fyre. The third had a thing like <u>a hatt band of lawn,</u>[218] of many cullours, which ever as his turne cam to be agaynst the opened hole, he seamed to cast toward the people, and the people did seme to be drawn to him ward, by the Casting of it toward them.

---

[213] 3. BLN.

[214] Ab illo, per illum, cum illo: "from him, through him, with him." -Ed.

[215] Qui caret hijs tribus: "Who lacks these three." -Ed.

[216] In ecclesia . . . Vanum: "In the church of God, he will work in vain." -Ed.

[217] Penitence.

[218] Lawn: "thin fabric." -Ed.

These three bodyes, thowgh they turned contynually, yet did the face or Cowntenance of that One Compownd hed, <u>stedyly and immoveably regard or loke into the Globe at the forsayd</u> hole therof.

H: A wonder to behold the heuen, much more this.

EK: Now this Ternarie separated it self, and the <u>hole or clyft</u> in the Globe <u>did shut to</u>. These three did <u>sit down</u> by Bobogel.

H: Sunt semper, et Cibus illorum est unus.[219]

Δ: Note: The first Ternarie, they semed to stand leaning to Bobogel. The Third Ternarie was set orderly and vicissim,[220] close by Bobogel his feete, one of these betwene two of the first; euer so that orderly one of the first, and one of the Third ternarie, one of the first and one of the third; one of the first and one of the third.

EK: Then cam the Ternarie A N A.[221]

They sayd, orderly thus,

1. Ab illo sed.
2. Cum illo sed,[222] looking on <u>his own belly</u>.

Δ: Then I demaunded of theyr Apparayle: and EK sayd that these were brauer than the former Ternary. Bobogel sayd, Aliqui a dignitate, Cæteri talia quia non sunt Digni.[223] This he sayd, pointing to theyr apparayle. Then the third sayd,

3. Per illum, Per illum, Per illum,[224] with a frowning cowntenance thrusting furth his hand.

---

219 Sunt semper . . . unus: "They are always, and their food is one." -Ed.

220 Vicissim: "in turns." -Ed.

221 4. ANA.

222 Ab illo sed. Cum illo sed: "from him only; with him only." -Ed.

223 Aliqui . . . Digni: "Some from worthiness, others are not worthy of any sort." -Ed.

224 Per illum, Per illum, Per illum: "Through him, through him, through him." -Ed.

EK: They ioyne to gither into <u>one hed</u> and <u>three bodyes</u>. The Hole of the Globe opened very wyde now. This one Compownd Hed <u>had many eyes</u>, <u>many noses</u>, many mowthes, as thowgh it were a Cahos[225] of Faces, in one hed, but three bodyes. One of this bodyes had in his hand a little Ball, like the other before, very white, but with twynkling brightnes in it. The other two bodyes, theyr hands were emptie.

EK: They turn in order agaynst the Hole of the Globe: But the People <u>regarded them</u> not: but at the comming of the hand with the Ball, against the hole, the people loked a little up at it.

Bob. sayd, Et quia carebant in ardentibus ignis.[226]

EK: These, being dissolued into theyr former state, go and sit (with <u>hevy</u> chere) by them that sat <u>affar of from</u> BOBOGEL. Theyr apparaill semed to be simple: <u>theyr good apparayle was gone</u>.

Δ: Here I fownd a certayn error in my writing of the first Notes: which I haue amended in the writing of this: But while that error did trubble me, the spirituall Creature sayd these wordes. Bob: The Fawt is in EK his remembrance, and not in his will. Note this,

LEE ar the Three that stand with me.
NAR are the Three that I reiect.
BLN are the Thre which are enterlincked with me.
ANA are the Three that are reiected.[227]

---

225 Cahos: "chaos." -Ed.

226 Et quia . . . ignis: "And because they were lacking in blazing fires." -Ed.

227 In the manuscript there is a line drawn from LEE to BLN, and another line from NAR to ANA. -Ed.

Bob. sayd, Omnes naturam ad, Sed, Nôn in illo.[228]

EK: The 30 remayning,[229] cam all away, and satt betwene Bobogel and the reiected Cumpany: and from that Cumpany[230] cam onely 7 to the Circle agayn. Euery of these 7, sett theyr feete, eche uppon a letter of the Circle, which letters are these,[231]

AOIDIAB.

EK: They say, In use,[232] we are perfect; Misused, we are Monsters. Sumus septem Januæ Naturæ, et sui ipsius qui novit Deum.[233]

EK: These 7, seme to vanish into wynde, or white smoke, and to fall into the Globe. And the six reiected, turn into a black smoke: and the rest of the 30[234] semed also converted into black smoke, and to fall into the Globe.

Bob. sayd, In sexto et septimo sunt omnia.[235]

EK: The six that were next him, semed to clyng hard and close to Bobogel. (Bob: Behold.) EK: They be ioyned all into One body, and becam like the sonne, into the forme of a bowle or Globe: and so moved up or rowled up the small narrow race, or line unworne, which remayned higher then the chayre, toward the top of the Diaphanous Globe, as before is declared, so that this Princely Noble man, and his six adherents [LEE:BLN], in this manner went out of sight.[236]

---

228 Omnes . . . in illo: "Everything towards nature, but not in him." -Ed.

229 Δ There remayned 10 tymes Three.

230 Δ of 30.

231 Note, by theyr sitting that they are indifferent: and so they say.

232 Δ They semed therfore to sit betwene the perfect and reiected: as indifferent.

233 Sumus . . . novit: "We are the seven gates of Nature, and of him who knew God." -Ed.

234 Δ: beside AOIDIAB.

235 6, 7. -Δ. In sexto . . . omnia: "All things are in the 6th and 7th." -Ed.

236 NOTE the narrow path, above the chayr.

H: <u>Formator</u> horum, <u>Secundus</u>[237] est in Heptagono.[238]

They are diuided into the day, as the other wer, before: But wheras the other are <u>chiefly</u> uppon that day which you <u>call Mon</u>day, so ar these to be <u>used onely on</u> the Sabaoth day.

Theyr use, is onely thus (obseruing the <u>former</u> order) with the <u>Circle</u> uppon the grownd.[239] <u>The first six,</u>[240] with theyr King and the <u>seale of theyr Prince</u>, taketh place in the whole body of the day: The other being <u>6 tymes six,</u>[241] are diuided into the partes of the day as before. The Letters onely where they stode, are theyr <u>names and Characters</u>. **What doth the heven behold or the earth conteyne, that is not (or may be) <u>sub</u>dued, <u>form</u>ed and made by these. What lerning, grown<u>ded uppon</u> wisdome, with the excellencies in**[242] **Nature, ca<u>nnot they</u> manifest? One in heuen they know.**

One and all in Man, they Know.

One and all in erth, they know.

Measure heuen by a parte, (my meaning is, by these few). Let God be Glorifyed: His name praysed. <u>His Creation</u>[243] **<u>well taken, and his Creatures, well used.</u>**[244]

---

[237] Δ Bornogo.

[238] Formatur . . . Heptagono: "The maker of these is the second in the Heptagon." -Ed.

[239] Note former. ergo. There is allso a circle on the grownd. Vide ante 3 folia: of my fete placed uppon the Tables: Ergo they shold seme to be on the grownd. -Δ (Vide ante 3 folia: "See three folios earlier." -Ed.)

[240] Δ: of the six orders.

[241] Practise. by 6.

[242] Sloane 3188 reads, "excellencies of" in Ashmole's handwriting, but CHM, HM, and Sloane 3677 all read, "excellencies in." -Ed.

[243] This boke sometymes called liber Creationis, & sometymes Tabulae Creationis. -Δ. ("The Book of Creation," the "Tables of Creation."-Ed.)

[244] HM cites this: "King Carmara, Novemb. 19, of King Bobogel, his princis Ministers." -Ed.

Δ: I craued for some playner Instruction, as concerning the use of the . . . and he answered,

H: Behold: Are thy eyes so blynde? Dost thow see and wilt not see? Thy mynde telleth thee. Thy understanding furdereth, and thy Judgment doth establish it. That as thow sawest a Body in three places, and of Three Compositions: Thowgh but two in forme, **So shall this work haue relation to 1:** tyme present **and present use, to 2:** Mysteries far exceding **it, And 3: Finally to a purpose and intent, wherby the Maiestie, and Name of God shall and may, and of force must appeare, with the Apparition of his** wonders, and mervayles, **yet unhard of.**[245]

Dixi.[246]

Δ: Than immediately after he began agayne, as followeth,

H: **Venito, veni (inquam) adesto Veni Rex. O Rex, Rex, Rex Aquarum,**[247] **Venito, venito inquam. Magna est tua; maior autem mea potestas. Deus noster, restat, regnat, et est, Quod, et sicut fuit.**[248]

EK: Then cam one and sayd,

------------ Parati sumus nomen eius Creatoris nostri, nomen, nomen laudare Nomen (inquam) Unius nunc   et viuentis.

Obscura sunt hæc animis obscuris. Vera et manifesta Veris et perfectis. Ecce adsunt.[249] EK: He that sayd this, is as thowgh he were a king,

---

[245] A Threfold use of this Doctrine.

[246] Dixi: "I have spoken." -Ed.

[247] Rex Aquarum. -Δ. ("The King of the Waters." -Ed)

[248] Venito . . . fuit: "Come, come (I say), be present. Come, O King. O King, King, King of the waters, come, come I say. You are great, but my power is greater still. Our God stands firm, rules, and is, that which he was." -Ed.

[249] Parati . . . adsunt: "We have been provided his name from our Creator, the name, to praise the name, the Name (I say) of One now [blank space in manuscript] and

with a Crown on his hed: His apparayle was a long robe whitish: But his left arme was very white, and his right arme, black.[250]

EK: There cam after this King a Cumpany of 42: and euery one of them had a letter in his forhed, and they were 7 in a row, and six, downward.

```
. . . . . . .
. . . . . . .
. . . . . . .
. . . . . . .
. . . . . . .
. . . . . . .
```

The King had written in his forhed, BABALEL.[251]

The first 7, (begynning from EK his left hand toward his right) had these letters, and the second, Thirdth &c had these letters as here appeare.

E	I	L	O	M	F	O
N	E	O	T	P	T	A
S	A	G	A	C	I	Y
O	N	E	D	P	O	N
N	O	O	N	M	A	N
E	T	E	V	L	G	L

H: At the next tyme, more.

---

living. These are dark/obscure to dark minds, but true and clear to true and perfect minds. Behold, they are present." -Ed.

[250] Note this Kings apparayle, and shew.

[251] King BABALEL

Δ: Omne quod viuit laudet Deum unum et trinum, in omne æuum.[252] Amen.

EK: The cloth draws.

Nouemb. 20 Tuesday, a meridie circa 2ā.

Δ: After a great half howre attending, and diuerse tymes our prayers to god, The black Cloth was pulled upward: and so vanished away. H appered sitting in his chayre, and his face toward me: and so looking abowt he paused a while: half a quarter of an howr. In the meane space cam one skypping lightly, a little boy, in a grene coate, and sayd, He is here, at an ynche.[253] Than he sayd, Hark. To me he sayd, Ha-sir-ha. Δ: What wilt thow say to me? [Grene Coate:] I am Multin his minister, wilt thow any thing with me? I cannot tarry. Δ: Then this skipiak[254] espyed a spirituall creature comming, and sayd, Ha, ar you there? Δ: And so went out of sight.

Δ: This was King BABALEL, with a crown of Gold on his hed, his garment whitish, and his right sleue on his arme, blak: and the left sleve very white. He seamed to stand uppon water.

The other 42 cam likewise and stode.

Bab: Veni princeps[255] 7 principum qui sunt Aquarum Principes. Ego sum Rex potens et mirabilis in aquis: cuius potestas est aquarum visceribus. Princeps iste[256] (Δ: pointing to a Prince, new come to sight

---

252 Omne . . . aecium: "May everyone living praise God, one and three, into all time." -Ed.

253 At an ynche: "nearby." -Ed.

254 Skipjack: "a dandy, skipping fellow." -Ed.

255 He calleth Befafes.

256 Veni . . . iste: "Come, O prince of the seven princes, who are princes of the Waters. I am the king, mighty and wonderful in the waters, whose power is in the depths of the waters. That prince . . ." -Ed.

which **had a <u>red long robe</u>, and a <u>cerclet</u> of gold on his hed**[257]) est
Tertius principum in Heptagonon.[258] Δ: I sayd Heptagono: he replyed,
Heptagonωn,[259] and sayd: Verè planè, et perspicuè dixi.

Bab: Mensurasti aquas?[260] Befafes answered, Factum est.[261]

Δ: I seemed to dowt of some matter here, and Befafes sayd, Thow
shalt be answered in any dowt. <u>I am thy frende. I haue fauored thee in
many things</u>.[262] Ph'ers[263] haue imagined vaynely of my name. <u>For thy
loue towards me</u>, Thow shalt know my name. I was <u>with Salomon</u>; I
was also (unknown) with Scotus.[264] I was, in respect of my powr:
unknown, in respect of my name. He called me Mares. Since, I was not
with any. <u>And I preserued thee from the powre of the wicked, when I
told thee things of truth to come. When I rid thy howse of wycked
ones, and was with thee in extremities. I was with thee. Behold I was
with thee throwghly.</u>

Δ: Then he bad EK Ax me, yf I knew Obelison. Δ: I had to do with
Obelison, but by reason of my Skryers nawghtynes, I was in dowt what
I might credit.   Bef: Thow shalt <u>know this for a most manifest
truth</u> hereafter. I am Obelison, the <u>fifth of the Seuenth</u>,[265] which haue
the skowrging of <u>Obelison the wicked</u>: but not wicked for euer, neyther

---

[257] The Prince his apparayle.

[258] . . . est Tertius principum in Heptagonon: ". . . is the third Principality in the
Heptagon." -Ed.

[259] Heptagono: "(in) the Heptagon." Dee seems to be checking or correcting Kelley
here. –Ed.

[260] Vere . . . aquas: "I have spoken quite plainly and distinctly. . . . Have you measured the waters?" -Ed.

[261] Factum est: "It is so." -Ed.

[262] Prince Befafes, my old frende unknown of me.

[263] Philosophers. -Ed.

[264] John Scotus Erigena (815?-877 theologian)? Michael Scot (introduced transla-
tions of Aristotle)? John Duns Scotus (1265?-1308 theologian)? –Ed.

[265] Δ The fifth of the seventh. I understand not this yet. Vide lib. 5. A° 1583 Maij 1.

accursed to the ende. <u>We Angels haue tymes, and our faultes are amended</u>.[266]

Δ: Shall I Note your name, by Befafes? He answered, My name is so, in dede: The Ægyptians called me Obelison in respect of my nature. Δ: I pray you what is the Etymologie of Obelison? Bef: <u>A pleasant deliuerer</u>.[267]

EK: The former <u>7, haue Crownes</u>.[268] Theyr letters stand betwene theyr feete.[269]

E I L O M F O &c.

Bef: Thow hast receyued these letters allready.
EK: <u>The water seameth, contynually to pass ouer these letters</u>.
Bab: I Gouern uppon Tuesday.

1. EK: **The first seuen take the water and throw it up, and it becometh clowdes.**
2. **The second throweth it up, and it becommeth <u>hayle and snow</u>.** One of <u>the first 7</u> sayde, Behold, Behold, Behold: All the <u>motion</u> of the waters, and the <u>saltnes</u> thereof is æqually assured by us. We giue good <u>success in battayles</u>, reduce ships & all manner of vessells that flote uppon the seas: Our make is great. Muse not [Δ], For whan the seas are trubbled, with the wickednes or uprore of man, our Authoritie giueth victory from him that is most Victorious. <u>Fishes and Monsters</u> of the sea, yea all that liueth therein, are well known with us. Behold we are (generally) the <u>Distributers of Gods Judgments uppon the waters that **couer the earth.**</u>

   EK: Than stept furth all the rest.

---

[266] NOTE: of wicked spirits, some restitution to favor.

[267] See. 4th Enochian Call: "obelisong" is translated "as pleasant deliverers." -Ed.

[268] Or Cerclets perhaps.

[269] HM reads, "Euery one of the 42 had a letter in his forhed. They were 7 in a row:

3. <u>The Third</u> seuen sayd, Some of us <u>conduct the waters</u> throwgh the earthe. Other of us, do <u>beawtify Nature</u> in her Composition. The <u>rest of us ar distributers</u> and Deliuerers <u>of the Threasures and the unknown</u> substances of the seas.[270]

Bab: Praysed be God which hath created us, from the begynning with Glory. His Glory be augmented.

EK: **Now the 42 diue into the Water and so vanish away: and Befafes, and Babalel also wer suddaynly gon.**

H standing up sayd, LO, **Thus thow seest the glory of Gods creatures: Whome <u>thow mayst use</u>,[271] with the consideration of the day, theyr king, theyr Prince, and his Character. <u>The King and prince gouern for the whole daye</u>.[272] The rest according <u>to the six partes of the day</u>.**

Use them, to the glory, prayse, and honor of him, which created them to the Laude and prayse of his Maiestie. A day is 24 howres. Δ: But whan doth that Day begyn?

H: Thow shalt be towght the rest.

H proceded, and sayd, Vitam dedit Deus omnibus Creaturis. Venite Veni <u>Ignis</u>, veni Vita mortalium (inquam) Venito. Adesdum. <u>Regnat Deus</u>. Ô Venite. Nam unus ille Regnat, et est Vita Viuentium.[273]

----

and 6, downward. But of the first 7 the letters became to be between theyr feet, and the water seamed contynually to pass over these letters." -Ed.

[270] Threasors in the seas.

[271] Practise.

[272] King and Prince govern the whole day.

[273] Δ: Whereas in the former Treatise, ther was a dowt of Butmono the fowrth, and Blisdon theyr offyces, being assigned here clere contrary: The dowt may be answered by the notes A. 1583, Maij 5 of the Table and my Character. Therefore I suspect some Intruder to have first .... -Δ. Vitam . . . Viuentium: "God gave life

EK: <u>Now there commeth a King,</u>[274] <u>and hath a Prince</u>[275] <u>next him</u> <u>and after them 42, like ghostes, or smokes, with out forme; hauing</u> <u>euery of them a little glittring spark of fire in the myddest of them.</u>

The first 7, are red, as blud.   }   The sparks of these were
The second 7, not so red.   }   greater then of
The third 7 like whitish smoke.   the rest.

The fowrth 7   }   are of diuerse cullours: All had firie sparks
The fifth   }   in theyr myddle. Euery spark had a letter in it.
The sixth

Verè beatus[276] (sayd this King that						
now cam.)	B	B	A	R	N	F	L
Δ: I pray you to tell me your name.	B	B	A	I	G	A	O
King: I am the fowrth King in the Table	B	B	A	L	P	A	E
and the two* and twentyth in number.	B	B	A	N	I	F	G
Δ: I understand in the Table of the names	B	B	O	S	N	I	A
collected from the 7 Tables of 49.	B	B	A	S	N	O	D

And in those tables taking of the first septenarie, Baligon for the first King; and in the second septenarie, Bobogel for the second King, and in the third septenarie, taking Babalel, so accownted the third, and in the fowrth septenarie, the first of septenarie is Bynepor, and so accownted the fowrth: but accownting euery one from Baligon he is the 22th: and so the fowrth and the two and twentith.

---

to all creatures. Come ye, come O fire. Come, O life of mortals Come (I say). Be present. God rules. O come. For he alone rules, and is the life of the living." -Ed.

[274] HM identifies this as King Bynepor. -Ed.

[275] Butmono. -Ed.

[276] Verè beatus: "Truly blessed." -Ed.

EK: A Voyce I here, saying, You shall begynne to work agayn, at 6 of the clok next.

Δ: Omnium bonorum largitori, laus perennis et immensa.277
Amen.

Δ: Abowt half a quarter of an howre after 6: we retorned to the work and the cloth was drawn away: H sitting in the chayre.

EK: There appeared a little ronning water very clere chrystalline: and on this side the 42 last specifyed.

Bynepor sayd: Lo, [and than he kneled down, and semed to pray, a prety while]. The generall state and condition of all things resteth onely and dependeth uppon the distribution, and participation of my exalted most especiall and glorified powr. My sanctification, glory, and renowne, allthowgh it had begynning, cannot, shall not nor will haue ending. He that Measureth, sayd,278 and I was the ende of his workmanship. I am like him, and of him, yet not as partaking nor adherent, but distant in One degree. The Fire that holdeth, or is, the first Principle of all things in generally,279 hath his universall and unmeasurable powre in the workmanship of my Creation. Visible and Invisible, were not, withoute my record. When he [Ipse280] cam, I was magnified by his comming, and I am sanctifyed, world Without ende.

Vita suprema,
Vita superior,

---

277 Omnium . . . immensa: "Perpetual and unlimited praise for the giver of all good." -Ed.

278 Ipse dixit. -Δ. ("He himself said." -Ed.)

279 Generaltye.

280 Ipse: "himself." -Ed.

et Infima, sunt meis mensurata manibus.[281] Notwithstanding, I am
not of my self, Neyther is my powre myne owne, Magnified by his
name: Behold I dubble <u>life from One</u>, unto a thowsand of Thowsands:
and One thowsand of thowsands, to a number, exceding cownt: I speak
in respect of mans Capacitie. <u>I am in all and all hath some being by me:</u>
yet my powre is nothing in respect of his powre, which hath sent me.
<u>Write this reuerently.</u> Note it with <u>Submission</u>: What I speak hath not
byn reuealed, no not in these last tymes, of <u>the second last world</u>.[282]
But I begynne <u>new worldes, new people, new kings</u>, & new knowledge
of a new Gouernment.[283] To be short,

> Vitam tradidit; deditque mihi potestatem
>
> esse, Viuere, et in perpetuum glorifica...
>
> Omnibus et ubique.[284]

As these cannot be comprehended, what they are, with mor...

So cannot any thing be browght to pas in me, <u>without a living sight,
and a perfect mynde</u>.[285] I Gouern uppon Thursday. For Instruction, the
rest as before. <u>Thow shalt work mervaylous mervaylously, by my
workmanship</u> in the highest. To whome[286] (with overshaddowing thy
light with life, and blessing you both, in his name of whome I am the
Image,) I prayse God.

EK: Now he descendeth into the Globe, and it becam very bright
there among the people: which, allso, at his comming, seamed to be
more cherefull.

---

281 Vita . . . manibus: "The highest life, the higher life, and the lowest life are measures by my hands." -Ed.

282 Note second last world.

283 Ecce, omnia Noua. -Δ. ("Behold, all things are new." -Ed.)

284 Vitam . . . ubique: "He surrenders life, and gives me power to be, and to live in
perpetual glory. Everything and everywhere." -Ed.

285 Note.

286 Δ I dowt, I did not here perfectly at this writing down.

H stode up and moved his hand, aboue his hed, cumpassing with it a loft.[287] After that cam a Cumpany, with a King,[288] and after him a prince.[289] <u>The king had a red robe on, and a crown on his hed.</u> The <u>Prince had a robe of many cullours</u>, and on his hed a Cerclet. **The Cumpany [42] seemed to stand rownd abowt a little hill of Claye. Behynde this Cumpany seamed to stand an innumerable multitude of ugly people, a far of:**[290] **Those which seeme to stand rownd abowt the little hill seme to haue in <u>the palmes of theyr hands</u>, letters, in order as here appereth.**

Δ: The king spake, Beholde, All <u>the Earth with her bowells and secrets what soeuer, are deliuered unto me.</u> And what I am there thow mayst know. I am great, But he, in whome I am, is greater then I. Unto <u>my</u> Prince, (my Subiect) <u>are deli- uered the keyes of the Mysteries of the earth. All these are Angells that gouern under him:</u> whose Gouernment is diuided, as before. <u>Use them, they are and shalbe at thy commaundement.</u>[291]

<u>Those that stand afarr</u> off are the Spirits of perdition, <u>which kepe earth with</u> her Threasor, for him &c: and so furth.[292] I haue sayd.

----

287 Cumpassing with it a loft: circling it around in the air. -Ed.

288 Δ Bnaspol.

289 Δ Blisdon.

290 An Innumerable Cumpany of ugly Creatures, a far of.

291 Vide Lib°. 5, 1583 Martij 26.

292 Vide de istis in libro Cracoviensi Junij 26. Treasure hid in earth, kept by wycked spirites. -Δ. See TFR, p. 180. -Ed.

H, standing up, sayd, His name is the fifth and the 29th: and his Prince his name, the fifth, and the 23th.[293] Δ: The first name, I understand in Tabula collecta, The second name I understand, for the fifth to be in Heptagono and the 23th to be so fownd the same, in Tabula collecta.

H: Venite, ubi nulla quies, sed stridor dentium.[294]

EK: Then cam the man agayn, with ugly fyrie flames out of his sides, which was here before, the last day.[295] H beckened with his hand unto him, and his coates went to gither, and so couered that horrible sight.

EK: **There appeareth a rownd Table, which 42 hold and toss, all in fyrie flames.**

H: Write quickly, thow [EK] canst not behold it.

EK: The first seameth to be a King[296] with a crown on his hed, and the &c.

Lo I gouern (as I[297] haue sayd before) All enchanters, Coniurers, witches, & Wicked spirites that are hated of God, and included for euer, in owteward darknes (except a few which remayn in a second payne, which gape and grone for the mercies of God, and haue tyme of Ioye, whose measures I haue, and kepe accownt of) are all at my gov- ernment.[298] By me, thow shalt cast oute **the powre of all wicked spirits. By me thow shalt know the** doings and practises of euill men, **and more then may be spoken or uttred to man.**

---

293 Bnaspol, Blisdon.

294 Venite . . . dentium: "**Come here,** where there is no peace, but only the gnashing of teeth." -Ed.

295 Prince Brorges. -Ed.

296 The King.

297 Mark who sayd so **before.** -Δ. This was Carmara at the beginning of Book 4. -Ed.

298 Note a great Secret of **spirits** in payn expecting release.

Blessed be his name, whose Glory is euerlasting fode to the Just, and Sempiternall[299]8 to the Wicked.

H: The 36[the] name, is the King his <u>name,</u>[300] And his Prince his name.[301] is the last [saue one] written in the Heptagonon.[302]

H: **Venite vos qui sub mea estis potestate.**[303]

EK: **Then cam bright <u>People</u> 42: And besides these, all <u>the Ayre swarmeth</u> with creatures. Theyr letters are in theyr forheds: these stand in a circle: they take the letters from theyr forheds, and set them in a Circle.**[304]

---

[299] Somwhat was not hard of me, or forgot. Perhaps Terror.

[300] Δ: Bnapsen.

[301] Δ: Brorges.

[302] Note A. 1583, Maij. Thus I considered In dede after a sort Brorges may be cownted as last, for the begyning secretly was with Bralges.

[303] Bralges sayd his government was of such: super fol. 4.b. -Δ. Venite . . . potestate: "Come you who are under my power." -Ed.

[304] The Circle of letters.

H: Of these, I am <u>Gouernor my self.</u>[305] Behold I am of <u>tyme pres-</u>
<u>ent</u>. I am of the <u>last Ternarie.</u>[306] Loke what may be wrowght, <u>in all</u>
<u>aëriall Actions</u>, I can distribute and bestow at my pleasure: my tyme
and day, is <u>Friday</u>. The day of the last before, is Saterday. The day of the
Fifth is Wensday.

H: Behold,

I haue towght thee. His name be blessed who raigneth and liueth for
euer.

Δ: Amen, Amen, Amen.

H: I will answer thee of all Dowtes herein (being demaunded of me) to
morrow. For, so I call it, for thy sake: Not, for that, it is so to me.

Δ: So he went away.

Δ: Then cam URIEL and MICHAEL, and an other (I think RAPHAEL)
and the chayre and table appered, as in the first boke hath byn shewed:
And also H had his peculier chayre, at his tymes of teaching me.

MICHAEL (sayd,[307]) **Mercifull is our God, and glorious is his name**
Which chuseth his creatures, according to his own Secret Judgment and
good pleasure.

---

[305] HM notes, "Prince Bagenol appeared not, by that name, yet. Note, the king him
self [Baligon, aka CARMARA] is governor ouer these." -Ed.

[306] The last Ternarie. That is expownded lib°. 5. Maij 5.

[307] Note, As Michael and Uriel, at the begynning of these revealed mysteries, were
present, and gaue Authority to Carmara, to order the whole Heptarchicall

This Arte is the <u>first part of</u> a <u>Threefold Art,</u>[308] ioyning Man (with the Knowledge of 1. the <u>WORLDE</u>, 2. the <u>GOVERNMENT</u> of his Creatures, and 3. the <u>SIGHT</u> of his Maiestie.):

Unto him (Ô, I say) unto him; which is

Strength, Medicine, and Mercie[309]

to those that feare him:

Amen.

Δ: Gloria, laus, honor, et perennis Jubilatio,

sit Deo nostro Omnipotenti,

Optimo, Maximoque.[310]Amen.

Δ: Note, Remember, and enquire what it meaneth, that no Mention is made of Bralges the Prince, Nor of Blumaza his king in this Treatise, being a certayn Repetition of the Heptagonum stellare, going next before.[311]

Reuelation, so, at the Conclusion, they appeared agayn and Raphael with them, and Michael concluded the second boke (of this particular Reuelation Heptarchicall,) with these words following. -Δ (HM).

[308] Prima pars Artis Triplicis: he termeth this afterward of three proportions in Esse. Consider these three principall points here. -Δ. Prima pars Artis Triplicis: "The first part of a triple art." -Ed.

[309] Annael.

[310] Gloria . . . Maximoque: "May glory, laud, honor, and eternal thanksgiving be to our God, almighty and all good." -Ed.

[311] 1588. On twelfth day at night as I considered the Method of this boke, this cam to my mynde. -Δ. Dee's diary fills in some of the events between this action and the next: "[1582] Nov. 22nd, E.K. went to London, and so the next day conveied by rode toward Blakley, and within ten dayes to returne. Nov. 24th, Saterday night I dremed that I was deade, and afterward my bowels wer taken out I walked and talked with diverse, and among other with the Lord Thresorer who was com to my howse to burn my bokes when I was dead, and thought he loked

Wensday: Nouemb 21. hora 7 a meridie

Δ: There appered the first table, covered with a cloth of silk changeable <u>cullour red and grene</u>:[312] with <u>a white cloth</u> under it: all hanging very low. The first Chayre allso: wherein Michael used to sit. And H did appere likewise, <u>and his peculier chayre</u>:[313] and he standing by it. But the Diaphanous Globe, and the people or world in it, <u>did not now appere</u>, and, bycause no voyce or word cam from those spirituall creatures, yet: I declared that I did attend theyr pleasure first, as a scholer comming in the presence of his Master, and whan they had sayd those things which were for us first, (at this instant) to lerne, that than, I wold move some dowtes of the premisses, as I was yesterday advised to do. H, he held up his rod (which had two portions or partes of it black and one, red): and sayde,

Ô quanta est hõis infirmitas et Corruptio, qui Angelis, idque suis bonis, fidem autem Deo, vix habet? Omnia mundana, fæces: Mundi Corruptiones in se habent: Deus noster, Deus noster, Deus (inquam) ille noster verus, cum Veris suis angelis, eique[314] inseruientibus Semper verus est. Pete quæ vis? Dixi: et quod dixi, obumbratum est veritate, iusticia et perfectione.[315]

---

sourely on me. [1583] Feb. 26th, I delivered my boke to the Lord Threasorer for the correction of the Calender. March 6th, I, and Mr. Adrian Gilbert and John Davis, did mete with Mr. Alderman Barnes, Mr. Townson and Mr. Yong and Mr. Hudson, abowt the N.W. voyage. March 18th, Mr. North from Poland, after he had byn with the Quene he cam to me. I receyved salutation from Alaski, Palatine in Poland; salutation by Mr. North who cam before to the Quene, and next to me was his message, hor. 12." Halliwell, ed., *The Private Diary of Dr. John Dee* (New York: AMS Press, 1968), pp. 18–19.

312 Note. The cullour red and grene of the Table of Covenant. Two chayres.

313 Two Chayres.

314 Idque.

315 O quanta . . . perfectione: "O how great is the weakness and corruption of mankind, that has little faith in angels and their good deeds, but hardly any faith in God. All worldly things contain the corruption of the world within them. Our

Ecce, (Δ: holding up the rod[316]).

Hîc (Δ: pointing to the ende of the rod).

Per hoc (Δ: pointing to the middle of it).

Et a Mensuræ fine, nos nostramque <u>mensurabis</u>

potestatem. Age (inquam) Quid vis?[317]

Δ: I, than, of the premisses used a little discourse: how they might parabolically,[318] betoken other more profownd matter, and litterally other: yet what sense so euer the premisses had, that theyr first rudiments and Text was to be made somwhat playner to me, then yet they were: bycause I dowted as well of the understanding of some of that, I had written, as allso of mys writing: eyther throwgh EK his mys reporting to me matter shewed to him, or by my mys-hering or negligent writing &c. To some part therof he sayd these words ensuing.

H: In umbra mortis non est æqualitas. **Obscurum enim nihil est quod per <u>illum</u> [EK] recepisti. Age.**[319]

H: **Thow hast a work of <u>three proportions</u> in esse;[320] of 7 in forme: which is of it self diuided by a number septenarie, of the <u>course, estate and determination of things aboue, things next, and things below</u>:**

God, our God, he (I say) our God is true, and is true with his true angels and those who ever serve him. Ask for what you wish. I have spoken, and what I have spoken that was obscure, was in truth, justice, and perfection." -Ed.

[316] Note of this Rod.

[317] Ecce . . . Hic . . . Per hoc . . . Et a Mensurae . . . vis? "Behold . . . here, . . . and here. . . . And from the end of the measure you will measure us and our power. Practice (I say). What do you wish?" -Ed.

[318] Parabolically: using parable. -Ed

[319] In umbra . . . Age: "In the shadow of death there is no equality. Nothing is obscure which you have received through him (E.K.). Practice." -Ed.

[320] A Threefold work.

which, of it self is pure perfect and without blemish.[321] Notwithstanding I will answer thee thus.

The 7 Kings are orderly conteyned in the first of the Seuens diuided
in generall numbers: whose names are expressed; published and perfectly formed within the first grownd and fowndacion of this Threefold
work.[322] The kings I meane with theyr Characters,[323] and the names of
theyr 7 liuing and semper adherent Ministers:[324] Whose names thow
mayst see not onely there written, but openly, and most playnely, truely,
and sincerely spoken of before:[325] as, by due examination of thy bokes
thow shalt manifestly perceyue. Notwithstanding, as euery king, in his
Maiestie, doth comprehend the dignitie of his whole seat and estate, so
I of my self being the First, haue the gouernment of my self perfectly, as
a mysterie known unto my self: which is a thing unlawfull to be published unto man and lawfull[326] in respect of the charge committed unto
us: and the slender Dignification of mans frayle estate; Which thow
mayst see in the Heptagonon: where, there wanteth a name: the rest of
the Cr... the utter Circumference of the Globe, are the Six Kings Or ...
following: according as they are written in the Mysteries of the ...
which do begynne the[327] Powres, with theyr Prince,[328] and theyr
Characters orderly taken, by and uppon the Heptagonon ...

Ô God, how easy is this first understanding. Thow hast byn told

---

[321] In HM, Dee attributes this to "Carmara, Nouemb. 21. in appendix of the second
boke." -Ed.

[322] Threfold Work.

[323] The Kings with their Characters.

[324] An, Aue, Rocle, Liba. I understand of Il, An, Aue, &c in the characters of the 7
kings.

[325] Filij Filiorum - An, Aue, &c. Examination to be made of these bokes. -Δ. Filii
Filiorum: "Sons of the Sons" -Ed.

[326] Δ fortè "Unlawfull" and was myshard.

[327] Forte: "their." –Ed.

[328] Princis.

perfectly, playnely and absolutely, not onely the <u>Condition, dignitie, and estate</u> of <u>all things that God hath framed</u>: But allso withall, thow wart deliuered the <u>most perfect forme and use of them.</u>[329]

But this will I tell thee (to the intent thow shalt know: and forby cause I wold not, thow sholdest be ignorant in <u>true Wisdome</u>) that those <u>Six</u> Names in and uppon the Heptagonum are Collected, do growe and are gathered from the names in generally aforesayd.[330]

Take the Names, I will teache thee to know them, which els, [without] by direction[331] thow canst not fynde.

 Loke thy First Table. I am called BALIGON <u>with men</u>. Thow hast Noted my name (which is secret) <u>among the Angels,</u>[332] begynning with this letter M, consisting of 7 letters, the last being an A.

I am called MARMARA: but otherwise CARMARA : but that letter <u>M, shall not be expressed</u>, &c.

Thow seest, next, BOBOGEL, He it is that is the Second King. Thow seest the name BORNOGO, to be the <u>first</u>[333] uppon the Heptagonum: <u>it is his Prince</u>. And therfore I did Note him with a Coronet, and not with a Crown: nay rather, but with a Cerclet abowt his hed. &c[334]

---

[329] Liber Creationis. Note, what hath bin tawght in this boke. -Δ. HM attributes this saying to Carmara, Nouemb. 21. Liber Creationis: "Book of Creation." -Ed.

[330] Δ: as may appere by the 49 names Collected.

[331] Δ: I suspect this to be an imperfect phrase.

[332] Name among Angels

[333] Δ = name expressed.

[334] Note Attire.

Δ: I concluded (of his instruction) the Kings and theyr Princes, theyr names to be thus lerned out of the Table Collected of 49, names, it is to weete,[335]

1	--Δ--	44
8	-----	2
*15	-----	9
22	-----	16
29	-----	23
36	-----	30
43	--Δ--	37

} modo retrogrado quasi[336]

** As far as I remember, he sayd, My Prince is in my self: which is a mysterie

~~My Coniecture (hereuppon, and uppon this retrograde respect to finde the princis among the 49 names in Tabula~~ *** ~~Collecta) is, that Baginol is the Prince under BALIGON: bycause the letters are all one: but the order of theyr places diuerse: and so is his prince conteyned in him self.~~

Rex   Princeps

~~Δ He then allowed of my Coniecture for these .6. but of his Prince~~
~~Δ I than sayd nothing: tyll at the fayr writing hereof, this, here added, cam into my mynde. How well, I know not yet: Novemb .23.~~

---

[335] It is to weete: "that is to say." -Ed.

[336] Modo retrogrado quasi: "now as if going backward." -Ed.

* Addendo 7 - fit hic processus. Ergo addendo 7, numero 43, proueniet 50: numerus: major 40 quam 49 per .1. qui respicere pt illum: primum Regem Baligon.[337]

** addendo 7, fit processus hic g°. Si 7 addantur numero 37: inde emerget 44. pro proximo principe.[338]

~~*** It is not Baginol, but Bagenol, with e not i, and therfore consider.~~

---

and farder he sayd, <u>The Characters of Kings, are in the **Globe**;</u>[339] <u>and of the Princis, in the Heptagonon.</u>

Δ: Note: from the 👉 on the last side, untyll these words finished, he was out of sight: and whan he had ended these words, he cam in sight agayn: and browght a thing in his hand like a sterre: ✡ or Heptagonum.

H: Beholde. <u>Euery one of these Princis hath</u>[340] <u>his peculier Table.</u> Thow hast Noted the <u>First Table</u> which begynneth, as I will tell thee.

1. 2: In BOBOGEL, that O, (the second letter) is the first of the Table OESNGLE and the second of Befafes, is the second, and the thirdth of the third: and the fowrth of the fowrth and the fifth of the fifth, and the sixth of the sixth, and E, (in the

---

[337] Addendo . . . Baligon: "This course is made by adding 7. Therefore adding 7 to the number 43 results in 50: a number one greater than 49, which may indicate the first king, Baligon." -Ed.

[338] Addendo . . . principe: "This course is made by adding 7. Therefore if 7 is added to the number 37, from there results 44 for the next prince." -Ed.

[339] Δ: Note that he calleth that contynually A Globe. Uppon such a globe Nalvage shewed out all the Calls.

[340] HM reads "must have." -Ed.

seuenth. Bnagole is the seuenth and last of this first seuen of this
first Table: <u>accownted the first</u>. ¶ AVZHILN.[341]

The second seuen by like order is gathered of Babalel, and
the rest of his septenarie. And so furth, to the ende downward as
thow didst before &c.

2. 3: In the second Table; L (the first letter therof) is out of Bobogel
his last letter, the second letter, is the sixth of Befafes; the third,
is the fifth of Basmelo &c and so you haue LEENARB.[342] For
the rest kepe that order downward to the ende of the last Name
Bamnode. Tranversim, quasi retrograde.[343]

3. 4: In the Third, begyn at the lower[344] letter [<u>of the latter</u>[345]
<u>worde</u>] of the last of the second seven: and so upward, toward
the right[346] hand: Δ: The last word is of second seven is
Bnagole: the last letter therof is e: which is the first of this
Third Table: and the i, in Brisfli, is the second, and the l in
Branglo the thirdth, and than so furth, upward, overthwart,
toward the left hand: till ye come to Bobogel, his second letter, being O. Then to N in Bonefor: e in Bermale: o in Bragiop.
&c.

4. 5: For the Fowrth, loke, Bobogel. Then loke to this fowrth Table
the first B of the Table is the first B of Bobogel. The second B of
this Table, is the B of Befafes. The third letter is <u>a</u>, the second letter of Basmelo. The fowrth letter, <u>R</u>, is the thirdth of Bernole.
The fifth is the fowrth of Branglo. The sixth, is the fifth of

---

[341] King . . . first . . . answering to Blumaza as I perceyued 1583 Maij 5, manè by
meditation: and of Necessity must be: yf the last be for Baligon.

[342] The next l is the last letter of Babalel, and then transversim as before, &c.

[343] Traversim quasi retrograde: "Going crosswise as if backwards." -Ed.

[344] Last.

[345] Last.

[346] Left.

Brisfli. The seuenth is the sixth of Bnagole. And so in to the next sevens downward orderly for the rest of the table.

5. 6: The Fifth begynneth from Bnagole upward: begynning at the last letter being e: and then upward croswise exactly tyll the B of Bobogel. And so of the next seuen, for the next: begynning at the n of Bonefon, and so furth.

6. 7: In the sixth, (the Infernall Table) The first is B of Bobogel, The second is A of the 15th: The third is N of the 22th: the fowrth, is the fowrth of the 29: The fifth of the 36: the sixth of the 43: and the seuenth of the 49: being E in Bamnode, two letters being taken in that last septenarie. The second septenarie begynneth at the first of the 15th, the second at the second of the 22th, (being Y), the third at the thirdth of the 29th, then the 4th of the 30th,: the 5th of the 43th.

7. 1: The Seuenth: the first A, is the A, of Baligon, and so downward all the second letters of the 7 kings: Then all the third letters, then all the fowrth letters, then all the fifth letters, then all the sixth letters only and finally the seventh and last letters of the first names of the Septenaries.

Δ: Note, this Table is made all of Kingly substance &c.

Δ: Now I trust I understand (meterly well,[347]) the making of the 7 Tables. I wold gladly here som instruction of the great Circular table (which you call the Globe) which hath the Kn... with theyr Characters; and so within, 7 tymes 7, seuen tymes . . . 7 tymes 6, seuen tymes furnished with letters and numbers . . . sorts.

H: That doth apperteyn to an other tyme.[348]

EK: The Cloth was lett down, and the stone did yield voyce but nothing visible but the forsayd blak cloth.

---

[347] Meterly well: "fairly well." -Ed.

[348] The use of the Circular Table (here before often called a Globe) at another tyme.

H: One thing is yet wanting: <u>a mete receptacle</u> &c. There is yet wanting <u>a stone</u> &c. One there is, most excellent, hid in the secret of the depth &c. In the uttermost part of the <u>Roman Possession</u>.

H: Write. All lawd, Glorie and honor be unto him, which rayneth for euer. Amen. Be of good Cumfort.

Lo, the mighty hand of God is uppon thee.

Thow shalt haue it. Thow shalt haue it, Thow shalt haue it. Dost thow see, loke and styr not from thy place: EK pointed toward it.

Δ: I see it not.

H: It is sanctified, blessed, and . . . .[349] in the use of his Creatures.

<u>**Thow shalt preuayle with it, with Kings, and with all Creatures of the world: Whose beauty (in vertue) shall be more worth then the Kingdomes of the earth.**</u>

Loke, if thow see it: But styr not, for the Angel of his powre is present.

EK loked toward my west wyndow, and saw there first uppon the matts by my bokes a thing, (to his thinking) as bigg as an egg: most bright, clere, and glorious: and <u>an angel</u> of the heyth of a little chylde <u>holding up the same thing</u> in his hand toward me: and that Angel had a <u>fyrey sword</u> in his hand &c.[350]

H: Go toward it; and take it up.

Δ: I went toward the place, which EK pointed to: and tyll I cam within two fote of it, I saw nothing: and then I saw like a shaddow on the grownd or matts hard by my bokes under the west wyndow. The shaddow was rowndysh, and less then the palm of my hand. I put my hand down uppon it, and I felt a thing cold and hard: which, (taking up, I) perceyued to be the stone before mentioned.[351]

---

[349] I omitted a word, and our memories could not yeld it, this perhaps, Dignifyed.

[350] An angel holding up the stone.

[351] This stone brought by the Angel is said to bee an nich thick in the following Mysteriorum Lib. 5. Ms. p. El. Ash: conceives it to have been of a lenticular

H: **Kepe it sincerely.**

Veritas in veritate: Deus in Deo, Unus in uno est.[352]

Let no mortall hand towche it, but thyne owne:[353]

Prayse God.

Δ: Illi qui venturus est Indicare Sæculum per ignem sit omnis honor, laus, et gloria, in sempiterna sæcula.[354] Amen.

---

forme, included in a circular limb upon the top of which a cross, & edgewise sett in the frame. -E.A. See action of 5 May 1583. -Ed.

[352] Veritas . . . uno est: "Truth is within truth, God within God, One is within one." -Ed.

[353] ☞ caue. -Δ. ("Beware." -Ed.)

[354] Illi . . . saecula: "May all honor, praise, and glory be to him who is to reveal the age through fire, forever and ever." Perhaps *indicere is intented: "to inflict (the age with fire)." Ashmole reads Iudicare: "to judge." -Ed.

Liber Mysteriorum

Quintus

1583 Martij 23.

Liber 6us.
Liber 7us[1]

---

[1] The words "Liber 6us. / Liber 7us." are in Ashmole's handwriting. -Ed.

Jesus †.

Anno 1583 Martij 23. Saterday a meridie.

Δ: EK being come, with Mr John Husey of Blokley. (on the 22 day of marche) and EK being desirous to understand somwhat of our spirituall frendes as concerning such matter as had falln out very strange to him and Mr Husey: abowt a certayne moniment of a boke and a skroll fownd in Northwik hill[2] by the direction and leading of such a spirituall Creature, as when they had gotten the same, and they endeuored by art to haue some exposition of the skroll, written in strange characters, they wer willed to repayre to me, and there they shold be answered: &c. which thing now they did.[3]

Being therfor now ready to receyue instructions of our frendes, there appered in the stone One,[4] in a foles cote, going abowt a clowde, which appered first in the stone. I charged him if he were the enemy of God to depart. He tore his clothes all, and appeared all hery under: and sayd, Penetrasti vim iniusticæ meæ.[5]

Δ: Glorifie God and depart. He sayd, Feci, Nam decedo.[6] He went away as it had byn a bunsh of fethers pulld in peces. The Clowd wexed bigger, and went all to the right hand. At length the Table appeared, But the Chayre seamed not to be of the same sort it was, but more Glorious. There appeared three, of which, two went away, and one tarryed behynde.

He sayd----------Auete.

---

2   The boke fownd in Northwik hill.

3   The scroll is shown below before the April 11th Action. It shows the locations of ten hidden treasures. -Ed.

4   Pilosus. -Δ ("Hairy." -Ed.)

5   Penetrasti . . . meae: "You penetrated the power of my iniquity." -Ed.

6   Feci, Nam decedo: "I am done, for I depart." -Ed.

Verum est, et incredibile.[7] He kneeled to the Chayre and spake, but his words could not be discerned.

Via, veritas, et virtus, unum sunt: et multiplex et admirabilis est eius magnitudo: Et venit ab ore tuo flatus, (et vitam habet) quo viuunt omnia, nutu, et illuminatione tua.

Aue Verbum, Aue rerum formatrix[8] et mensura eorum quæ fuerunt, sunt, et erunt: Illuminasti oculos creaturarum monimentis et admonitionibus planis: Vita bonis, mors autem impijs, et a consideratione tua abiectis. Quanta et innumerabiliæ sunt (Iustitia) dona tua? O remiges varpax. Kyrie eleyson.[9]

Δ: All this he sayd Kneeling to the chayre; and then he rose; and I sayde, O beata Trinitas, mitte lucem et veritatem tuam, ut ipam me ducant ad montem sanctum, et ad tabernacula tua.

Me: Ubi, non increduli.

Δ: Nos non sumus increduli: sed spes nostra viuit æterna et Omnipotens est Veritas, fons vitæ.

Me: Adduxi vobis aquam[10] ex eodem riuulo. Medicina verò est imperfectionibus et necessitatibus vestris. Intelligite nunc et quis sum, et quibus ornatus. Bibite, et accipite Ossibus vestris pinguedinen. Multæ namque sunt mortalium imperfectiones. habeo, et habebitis: Adduxi, et videbiter. Verbum est Lumen illud quo omnis imperfectio

---

7   Auete. Verum est, et incredibile: "Greetings. It is the truth, and incredible." -Ed.

8   Iustitia. -Δ ("Justice" -Ed.)

9   Via . . . eleyson: "The way, the truth, and the virtue are one, and his greatness is manifold and wonderful. And the breath comes from your mouth (and has life) from which everything lives, by your command and your light. Hail the word, hail the creator of things and of their measure which have been, are, and will be. You have illuminated the eyes of the creatures by reminders and plain warnings. Life to the good, but death to the wicked, and those cast from your consideration. How great and innumerable are your gifts? O remiges varpax. Lord have mercy." -Ed.

10   Aqua. -Δ ("Water." -Ed)

aboletur. Credentes introibu... in Sanctum eius. vbi potio, et <u>Medicina</u> sempiterna.[11]

Cogitasti verè. Sum etiam, et Credas. Nam veritate et iustitia, vera et perfecta sunt verba et disciplina eius.[12] What willt thow?

Δ: Recte sapere.[13] Me: <u>Thow hast it.</u>

Δ: I perceyue it not otherwise, then that I beleue, it may be the decree of the highest.

Δ: He shewed a Tree, and a great deale of water at the roote or botom of it: and he sayd, Me: Hath this Tree, now, any frute?

Δ: I see it not. But the skryer may say.

EK: The water commeth up the tree, and it swelleth, and it hath frute, great, fayre, and red.

Me: Lo I eate of it my self, and it lighteth the harts of those that are chosen. [He semeth to eate.] <u>So is it in thee.</u>

Δ: Ecce seruus Domini, fiat Decretum eius in me (iuxta misericordiam eius) de me pronunciatum.[14]

Me: Go and thow shallt receyue. Tary, and you shall receyue slepe, and you shall see, But watch, and your eyes shall be fully opened. One

---

11 Loquitur de mea cogitatione, quod esset Raphaël. -Δ. ("He speaks concerning my thought that he may be Raphael." -Ed.)

12 O Beata Trinitas . . . eius: "O blessed Trinity, send your light and your truth, that they may lead me to the holy mountain and to your tent. Me: Where, O unbelievers? Δ: We are not unbelievers, but our hope is alive, and the eternal and almighty truth is the fountain of life. Me: I brought you water from that same stream. It is a true medicine for your imperfections and needs. Understand now both who I am and for whom I was adorned. Drink and receive the abundance for your bones [can also be figurative: innermost part, soul]. For many are the imperfections of mortals. I have and you (pl) will have. I brought, and he shall be seen. The word is that light that blots out all imperfections. The faithful will enter into his blessedness. Wherein is the potion and eternal medicine. You thought correctly [see previous footnote]: I am indeed as you believe. For by truth and justice, his words and teachings are true and complete." -Ed.

13 Recte sapere: "To perceive correctly." -Ed.

14 Ecce seruus . . . pronunciatum: "Behold the servant of the Lord, Let his decree be for me (like his mercy) as was declared about me." -Ed.

thing, which is **the growmd and element of thy desyre, is allredy perfyted.**[15]

Yt seemeth that you beleue not.[16] But I haue sayde, as he hath sayd and his worde shall endure for euer. For he shall, and will performe it, for he liueth for euer. **Oute of Seuen thow hast byn instructed most perfectly of the lesser part,**[17] the rest I haue browght you, in this my vessell; A medicine sufficient to extinguish and quenche oute the enemy, to our felicitie: Muse not, thowgh I say ours: for we all liue in tasting of this liquor. His Hed is a marble stone.[18] His hart is the blud of a dragon. His leggs are the tops of the Northen Mowntaynes. His eyes are bright, and his face of many Cullours, eche substance amongst the turmoyle and trubble of nothing. For as then, they were Nothing: Had a forme applyable and necessary according to theyr quantitie and secret qualitie. The heuens are lightened by his two eyes: wherof the one sight is brighter then the other. Aboue and in him self which is by him self, and in no other, is this great and vertuous fowntayne. In nature Intellectuall he hath watred the plantes of her beauty, and stroked up the garments of her felicitie. In her darkest members entreth in the taste and sauour of this percing Medicine; reviving and recalling all things past present and to come, unto theyr lively and dignified perfection. My words ar sentences. My sentences, wisdome; My wisdome the ende in my message of all things. Mighty and glorious is the Vertue of it, whose springs do endure, and are clere for euer: Whose name be blessed.

Δ: Amen. I respect the tyme. God be with you.

---

15 Perfyted: "perfected." -Ed.

16 Increduli. -Δ ("Unbelievers." -Ed.)

17 HM identifies this as Raphael. -Ed.

18 A parable.

Martij 24. Sonday: morning abowt 8.

Δ: The Table appeared, and the Chayre: and he who appeared yesterday: kneeling or rather lying prostrate on his face, as if he were a slepe:
He lay a long while.

A thing like a lambs hed did seeme to lik him, and then he rose and
wiped his face, as thowgh he had wept.

Me, he sayd, <u>Signa sunt hæc vobis, humilitatis et pænitentiæ; quæ
facio omnia, vestra, non mea sunt.</u>[19] Laudetur verbum eius in Cælo,
laudetur etiam et in terris: Investigate potentiam in humilitate loquelæ
eius, et videbitis gloriam frontis eius. Misericors namque et omnipotens
est gloria virtutis eius. Vana sunt, corruptionibus suis; Necessaria verò
Necessitatibus vestris. Nam fecit omnia ad laudem eius: et opera
manuum suarum (Ecce) collaudant lumen vultus eius. <u>Adinvicem dilig-
ite</u> Humilitate viuite. Medicina verò mea (quæ eius est) <u>omnia
resanabit.</u>[20]

The feldes wither without the drops of his Mercie. Mans Memorie
is dull, unleast it taste of the sprinkling of this vessell. [EK: He hath a
great thing under his gown.]

<u>Nature and reason</u>[21] haue disputed profowndly and truely by the
sauour hereof: it perceth therfore depely. But understanding and reason
haue eleuated and lifted up the dignitie and worthynes of Mans Memorie,
by taste hereof. The Immeasurable and unspeakable begynnings (yea with

---

[19] Note hereby to consider theyr actions, gestures and other circumstances.

[20] Signa sunt . . . resanabit: "These are signs to you (pl) of humility and of repen-
tance; which (signs) I make everything yours; they are not mine. May his word
be praised in heaven, and may he also be praised on earth. Discover power in the
humility of his speech (or language) and you (pl) will see the glory of his brow.
For the glory of his power is merciful and almighty. Vanities exist in his seduc-
tions; Necessities exist in your true needs. For he made all things for his praise:
and (behold) his handiwork praises the light of his face. Love one another; live
with humility. Truly, my medicine (which is his) will convey everything." -Ed.

[21] Nature ∴ Reason ∴

the begynner and Principle therof), are exactly (after a sort) and perfectly known of them. Yt hath towght from the earth unto the heauens: from the heven, unto his seat: from his seate, into his Diuinitie. From his Diuinitie, a Capable measuring of his unmeasurable mercies. It is true, most true, and true shalbe for euer. That from the lowest grass to the highest tree, [from] the smallest valley, to the greatest mowntayn; yea, euen in the distinction, betwixt light and darknes: the measure whereof is the deapest: yea (I say) it hath towght a Iudgment. When he axed wisdome, and forsoke the world, he receyued it: and it measured the things of the world. Great are the inward eyes, and greater are the meanes, which deliuer things subiect or obiect unto them.

Finally it procedeth from him, that procedeth: Whereunto the first was <u>formed, after, and not like</u>. Whose fote slipping hath dasshed his hed in peces, and it becam dark: untill agayn, the Medecine which I haue browght, revived his slombring. Hereby, he, not onely knew **all** things,[22] but the <u>measure and true use therof</u>. Yf the body haue no inward fyre, it presently falleth. Euery Organ is voyde of qualitie, unleast <u>a meane</u> be adiected. So, is all that thow hast before, <u>more wonderfull, then, as yet, profitable</u>, unleast thow be <u>directed</u> and led-in <u>unto the true use and order of the same</u>.[23] Great are my words, and great is thy thowght: Greater shalbe the ende of these Gods Mercies.

New worlds, shall spring of these.

New manners: strange men: The true light, and <u>thorny path</u>, openly seen. All things in one, and yet, this is but <u>a vision</u>. Wonderfull and great are the purposes of him, whose Medicine I carry. I haue sayde.

Δ: He lay down agayn, a good while, and at length he rose: after my long prayer and confession made to god, and my discourse to him, &c.

---

22 Note Adam, before his fall, knew all things.

23 The true use and order of the premises.

EK: He plucketh out a boke: all the leaues are, as thowgh they were gold, and it semeth written <u>with blud, not dry</u>.

Δ: He sayd, Cownt. Δ: He turned ouer the leaues, but EK could not well cownt them: whereuppon he sayd: <u>I will raze out</u>[24] <u>thy dulnes, and at length, make thee clere</u>.

EK: There are 48 leaues.

Me: Et finis est.[25] <u>One is one</u>; neyther is, was or <u>shalbe known</u>: And yet <u>there are iust so many</u>. These haue so many **names**, of the so many Mysteries, that **went** before. This is the second and the Third: The Third and the last.[26] <u>This is the measure of the whole</u>.

Ô what is man, that is worthy to know these Secrets? Heavy are his Wickednesses, Mighty is his synne. <u>These shallt thow know: These shall you use</u>.[27] The One is a Master, the other is a Minister. The One, is a hand, the other is a finger: Grutch not. Neyther let wickednes tempt you: <u>loue togither</u>. Be contented with your calling: For, all beasts see not a like: yet are they all Creatures: Vessels, not of one bignes, yet are they all full. <u>Both, most sufficient</u>, but according <u>to fayth</u>, and understanding of Conscience. Yet must there be <u>a third</u>; whom, God doth not yet chuse. The tyme shalbe short: the matter great, the ende greater. Ask now what thow wilt and he shall answer thee.

EK: There appered one like my self laying his two armes, one, on EK his sholder: and the other on a man his sholder, unknown to us, but somwhat like to Mr Adrian Gilbert,[28] &c.

---

24   Raze out: "erase." -Ed.

25   Et finis est: "And it is the end." -Ed.

26   Note of this boke.

27   J Dee, and EK.

28   Adrian Gilbert, half-brother to Sir Walter Raleigh, was a frequent visitor to Mortlake. He eventually was allowed to participate in some of the actions. Earlier in this same year (1583), Dee started plans to colonize North America with Adrian Gilbert and John Davis. During subsequent actions, Dee consults the angels about this proposed venture.

Δ: Ys it your will to procede in this matter, you now haue begonne withall: or will you of these characters and places of Threasor hid (here portrayled by picture), say any thing?

Me: As thow wilt. Δ: As the will of God is, so will I. The will of God you know, better than I.

Me: The æternall liquor be uppon you. Ones more, what wilt thow?

Δ: I do prefer the heuenly liquor, before all things, and do desire to be bedewed, with the supercælestiall dew thereof.

Me: Consider the former tree.

Δ: The tre with the water at the fote?

Me: <u>Thow hast sayd</u>. His growing <u>powre</u>, bringeth <u>furth</u> Act.[29] Remember the <u>Prince and Subiects</u>, which haue powre (as is told thee) of Erthly Bowels (The thing there, [~~whose~~] which you desire of me, is no parte of my charge), <u>Call him</u>: It is his office: <u>for by his ministers it hath byn shewed.</u>[30] God doth impart his mercy, to those he loueth, in all necessitie: whether of the one, or of the other, where it is dew: I leave it: his Office is to speak it. Notwithstanding liue in truth and humilitie: <u>Use God his Creatures, to his glorie</u>, and thy Necessitie, the proffit of thy own lymms, and cutting out of all Canker and rotten flesh. Thow understandest: <u>For thy eyes shalbe opened</u>. Amen.

EK: He spreddeth his hands abroade, and goeth away, and putteth his boke in his bosom as he goeth.

Δ: Gloria patri.[31] &c. Amen.

---

29 Potentia, Actus. -Δ ("Power, Deed." -Ed.)

30 Δ Blisdon is the prince under Bnaspol the king. Vide sup. Lib. 4: A°. 1587. Circa Maiu: Quidam Ben, (spiritualis Creatura) dixit ipi EK, se custodinisse illum pulverem et librum Dunstani, &c. -Δ. (Vide sup. ...: "See above in book 4. Around May 1587 one Ben (a spiritual creature) said to EK that he himself had guarded that powder and Book of Dunstan.") See TFR Actio Tertia, May 23, p. 27 (pages separately numbered). -Ed.

31 Gloria patri: "Glory be to the Father." -Ed.

Martij 26. hor. 10 ante Meridiem.

First, appered a clowd: and that vanished away: Three cam in, they made Cursy to the chayre: and two went away. Then the third which remayned, lay down on the grownd, as before. There cam like a lambs hed,[32] and licked him. He sayd then, as followeth: being stand up,

Magna sunt, Alla quæ dixisti,[33] making cursy to the chayre. There was a sownd hard before. After a while he sayd,

Me: Thy Kingdom is established in eternitie. Thy hands are invisible, and no man can distinguish thy mercies. I attend your desire.

Δ: As concerning the Characters, and shew of the ten places, we are desirous to know whyther we may require now Bnaspol, or other under him, to say unto us, that, which may content us, for the Case as it standeth with us.

Me: The buylder of the Temple was riche, before it was adorned. With Wisdome, cam the Instruments necessarie for mans worldly use. He hideth no light from those he loveth: neyther shutteth up his tents from such as seke him. Yf one be great, Ô how small is the other? How small therfore is the mynde, and how much weakened that desireth those trifles? But as the smallest thing is feefest to the smallest use, so is the existimation of things of light accownt, necessary for the lightnes and vanitie of this world. A part (Notwithstanding) may beawtify the whole, and a small thing, may cure a great infirmitie. I told thee before, that my fete are not placed uppon such brittle and crakling sand, neyther are my lipps occupied with the vanitie of nothing. I will not[34] manifest in any point, the thing which thow desyrest, neyther is it any part of my charge.

I haue byn thy scholemaster and director to the Sterne, to rule the

---

32 A lambs hed, may be a token of our humilitie required, &c.

33 Magna . . . dixisti: "Great are the things that I have said." -Ed.

34 Note.

reason therof, <u>with those, which can reache the</u> Iudgment therof. <u>All those before spoken of, are subiect to thy call.</u>[35] This vessell <u>at all tymes</u> they greatly accept. Yet <u>haue they times</u> and <u>seasons:</u>[36] When <u>order</u> breaketh in her self, the labor is in vayne. Euery thing is for and to an ende. <u>Of frendeship</u>, <u>at any time,</u>[37] <u>thow mayst see them, and</u> Know what <u>thow willt.</u>

But One thing differeth, the Ende, and the Begynning. That onely, is the El, rod, or measure which all ready is deliuered. <u>The stroke</u> of which, bringeth all things, in theyr degree, to an ende: as far as the seven (magnificencie of euery Seuen) stretcheth out it self.

<u>Euery one</u>, (to be short) shall <u>at all times</u> and seasons,[38] shew thee <u>direction in any thing.</u> But, SO, thow canst <u>not use them</u>, in the determination, and full ende of euery practise. It is one thing to affectionate; and an other to effect. What thow seest, is true, and to a former[39] commoditie: For, with Furderance, euery thing in Nature is ayded.

Δ: ---

Reade ouer that, which now, lastly, I declared: Then see, if you be not answered.

Δ: ---

Therfore mayst thow <u>know, what that is</u>, allthowgh thow do not, yet, or presently, put it in <u>practise, by him</u>, whose <u>Charge it is, to deliuer it.</u>[40]

Δ: Of your so greatly commended liquor I am desirous to haue farder understanding.

---

[35] NOTE.

[36] Note. All tymes, Speciall tymes.

[37] Of frendship, at any tyme.

[38] Note.

[39] Furder.

[40] NOTE Whose charge it is to deliuer it.

Me: What liquor is more liuely then the dew of Truth, proceding from a fowntayn most swete and delectable? Euen that veritie which thy mowth hath preached of.[41] What water recreateth more, or cooleth ignorance deeper than the knowledg of our Celestiall speche?[42] your voyces are but fayned: shaddows of the wordes and voyces that substantially do comprehend euery substance in his kinde. The things which you do loke on, bycause you see them not in dede, you allso do name them amysse: you are confownded, for your offenses: and dispersed for your punishments: But we are all one, and are fully understanding. We open the eare, and the passage thereof, from the sonne in the morning to the sonne at night. Distance is nothing with us, unleast it be the distance, which separateth the wicked from his mercy. Secrets there are none, but that buried are in the shaddow of mans Sowle.

We see all things: and Nothing is hid from us: respecting our Creation. The waters shall stand, if they here theyr own speche. The heuens shall move, and shew them selues, when they know theyr thunder. Hell shall tremble, whan they know what is spoken to them.[43] The first[44] excepted, No man euer was, is, or shall be (excepted where I except) that euer shall understand, hath or doth know the least part (ô it is incomprehensible) of this Vessel. He named all things (which knew it) and they are so in dede, and shalbe so for euer.

Thow shallt speak with us;[45] And we will be spoken with, of thee. Three they are excepted, which taken from amongst you, as they were, do yet speak with us, which are provided in the three laws to destroy

---

[41]   Veritas. -Δ. ("Truth, verity." -Ed.)

[42]   Lingua et Vox Angelica. -Δ. ("Angelic language and voice." -Ed.)

[43]   The Powre of the primitiue diuine or Angelicall speche.

[44]   ADAM.

[45]   Angelorum Colloquia -Δ. ("Conversation of angels." -Ed.)

that Monstre.[46] They are fed with cælestiall fode, and they, talking, speak all understanding. This it is, I take God, (onely him that created me) to recorde. It is determined: else wold I not: And may be undetermined, yf you break his commaundements.[47]

A Stone it is that perceth[48] down all things before it; and kepeth them under him, as the heuens do a clowde. What art thow, (O god,) and how mighty ar the drops of thy mercy, that preparedst man before to examin thy Mysteries? The plagues of those that plagued them selues, shall fall uppon you, yf you transgress[49] one iote of your eye-sight:

For, What you desire, is graunted: and if you loue him, you shall endure for euer. I am not as a clowde, sheuered[50] with the wynde: nor as a garment, that waxeth olde, and torn in peces: But I am for euer (bycause my message is such) and my truth, shall endure for euer.

Beholde, Beholde, yea let heven and earth behold: For with this, they were created: and it is the voyce and speche of him, which proceded from the first, and is the first; whose glorious name be exalted in his own horn of honor.[51] Lo, this it is. [EK: He sheweth a boke, as he did before all gold.] And it is truth; Whose truth shall endure for euer.

---

46   Tres ab hominibus in cælos rapti cum Angelis conversantes. Fortè, 'Enoch, Elias, Jo . . .' -Δ. ("Three carried off to heaven keeping company with angels. Perhaps Enoch, Elias, and John [the Baptist]." -Ed.)

47   NOTE. -Δ. In the manuscript this last sentence is heavily underscored. -Ed.

48   Fortè: "presseth."

49   Note.

50   Shivered: "shattered." -Ed.

51   The boke, the first Language of God Christ.

EK: The leaues of the boke, are all lyned: full of square places, and those square places haue characters in them, some more then other:, and they all written with cullour, like blud, not yet dry.[52] 49 square spaces, euery way, were on euery leaf, which made in all .2401. square places. He wiped his finger on the top of the Table, and there cam out aboue the Table certayn Characters[53] enclosed in no lines: but standing by them selues, and points betwene them. He pointed orderly to them with his finger, and loked toward the skryer at euery pointing.

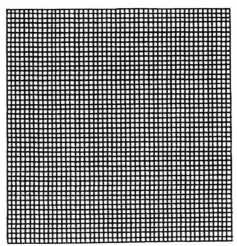

Me: Note what they are.

~ · ꓶ · ꓛ · ꓭ · ꓮ · ꓜ · ꓨ · ꓝ · ꓴ · ꓵ · ꓬ · ꓯ · ꓡ · ꓨ · ꓹ · ꓠ · ꓩ · ꓩ · ꓩ · ꓩ ·

Δ: They are Noted.

EK: He toke from under the Table, a thing like a great globe, and set that in the chayre: and uppon that Globe, layd the boke. He pointeth to the characters: and cownteth them with his finger, being 21, and begynning from the right hand, toward the left. He putteth-off the Crown of gold, from his hed: and layeth it, on the Table. His here appereth yellow. He maketh cursy: and from under the Table taketh a rod of gold in his hand, being diuided into three distinctions.[54] He putteth the ende of the rod on the first of the Characters, and sayeth, Pa:

---

52   The cullor of the Letters.

53   21 Characters.

54   Δ By his often taking things from under the table it shold seme that there shold be some shelf made under our Table.

and there appered in english, or latin letters, Pa: He sayd, veh: and there appered veh in writing: Then Ged: and after that he sayd, Unus Unus Unus, Magnus, Magnus, Magnus, es.[55] Then he pointed to an other, and sayd Gal, and there appeared Gal: Then or [the voyce seemed Orh.] Then un [the sownd semed und.] Then Graph: [The sownd as Grakpha, in the throte.] Then Tal, [in sownd stall or xtall.] Then gon. Then na [but in sownd Nach as it were in the nose.] Then ur, [in sownd our or ourh.] Than mals, [in sownd machls.] Then Ger, [in sownd, gierh.] Then drux, [in sownd drovx.] Then Pal: the p being sownded remissly. Then med. He sayd, Magna est gloria eius.[56] Ceph, sownded like Keph, But before that, was Don: Then van, Fam, Then Gisg.

Ʋ	Pa	b
к	veh	c
Ʊ	ged	g
Y	gal	d
ʔ	or	f
ƶ	un	a
ꝗ	graph	e
ʋ	Tal	m
ꜿ	Gon	i
ꝏ	na	hath
ꝣ	vr	l
Ω	mals	þ
ʊ	ger	q
Ⴝ	drux	n
ͳ	Pal	x
Ⳑ	med	o
c	don	r
Ⱨ	ceph	ꝛ
χ	van	u
ꝗ	fam	ſ
ᴎ	Gisg	t

Then he lay down before it: and there cam two lines and parted the 21 letters into 3 partes, eche being of 7. He sayd, Numerus ô perfectissimus, Unus et Trinus. Gloria tibi,[57] Amen.

---

55   Unus . . . es: "You are One, One, One, Great, Great, Great." -Ed.

56   Magna . . . eius: "Great is his glory." -Ed.

57   Numerus . . . tibi: "The number, O most perfect, One and Threefold. Glory be to you." -Ed.

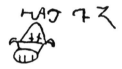

Then he put on his Crown, and pluckt a black veale before all in the Chayre. He sayd, Remember to lerne those names without boke, and to know them.

Δ Thus I deciphred them after a day or two or three.

Martij 26. a meridie + Tuesday hor. 5½

First there was a great noyce of harmony, hard. There appeared two great Armies fighting, and much bludshed on both sides.[58] One Captaine is in red harness, the Contrary Captayn, is white and grene. There appered Flags with a croked tree, or like a ragged staff, or cudgell, in them: and they were on the red Capitayns side. He and his soldiers had the worse and were putto flight, and they ran away. The Captayn with the white and grene was Master of the felde: and assembled and gathered his men to gather after the Victorie. Now this Capteyn goeth to a town and semeth with his hand to heave up the towne, being a big towne. There was a voyce hard, saying thus, — So shall it be, with 21 more.

Δ: Wyth what one and twenty?

A voyce:—As yet, you can not know. This shall happen, before the Sonne hath twise gon his course.[59]

---

58 A battle foreshewed.

59 Before two yeres finished, Ergo before A°. 1585, Martij 26.

EK: Now the Capteyn appeared alone, on fote, in his harness. He hold-eth up his hands to heven: He is now vanished away. I meane the Capteyn in white and grene. Now appeareth the red cloth before the chayre. There come in three: they all make cursy: and two of them went away.

Δ: Our desyre is to know what we are to think of the Man which cam out of my Oratory and layd the fyry Ball at Mr Adrian Gilbert his fete yesterday, as he sat in my study with Mr Kelly and me: whether it were any Illusion, or the act of any seducer?

Me: <u>No wicked powre **shall enter** into this place</u>.[60] Neyther shall Iniquitie range where the fyre of his percing Judgment <u>and election</u>[61] doth light, which shall quicken his deadness, and revive <u>his courrage to the auancement of the name of him, which liueth now</u>. He chose with fire and lightened theyr harts, and they immediately understode and felt the Illumination of his glory.[62]

What wilt thow?

Δ:

To the performance of the glorie and encreasing of his name, which shortly maketh an ende with for euer.

Δ: This phrase, <u>for euer</u>, is somwhat dark.

Me: **With this world**, <u>for euer</u>. Δ: This giveth some light.

EK: The stone is become very dark.

Me: As the Buylding is grownded and ended uppon Three, So must the mysteries hereof be <u>practised With **Three**</u>. The fowrth is the Boke, which, Lo, is here present.

Δ: Must Adrian Gilbert, be made priuie of these Mysteries?

Me: Thow hast sayde.[63]

---

[60] NOTE.

[61] Election.

[62] The Apostles on Whitson Sonday.

[63] A. Gilbert may be made priuie, but he is not to be a Practiser.

Δ: May I note to your name any peculier Character or Syllable to distinguish your speches from ours or others?

Me: Medicina sum.[64]

Δ: I may then use this syllable Me, to Note Medicina or Medicus Dei.[65]

Me: Behold, these things, shall God bring to <u>pass by his hands whose mynde he hath now newly set on fyre.</u>[66] The corners and <u>streights of the earth</u> shall be measured to the depth: And strange shalbe the wonders that are Creeping into new worldes. <u>Tyme shalbe altred, with the difference of day and night.</u>[67] All things haue grown allmost to theyr fullness. But beware of <u>Pride</u>. We teache duty, Humbleness, and submission. <u>Shortly</u> shall these things come to passe.

Δ: Than, this Adrian Gilbert shall cary the <u>name of Jesus</u> among the Infidells to the great glory of god, and the recouery of those miserable people from the mowth of hell into which, for many hunderd yeres past, and yet contynually they do fall, &c.

Me: <u>Who</u> made thy mowth to <u>prophesy</u>? or, <u>who</u>* [Of God] opened the eyes of thy understanding? Who annoynted thy Jaws, or fed thee with unknown meate. <u>Euen he</u>* it is, <u>that pricked these things forward, and shall use you as his</u> Instruments to a <u>mightie honor.</u>

Δ: May we require description[68] of the Cuntryes, for his better instruction, &c.

\----------------------------

Me: <u>Let darknes go behinde</u> thee, and <u>tempt him</u> not, that iudgeth.[69] <u>These things belong not to my charge.</u> Thow knowest <u>them, which are</u>

---

64   Medicina sum: "I am the medicine." -Ed.

65   Medicina or Medicus Dei: "God's medicine or doctor." -Ed.

66   A Gilbert, his task.

67   Note, a prophesy.

68   Description geographicall.

69   Tenebrae post dorsum. -Δ ("Darkness behind the back." -Ed.)

sufficient,[70] whan short time shall serue, for the whole instruction.[71] Greater nede were to enquire How or by what meanes thow mayst be made worthy;[72] and, so, consequently, haue knowledge for the knowing, hauing and using of this cælestiall medicine.

Forget not.

I instructed thee before-hand, and told thee, that both of you must iointly[73] lerne those holy letters (For, so, I may boldely call them) in memory: with theyr names: to the intent, that the finger may point to the hed, and the hed to the understanding of his charge:

Δ: You perceyue that I haue diuerse affayres which at this present do withdraw me from peculier diligence using to these Characters and theyr names lerning by hart: And therfore I trust, I shall not offend, if I bestow all the convenient leysor[74] that I shall get, abowt the lerning hereof.

Me: Peace, Thow talkest, as thowgh, thow understodest not. We know thee, we see thee in thy hart: Nor one thing shall not let an other. For short is the time, that shall bring these things to profe: Wherein he that liueth, shall approve him self aliue.[75] Beautifull are the footesteps of his comming, and great is the reuenge of the wicked.

O Liber, Liber, Liber, bonis vita, malis vero mors ipsa. Magna sunt mirabilia in te inclusa: et magnum est nomen Sigilli tui

Lumen Medicinæ meæ, vobis.[76]

---

70   For discoveries making of the seas and theyr bownds.

71   Instruction requisite.

72   Note.

73   Both ioyntly EK and J:D:

74   Leysor: "leisure." -Ed.

75   God will shew himself aliue.

76   O liber . . . vobis: "O book, book, book, life to the good, but truly death itself for the wicked. Great are the wonders sealed up inside you, and great is the name of your seal. The light of my medicine, for you." -Ed.

EK: He holdeth his hands abroad. He draweth the Curten.

Δ: Gloria Laus et honor Deo patri et F. et SS.[77] Amen.

Martij 28. Thursday morning. Mawndy Thursday.

A voyce: Pereant omnes <u>qui insidiantur</u>[78] virtuti nominis mei: et qui Lumen absconderunt Iustitia mea.[79]

EK: Now the veale is pluckt away.

Three appeare, as before time.

All three sayd,—Multa nos, quia multa patitur ipem.[80]

EK: The two go away, and the Third remayneth who is like in all points to him, who yesterday <u>to me alone</u>, in your absence had declared himself to be an Illuder. Δ: NOTE, for the better understanding of this dayes Act it may be remembred that E. Kelly, while I, (John Dee) was at London, yesterday (being wensday) had used meanes to haue conference, with the good Creatures, with whome we haue dealing iointly: and that there appeared one <u>very like unto our good frende</u>, who toke apon him to be <u>**the same**</u>, and now semed to be <u>constrayned</u>[81] <u>by EK</u> to tell the truth: and therfore his outward beautifull apparell semed to go of, and his body appered hery and he confessed that he was an Illuder[82] &c. Whereuppon EK was in a great perplexitie of mynde, and was

---

77 Gloria Laus et honor Deo p<at>ri et F<ilio> et S<piritui> S<ancto>: "Glory, praise, and honor to God the Father, and to the Son, and to the Holy Spirit." -Ed.

78 Insidiatores. -Δ. ("Traitors." -Ed.)

79 Pereant . . . mea: "May everyone perish who betray the virtue of my name: and who have hidden the light of my justice." -Ed.

80 Multa . . . ipem: "Reprove us, because he himself suffers much." -Ed.

81 Constrayned: "forced." -Ed.

82 Pilosus. -Δ ("Hairy." -Ed.)

ready to haue gone his way. And at my comming home told me a long
processe of this Tragicall Act. But I comforted him, and wold not yeld
to his opinion, But did declare my confidence in the goodnes of God:
for that we craved at his hands, things good and necessarie: and that
therefore he wold not giue his childern a stone for bred, or a scorpion
for nedefull food required &c.[83] And this morning the matter was
propownded by me, and thereuppon the former sayings wer used, and
all the consequences of matter, which hereafter is recorded.

Δ: The veritie I require of yesterdays doings with EK on my absence.

Camikas zure, he sayd, holding his hands to heuen.

EK: He walketh up and down and semeth angry: and did beat his
hands togither. There commeth a little streame of fire whitish from
aboue: and cam to his hed. He kneleth down before the Chayre, and
loketh up, and sayde,

Me: Oh how brittle are the works of thy hands [he looked up]
whose Imperfections are now more innumerable then the sands of the
sea: or clowds that were lifted up since the begynning of the world.
Darknes dare presume to place him self in Lightnes: yea dishonor, (o
God) to dwell in place of glory: His lying lipps presume against Truth:
whilest thow suffredst his old and withered face to be garnished with
thy beawty. Heavines[84] is his seat; yet are his lipps myrthfull: and little
there that separateth him from the dignitie of honor: But his ponishment is sufficient, his dishonor unspeakable, and his damnation for
euer: which how bitter it is, great and unspeakable, Thow, ô thow (I
say) that liuest (which hast estranged him so far from thy glory) makest
onely manifest. But yet how long shall the sonnes of men puff up them
selues with bragging and boasting of that they see not? But (alas) All

---

83   See. Matthew 7:9; Luke 11:11–12. -Ed.

84   Heaviness: "sorrow." -Ed.

things are confownded, and are contrary to thy commaundements: some onely which differ, remayn with concordant myndes praysing thee, and lifting up thy name, as much as strength performeth. But herein is thy glory and long sufferance manifest, in that thow dost not onely with greif behold theyr synnes, but like a iust iudge, <u>fauorably doth ponder the greatnes of theyr enemies, which infect theyr myndes, and blynde the light, which thow hast given</u> unto theyr understanding, with inflammations bodyly, instigations worldly, and tentations innumerable. Great therfore and most great, and none greater can be, which deridest the Aduersarie, and healest the weak: whose smallnes of habilitie thow canst augment, wherein the mysteries of thy great glorie and might, is manifest. Thy seal yeld prayses, with incessant and dutifull obedience. Thy name be magnified, thy mercy published to thy glory: Holy Holy, yea great and most holy, is thy euerlasting kindenes for euer.

EK: Now he standeth up, and sayd,

Me: As I haue all ready told,[85] from whome I cam, so haue I not hydden, what I am, or what message I bring; why it is sent, it is allso written. How long shall I perswade to stedfastnes? But the greater your measures are the greater shalbe the quantitie. These afflictions are necessary. For herin is a measure to distinguish[86] from falshode, light from darknes, and honor from dishonor. <u>The more they are like us,</u> or shew them selues so, (for, nothing can be more dislike) the more they are Judges of theyr own damnation. <u>Yea, if his strength had byn great, he wold haue devoured thy sowle.</u> [Loking to EK.] But whome God <u>hath chosen,</u> shall none overturne. Brag not: eyther Credyt my words by thyne owne reason. But Consider that diuerse may be dishonored, yea thowgh they be in honor: yet shallt not thow neyther be ouerturned

---

85 Raphaëlis officium. -Δ. ("Raphael's office." -Ed.)

86 Fortè, truth.

with the one wynde nor the other: <u>thowgh the afflictions that shall follow thee, be great and hard.</u>[87] In my words are no error: neyther haue
you fownd my lipps untrue. Whan I kneeled, I spake for you. But I haue
promised that <u>No unclean</u> thing shall <u>prevayle</u> within <u>this place</u>.
Neyther am I a revenging spirit nor of any such office. I quicken the
dead, revive them that are falln and cure or sow up the wowndes, which
they are permitted to work uppon man, as tokens of God his Iustice.

I call the same god, (whome I haue called before) to recorde, that
these words are true, my sayings iust, and his mercies more perfect.
Whilest heven endureth and earth lasteth, <u>never shall be razed out the
Memorie of these Actions.</u>[88] Use Humilitie: Reioyce whan the enemy is
discomforted in his traynes,[89] and inventions: A ponishment so great,
Et cætera. <u>Whan I yoked your feathers</u>[90] to gither, I ioyned them not
for a while. Your flying is to be considered in quantitie, qualitie and
Relation.

Thank God: Be mercifull: forget your synnes: and prepare your
selues, For great and wonderfull is the <u>immediate powre</u> of him that
illuminateth from aboue. It shall light apon you: <u>For those that are
present with him, liued with him, eat and drank with him,</u> [and] were
instructed by him, Were but hearers onely: At length God was glorified,
in one instant all things browght unto theyr remembrance: yea some of
them taken to behold the heavens, and the earthly glory. I haue sayd.

Δ:

Me: Behold. Veniat vindictum dei, et percutiat linguam mentientem.[91]

---

[87] Afflictions to EK.

[88] Note the durance of these Memorialls.

[89] Traynes: deceits. -Ed.

[90] Note of the vision which was shewed A°. 1582.

[91] Veniat . . . mentientem: "May the vengeance of God come, and may it may smite
the lying tongue." -Ed.

EK: He goeth his waye and taketh all with him, Table, Chayre, and Curten and all. There cam in a great many with flaming swords, and bring in the wicked spirit, who yesterday delt so diuilishly with EK. One of them holding him by the arme, sayde, Speak now for your self, you could speak yesterday. They all drew theyr swords: they sknorked fire. And there seamed a water to com in, but it went away again.

A voyce:—Dicat, nam nrm non est.[92]

EK: Now is the Skroll with the Characters browght in, which was fownd by spirituall direction this month, the 12 day, abowt 10½ after none by Mr Kelly and Master Husy.[93] He semeth now as like our good frende, as may be. Our frende cam with a sponge and annoynted the wicked spirit his lipps.

A voyce:—Els could I not speak.

Δ: Seing now thow canst speak, answer me.

The wicked, sayd:—Ask quickly.

Δ: What is thy Name?—The wicked answered, Gargat.

Δ: What is the sentence of that skroll?— Gar: I know not.

Δ: In the name of Jesus, I charge thee to tell me the truth as concerning That roll here shewed.—Gar: I haue cownterfeted this roll, and browght it: for it is not the true roll.[94]

Δ: After many words betwene him and me, and the more, bycause he denyed that he knew of any Glorie belonging to God, I urged him so, at length with short and euident argument, that he answered, he must confess the powre and glorie of god: and sayd, that he was damned for euer: and did wish damnation to me. And I requested God to use his Justice on him, for the glory of his name. Then he entreated me somwhile, and somwhile derided me, saying, Art thow so lusty? &c.

---

92 Dicat . . . non est: "He may speak, for he is not one of us." -Ed.

93 The finding of the skroll, of the Treasors.

94 Cownterfeted Roll. -Δ. Vide infra pag. 152, 153 &c. -E.A.

Δ: All the Cumpany fell on him, and hewed him in peces: and digged a hole in the earth, with theyr swords, and he fell in, and after that was a myghty roaring hard.

A voyce:—Sic soleo iniustis.[95]

Δ: The Cumpany went away. There cam a fire and seamed to burn all the howse.

A voyce:—Purifica Domine sanctum tuum, et dele iniquitatem inimicorum nostrorum.[96]

Δ: Then returned our frende, ᵐᵉ , and all seemed light and bright agayn: likewise all the furniture, of Table, Chayre, Globe in the chayre covered with a red covering &c.

Me: Visio vera, verè denotatur. Denotetur etiam ad gloriam Dei.[97]

☞ Δ: Master Kelly, is your dowt of the spirit, now taken away?

EK: Ye truely, I beseche God to forgive me.

Me: Dixisti, et factum.[98]

Δ: As concerning Adrian Gilbert, there might be some dowte in common externall Judgment, of his aptnes to the performance of the voyage with the appertenances, But the Secret of God his prouidence, I will not meddle withall: for he can make infants speak, and the dum to shew furth his glory &c.

Me: Yf God be mighty, acknowledge his powre. Who made the Sonne of nothing? or man, so brittle a substance? Nature thrusteth up her sholders amongst trees and herbs, like a <u>ientle</u> fyre: In beasts and all the creatures of the feelde, waters, and earth, in a palpable imagination: Amongst the sonns of men, she auanceth her self, wholy in

---

[95]   Sic soleo iniustis: "So I am accustomed to unrighteous people." -Ed.

[96]   Purificata . . . nostrorum: "Cleanse, O Lord, your holy one, and destroy the wickness of our enemies." -Ed.

[97]   Write. -Δ. Visio . . . Dei: "The true vision is truly noted, and it will be noted for the glory of God." -Ed.

[98]   Dixisti, et factum: "I have spoken, and it is so." -Ed.

the light of understanding. In all these she walketh by her own qualitie, mixing the quantities, with her before iudged proportion.
Amongst all these is some distinction, yet all in theyr kindes are perfectly and substantially norrished. Yf Nature haue such powre, What
powre hath our God, and how great is his might in those in whome
He kindleth a sowle, understanding. The strength of 1. body, and 2.
inward man, with 3. <u>the strength of him that allso leadeth him,</u>[99] are
augmented and diminished at his pleasure. Yf earth, in myxture
become fyre, hom much more shall he encrease, whome God hath
strengthened: yf he wold haue <u>conquered with thowsands, he wold
not haue sent back the dogged harted people</u>. Yf riches or renown
were his felicitie, he wold haue kindled the twelue Lamps[100] of his
æternall light, on a higher mowntayne: But he chose them in the
Valleys, and from the watering places. I think this be sufficient to
confirme your understanding.

Δ: I trust, God be not offended with this matter propownded &c.

Me: He is pleased: And it is enowgh. Eternitie is mighty and glorious to the righteous.

Δ: Whan shall I make him[101] priuie of these things?

Me: Whan thow wilt. For euery thing is acceptable with those that
are accepted. <u>See thow cownsayle him, and be his Father.</u>

Δ: As concerning John Dauis,[102] we are to ax somwhat &c.

Me: <u>John Dauis, is not of my Kalender. Lern of them, of whome</u>

---

99 Δ Note Body, sowle, spirit.

100 The 12 Apostles.

101 A. G.

102 John Davis is mentioned in Dee's diary as early as 1577, but Dee probably knew
him as a boy. He was evidently one of Dee's pupils, and one of the principal play-
ers in the search for the Northwest Passage. He stole at least seventy books from
Dee's library after Dee left for Europe in 1583. See Julian Roberts and Andrew
Watson, *John Dee's Library Catalogue* (London: The Bibliographical Society,
1990), p. 50.

<u>it is</u> necessary. Be not negligent, in lerning the things before prescribed.[103]

God be emongst you.

EK: He hath drawn the curten of red.

Δ: Soli Deo sit omnis honor et gloria.[104] Amen.

Mawndy Thursday, after None. hor 3½

Δ: The Veale being drawn away after a quarter of an howre (almost) after the first motion made by me. Three cam in, and made obedience to the chayre. Two went away, and the third remayned there, as before.

Δ: As concerning the Kalender to be reformed, I am grieved that her Maiestie will not <u>reforme it in the best termes of veritie.</u>[105] And as for the priuiledge for Mr Adrian Gilbert his voyage, I think not well of it, that Royalties shold not be graunted. Therfore both these points, respecting her Maiestie, I wold gladly haue cownsayle, such as in the Judgment of the highest might be most for my behofe, to follow.

Me: In one gouernment there are sundry principall partes: Euery part in subdiuision conteyneth many and sundry offices. Many Offices

---

[103] Lern the Alfabet.

[104] Soli . . . gloria: "May all honor and glory be to God alone." -Ed.

[105] The reformation of the Kalendar. -Δ. On 24 February 1582, Pope Gregory XIII ordered the use of the "Gregorian" calendar, and the English court deliberated over its response. Dee was one of the authorities commissioned for a report. According to his diary, Dee delivered his proposal to reform the calendar to Lord Burghley, Treasurer of England on 26 February 1583. It caused considerable controversy. The court opinions were all favorable, and the Queen approved a draft proclamation to adopt the reform, but it was rejected by the bishops because they didn't want to appear to be following the Catholic lead. -Ed.

require many disposers: yet hath euery disposition continually some partition in his qualitie. All things, one thing: And one thing, something: some thing, many things, and many things, most innumerable. The heuens in proportion are gouerned universally of a few; particularly of many: eche place possesseth his diuision: and euery thing diuided, his propertie. Princis ar governors which move and stir them up to work, as it is provided, and to behold in speculation How euery particular Action, shall haue due, perfect, and appropriated Locall being, motion and Condition. Subiects, (yea, the Highest) are stirred up, by theyr propre Angels:[106] The inferior sort do follow the disposition of theyr leaders. Vertue and Vice dwell euery where. Light and darknes, are allwayes intermedled.

Consider, How I speak it.

The myndes of all that move, euen unto the least qualitie in Nature, haue of them selues propre vertues: and therfore propre Instigators.[107] I call to memory thy words, the manner of thy speche, and the secret purpose or meaning, whereunto it is uttred. I see thy Infirmities, and know what thow desyrest. But mark me, whom God commonly choseth,[108] shalbe whom the Princis of the Erth do disdayn. Consider, how the prophet that slew that Monstrous Gyant, had his election.[109]

God respecteth not princis, particularly, so much as the state of his whole people. For in Princis mowthes, is there poyson, as well as proverbs. And in one hart, more Synne, then a whole world can conteyn. Yt is not myne office to meddle with theyr vanities, neyther is it a part of my pageant to towch any thing that tasteth not of Medicine. But, what? doth thy mynde reply? Dost thow think, that my cownsayle

---

[106] Angeli proprij. -Δ ("Proper angels." -Ed.)

[107] Peculier and propre Instigators.

[108] God his Elect.

[109] The reference is to David and Goliath. -Ed.

herin, to a grieved mynde, is, (thowgh it can be) Medicinall? Peraduenture[110] thow thinkest I am not, [in] thy marrow: yes I haue byn <u>long in the highest part of thy body,</u>[111] and therfore ame somthing perswaded of thy meaning.

Δ: In dede, I thowght that your good Cownsaile, was or might be a remedie and a medicine to my afflicted mynde, for this unseamely doing, in the two former points expressed.

Me: Behold, where unto thy earthly man wold seduce thee. Dost thow think, that <u>if it pleas god, it shall not please the Prince?</u> **if it be necessarie, all ready** <u>prepared</u>?

Secretum dico.[112]

For all things are Limited, with a full measuration, and unserchable forsight: yea, I say, <u>all ready</u>, unto the ende. Be not discomforted. Quayle not at the blast of a small tempest: <u>For those that speak thee fayre,</u>[113] <u>haue dissembling harts, and priuilie do they shote at thee, with arrows of reproche.</u> Whan they[114] shall haue nede of thee: I meane, of the help of God, throwgh thee, (some shut up, some entangled, some gadding[115] like <u>masterles Doggs,</u>) Than shall they gladly seke thee and desire to finde thee. They shall smell oute thy fote steps, <u>and thow shallt not see them.</u> The key of theyr Cares shalt thow be Master of: And they them selues shall not unlok theyr own grievousness. Yea they shall say, Oh let the earth devowr us. But I am to long. I

---

[110] Peradventure: "perhaps." -Ed.

[111] Δ: Raphael long tyme visiting my hed.

[112] A secret. -Δ. Secretum dico: "I declare a secret." -Ed.

[113] Lingua dolosa. -Δ ("Deceitful speech." -Ed.)

[114] England.

[115] Gadding: "wandering." -Ed.

answer thee, all thowgh it be not my office,[116] to declare that thow desirest: yet for that thow desyrest my Medicine. <u>I say, Thow shalt preuayle agaynst them,[117] yea euen agaynst the Mightiest</u>. As thow wilt, so shall it be in God his blessings.

Beware of <u>Vayne glory. Use few wordes</u>.

Thy weapons, are small, But <u>thy Conquest</u> shalbe great. Lo. Doth this satisfy thee? Haue a firme faith. It is the greatest lesson. Be it unto thee as thow hast deliuered. One thing, I answer thee, for all Officis. Thow hast in Subiection all Offices. <u>Use them when it pleas thee, And as thy Instruction hath byn</u>.

I haue sayde.

Δ: As things be planted here, for preparation of Table, Sigillum Dei &c, which things are not portable with eas: So, bycause I think, that some seruices to be done in gods purposes by me, <u>will require other</u> places <u>than this howse</u>, so shall diuerse my practises haue (as I think) a more compendious manner, and redy, to be executed in any place &c.

Me: Truely thow hast sayd, and so shall it fall unto thee. As I am here in this place, and yet in dede not, So, here: So shall it fall oute, and follow in the Mysteries of your Associated Operation.

<u>The other[118] shall be, but, as a necessary help to the first Practises, to plant the Tree: which being confirmed and strongly rooted shall bring furth frute, most abundantly.[119]</u> The <u>Erth and the tree</u>, can <u>not be separated</u>. This is the ende, and true it is. Let him be record, whom I beare record of here,

---

116 Note, each in his Office.

117 Prævalescentia. -Δ ("Prevailing against." -Ed.)

118 Δ: and EK, and A. Gilbert.

119 The erth   — 1. EK
    The Tree   — 2. Δ
    The planter — 3. AG

And so, with thee, Amen.

I must help thee. <u>Lerne ioyntly</u> the Elements or grownds of this heuenly doctrine;[120] <u>the ende and Consummation of all thy desired thirst: in the which God shall performe thee, thy Philosophicall Harmonie in prayer.</u>[121] Thow knowest what I mean.

The Æternall physitien minister his heuenly grace and continuall blessings uppon you, to the Glorie of his name, execution of your procedings, and holy and <u>insatiable desires.</u>

> Δ: Amen: Omnipotenti Deo, nostro,
> Creatori Redemptori et
> Santificatori, omnis honor
> laus et gratiarum actio.[122]
> Amen.

Jesus.

On good friday; After None

Δ: There was a savor of fire felt by EK. There semed one with a sword, suddenly to thrust out of the stone at EK his hed. Whereat he started; and sayd he felt a thing (immediately) creeping within his hed, and in that pang becam all in a sweat. And he remayned much misliking the

---

[120] Note Lerne The Alfabet.

[121] Δ Philosophicall Harmonie in prayer, is ment by the prayer which I dayly use, & often: Deus in a m ind a a m f G P e F e S &c. -Δ. Apparently "Deus in adiutorium meum intende: Domine ad adiuvandam me festina: Gloria Patri et Filio et Spiritui Sancto" ("O God, be pleased to deliver me; O Lord, hasten to help me. Glory be to the Father, and to the Son, and to the Holy Spirit"), based on Psalm 70. Compare with Dee's prayer at the beginning of Liber 1. -Ed.

[122] Omnipotenti . . . actio: "All honor, praise, and thanksgiving be to our almighty God, creator, redeemer, and sanctifier." -Ed.

moving and creeping of the thing in his hed. At a quarter of an howre ende it cam to one place: and so ceased somwhat: & then the Curten was drawn away: and there appeared the Table, and the chayre covered. Then cam three, two went away and the one remayned: as before was used.

EK held the paper of the letters in his hand: and $\overset{\star}{Me}$ bad him put it out of his hand.

Me: The taste of this mercifull potion, yea the savour onely of the vessell worketh most extremely agaynst the maymed drowsines of ignorance. Yf the hand be heavy, how weighty and ponderous shall the whole world be? What will ye?

Δ: This he sayd uppon our silence after his former words. I answered, we desyred to lerne the Mysteries of the boke. The Boke now appeared (the cover of the chayre being taken away) the boke lying uppon a rownd thing: which EK, was not yet able to discern what it is.

The first side of the first leaffe of the boke appeared full of the former letters, euery side hauing 49 tymes 49 square places, <u>with letters: some more then other</u>.

Me: Euery side conteyneth 2400 and one od <u>letter.</u>[123]

EK: All the letters semed to be of bluddy cullor, and wet. The lines betwene the squares, semed to be like a shaddow. In the first square were 7 letters.

Me: Say after me: But pray first, ere you begynne. Δ: We prayed.

EK: All became blak as pych in the boke.

Then it becam light agayne.

---

123   49
    <u>49</u>
    441
    <u>196</u>
    2401

Now he pointeth up, with his rod of gold diuided into 3 equal parts, which rod he toke from under the Table.

Me: 1.   {   Keph van [He lifted his face to heven.]
               Don graph fam veh na

EK: Now he kneleth down; and holdeth up his hands:
The letters of the first square, ar 7.

7	6	5	4	3	2	1

Now he pointeth to the second.

2. Med gal [EK: He turneth him self abowt.]
3. un gal un Mals na.

Me: Twise seven, Thre and All one: and his mercy endureth for euer.

4. Tal un vrh.

5. Fam graph Fam.

6. Ged graph drux med.

7. un van.

8. Tal un don ur un <u>drux.</u> Sownded as δρυξ

9. Med.

10. Tal van fam mals un.

11. un ged gon med gal.

12. Mals un drux.

13. Ged un.

14. Fam graph fam.

15. ged un tal mals graph gal un keph

16. veh un mals veh drux graph na   [capcneh]

17. ged med.

18. med gal.

19. Fam graph tal graph ur un pa van ged graph drux

20. Gal med tal drux un.

21. mals na gon un tal

22. ged un

23. van un drux veh don un drux.[124]

24. Van don graph mals don graph fam

EK: Now he seemeth to wepe, and knock his brest. He pointeth with the rod, up, agayn, and sayd,

25. un gal graph mals gal

26. un keph graph

27. Gal don van keph

28. Gisg un don gal graph tal un na.

---

[124] 100.

29. van un
30. veh graph fam gisg fam
31. ged don un mals un gal. He stayed here a good while.
32. fam graph gal
33. van drux pa un don
34. gal med tal gon med urh
35. un gal graph mals med un gal
39. 38.37.36. <u>veh na graph van un veh na / Tal un na / Med fam</u>
    <u>fam na graph / gal un mals na /</u>
40. med drux gon keph gal un don. This is a word.
41. mals un drux ged graph mals na gon.

EK: Now he walked up and down before the chayre: and cam agayn
and pointed. The letters now following seme to be written with Clay.

42. Med gal un tal na
43. ged graph tal graph gal fam un ur: eight letters[125]
44. un
45. gal gon drux med keph un
46. na med pal mals med don. Now he walketh agayn, and loketh
    upward.

Then he pointed agayn.

47. Un gal mals van drux
48. Gal un don
49. ged un don tal graph fam: He walked betwene the shewing of
    tal and graph. There are six letters in that word.

---

[125] 100.

Me: Say after me (Shall I speak the Mysteries of thy glory, which thow hast secreted from the Inhabitants uppon the erth? Yea lord, it is thy will, whose hed is high, and fete euery where, redy to revenge the blud of Innocents, and <u>to call home the lost shepe</u>.)

Say after me,

1. zuresk[126] od adaph mal zez[127] geno au marlan oh muzpa agiod pan ga zez[128] gamphedax[129] Kapene[130] go[le] od Semelábugen donkna[131] fian[132] ga vankran vreprez[133] ádeph[134] arxe[135] drux[136] Tardemah va tzests[137] grapad. zed unba[138] domiól adepóad chieuak mah oshe daph Onixdar[139] pangepi adamh gemedsol a dinoxa hoxpor adpun dar garmes.[140]

   Me: I teache. Let this lesson instruct thee to read all that shalbe gathered out of this boke hereafter. It is <u>not to be</u>

---

[126] Zuresch. Veresk and Zuresk are all one. Δ Perchaunce Zuresch, with ch, for k, and so the word shalbe of 7 letters.

[127] Ses: the letters giue.

[128] Ses.

[129] Gampedaz.

[130] Kaphene.

[131] Domka.

[132] Phiam

[133] Vrepres

[134] Adepd.

[135] Aze.

[136] Druz.

[137] Keztz/cests.

[138] Unbar.

[139] Onizdar.

[140] Gharmes.

spoken,[141] <u>but in the time of his own time</u>. It shalbe sufficient to instruct thee: Fare well.

EK: Now he couereth the boke with the veale.

Δ: Prayses and Thankes be rendred to god, of us his sely[142] ones, now and euer. Amen.

Δ: Note. All the former letters and words in the squares, were onely in the first or upper row, begynning at the right hand, and so going orderly to the left. And secondly Note that this lesson he red, pointing with his rod orderly uppon the same forsaid first row.

Martij 31. Easter day after none abowt 4.

EK hard first a sownd of Musicall harmonie.

Δ: The Veale was pluckt away.

Three cam in, two went away, as was before accustomed.

EK: Now he lyeth down. He riseth and pulleth the veale from the chayre. That veale was of cullor as a raynbow. The boke appeared playne and evidently on the globe in the chayre. EK felt the thing ronne in his hed as the other day it did. Me taketh out the rod from under the Table: He sayd,

Æternitas in Cælo.

Δ: Uppon my staying from speche, he sayd, What wilt thow?

Δ: The proceding instruction necessary for understanding of the boke.

---

[141] Δ It is not to be spoken or interpreted, but whan the <u>time</u> appointed is come.
[142] Sely: "pitiable." -Ed.

Me: Mensuratur.[143] Δ: He putteth up his rod to the boke.

Me: Sint oculi illorum clari, ut intelligant.[144] [He held up his hands and semed to pray.] He pointed now to the second row of the 49 rows of the first page of the boke, and sayd,

Secundus a primo.[145]

1. Gon na graph na van fam veh na [Now he walketh up and down.]

2. Ged don med drux na un gal med Keph [He walketh agayn.]

3. Un don gal graph drux   [He walked agayn.]

4. med

5. drux un   [He walked.]

6. ged graph tal mals [He walketh.] un ur med. [7 letters.]

7. med gon veh un fam tal un drux

8. van un drux gal don graph fam

9. med don gal un

10. van graph van graph gon un na

11. drux med fam

12. mals ur gon ged drux un mals na graph

13. Keph un tal mals med drux med drux

14. un drux graph mals na

15. med mals na graph ~~veh~~ gal [Here, veh or gal is indifferent.]

16. un

17. Tal graph gal med ~~[Keph]~~ [or rather] pal [So it shalbe better understode.[146]]

18. Tal un don van drux graph

---

19. ged graph drux un
20. mals don graph fam [Now he walketh.]
21. drux med
22. gal un fam tal un gisg
23. van med don gisg fam
24. tal un drux ged graph gisg [So it is.]
25. un

    gal graph van drux graph

26. gal un tal mals na
27. drux un pal gisg
28. med fam
29. van un drux gal graph tal na drux un pal un gisg [12 letters.]
30. med don med mals na un fam
31. van med don
32. tal gon drux med gal un ur
33. un tal van gal un fam
34. ged graph don
35. mals un
36. med
37. gal un pal keph van tal
38. pa un drux veh graph fam
39. med don gal un drux [Now he maketh low obeysance to the chayreward.]
40. Mals un Incomprehensibilis es in æternitate tua.[147]
41. Mals don graph fam
42. van tal pa ur med fam gal un
43. van med don pal
44. drux un gal med drux

---

[147] Incomprehensilibis . . . tua: "You are incomprehensible in your eternity." -Ed.

45. mals un gisg don med mals na graph fam.

46. van drux gal graph fam.

47. un gal med drux.

48. ged un drux graph pa drux[148] fam.

49. gon na graph na van gal keph

     Me: Shall I rede it? Δ: We pray you.

2. <u>Ihehusch</u> Gronadox[149] arden, o na gémpalo micasman[150] van-
dres orda beuegiah[151] noz[152] plígnase zampónon aneph[153]
Ophad[154] a medox[155] marúne gena pras[156] no dasmat. Vorts
manget a-deüne[157] damph. naxt os vandeminaxat.[158] Oróphas
vor mínodal amúdas ger pa o daxzum banzes[159] ordan ma pres
umblosda vorx nadon patróphes undes adon ganebus Ihehudz

Δ: Gehudz consisteth of 6 letters: But, Gon na graph na van gal keph,
consisteth of 7. I wold gladly be resolued of that dowt if it pleas you.

EK: He boweth down, and put the rod away, and than Kneled
down.

---

148 Δ: Fortè, van. Axe this dowte.

149 Gronhadoz.

150 Oicasman.

151 Veueiah.

152 Nos.

153 There is a stop.

154 Ophed.

155 Medoz.

156 Pres.

157 Δ: Note: A-deüne must be pronownced as one worde: like as Res-publica, in latin:
els here wold seme to be 50 words but, A-deüne, cam out of one square.

158 Vandemhnaxat.

159 Bances.

Δ: He rose and axed me, What wilt thow?

Δ: The former question to be soluted. Me: Thow hast written fals: for, it must be <u>Ihehudz</u>, and so it is of 7 letters.

Δ: Yf euery side conteyne 49 rows, and euery row will require so much tyme to be receyued as this hath done it may seme that very long time will be requisite to this doctrine receyuing: But if it be gods good liking, we wold fayne haue some abridgment or compendious manner, wherby we might the soner be in the work of Gods servyce.

EK: The Chayre and the Table <u>are snatched away,</u>[160] and seme to fly toward heven. And nothing appeared in the stone at all: But was all transparent clere.

Δ: What this snatching away of Chayre and Table doth meane we know not: But if the Lord be offended with his yonglings, and Novices in thes Mysteries, for propownding or requiring a compendious Method &c, Then we are very sorry, and ax forgivenes for the rashnes of our lipps: and desyre his maiestie not to deale so rigorously with us: as thowgh we had sufficient wisdom or warning, to beware of such motions or requests making <u>to his ministers. Let it not be so sayd of the holy one of Israel</u>: but let his mercies abownd with us to his glorie. Amen.

EK: Now commeth all down agayn, as before.

Me: What are the Sonnes of men, that they put time in her own bosom? or measure a Judgment that is unsearchable?

Δ:

Me: I help thy imperfections: What, man thinketh wisdome, is error in our sight. But bicause my Nature is to cure, and set up those that fall, Thus much understand.

As I haue sayde: The <u>49 partes of this boke</u>[161] - 49 voyces,

---

[160] Δ Note and take hede from hence forward.

[161] Of the boke.

Whereunto the so many powres, with theyr inferiors and subiects,[162] haue byn, are, and shalbe obedient.

Euery Element in this mysterie is a world of understanding. Euery one knoweth here what is his due obedience: and this shall differ thee in speche from a mortall creature.[163]

Consider with thy self, How thow striuest against thyne own light, and shaddowest the windows of thyne own understanding.

I haue sayde: Be it unto thee, as God will. I am not a powre or whirlewynde that giueth occasion of offence.

Longe sumus a peruersitate destructionis.[164] Thus much I haue sayd, for thy reformation and understanding.

Δ:[165]

Me: Lo, untill the Secrets of this boke be written, I come no more: neyther of me shall you haue any apparition. Yet, in powre, my office shall be here.[166]

Say, what you here, for euery word shall be named unto you: it is somwhat a shorter way, and more according to your desyre.

Euery Element[167] hath 49 manner of understandings. Therin is comprehended so many languages.[168] They are all spoken at ones, and seuerally, by them selues, by distinction may be spoken. Untill thow come to the Citie, thow canst not behold the beawty thereof.

Nihil hic est, quod non est perfectum.[169]

---

162 49 Powres with theyr Inferiors, vide sup. 48 after a sort: and 1. vide Martij 24.

163 Angelicall Language.

164 Longe . . . destructionis: "We are far away from the perversity of destruction." -Ed.

165 There are approximately three blank lines here. -Ed.

166 Raphaël is to be absent for a certayn time: but his powre shall be here.

167 Of the boke.

168 Languages.

169 Nihil . . . perfectum: "Nothing is here which is not perfect." -Ed.

I go. I haue sayde, (and it is true,) No unclean thing shall enter: Much less, then, <u>here</u>: For, it is the <u>sight of whose Maiestie</u> we tremble and quake at. <u>He shall teache, of himself</u>; for, we are not worthy.[170] What then, of your selues? But such is his great and singular fauor, that, he is of him self, and with those, whom he choseth.[171] <u>For, the ende of all things is at hand,</u>[172] and Powre must distinguish, or els nothing can prevayle. What you here, yea what thow feelest, by thy finger, Recorde; and seale sure. This is all, and in this is conteyned all, that comprehendeth all, The allmighty powre and profunditie of his glory.

What els?

As thow seest, and till he see, whose sight,[173] is the light of this his own powre, His might is great. The dew of his stedfastnes and glorious perfection hold up and rectify the weaknes of your fragilitie: Make you strong to the ende of his workmanship to whome I commit you.

EK: He plucketh the veale ouer all.

A voyce afterward:—Ne Ne Ne na Jabes.

Δ: Sanctus Sanctus Sanctus Dominus Deus Zebaoth: Pleni sunt cæli et terra gloria Maiestatis eius. Cui soli omnis honor, laus et gloria.[174]

Amen.

---

[170] Δ Note, that we shalbe Theodidacti, of god him self and no Angel herein. -Δ. Theodidacti: "taught by God." -Ed.

[171] Potentia. -Δ. ("Power." -Ed.)

[172] The ende of all things is at hand.

[173] The sight of god.

[174] Sanctus . . . gloria: "Holy, holy, holy, Lord God of Hosts. Heaven and earth are filled with the glory of his majesty. To him alone is all honor, praise, and glory." -Ed.

1583 Aprilis 2. Tuesday. Jesus + before none

Δ: A noyce like a Thunder was first hard. The Chayre and Table appered. There appered fyre in the chayre, and burnt away the veale or covering therof. The cullor of the flame of the fire was as of Aqua vitæ burnt.

A voyce:—Sum.[175]

EK: There goeth a clowd or smoke from the chayre, and covereth the Table. That smoke filled all the place.

A voyce:—Impleta sunt omnia gloria et honore tuo.[176]

EK: All is become clere, saue the Table which remayned couered with the clowde still.

🕮 A great thunder began agayn, and the chayre remayned all in fire. Now the boke appeareth euidently, lying uppon the Globe in the chayre and the letters appered wet styll, as yf they were blud. There appered fire to be thrown oute of the stone, uppon EK.[177]

The sownd of many voyces semed to pronownce this: Let all things prayse him and extoll his name for euer.

EK: The fire is still in the chayre, but so transparent, that the boke and letters therof may well be seen.

EK felt his hed as if it were on fire.

A voyce:—Sic soleo errores hominum purificare.[178]

A voyce:—Say what you see.

EK: I see letters, as I saw before.

A voyce:—Moue not from your places;[179] for, this place is holy.

---

175 Sum: "I am." -Ed.

176 Impleta . . . tuo: "All things have been fulfilled to your glory and honor." -Ed.

177 Note, fire.

178 Sic . . . purificare: "So I am accustomed to cleansing the errors of the people." -Ed.

179 Moue not from your places.

A voyce:—Read.—EK: I cannot.

Δ: You shold haue lerned the characters perfectly and theyr names, that you mowght now haue redyly named them to me as you shold see them. Then there flashed fire uppon EK agayne.[180]

A voyce:—<u>Say what thow thinkest</u>. Δ: He sayd so to EK.

EK: My hed is all on fire.

A voyce:—What thow thinkest, euery word, that speak.

EK: I can read all, now, most perfectly: and in the Third row[181] thus I see to be red,

3. Palce[182] duxma ge na dem oh elóg da ved ge ma fedes o ned a
    tha lepah nes din. Ihehudétha dan vangem onphe dabin oh nax
    palse ge dah maz gem fatesged oh mal dan gemph naha Lax ru
    lutúdah ages nagel osch. macom adeph a dosch ma handa.

EK: Now it thundreth agayn.

A voyce:—Ego sum qui in te. Mihi ergo qui Sum.

Δ: Non nobis domine non nobis, sed nomini tuo damus gloriam.[183]

Δ: Then EK red the fowrth row, as followeth,

4. Pah o mata nax lasco vana ar von zimah la de de pah o gram nes
    ca pan amphan van zebog ahah dauez öl ga. van gedo oha ne daph
    aged onédon pan le ges ma gas axa nah alpod ne alida phar or ad
    gamésad argla nado oges.

Δ: Blessed be the name of the Highest, who giueth light and understanding.

---

180 Fire agayn.

181 The Third row of the first page.

182 Palse/Palze. I dowt which of these 3 must serve: c,s,z.

183 Ego sum . . . gloriam: "I am the one who is within you. Therefore I am the one who is for myself. Δ: Not for us, O Lord, not for us, but for your name may we give glory." -Ed.

EK: It thundreth agayn. All is covered.

A voyce:—Orate.[184]

Δ: We prayed: and returning to the work agayn, the fire covered all still and EK hard voyces, singing (as a far of) very melodiously. Then all became euident agayn unto EK his perfect Judgment.

Δ: EK then red thus,[185]

5. Mabeth ar mices[186] achaph pax mara geduth alídes orcánor manch[187] arseth. olontax ar geban vox portex ah pamo. agématon buríse ganport. vdríos pasch. Machel len arvin zembuges. vox mara. gons Ihehusch dah pársodan maäh alsplan donglses adípr[188] agínot. archad[189] dons a dax van famlet a dex arge pa gens.

----

6. Van danzan oripat es vami gest ageff ormaténodah zálpala doniton pasdaes[190] gánpogan Undanpel adin achaph máradon oxámax anólphe dan ieh voxad mar vox ihedutharh aggs pal med lefe. IAN lefa dox parnix O droes[191] marsíbleh aho dan adeph uloh iads ascleh da verox ans dalph che damph lam achos.[192]

---

184 Orate: "Pray." -Ed.

185 The fifth row.

186 Pronownced mises.

187 Mansh.

188 Adíper. It is significatiue.

189 Arkad.

190 Pasdas.

191 Dros.

192 Akos.

EK: There is a great Thundring agayn.

Δ: It is the hand of the highest, who will get him honor by his own works.

EK: The Voyce and sownd of pleasantnes and reioycing was hard: and all was dark.

A small voyce:—Locus est hic sanctus.[193]

An other voyce:—Sacer est a te Domine.[194]

EK: All is now opened agayne.

Δ: Then EK, red thus,[195]

7. Amídan gah[196] lesco van gedon amchih ax or madol cramsa ne dah vadgs lesgamph[197] ar: mara panosch aschedh or samhám-pors asco*. pacadabaah <u>asto</u>[198] a vdrios archads ors arni. pamphíca lan gebed druxarh fres adma. nah pamphes eä van-glor brisfog mahad. no poho a palgeh donla def archas NA Degel.

----

8. Vnaem[199] palugh agan drosad ger max fa lefe pandas mars langed undes mar. pachad odídos martíbah v'dramah noges gar. lenges argrasphe drulthe las aséraphos. gamled cam led caph Snicol lumrad v ma. pa granse paphres a drinox a demphe NA. geníle o danpha. NA ges a ne gaph a.

---

[193] Locus sanctus. -Δ. Locus est hic sanctus: "This place is holy." -Ed.

[194] Sacer est a te Domine: "It is consecrated to you, O Lord." -Ed.

[195] The Seventh row.

[196] Iah.

[197] Lesgomph.

[198] Asco, with a prick ouer the o, is to be pronownced as Asto.

[199] Vnam.

EK: The sownd of Melodie, begynneth agayne.

Δ: The fire cam from EK his eyes, and went into the stone againe. And then, he could not perceyue, or read one worde.[200] The Fyre flashed very thick and all was couered with a veale.

Δ: Prayse we the lord, and extoll his name. For, his hand hath wrought wundrous works, for his owne glorie.

Amen.

Aprilis .3. Wensday, Forenone †

Δ: First the Curten was drawn away: and then all appeared on fire: The whole place all ouer. EK hard voyces, but could not discern any thing but the hummering of them.

Δ: There cam fire agayn (out of the stone) uppon EK, all his body ouer.

EK: The fire so diminisheth it self that the boke may be perceyved.

A voyce:—Magnus Magnus Magnus.[201]

An other voyce:—Locus sacer et acceptabilis Deo.[202]

EK fellt the fire to gather up into his hed. Shortly after he could read the boke, as he could do yesterday.

Ʂꜣꜣꝡ ꞷꞁꝡ

9. Vlla[203] doh aco par semná gan var se gar on dun. sebo dax se pal genso vax necra par sesqui nat. axo nat sesqui ax[204] olna

---

200 Note this Mysterie of god his powre drawn to him self agayne.

201 Magnus Magnus Magnus: "Great, Great, Great." -Ed.

202 Locus . . . Deo: "A place consecrated and acceptable to God." -Ed.

203 Of the first character of Vlla, I dowt.

204 Ex.

dam var gen vox nap vax. Vro[205] varca cas nol undat vom
Sangef famsed oh. sih ádra gad gesco vansax ora gal parsa.

----

10. Varo. nab vbrah NA pa uotol ged ade pa cem[206] na dax. van
sebrá dah oghe aschin o nap gem phe axo or. nec a ve da pengon
a moroh ah óha aspáh. niz ab vrdráh[207] <u>gohed</u>[208] a carnat dan
faxmal gamph. gamph nacro vax asclad caf prac crúscanse.[209]

----

11. gam. ohe gemph ubráh-ax.[210] orpna[211] nex-or napo, gemlo. a
cheph[212] can sedló pam-geman ange hanzu <u>ALLA</u>.[213] Cáppo-se
damo gam-vas oro-dax-vá ges-pálo palme pola.[214]

EK: All these, (now red,) fall out and all the rows, before, likewise.
A voyce:—Prayse God.
Δ: We prayed. And after, was this shewed,[215]

---

[205] The V has an umlaut in the manuscript. -Ed.

[206] Sem.

[207] Vdráh.

[208] Iohed. gohed, pronownced as Iohed, signifieth One euerlasting and all things
descending uppon one, and gohed Ascha is as much to say as One god.

[209] Canse, signifieth mightie: and Cruscanse, more mightie.

[210] All these which haue lines under them [Here they are hyphenated. -Ed.] are eche
but one word of diuerse syllables: being 9 words of them.

[211] The a produced.

[212] The last h remissly sownded.

[213] This word is circled in the manuscript.

[214] Pola and Pala signifie two: Pola signifieth two together, and Pala signifieth two
separated.

[215] Δ This was a parcell of a row, which onely appered by him self.

Gals-ange no-témpa-ro sama dan genzé axe. falod amruh ácurtoh
saxx par mano gan vax no.[216] gramfa gem sadglá[217] loh vrox sappóh
iad ah oha unra.

Δ: Now appeared an other row.

12. Se[218] gors axol ma pa a oh la sabúlan. Caph ardox anpho nad
v'rnah ud ago lan vans.[219] v'xa grad órno dax palmes árisso dan
vnra. vánsample galse not zablis óphide ALLA loh. gaslah osson luze
adaö max vanget or dámo ans. leóz dasch léöha dan se gla'spa neh.

All becam dark, and it thundred.
A voyce:—Prayse God.
Δ: We prayed.
Δ: Now appered three or fowr rows to gither. The boke seemed to
fly, as if it wold fly a peces (the fyre remayning) and to make a great
sturring in the place where it lay.

13. Amprí apx ard ardo argá[220] argés argáh ax. osch nedo les icás.
han andam von ga lax man. nosch. dóngo a yntar cey[221] lude
asch úrise alpé gem var dancet.[222] nap alped v'rsbe temps a vod

---

216 In margin, but later crossed out: Δ At 'no.', ende 49, and so here ar 10 over.

217 "á" must be sownded long.

218 This "se" is the nine and fortyth word longing to them before.

219 Vns.

220 "A" long.

221 Sey.

222 Danset.

nos gema o ulon máncepax oxné pricos a gót. zalpa ne doxam
órne.[223]

----

14. Admag apa ascò[224] tar. gans oärz am seph selqui quisben
almán. gons sa ieh mársibleh gron áscabb gamat. neý aden vdan
phand sempés nan narran al. cáno géme dansé álde nótes par-
célah arb ner ga lum pancu[225] príscas ábra músce[226] an nox.
napód[227] a on dan sem ges asche[228]

EK: A sownd of many voyces, sayd, —Orate.[229]

15. Mica suráscha para te gámmes ádrios NA danos. vra lad pacad
ur gesme crus[230] a prásep ed. a palse nax varno zum. zancú
asdom baged V'rmigar orch phaphes ustrá nox affod masco
gax cámles vnsanba a oh la gras par quas. cónsaqual lat gem-
dax tantat ba vod. talpah ian.

----

16. Gescó[231] a taffom ges nat gam. pamphé ordáquaf cesto

---

223   ⌒ this with a prick betokeneth "y."

224 Pronownce "Asto."

225 Pansu.

226 Musse

227 ó long.

228 Aske. E.K. understode the Language: and wold haue spoken somwhat, but he
was willed to stay.

229 Orate: "Pray." -Ed.

230 Pronownce as we do cruse a cup.

231 ó long.

chídmap[232] mischná ia-ísg.[233] iaiálphzudph a dancét[234] vnban
caf ránsembloh. daf-ma[235] vp aschem graos[236] chrámsa[237] asco
dah. vímna gen álde os papéam och láuan vnad. oh drosad
údrios nagel panzo ab sescú. Vórge afcál[238] vslaffda mórsab
gaf[239] ham de Peleh asca.

Δ: This went away, when it was read. It waxed dark.
A voyce:—Orate.[240] Δ: We prayed.
EK: It beginneth to clere.
A voyce to EK:—Say.

17. Ar'tosa geme oh gálsagen[241] axa loph gebed adóp: zarcas vr
vánta pas ámphe nóde alpan. nócas se ga ormácased lax naph
talpt. pámphicas[242] sandam Voscméh iodh asclad ar. phan gas
málse a quaz nam vngem vansel gembúgel a gémbusez á-ro[243]
tehl alts murt valtab bániffa faxed ar chlyfod

---

[232] Kidmap.

[233] Sempiternall One and indiuisible God.

[234] Dansét.

[235] A very long.

[236] Gras.

[237] a reverent word, the first 'a' very long, and is, be it made with powre.

[238] Ahal, iently, and the 'a' long.

[239] "A" long.

[240] Orate: "Pray." -Ed.

[241] The diuine powre creating the angel of the sonne.

[242] 4 manner of constructions in that one word.

[243] A-ro is one word diuided, as res-publica, and here this word is diuided into two squares, and so there are 49.

18. A tam nat. glun asdeh ahlud gádre fam Shing la dan. guinsé[244]
    <u>life</u>[245] arilsar zabulan cheuá<u>ch</u>[246] se. amph lesche andam var
    ges ar phex are.[247] <u>NA</u>[248] tax páchel lapídox ar da vax malcos.
    vna gra tassox varmára ud ga les vns ap se. ne da ox lat ges ar.

Now it waxeth dark. Δ: We must pray: (sayd I) and so we did. But
EK prayed perfectly in this Angels language &c.

19. Asmo dahán pan casme co caph al oh.
    san ged a b<u>ansaa</u>[249] un adon a seb Ian.
    agláho dánfa zúna cap orcha[250] dah os.
    fámsah ON naä̈b[251] ab nagah geha fastod.
    hansey om hauan lagra gem gas mal.
    parcóg[252] dax nedo va geda leb ar'ua ne cap sem[253] carvan.

    ----

20. Onsem gelhóldim geb abníh ian.
    oxpha bas cappó cars órdriph grip gars.
    of víndres nah ges páhado vllónooh can vaz a.
    fam gisril ag nóhol sep gérba dot vánca NA.

---

[244] E long.

[245] <u>Life lephe lurfando</u> is a strong charge to the wicked to tell the truth: Δ This he
sayd to my demand of this phrase wherof I had mention many yeres since.

[246] A long.

[247] Pronownce "ar."

[248] <u>NA</u> - The name of the Trinitie, One separable for a while.

[249] "A" long; onely one "a" sownded for "aa."

[250] Orka.

[251] "ä" sounded as "au."

[252] The 'g' not expressly sownded.

[253] In eius loco. ("In this place." -Ed.)

sem <u>ah-pa</u>[254] nex <u>ar-pah</u> lad vamó iar séque.

Vad ro garb. ah sem dan van ged ah paleu[255]

Now, the fire shot oute of EK his eyes, into the stone, agayne. And by and by he understode nothing of all, neyther could reade any thing: nor remember what he had sayde. All became dark. Then was the curten drawne, and so we ended.

> Δ: Gloria patri et filio et spiritui sancto
> nunc et semper.[256]
> Amen.

Aprilis .3. Wensday + After none hor 5¼

Δ: A prety while, the veale remayned ouer all: then it was taken away. First fire was thrown uppon EK out of the stone. Many voyces concordantly sayd, —Bonum est ô Deus, quia Bonitas ipa es.[257]

An other voyce:—   Et magnum, quia tu magnitudo ipsius Magnitudinis.[258]

A voyce:—   Ádgmach ádgmach ádgmach [= much glory]

A great voyce:—   Sum, et sacer est hic locus.[259]

---

[254] It is but one word.

[255] Sownded, palef.

[256] Gloria . . . semper: "Glory be to the Father and the Son and the Holy Spirit now and forever." -Ed.

[257] Bonum . . . es: "It is good, O God, for you are goodness itself." -Ed.

[258] Et magnum . . . Magnitudinis: "And great because of the size of greatness itself." -Ed.

[259] Sum . . . locus: "I am, and this place is, holy." -Ed.

A voyce:—   Ádgmach ádgmach ádgmach húcacha.

Δ: Then EK read the row on this manner,

21. Padohómagebs[260] galpz <u>arps</u>[261] apá nal Si. gámvagad al pódma
    gan NA. vr cas nátmaz ándiglon ar'mbu.[262] zántclumbar ar
    noxócharmah. Sapoh lan gamnox vxála vors. Sábse cap vax mar
    vinco.[263] Labandáho nas gampbox arce.[264] dah gorhahálpstd
    gascámpho[265] lan ge. Béfes argédco[266] nax arzulgh[267] <u>orh.</u>[268]
    sémhaham[269] vn'cal laf garp oxox. Loangah.[270]

---

[260] Padohómaghebs.

[261] Rede as arch.

[262] A piller of light stode before the boke.

[263] In margin, but crossed out: "Vin in vinco must be pronowced long as if it were a
    dubble i."

[264] Arse.

[265] Or, gáscampho - why didst thow so: as god sayd to Lucifer. The word hath 64
    significations.

[266] =cum humilitate aduocamus te cum adoratione Trinitas. ("[Befafes] with humil-
    ity we call you, with adoration of the Trinity." -Ed.)

[267] This is the name of the spirit contrary to Befafes.

[268] In margin: "~~Orh = Deus sine fine. Gorh = Deus a Deo.~~

    Befes, the vocatiue case of Befafes.

    ~~Befes, is as much to say as 'come Befafes and see us'.~~

    Befafes ô, is to call uppon him as on god. Befafes oh, is as muche to say, 'come
    Befafes and beare witness."

    Also in margin: "Befafes his Etymologie is as much to say as, 'Lumen a Lumine'.
    Spiritus orh secundus est in grada imperfectionis tenebrarum. = Δ. How can orh
    signifie 'Deus sine fine' if it be the name of a wicked spirit?" (Deus sine fine:
    "God without end"; Deus a Deo: "God from God"; lumen a lumine: "light from
    the light"; Spiritus orh . . . tenebrarum: "The spirit orh is the second in the scale
    of imperfections of darkness"; Deus sine fine: "God without end." -Ed.)

[269] This word hath 72 significations.

[270] Of two syllables.

Δ: Now appered Raphael [⟨symbol⟩] or one like him, and sayde,
Salus vobis in illo qui vobiscum.[271]

I am a medicine that must prevayle against your infirmities: and am
come to teache, and byd take hede. Yf you use <u>dubble repetition</u>, in the
things that follow, you shall both write and work and all at ones: which
mans nature can not performe. The trubbles were so great that might
ensue thereof, that your strength were nothing to preuayle against
them. <u>When it is written, reade it no more with voyce</u>, till it <u>be in prac-</u>
tise. All wants shalbe opened unto you. Where I fownd you, (with him,
and there,) I leave you. <u>Cumfortable Instruction is a necessarie</u>
Medicine.

    Farewell.

EK: The boke and the Chayre, and the rest were all out of sight while
Raphael spake, and he lay down prostrate. EK saw a great multitude in
the farder side of the stone. They all cam into the stone, and axed,

    What now?
    How now?

Vors mábberan = how now: what hast thow to do with us?

Δ: As I began thus to say (<u>The God of powre, of wisdom</u>,) they all
interrupted my entended prayer to god for help &c and sayd, We go
We go.

Δ: And so they went away.

Then the boke and the rest cam in agayne.

A voyce:—One Note more, I haue to tell thee. <u>Ax him not, What he</u>
<u>sayeth</u>, but write as thow hearest: for it is true.

Δ: Then, o lord, make my hearing sharp and strong, to perceyue sufficiently as the case requireth.

---

271 Salus . . . vobiscum: "Welcome (lit. health) to you in him who is with you." -Ed.

Rap:—Be it unto thee.

Δ: Then EK red as followeth,

22. <u>ors lah</u> gemphe nahoh <u>ama-natoph</u> des garhul vanseph iuma lat
   <u>gedos lubah</u> aha last gesto Vars macom des curad <u>vals mors</u>
   gaph gemsed pa campha zednu ábfada máses lófgono
   Luruandah[272] lesog iamle padel arphe nades gulsad maf gescon
   lampharsad <u>surem paphe arbasa</u> arzusen agsde ghehol max
   vrdra paf gals macrom finistab gelsaphan asten Vrnah[273]

A Voyce: Whatsoeuer thow settest down shalbe true.

Δ: I thank god most hartilie: The case allso requireth it so to be.

23. Asch val íamles árcasa árcasan arcúsma íabso gliden paha
   pacadúra gebne[274] óscaroh gádne au[275] arua las genost cásme
   palsi uran vad gadeth axam pambo cásmala sámnefa gárdomas
   árxad pámses gémulch gápes lof lachef ástma vates[276] garnsnas
   orue gad garmah sar'quel rúsan gages drusala phímacar aldech
   oscom lat garset panóston.[277]

----

24. gude laz miz lábac vsca losd pa Cópad dem sebas gad váncro
   umas ges umas umas ges gabre umas umáscala um'phazes

---

[272] Larvandah.

[273] Δ Note these 55 wordes stand in 49 places: [ors lah, ama natoph, gedos lubah,
vals mors] of which 55, some two stand in a square place, some three, [surem
paphe arbasa] as I haue noted.

[274] Iebne.

[275] Af.

[276] Bates.

[277] There are no points neyther in the last before. They be parcells of Invitations very
pleasant to good Angels. Before was, as it were a preface of the Creation and distinction of Angels &c.

umphagám maaga mosel iahal loges[278] vapron fémse dapax orgen[279] láscod ia láscoda vága am lascafes iarques préso tamísel vnsnapha <u>ia dron</u> goscam lápe voxa chimlah aueaux losge auióxan lárgemah.

----

25. zureth axad lomah ied gura vancrásma ied sesch lapod vonse avó avé lamsage zimah zemah zúmacah Vormex artman voz vozcha tolcas zapne zarvex zorquem allahah gibúrod[280] Ampátraton zimegauna[281] zonze zámca aschma[282] vlpa tapa van vorxvam drusad Caph castárago grúmna can'caphes absacáncaphes zúmbala teuort granx zumcot lu graf saxma Cape.

----

26. Col age lam gem fam tepham vra ap du ca sampat vóxham Lúnzapha axquem Bobagélzod gaphémse lan'se agni cam setquo teth gaphad oxámarah gímnephad vox'canah vrn dage[283] paphcod zámbuges zambe ach oha zambúges gásca lunpel zadphe zómephol zun zadchal ureseh varún pachádah gusels vx amna pa granna oh vz

----

Δ: I think it will be dark by and by, and our Cumpany will expect

----

278 Loghes.

279 Orghen.

280 Ghibúrod.

281 Zimegafna.

282 Askma.

283 Daie.

our comming down to supper. Therfore, if, without offence we might now leave of, it might seme good so to do.

A voyce:—gemeganza = your will be done.

Δ: As I was discoursing with EK after we had done, and he seamed yet skylfull and hable to say much of the understanding of the premisses, and began to declare somwhat, How they did all apperteyne to Good Angels, suddenly there cam the fyre from his eyes into the stone agayne. And than he could say no more: nor remember any thing of that he had hard seen or understode less than half a quarter of an howre before.

Δ: Deo nostro Viuo Vero et Omnipotenti
sit omnis laus et graz actio
nunc et semper.[284] Amen.

Aprilis 4 Thursday + mane hor. 5½

Δ: I made a prayer.

Δ: A voyce:—Quia ipem Deus Deus Deus noster cuius misericordia infinita.[285]

Δ: The fire, immediately did shote out of the stone into EK, as before. His tung thereuppon did quake in his mowth.

---

[284] Deo . . . semper: "To our God, living, true, and almighty, be all praise and thanksgiving, now and ever." -Ed.

[285] Quia . . . infinita: "Because God himself, God, our God, whose infinite mercy." -Ed.

EK: The Veale hangeth yet before.

Δ: Then, all being uncouered, thus he red.

27. Atra cas carmax pabámsed gero adol macom vaxt gestes[286]
ladúch carse ámages[287] dascal panselogen dursca zureóch pam-
casáh vsca huädrongúnda malue ior. gáscama af orthox VAN-
CORHG aspe zubra vaacääh gandeuá arinmaphel vax oh saoh
abra iehudeh gamphe vndáxa casmat lafet vncas laphet
vanascor torx glust hahaha enséde gumah galseds.

----

28. Pacádpha palzé zuma carphah uzad capaden v'lsage[288] EXCOL-
PHAG-MARTBH iasmadel vóscon sem abnérda tohcoth[289]
iamphala páhath órcheth iesmog pasque Labääh agas lada vng
lasco ied ampha leda pageh gemze axax ózed caphzed campha
voxal luthed gedan[290] famech[291] ártsnad gathad zuresch pascha
lo guma[292] hálphe dax vancron patel zurad

----

29. Canda lahad Bóbagen afna vorzed phadel NOBTDAMBTH
gáscala oxad vanges[293] vodoth mured achna[294] adcol damath

---

[286] Iestes.

[287] Amaies.

[288] Vlsaie.

[289] This name comprehendeth the number of all the fayries - who are diuels next to
the state and condition of man etc.

[290] Iedan.

[291] Famek.

[292] Iuma.

[293] Vanies.

[294] Akna.

zesvamcul pacadáah zimles zoraston geh galze mazad pethel cusma iaphes huráscah órphade loscad mages[295] mat lúmfamge detchel[296] orze cámalah vndan <u>padgze</u>[297] páthmataph zumad lepháda oháäx vlschan[298] zembloh agne phamgah iudad capex Luzad vemech arse

----

30. Onda gams luzgaph vxan genzed[299] pádex CÓNGAM-PHLGH[300] ascath gadpham zurdah zamge gloghcha sapax tastel vn'sada phatheth zúncapha oxamáchad semteph ascle zuncas magzed dulm pamfra húsage axad exóradad casmet ámphigel adcath luza pathem nécotheth gesch[301] labba doh dóxa vascheth hoxan lamésde lampha iodoch gonzah hamges[302] glutha óxmogel[303] démapha vz'ed ascraph.

----

31. zudath chádgama[304] ómsage[305] hor gadsa gézes ORPHÁM-ZAM<u>NAHE</u>[306] gedod asphed voxa gémgah lath gáphes

---

295 Maies.

296 Detkel.

297 Pagze. = iustitia a numine diuino sine labe. Δ ("Justice from divine power without defect." -Ed.)

298 Vlskan

299 Ienzed.

300 Congamfilgh. = fide that reviveth mans brest, The holy ghoste. -Δ (Fide: "in faith." -Ed.)

301 Iesk.

302 Hamies.

303 Oxmoiel.

304 Kadgama.

305 Omsaie.

306 Na.

zembloth chasca olphe dax marpha <u>lothe</u> sool[307] separ
marges[308] bosqui laxa cosneth gonse dadg voxma v'mage vnx
gascheth lood admah loo[309] ga zem-chá-na-phe am'-na-la ia
pacheth nox-da a-mah

----

32. Gedox al SEM-GA-NA-DA-BAH ongagágeda phachel loódath
    haxna gu-na-pá-ge-pha al se geda oh oöda géhoph pachad enol
    adax loges famgah laxqui hasche vadol vóms-a-na gax-ma-deph-
    na-zad gel panca vam Sesquin oxal genoph voödal u-má-da-bah

----

33. Asge lun <u>zumia</u> paxchádma enohol duran ORCHLÓD-
    MAPHAG mages oschan lod bunda cap luzan lorpha leuándah
    orxzed famzad ge-nós-o-dath[310] phasélma gesda chom-gas-
    naph-geth-nag g<u>ot</u>h[311] ládmano Vmvar gezen vax gulzad
    margas luxt lapch iudath zomze van goth dah vorx guna ia ada
    Vox-há-ma-na

----

34. Arze galsam vnza vcha pasel noxda Nobróschom[312] gu-na-dé-pho-
    gas dúnseph man-cax-mal-cás-mah ied-hah-mel-cár-na zemphe
    vncah lethoph both-ned-ga-phí-cas-mel ioth-hath-cha-sad ma-ne-
    ded-ma-gon zuna gothel pascheph nodax vam phath mata[313]

---

307 Sol.

308 Maries.

309 Lo.

310 21, words hither.

311 O long.

312 In great letters.

313 Δ Here are but 48 words: I dowt that there lacketh one.

A voyce: Orate. Δ: We prayed.

35. Aphath zunca voxmor can zadcheth[314] napha. VOR-
DOMPHÁNCHES ga-ues-go-sa-del gurah leth agsnah orza
max pace ieth cas lad fam pahógama zon-chás-pha-ma zum-
blés-cha-phax var-gat-ma-gas-ter ne-ho-gat-ma-gan vn-ga-
phax-ma-la gegath laxqu goga lab naches[315]

Δ: Thereuppon the Vele was drawn, and the fire cam from EK
his eyes again into the stone.

Δ: Deo opt. Max. omnis honor
laus et gloria.[316] Amen.

Aprilis .5. Friday + a meridie hora 5¼

Δ: The Vele was taken away, without any speche used by me or EK. The
boke and all the former furniture appeared very bright.

Δ: I made a prayer to god, begynning, Expectãs expectaui Dominum[317] &c.

EK: I here the sownd of men playing very melodiously on
Instruments and singing.

---

314 Zadketh.

315 Here seme to be to many by 3 or 4.

316 Deo . . . gloria: "To God all good, all honor, praise, and glory." -Ed.

317 Expectas expectaui Dominum: "I waited patiently for the Lord" (Psalm 40:1/
Vulgate 39:1). -Ed.

A Voyce:—Serue God and take hede of Nettels.[318] Δ: This was spoken to EK in respect of a great anger he was-in yesternight, by reason that one had done him inurie in speche at my table. [Charles Sled.]

EK: There appere a great many, a far of; as thowgh they appered beyond the top of a howse: and so semed far of behinde the stone: and they seme to haue no heds.

A Voyce:—A peculier people, and shalbe restored.[319]

Δ: After this voyce, the sayd hedles-people disäpered. Then all appered fyre, and a clowd covered all: and in the top of the fyre in the chayre, appered three faces, and seemed to shute and close in one. The faces seemed, eche to turn rownd, and so to ioyne in one afterward.

A Voyce:—Prayse him in his glorie and worship him, in his truth.

Δ: The fire entred into EK.

A voyce:—Orate.[320] Δ: We prayed.

Δ: Then thus appeared,

36. gedóthar argo fa adóphanah gamsech olneh várasah iusmach [= begotten.]

A voyce:—Interpret not, till your understanding be furnished.[321]

---

[318] Take hede of Nettels.

[319] Perhaps the Jues shall be restored. -Δ. Dee sees "headless" as a metaphor for the fact that the Jews have no central authority like the Pope. Dee's meaning is most likely to be that the vision is a prophecy that the Jews will be readmitted into England where they had been expelled in 1290/91. They were, in fact, readmitted into England in 1655 after petitions from Menasseh Ben Israel. See David S. Katz, *Philo-Semitism and the Readmission of the Jews to England* (Oxford: Clarendon Press, 1982), chapter three for details. There is more on this in his most recent book, *The Jews in the History of England* (Oxford: Clarendon Press, 1994). According to Dr. Katz (private communication), "Dee had good reason to think this might happen in his lifetime." -Ed.

[320] Orate: "Pray." -Ed.

[321] Interprete not yet.

Vschna pháol doa vah oho lazed la-zu-red ámma donax valesto
acaph lámphages ronox ganma iudreth loth adágma gonsaph
godálga phareph iadsma zema loa ag-náph-ag-on zu-na-ha[322] al
me io-náp-ha-cas zeda ox arni

----

37. Adgzelga[323] olms vánaph osma vages otholl <u>dox an ga had</u>[324]
latqui dónaphe zu gar. phamah[325] nordeph gasmat gasque gasla
gas NA gasmaphés gasmagél gasnúnabe vamsech ábsechel
gúlapha axnécho demsa pámbochaph iehúsa gadaámah nosad
iurés chy almse orsa vax marde zun éffa mochoéffa zuréheffa
asga Lubeth bethlémcha máxiche iehúscoth iaphan órnada
vamne od ghim-noh

----

38. <u>Arph</u>e[326] lamse gaphnedg[327] argaph zonze zumcoth <u>O'mdopa-
dáphaab</u>[328] nulech[329] gaartha ancáphama soldémcah casdra
vges lapha ludasphándo ga-lú-ba-noh ap-á-cha-na[330] iedeph
zembloh zamgýssel chéuacha laquet lozódma ierinth onaph
uzad máspela gýman orphámmagah iu-mes-ba-lé-go archán-
phame. zamcheth zoach[331]

---

[322] Zunah.

[323] Ag-zel-ia.

[324] Doxaniahad. one word.

[325] Fáma = I will giue.

[326] = I desire thee O god.

[327] Gaphned.

[328] This was put in and out a good while before EK could haue a perfect vew to rede it.

[329] Nuleg.

[330] = The slymie things made of dust.

[331] Zoah. Δ Here seme to want 5 or 6 names.

----

39. Am'chama zeuoth luthámba ganeph iamda ox oho iephad made
noxa voscaph bámgephes noschol apeth iale lod ga NA-zuma
datques vorzad nu-mech[332] apheth nudach caseth iotha lax
arseth armi pli ca tar bám a co[333] zamgeph gaseth vrnod arispa
iex ban Setha. oh lagnaph dothoth brazed vamchach odoámaäh
zembles gunza naspolge gáthme orsoth zurath vámeth anseh.[334]

----

40. Zalpe íedmacha ámphas nethoth alphax durah gethos aschéph
nethoth iubad laxmah ionsa max dan do násdoga mátastos[335]
lateth vnchas amse Jacaph zembloágauh[336] ad-pha-má-gel lud-
cha-dám-sa am-phí-ca-tol ar-nó-pa-a a-da-pa-gé-moh no-dás-ma
mac-hes-tép-ho-lon

----

41. Lumbor iemásch onzed gam-phi-dá-rah. gom-ás-cha-pa zeba
zun amph naho zucath uomplínanoháhal machal lozma dauan-
geth búches lauax orxod maches donchaph luzath marpheth oz
lanva don gáuah oschol lúmasa phedeph omsa nax do-má-ge-re
an-ge-no-phá-cha pha-cha-dó-na

----

42. óschala zamges onphá gemes phaches nolpha daxeth machés-
machoh vastnálpoh gemas nach loscheph daphmech noth

---

[332] Nu-mech is two wordes.

[333] One word.

[334] These last two words are in one square.

[335] = The furious and perpetuall fire enclosed for the ponishment of them that are banished from the glory. One word of 7 syllables: 4 in the first part and 3 in the last.

[336] Zembloágaf.

chales zunech maschol <u>Lu</u>[337] gasnaph malces gethcaph
madena[338] oäh gemsah pa luseth <u>iorbástamax</u> elcaph rusam
phanes domsath gel[339] pachadóra amáxchano lu-ma-gé-no
ar-ma-cha-phá-me-lon adro micho natath iamesebáchola doná-
docha.

Δ: The fire went from EK his eyes to the stone agayn. Then EK
his understanding was gone allso.

> Δ: Deo soli sit omnis laus honor
> et gloria per infinita sæculor
> sæcula.[340] Amen.

Aprilis 6. Saterday affore none hora 10¼

Δ: The fire shot into EK, as before was used: wherat he startled. All was
uncovered, as the manner was. But EK had such a whirling and beating
inwardly in his hed, that he could not use any Judgment to discerne
what appered, for half a quarter of an howre almost.

A Voyce:—SVM.[341]

And agayn—a voyce:—Gahoachma [= Sum quod sum,[342] EK
expownded it.].

----

337 Lu = from one.

338 Madna.

339 Iel.

340 Deo . . . saecula: "To God alone be all praise, honor, and glory, through endless
ages upon ages." -Ed.

341 Sum: "I am." -Ed.

342 Sum quod sum: "I am that I am." -Ed.

43. Asmar gehótha gabseph achándas vnáscor sátquama látquataf
hun gánses <u>luximágelo</u> ásquapa <u>lochath</u>[343] anses dosam váthne
gálsador ansech gódamah vonsepaléscoh ádmacah lu zámpha
oh adma zemblodárma varmíga zuna thotob am-phi-cha-nó-sa
ge-mi-cha-na-dá-bah Va-de-ma-do Va-se-la-pa-gé-do

----

44. A-mas-ca-ba-lo-no-cha a-nó-dah a-du-ra-dá-mah go-na-de-
pha-ge-no v-na-cha-pes-ma-cho ge-mi-na-do-cha-pa-mi-ca
vu-am-sa-pá-la-ge <u>vocórthmoth achepasmácapha</u> em-ca-ni-do-
bah gedóah

----

45. Nostoah[344] geuámna da oscha lus palpal medna go-rum-ba-ló-
geph a-cap-na-pá-da-pha Vol-sé-ma go-no-gé-do-cha am-bu-sá-
ba-loh ge-mú-sa-cha va-mi-li-ó-pha zum-ne-ga-da-phá-ge-pha
<u>iuréhoh</u>

This last word was hid a prety while with a rym like a thin bladder affore it: and when it was perfectly seen then there appered a
bluddy cross over it. It is a Word signifying what <u>Christ did in hel</u>.

----

46. Zém-no-da amni fa chebseth vsángrada bo-sa-dó-ma zú-ma-
coh a-phi-na-bá-cha buzádbazu a-ma-cha-pa-do-mi-cha
zu-ma-ne-pas-só NA vuamanábadoth zum-ble-gám-pha zum-
ble-cap-há-ma-cha[345]

---

343 Locat.

344 Nostah = it was in the begynning.

345 Δ Here seme to lack 5 words.

EK: All is couered with darknes. Terrible flashes of fire appered and they semed to wreath and wrap, one abowt an other. In the fire ouer the chayre appered, the three heds which appeared before.

A Voyce:—Laua zuráah.[346]

Δ: After our prayers was a very hevenly noyce hard.

47. Zudneph arni ioh pan zedco lamga nahad lébale nochas arni cans lósmo iana olna dax zémblocha zedman púsatha vámo mah oxex párzu drána ánza pasel lúmah cóxech á-da-max gón-boh alze dah lúsache[347] asneph gedma noxdrúma Vamcáph-napham ástichel <u>rátrugem</u>[348] abnath lonsas masqueth tauínar tadna gehodód gaphrámsana asclor drusáxpa

----

48. <u>Amgédpha</u>[349] lazad ampha ladmaáchel <u>galdamicháël</u> Vn'za dédma Luz zácheph pílathob ganó vamah zúnasch zemblagen ónman zuth catas max ordru iadse lamad caphícha aschal luz. ampna zod-mí-na-da ex-cá-pha-nog sal-gém-pha-ne Om vrza lat quartphe lasque deth ürad ox-ma-ná gam-ges

----

[The 49th row followeth after 2 leaves: Arney vah nol, &c.]

Δ: Now the boke was couered with a <u>blew silk</u> sindall[350] and uppon that blew covering appered letters of gold, conteyning these words,

---

[346] = Use humilitie in prayers to God, that is fervently pray. It signifieth, <u>Pray into god.</u>

[347] Δ pronownce as <u>che</u> in chery.

[348] Δ ratrugeem is one of the 7 words on the side of the Table first prescribed.

[349] = I will begynne a new.

[350] Note this covering to be made for the boke. = Δ. Sindall: "sendal, a thin light silk." -Ed.

Amzes naghézes Hardeh[351]

EK: It signifieth, the universall name of him that created universally be praysed and extolled for euer.

Δ: Amen

A Clowde covered the boke.
A Voyce:—Mighty is thy Name (ô lorde) for euer.
EK: It lightneth.
A Voyce:—The place is Holy: stur not [sayd the three heds].

Δ: Now appered to EK, some imperfection passed in the eleuenth row. And that we wer towght how to amend it: and so we did.

Δ: Then the firy light went from EK into the stone agayn: and his inspired perceyuerance and understanding was gone: as often before it used to be.

Δ: Gloriam laudemque nostri Creatoris, omnes Creaturæ. indesinenter resonent:[352] Amen.

Halleluiah Halleluiah Halleluiah
Amen.

Aprilis 6. Saterday after none.

Δ: The Table, Chayre, boke and fyre appeared. And while I went into my oratorie[353] to pray, fire cam thrise out of the stone uppon EK, as he was at prayer, at my table in my study.

----

351 Note this to be pronownced rowndly to gither.

352 Gloriam . . . resonent: "May all creatures continually resound the glory and praise of our Creator." -Ed.

353 Oratory: a small private chapel. -Ed.

EK hard a voyce out of the fyre, saying,

Why do the <u>Children of men prolong the time</u> of theyr perfect felicitie: or why are they dedicated to vanitie? Many things ar yet to come: Notwithstanding, the Time must be shortned,

I AM THAT I AM.

A voyce: Veniet[354] Vox eius, ut dicat filijs hominum quæ ventura sunt.[355]

EK: here is a man, in white, come in, like Uriel, who cam first into the stone.

Δ: Benedictus qui venit in nomine Domini.[356]—Ur: Amen.

Ur:—I teache: EK sayd that he turned toward me.

Ur: What willt thow I shall answer thee, as concerning this work?

EK: He hath a ball of fire in his left hand and in his right hand a Triangle of fyre.

Δ: What is the most nedefull for us to lerne herin, that is my chief desire.

Uriel:—Fowre monthes, are yet to come: The fifth is the begynning of great miserie, <u>to the heauens</u>, to the earth and to all liuing Creatures.[357] Therfore must thow nedes attend uppon the will of God: Things must then be put in practise. A thing that knitteth up all must of

---

[354] The manuscript has an "a" (or Δ?) over the second "e" in "veniet." -Ed.

[355] Veniet . . . sunt: "His voice will come, that he may tell the sons of men what is coming" Sloane 3677 also has an "a" over the second "e" of "veniet." With this proposed amendment the statement would start: "May his voice come. . . " -Ed.

[356] Benedictus . . . Domini: "Blessed in he who comes in the name of the Lord." -Ed.

[357] A prophesy very dreadfull now at hand.

force conteyn many celestiall Vertues. Therfore, in these doings, must things be finished spedyly,[358] and with reuerence.

This, is the light, wherewith thow shalt be Kindled.[359]

This is it, that shall renew thee: yea agayn and agayn, and, seventy seuen tymes, agayn.

Then shall thy eyes be clered from the dymnes. Thow shalt perceyue these[360] things which haue not byn seen, No, not amongst the Sonnes of men.

This[361] other haue I browght, whereof I will, now, bestow the seventith part of the first part of seuenty seuen. The residue shall be fullfilled, in, and with thee; In, (I say,) and to gither, with thee. Behold (sayth the lord) I will breath uppon men, and they shall haue the spirit of Understanding.

In 40 dayes[362] must the boke of the Secrets, and key of this world be Written: euen as it is manifest to the one of you in sight, and to the other in faith. Therfore haue I browght it to the wyndow of thy senses, and dores of thy Imagination: to the ende he may see and performe the tyme of God his Abridgment.[363] That shalt, thow,[364] write down in his propre and sanctified distinctions.

---

[358] Spedily & reuerently.

[359] Uriel held up now the triangle of fire ☞ .

[360] Those.

[361] Uriel now holding up the Ball of fire in his left hand, sayd as is here written: ☞ .

[362] If from the first day of writing we accownt than from good friday the reckoning doth begynne: and so ende this.

[363] The Abridgment of time.

[364] Speaking to Δ.

This other, (pointing to EK) shall haue it <u>allwayes</u> before him, and shall <u>daylie</u> performe the office to him committed. <u>Which if he do not, the Lord shall raze his name from the number of the blessed, and those that are annoynted with his blud.</u>[365]

For, behold, what man, can speak, or talk with the spirit of God? No flesh is hable to stand, whan the <u>voyce of his Thunder</u>[366] shall <u>present the parte of the next leaf unto sight.</u>

You haue wauering myndes, and are drawn away with the World: But brittle is the state therof: Small therfore are the Vanities of his Illusion.

Be of sownd faith. Beleue. Great is the reward of those that are faithfull. God Will not be dishonored, neyther will suffer them to receyue dishonor, that honor him in holiness.

Behold, Behold, Mark ô and Behold: Eache line hath stretched him self, euen to his ende:[367] and the Middst is glorious to the good, and dishonor to the wicked. Heuen and erth must decay: so, shall not the words of this Testimonie.

Δ: Ecce seruus et misellus homuncio Dei nostri, fiat mihi iuxta beneplacitum voluntatis suæ:[368] &c.

Δ: Uriel toke a little of the fire in his left hand and flung it at EK: and it went in at his mowth.[369]

Ur: My message is done.

Δ: May I Note Ur, (meaning Uriel,) for your name who now deale with us?—Ur:—I am so.

---

[365] The danger thretned, if EK do not his dutie.

[366] Note a terrible thing.

[367] The ende of all.

[368] Ecce . . . suae: "Behold this servant and wretched little man; let it be to me whatever is most pleasing to his will." -Ed.

[369] Note, by the place here before what measure in proportion of powr and understanding this was, in respect of the white ball of fyre.

Δ: I pray you to give us advise what we are to doo in our affayres.

Ur: It is sayde.

Δ: He sayd to EK, Tell him, I haue told him, and seemed to smile.

Δ: Of Mistres Haward (Jentlewoman[370] of her Maiesties priuie chamber) I wold fayn know, wherfore we were not warned of her comming? She hath caused us, now, for an howre or two, to intermit our exercise? Is it the Will of god, that for her great charitie used toward many, (as in procuring the Quenes Maiesties Almes to many nedy persons) the lord entendeth to be mercifull to her? I meane at the pynche of these great miseries ensuing, now (by you) told of. And that by her, I may do good seruice concerning the Quenes Maiesties Cumfort?

Ur:—Who is he, that opened thy mowth, or hath told thee of things to come? What thow hast sayd, is sayde. Mark the ende.[371]

It is a sufficient answer.

Ur:—Loke up.—Δ: He sayd so to EK: who loking up, saw the boke, the chayre and the Globe a part, abroad, out of the stone, and then, none remayning in the stone to be seene: and it cam nearer & nearer to him, and it burned, as before.

Ur: So, set down, what thow seest. [Δ: The boke and writing was made very playne to him.]

> What thow seest, deliuer unto him.
> As it is his will, so be it unto thee:
> Do thy duty, whereunto thow art moved,
> and it shalbe sufficient.

Farewell, for a time.

---

370 Jentlewoman: "noblewoman." -Ed.

371 Mistres Francis Haward elected to taste of god his great mercy for her charitable hart, &c.

EK: Now is all couered with a white clowde, such an one as I saw not yet.

Δ: We put up the stone: and the former boke and other furniture, appeared uppon the table hard by EK: and he was to write out as he saw: which he began to do, both in character and words: but it was to cumbersome to him: and therfore he wrote onely the words in latin lettres.

Δ: After he had written 28 lines there in that paper boke, the first word being <u>Arney</u>, and the last, being <u>nah</u> suddenly all was taken away out of his sight: and so likewise his understanding of that he had written was quite gone. For, contynually as he wrote, he understode the language and sense thereof, as if it had byn english.

Δ: After he had finished that second page[372] of the first leafe, I then did copy it out as followeth.

ᴤᴧᴤ ᴟᴤᴧ ᴨᴧᴈᴧᴤ

49.[373] Arney[374] vah nol gadeth[375] adney ox vals nath gemseh ah orza val gemáh, oh gedvá on zembáh nohhad vomfah olden ampha nols admácha nonsah vamfas ornad, alphol andax o'rzadah vos ansoh hanzah voh adma iohá notma goth vamsed adges onseple ondemax orzan, vnfa onmah vndabra gonsah gols nahad NA.

---

[372] Forte Row.

[373] This was originally numbered 1, the next 2, and so on. These were each crossed out later and renumbered 49, 1, etc. See the note at the end of the 49th row. -Ed.

[374] Δ forte: Asney.

[375] Iadeth.

1. Oxar varmol pan sampas os al pans orney a<u>n</u>ds<u>u</u> alsaph
   o<u>u</u>cha[376] cosdám on-za-go-les natmátatp max, olnah von ganse
   pacath olnoh vor nasquah loth adnay nonsah oxansah vals
   nodax vonqueth lan sandquat ox arda'nh onzâbel ormach
   douquin astmax arpagels ontipodah omvah nosch als mantquts,
   <u>armad</u>[377] notgals. Vantantquah +

In[378] the tables	drux	1
expressed	na	2
drux	ger	3
na	pa	4
ger	van	5
pa	or	6
van	pal	7
or	med	8
pal	gal	9
med	cheph	10
gál *letters names,*	vr	11
ceph *used in sense*	fam	12
vr	ged	13
fam	vn	14
ged	mals	15
vn		
mals		

---

376 I dowt which is n and which is u.

377 A dowte whether "ar made" be two words or one.

378 The following notes are found on a separate sheet of paper: -Ed.

veh
graph   16   15
gisg   17   16
+ mals   18   17
don   19   18
gon   20   19
tal   21   20

I finde diuerse dowts which I cannot order, to my contentment.[379]

1. How many of my ruled leaves, shall I tak for the writing of the first leafe?
2. How shall I make the distinctions of the last 9 lines of the first leafe answerable to all the former words: how is more then two hundred & some are of 3 hundred letters, & top 9 rows have but 49 letters.
3. how shall I do for the true orthographie, Seing g and C and p &c haue so diuerse sownds, & not allwayes one: as g sometymes as gh & sometymes as J. And C sometymes is like K, sometymes is like S. p sometymes is like ph, & sometymes is p—& sometymes f.
4. The number of the words in the first leafe,—every row, is not all one; nor 49 allwayes.
5. of the 2nd Table, when is to be set down all the tables following, all the table ... will not agree to fill up ...all places & to set down the ... perfectly.

2. Ondroh als vrh. panchah orn sandvah loh andah nol pan, sedmah zugeh als ab-mi-cad-am-pâ-get ordomph, axah gethol vav axel anthath gorsan vax parsah vort lanq an'damsah getheol, vrchan navádah o'xembles armax lothar, vos antath, orsé vax alnoth, other mals olnah gethom várdamach, alls;[380] Orgeth

----

379 In margin at top of page: "solgars." See TFR, p. 5, where "solgars" is prescribed as a cure. -Ed.

380 Δ Ω.

3. Or pasquah omzádah vorts, ange'nodah varsáua onch aldúmph, ánget ónsaual gálta oth aneth ax pa gesné ouád ax orneh al-dum-bá-ges vos-cómph alze ax, orzad andah gost astoh nadah vortes, astmah notesma goth nathad omza, geth altéth ox, degáth onda voxa gemnaché adna dansa als alst

----

4. arsah. Orthath ols gast ardoh max vármah doth novámq lath, adnab gothan, ardri'noh astómagel arpáget asteth arde obzá, ols NA[381] gem-na-pá-la-ba-m'i-da orsat nahah Odmázen an'-dulphel, ox ambrássah oxah géth nor vamfah genoh daqueth als astna, oh tatóh, alsah goth necor andeoh neo alda nah[382]

----

5. Vanlah oha demagens on sunfah, paphah olemneh, ózadcha lax ornah vor adme ox vastmah gu labazna, gamnácho asthmah ochádo landrídah vons sah, lúgho iahat nabscham nohads van-dispa rossámod androch alphoh, zúmbloh ásnah gonfageph aldeh lo dah vax orh asmo, gad au dansequa deo, dath vax nograh vor segbat Mon.

----

6. Arni olbah galpa lohánaha gáu-pu-ma-gén-sah ollo var se darsah goho ál-bu-mi-clá-má-ca-pá-loth ieho nad veslah vors ardno inmony asquam rath als vásmah génda loggahah astmu.[383]

---

[381] This word is circled in the manuscript. —Ed.

[382] Here seme to be 50 names: and so, one to many.

[383] Here are but 38.

----

7. Arnah notah lax vart luhoh désmaph, ol ca-pra-mi-na-cah[384] ox-and-an-vah gem-ne-lo-ri-pli-ton-pha ac-cam-plah-no-stapha or-max-a-da-ha-har or-zem-bli-zad-mah pan-che-fe-lo-ge-doh áschah ólmah ledóh vaxma

----

8. Gans na cap lan seda ax nor vorza vo laspral onsa gem gemah noph gázo na von santfa nostradg ansel vnsa pah vort velsa or alda viax nor adroh semneh ols vandésqual olzah nolpax pahah lothor ax ru vansar glímnaph gath ardot ardri axa noh gaga leth arde maxa.

----

9. Corsal mabah noplich alps arsod vord vanfax oriox nabat gemnepoh laphet Ióda nat vombal nams ar geth alloah néphirt. lauda noxa voxtaf ardno ándroch labmageh ossu állmaglo ardot nalbar vanse dar-to vorts parsan vr vnrah vor gádeth leth orze nax vomreh agelpha, legar or nembla ar vah Su.[385]

----

10. Zanchcumáchaseph, ol-za-mi-nó-ah Vals-e-bú-ra-ah no-da-li-gá-nax or-sáp-na-go dar-ság-na-pha nob-si-blith ar-mi-pyth ar-se-pó-lo-ni-tan-tons Jem-búl-sa-mar le-bó-ge axpar or-ná-za ol-dax-ar-da-co-ah[386]

----

384 Ce-.

385 48.

386 Here are 54.

11. Semno ah al-chi-do-á-cha-da Sel-pag-in-o-dah a-da-hu-bá-mi-ca-noh <u>dam pah gli ás cha nor</u> ox-om-pa-mi-na-pho <u>lemp, na, gón sa pha</u> ne co ál pha <u>as pa gé mo cal</u> na <u>tú ra ge</u>[387]

----

12. <u>Sen gál se quar</u> <u>rus fa glan súx taft</u> ormaca <u>ox i no dál ge brah</u> <u>nop tar ná gel</u> <u>vom na ches pál ma cax</u>, arsep <u>as dón sadg</u> <u>asc lan fán che dah</u> <u>nor vi car máx coh</u> <u>zum bla zánpha</u> ad geh <u>do ca ba ah</u>

----

13. Ar gém na ca pál fax, <u>or nído hab cás pigan alpuh</u> gágah loth <u>ral sá bra dan</u> <u>go sá pax</u> <u>vólsan qués tan</u> ondapha opicab <u>or zy lá pa</u> a-chra-pa-má-les <u>ad má car pah</u> oxalps <u>on dá pa,</u> <u>gém na de vór guse</u>

----

14. Lat gans sa par sat lastéah lor ádah nóxax ardéphis nónson andoh gv'mzi vor sab líboh <u>ad ni sa pa loth</u> gaho lar va noxa oho lan sempah noxa Vriah sephah lúsaz odgálsax nottaph ax v'rnoc árpos arta zem zubah lothor gas lubah vom <u>zá da</u> <u>phi cár no</u>

----

15. As-só-ta-phe on-dah vor ban sanphar pa loth agno iam nésroh am algórs vrrábah geuseh alde ox nah vors púrblox ámphicab nóstrohh admág[388] or napsú asmo lon gamphi arbel nof ámphi

----

[387] 50 words.

[388] Admad.

on Saubloth aschi nur laffax las doxa pra gem a Sestrox amphi
nax var sembbh[389]

----

16. Angésel oxcapácad onz adq ochádah ólzah vor náh orpogó-
    graphel al sa gem <u>ua ca pí coh</u> <u>vl da pa pór sah</u> naxor vonsa rons
    vrbanf <u>lab dún zaph</u> algadef loh gem vortaóh amph ahoha za
    vaxorza leph[390] oxor neoh ah va du-na-ca <u>pi ca lodox</u> ard nah.

----

17. Iahod <u>vox ar pi cah</u> <u>lot tár pi ges</u> <u>nol zim na plah</u> <u>ge ó gra plih</u>
    <u>ne gó ah</u> <u>va lu gán zed</u> <u>am phí la doh</u> <u>zan veh</u> al nex oh al pha ze
    goth gedóth axor van zebá <u>al cá pa</u> Luma ges ard <u>de oh ah</u>[391]

----

18. Onchas lagod van Sebageh oxangam pah gos dah manzeh ocon-
    dah vardol Sebagh ol madan NA ohal Sepaget, otoxen narvah
    lubatan ansem nofet au naba notoh ax arsah mans Vstgam
    pahod pah mal sednah gestons amphes al manso gapalebâton
    arra nax vamfes amah dot agen nalphat ar zamne oh Sages

----

19. nax lerua nath Zembloh axpadabamah Sanzápas gunzan-
    quah[392] ona var demneh gah lod vmnah doxa val tarquat mans
    ol gem nageph au zanbat vx anzach al pambóha naxtath ol nada
    vam nonsal aua nal gedot vorx alge lah despa gu prominabâmî-
    gah olpaz ord gamnat lem paz cath normadah on demq

---

[389] Sembeth.

[390] Lefe.

[391] Here seme to be 50.

[392] Of the "n" and "u" of this word I dowt.

----

20. Laffah ie ogg dalseph abrimanadg oldomph ledothnar ymnachar
    onze vam sepno voxauaret ol zantqur amph nas Sages om nartal
    vor miscam bemcax lappad gesso drux capgol ass letnar vom[393]
    sausah or gamprida ornat vol asmd onza duh get hansa gorh
    hubra galsaropah nequax dap gemno ab pnidah noxd lumbam

----

21. al gethroz ax arvan oh zempal guh arvax no demnat ar pam-
    bals nop nonsal geh axor pam vartop ab vbrah cardax lon
    songes au dumax ar nephar lu gemne om Asda vorts vmrod val
    manqh noh Sam, naga vrbrast Lurvandax vpplod dam zurtax
    loa an avarn nar gemplicabnadah oxa

----

22. nooa Babna ampha dum nonsap vrs daluah marsasqual orma
    nabath Sabaothal netma vol sempra isch laue ondeh noh sem-
    blax or mansa macapal vngenel vorsepax vrsabada noxanquah
    vndalph asmoh vxa na Gaspar vmpaxal Lapproh Iadd nomval
    vp setquam nol astma vors: vrdem gnasplat bef affafefafed
    noxtah Volls laydam ovs nac

----

23. cedah or manveh geh axax nolsp damva dor demgoh apoxan
    Subliganaxnarod orchal vamnad vez gemlehox ar drulalpa ax
    vr samfah oladmax vr sappoh Luah vr pabmax luro lam faxno
    dem vombres adusx or sembal on vamne oh lemne val se quap
    vn nap nastosm dah voz mazax lumato games on neda.[394]

---

[393] At vom was a + to note the ende of a line: But both these mak but 49 names.

[394] 51 words.

----

24. voh gemse[395] ax pah losquan nof afma dol vamna vn samses
oh set, quamsa ol danfa dot santa on anma ol subracah
Babalad vansag olso pas gonred vorn chechust axaroh rugho
am nadom val sequot ne texpa vors vrs al pam vans na tomva-
mal ansipamals notems anq$_e$ arxe al

----

25. pangef offd ne pamfah aliboh a nostâfâges almesed vrmast
geus vrmax au semblox satq quayntah luzez arne noh pamna
sams bantes orn volsax vors vnisapa monsel dah nax ah pah
vomreb doth danséqox anzazed onz anfal nom vamreh volts
vrnacapácapah noshan yalt gelfay nor sentqbt onbanzar luntaf
val sentepax

----

26. ornisa nor Pampals anz alpah nox noxa gendah von gamne
dah vors ad na lepnazu acheldaph var honza gune alsaph nal
vomsan vns alpd a domph ar zemnip ans vrnach vancef ban
yanzem ob aha vons nabrah vh asmo drat vormez al pasquar
no gems nah zem lasquith apsantah

----

27. Vol zans alphi ne gansad ol pam ro dah vor vngef a deoh nad
vnsemel apodmacah vnsap val vndar ban cefna dux hansel yax
nolpah volts quayntah gam vemneg oh asq al panst ans vntah
hunsansa Apnad ratq a sanst nel odogamanázar. olzah guh oh
nah varsa vpangah neoh aho

----

[395] Iemse.

----

28. Notgah ox vr auonsad vl dath nox lat ges orn val sedcoh leth
    arney vas ars galep odámpha nol axar vox apracas nolph admi
    adpálsah noh vrh gednach vax varsablox vrdam pagel admax
    lor vamtage oxandah lamfó nor vorsah axpáa, ols nugaphar
    ádras vxár nostrílgan ampacoh vortes lesqual exoh.

----

29. Ses vah nómre gal sables orzah, get les part, ox ar se de cól-
    machu ardéh lox gempha lar vamra goh naxa vors admah
    gebah, semfúgel admá geod alzeh orzam vánchet.[396] oxam
    prah geh orzad Val nexo, vam seleph oxa, noha par gúmsah
    askeph nox adroh lestof ad moxa nonsúrrach

----

30. Vomchál <u>as pu gán san var,</u> <u>sem quáh lah</u> set gedoh argli
    oranza vor zina sedcátah zuréhoh admich, ors arsah varsab,
    oliba vortes lúnsanfah, adnah vor semquáx, vorsan lap varsah
    gebdah voxlar geoh, gemfel ad gvns. aldah gor vanlah, gehu-
    dan vor sableth, gedvel ax ors, manch var sembloh.[397]

----

31. <u>Ar dam fa gé do hah</u> Luxh arcan Mans lubrah vor semblas
    adna gor partat, nor vílso ádchu apri sed amphle nox arua
    getol. Vor sambla geth, arse pax vor sah. gelh aho gethmah or
    gemfa nah prax chilad ascham na prah oxáh var setqua lexoh
    vor sámbleh zubrah.

----

[396] Vanket.

[397] 48.

----

32. Lax or setquáh vah lox rémah Nol sadma vort, famfa le gem
    nah or sepah vartef a geh Oha lon gaza Onsa ges adrux: vom-
    balzah ah vaxtal. noh sedo lam, vom tántas oxárzah Mechól va
    zebn geth adna vax, ormacha lorni adrah, Gens arnah vor,
    Arsad odíscoh alidah nepho.

----

33. Hastan bah ges loh ru mal; vrabro den varsah, Mah rox idah
    ru gebna demphe, ors amvi ar, Genbá, óxad va ges lath vriop:
    nal pas <u>vi me ró to</u> ád-na-vah ged anse lah verbrod vn gelpa,
    <u>lux árd do ah</u> vast vor Ge-ma-fá-noh

----

34. Amles ondanpha[398] noxt vradah gel núbrod <u>Arb á cha lo pe</u>
    <u>go há pa ra</u> <u>zem che pár ma la</u> <u>Na bu-rá doh</u> gem la pa
    or-zín fax nol ad micápar <u>vó si pi cá la ton</u> andrah vox ardno,
    <u>get na ca ploh</u> gál-z<u>un</u>

----

35. <u>O'r ge mah</u> luza <u>cá poh</u> nox tráh víoxah nebo hu <u>ge o mí lah</u>
    <u>cox chá dah</u> or na hú da <u>vol sa pah</u>: <u>No bro ch</u>, <u>ál pa</u> chídomph
    náb la grux la <u>vx ar gá fam gel</u> <u>ne do gá lah</u> <u>vo sa pah</u>

----

36. <u>Gu la gé dop</u> <u>áx ix</u> <u>óx a max</u> <u>lun fá gem pah</u> orsa dev'lmah
    <u>Gé pa cha</u> <u>vor sí ma coh</u> alduth gempfa: <u>Nox gal max</u> <u>ar hú gaf</u>
    <u>gli nó rob</u> <u>va gen lá car</u> du zum <u>ox am' pli zam</u> zu latmah
    <u>ge gé ma</u> ohahah

---

398 Corrected from "ondanfaha." -Ed.

----

37. <u>Ga lá pa</u> <u>drux váx ma</u> geb lá geb <u>or ché plon</u> <u>gan zéd ah</u> <u>Vox ár vox</u> gelet ar gahad, <u>gan pá gan</u> doruminaplah vor zinach <u>cû pa chef</u> ardrah <u>óx ox</u> <u>pol sa gal máx nah</u> guth ardéth on zupra <u>cró cro gah</u> <u>var sa má nal</u>

----

38. <u>Ar sa bá choas</u> noh al geh oh, <u>ax ár pa gal</u> olza déh <u>or za zú max</u> exoh eh, or cah pal donzahá onza zethas: <u>nor sáp se pah</u> onzap a palmah aldoh voh náblebah gemnápam os malsa or naoh <u>zar bu lagém pah</u> <u>ne-ó ha brah</u>

----

39. Tal gep ar sep nah doh, vors alsa doh necoh am ar geth na ges alpran odox malsápnah, gohor ahoh gadmah ol dáneph aludar dón-za-gab ól-sa-gah nebthuh or sapnar balgonph nep gemloh, ax amna[399] duth achár laspá, vohá, náxvolh gas vergol ah pratnom geá[400] nostúamph

----

40. <u>Va'n sa pal sah</u> <u>gón so gon</u> <u>gé la bu rá doh</u> tato lang, <u>ge mé fe ran</u> <u>ón da pans</u> ge lá brah: <u>or pa gé mal</u> <u>on sán' fan gen</u> ólc ma cha lan <u>Von sé gor</u> <u>a prí cas</u> <u>nor vá gel</u> <u>om brá cau</u> cohadal.

----

[399] The copy had "ouhna." I cowld not conjecture.

[400] Iea.

a d r o s,a,c l o d f a c,d o g é p n a h,l a p c a h,m o c d á c o d e,f a m ó n,t u a l c,d o m,

v r á s n a g e p h,a m p h i d o n,g á n s e l,v a x,ó r e h a m a h,v ó r s a f a n s a,u c a s

d a m í f a g a,n á b u l a x,o r s a g e h,n a m'v a h,o c a ɽ,l u n s a n g e l,c a r p a c o a.

l u n s e m n e p h,o d á r n a c h o h,z e m b l o h,o b l í c a n d o n,g a l s o r x v l á g a,

f ó m n a p h,a p á n s a g e h,l o n s ú g a l a n,g r a s t,v b l á n s o,a r n o x,v o n s á o

t a l t é m a p h e c h,ó r m a c h a d á g e n o x,v r s t á m v a h,n a d v a r e h,o n s,a r g

z u c á n z u,n a p l i o r a h,n o r g e,h a h a n a h a,v s p l a h,g r a d ú n v a h,n a v i o,

a r s a h,v ó n r o g e n,d a h v a l a h,o r z a p,c v l,c a r s e d,a,p o r s a l,q á s t a v a,

g a n f ú m a r a b ó m o n a h,g á s t a g e s,ó r d o l p h,n a q a s,o r g e m v a h,n o x a d.

Δ: And this is the late ende of the second page of the first leafe of this excellent boke. The other leaves are written, apart, in an other boke[401] as may appere. But with these 9 rowes and the former 41, doth arise the some of 50: which is one more then 49: Therfore I am not onely of this but of diuerse other imperfections yet remayning in this page, to ax the solution and reformation.

Δ: Whan I had told this my dowte to EK, he answered me that the first row of these last .50. before set downe, was the last of the first page of this first leafe: and true it is that in the first page were first sett down 48 rows, of which eight and fortith row begynneth with this word Amgédpha &c And therfore the next row following, (begynning with Arney vah nol gadeth &c) is the nyne and fortyth row of the first page and so the last row of that page: And therby allso the second page of the first leaf hath these 49 rowes here noted: And so is one dowte taken away: The other is of the numbers of words in some of the 49 rows of this second page.

---

401 An other boke: British Library, Sloane manuscript 3189 contains the bulk of the angelic book. -Ed.

Aprilis 10. hor. 9.

Δ: As we wer talking of the Macedonian (the grecian), who yesterday cam with Mr. Sanford his letters, there appeared in the corner of my study a blak shadow: and I did charge that shaddow to declare who he was: There cam a voyce and sayd that it was the Macedonian: and abowt his hat was written in great letters this word, καταρικτο— , which EK wrote out and it signifieth maculosus,[402] or condemnatus[403] &c. and the Voyce sayd, that word was sufficient

adding Est,[404]
Δ: God be thanked and praysed.

To me deliuered by Mr.
Edward Kelly
1583. Martij 22
Friday

Mr. Husy cam with
him from blokley[405]

---

402 Polluted. -Ed.

403 In marg.: ~~firmus~~ ("strong"). condemnatus: "condemned." -Ed.

404 Est: "He is." -Ed.

405 This note is on the reverse side of the following diagram. -Ed.

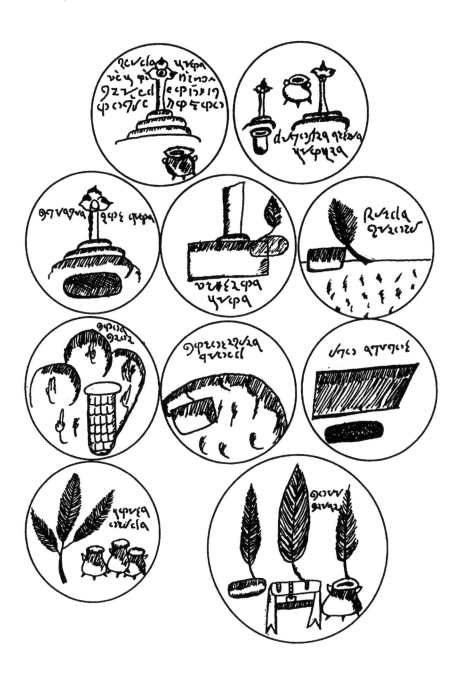

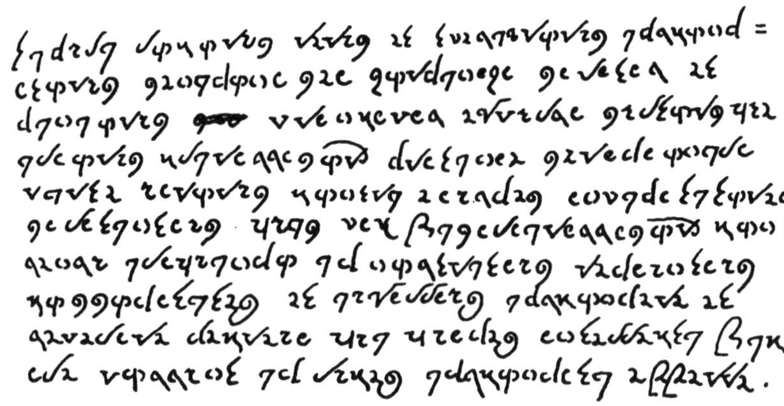

Aprilis .11. Thursday

Δ: After my comming home from the court abowt 4 of the clok after none, and after my being in my study a while, it cam into my hed to assay[406] to deciphre the cifre which before is spoken of, and was browght me by EK,[407] as he was willed to do. And at the first I was half out of all hope: but yet making many assayes, and gessing at it (at the length) to be latine, I fownd this to be the true Alfabet. God giving me the perseyverance.

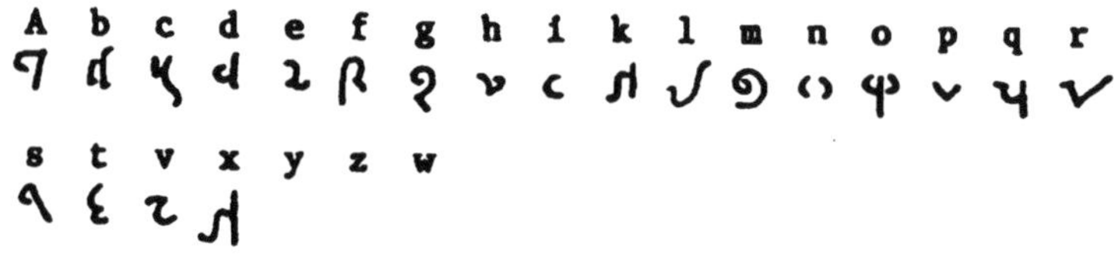
A b c d e f g h i k l m n o p q r
s t v x y z w

And, the first longer writing, was thus:

406 Assay: "try." -Ed.

407 They wer fownd at Huets Cross as the spirituall creature affirmed when he led them to the finding of this Moniment was & a boke of Magik & Alchimie. Perhaps that is the Cros called Huteos Cros being the fowrth of them below.

Tabula locorum rerum et Thesaurorum absconditorum Menaboni, mei Gordanili, militis, et Danaorum Principis, expulsi, multorumque aliorum clarissimorum (Britanie meridionali parte) virorum, contra eiusdem inhabitatores militantium: quam, hîc, familiarissimorum consensu, aliquando ad nostratium rediuntium commoditatem et auxilium abscondere et sepelire decreui: qua quidem intellecta, facile possunt ad lucem abscondita efferre.[408]

And the Notes of the ten places, here by, affixed: are thus to be red orderly:

1 Gilds cros hic o ..... mer id io onali ot on	2 blankis[409] Suters croces	
3 Marsars got cros	4 Huteos cros	5 Fleds grenul
6 Mons Mene	7 Mountegles arnid	8 Lan sapant
9 Corts nelds		10 Mnrr[410] Merse

----

408 Note J. Dee. The last being of the Danes here, was abowt the year 1040. (Tabula ... effere: "The table of places of things and hidden treasures of Menabon, my Gordanil, soldier and banished prince of the Danes, and of many other famous men [in the southern part of Britain], and of native soldiers who fought against the same. With the agreement of closest friends I decided to hide this away and bury it for the convenience and help of our countrymen who may return at some time. By this when understood, they can easily bring [lit. expose] the hidden to light." -Ed.)

409 Of this ♫ "k" I dowt yet.

410 Δ fortè Marr.

Aprilis 15. Monday

Δ: As EK was writing the <u>eightenth leaf which was of the spirites of the</u> <u>earth,</u> (in the after none abowt 4½ of the clok) he red a parcell therof, playnely & alowde to him self, and thereuppon suddenly at his syde appeared three or fowre spirituall creatures like laboring men, having spades in theyr hands & theyr heares hangyng abowt theyr eares, and hastyly asked EK what he wold have, & <u>wherfor he called them</u>. He answered that he called them not. & they replyed, & sayed that he called them: Then I began to say, they lyed: for his intent was not to call them, but onely to read and repeat that which he had written: and that <u>euery man who readeth a prayer to perceyue the sense thereof, prayeth</u> <u>not</u>. No more, did he call them. And I bad them be packing out of the place: and thereuppon remoued from my desk (where I was ruling of paper for his writing) to the grene chayre which was by my Chymney: and presently he cryed out and sayd they <u>had nipped him and broken</u> <u>his left arme by the wrest</u>: and he shewed the bare arme and there appered both on the upper syde and lower side imprinted depe-in, two circles as broad as grotes[411] thus:

very red: And I seeing that, sowght for a stik, and in the meane while, <u>they assalted him</u>, and he rose, and cryed to me (saying) they come flying on me, they come; and he put the stole, which he sat on, betwene him and them. But still they cam gaping, or gyrning[412] at him. Then I axed him where they were: and he poynted to the place: and then I toke the stik and cam to the place, and in the name of Jesus commaunded

---

[411] Grotes: silver fourpence pieces used from the 14th to the 17th century. -Ed.

[412] Gyrning: "snarling." -Ed.

those Baggagis to avoyde and smitt a cross stroke at them: and presently they avoyded.[413]

All thanks be to the onely one Almighty, and everlasting God Whose name be praysed now & ever. Amen.

Aprilis 18[414]. *Thursday morning .hor. 8. Circiter*

Δ: As EK cam to write-out the Tables according as he was wont: and to haue the letters appearing in the ayre hard by him, he saw nothing but a blak clowde seven-cornered. And after I <u>had put the stone agayne into the frame,</u>[415]and thereuppon did make long and oft request, for answer hauing, There appered nothing, neyther was anything seen in the stone. Then I fell to prayer agayn, and at length, there appeared written uppon, or yssuing out of the clowde, this sentence.

<u>He promised, be not carful</u>: Δ: Note here are iust 21 letters.[416]

EK: The letters semed to stand at fingers endes, (being 21): and so euery finger had a letter on it: and the fingers semed to be placed at the Corners of the Heptagonall clowde: and as sone as the sentence was red the fingers which seemed to issue out of the Heptagonum, did shrink in agayn and disapere.

Δ: All laude honor and thanksgiving, be to the highest, our most louing mercifull and almighty God, now and euer. Amen.

---

413 Avoyded: "departed." -Ed.

414 Note. Now 30 Tables being written since good friday: and days only 21 passed since good friday.

415 The stone out of the frame.

416 Δ as who shold say, αυτοζ ειψα, ipe dixit: nr Deus. -Δ. (Autos . . . Deus: "he said himself, 'our God.'" -Ed.)

Thursday. Aprilis 18. after dynner

Δ: We being desirous to know the cause of this stay making, in the Tables shewing as before was accustomed; and now (24 leaves being written,) a dark clowde to hang in the place of a glorious boke, did greatly disquiet our myndes, and browght us in feare of some offence lately committed, by any one, or both of us, whereby the Indignation of the lord might be kingled against us. Hereuppon we prayed severally; and at length, (no alteration, or better Cumfert hapening to us,) I prayed in the hearing of EK, (by my desk, on my knees) in great agony of mynde; and Behold, there appeared one standing uppon, or rather somwhat behynde the Heptagonall clowde who sayd,

I am sent, to understand the cause of your greif, and to answer your dowtes.

Δ: I, then, declared my mynde breifly, according to the effect of my prayer. Whereunto he answered at large, <u>reproving my appointing of god a tyme</u> or to abridge the tyme spoken of: and among his manifold grave speaches he had these words,

> Prepare all things,[417] For tyme is at hand.
> <u>His Justice is great</u>; and his arme stronge.

How darest thow dowt or dreame, saying: Lo, God, this may be done in shorter time &c. But such is flesh.

> Be rocks in faith.
> It is not the manner of us, good Angels,[418] <u>to be trubbled so oft</u>.

---

[417] Prepare all things.

[418] Good Angels.

☞ At the time appointed, thow shalt practise: <u>While sorrow shall be measured, thow shalt bynde up thy fardell.</u>[419] Great is the light of Gods sinceritie. Appoint God no tyme. Fullfill that which is commaunded. God maketh clere when it pleaseth him. Be you constant and avoyde Temptations: For True it is, that is sayde: And lastly I say,

> <u>It shall be performed.</u>

What is it now thow woldest desyre to be made playner?

Δ: Still he proceded uppon my answers: and at length he sayd,

> Neyther is the time of mans Justification known **untyll** he
> hath byn tried.[420]

You are chosen by God his mercy <u>to an ende</u>[421] and purpose: Which ende shall be made manifest <u>by the first begynning</u> in knowledg in these Mysteries.

God shall make clere whan it pleaseth him: & open all the secrets of wisdome whan he unlocketh. <u>Therfore **Seke not to know the mysteries of this boke, tyll the very howre**</u>[422] **that he shall call thee.** For then shall his powre be so full amongst you, that the flesh shall not be perceyued, in respect of his great glory.

But was there euer any, that tasted of <u>gods mercies so assuredly, that wanted due reverence?</u>[423] Can you bow to Nature, and will not honor the workman? Is it not sayd, that <u>this place is holy? What are the works of holines?</u> I do aduertise you: for, God will be honored. <u>Neyther will he be wrasted, in any thing he speaketh.</u> Think not, that you could

---

[419] Fardel: "pack." -Ed

[420] Tyme of Iustification known than.

[421] The ende of our election.

[422] Tyll the very howre.

[423] Want of due reuerence using in our actions is reproved.

speak or talk with me, unleast I did greatly abase my self, in <u>taking uppon</u>
<u>me so unlikely a thing in forme, as to my self, &c.</u>[424] But he doth this not
for your causes, not for your deserts, but for the Glorie of his owne name.

One is not to be lightened, but all. And, which all? The two **fethered**
fowle togither with **the Capitayn**.

Ask What thow wilt: for, untyll the <u>40 dayes</u>[425] <u>be ended</u>, shalt
thow haue <u>no</u> one more shew of us.

Δ: Whether shall we give Cownsayle, or consent to <u>the Captayne</u>[426]
to go down into his Cuntry, as, presently he entendeth.

Ur:—As he listeth. Δ: EK sayd that this was Uriel who now had
appered and answered all this.

Ur:—I will ask thee one question. Haue we any voyce or no?

Δ: I do think you haue no organs or instruments apt for voyce: but
are mere spirituall and nothing corporall: but that you haue the powre
and property from god to insinuate your message or meaning to eare or
eye, in such sort as mans Imagination shall be, that both they here and
see you sensibly.

Ur:—We haue no voyce but a full noyce that filleth euery place:[427]
which whan you ones taste of, Distance shall make no separation. Let
there one come that may better answer: not in respect of thy self but
one, **more nerer to thy estate.**[428]—Do thy Duty.

Δ: He sayd this, to one who cam in, and he departed him self.

Δ: This new come Creature sayd, Wold you haue any thing with
me, Il?[429]

---

[424] Angels abase themselues, to pleasure man by theyr instructions, when they tak
uppon them, or use any sensible evidence of themselves or voyces, &c.

[425] 40 dayes.

[426] A.G. -Δ. (Adrian Gilbert. -Ed.)

[427] Vox angelorum.

[428] Uriel putteth one into his place.

[429] Il or El.

Δ: Who art thow: Art thow one that <u>loveth and honoreth our Creator?</u>

Il: Will you see my hart?—EK: He openeth his body and sheweth his hart: and theron appered written <u>EL</u>.

Δ: He semed to be a very mery Creature, and skypped here and there, his apparell was like as of a vyce in a play: and so was his gesture[430] and his skoffing, as the outward shew therof was to be vulgarly[431] demed: but I did carefully ponder the pith of the words which he spake: and so forbare to write very much which he spake at the begynning by reason EK did so much mislike him, and in a manner toke him to <u>be an Illuder</u>.

Δ: As you are appointed to answer us by the Messager of God, so answer us, (who desyre pure and playne verity,) as may be correspondent to his Credit that assigned you, and to the honor of God who Created us.

Il:—My answer is Threefold:[432]—I answer by gesture, by my apparayle, & will answer thee by my wordes.

Δ: Do you know where the Arabik boke[433] is that I had: which was written in tables and numbers?[434]

Il:—It is in Scotland:—A minister hath it; it is nothing worth. The boke conteyneth fals and illuding Witchcrafts. All lawde honor and prayse be to the One and euerlasting God: for euer and euer.[435]

Δ: The Lord Threasoror,[436] hath he, any bokes belonging to Soyga?
Il:—<u>He hath none: but certayn Introductions to all artes.</u>

Δ: But it was reported to me by this Skryer[437] that he had: certayn

---

430 Gesture: "general behavior." -Ed.

431 Vulgarly: "commonly." -Ed.

432 Note, Threfold answer.

433 Liber Arabicus. -Δ. ("Arabic book." -Ed.)

434 This probably does not refer to the book *Soyga*. -Ed.

435 EK he Kneleth down.

436 Lord Treasurer: William Cecil, Lord Burghley. -Ed.

437 Note.

peculier bokes perteyning to Soyga: otherwise named ysoga, and Agyos, literis transpositis.[438]

Il:—Soyga signifieth not Agyos. <u>Soyga alca miketh.</u>

Δ: What signifieth those wordes? <u>The true measure of the Will of God in iudgment which is by Wisdome.</u>

Δ: What language is that, I pray you? Il:—A language towght in Paradise.[439]

Δ: To whome? Il:—By infusion, to Adam. Δ: To whome did Adam use it? Il:—Unto Chevah.[440] Δ: Did his posteritie use the same?

Il:—<u>Yea, untyll the Ayrie Towre[441] was destroyed.</u>

Δ: Be there any letters of that language yet extant among us mortall men?

Il: .... that there be. Δ: Where are they? Il:—ô, syr, I shall make you in loue with your Masterships boke.

Δ: Did Adam write any thing in that language? Il:—That is no question.

Δ: Belike than, they were deliuered from one to an other by tradition or els Enoch[442] his boke, or prophesie, doth, or may seme, to be written in the same language: bycause mention is made of it in the new Testament in Jude his Epistle where he hath, Prophetauit autem de his Septimus ab Adam, Enoch, dicens, Ecce venit Dominus in sanctis millibus suis, facere iudicium contra omnes, et arguere omnes impios, de omnibus operibus impietatis eorum, quibus impiè egerunt, et de omnibus duris, quæ locuti sunt contra Deum peccatores impij &c.[443]

---

[438] In Sloane 3677, Ashmole notes: "1674 The Duke of Lauderdale hath a folio MS which was Dr. Dees with these words in the first page, Aldaraia sive Soyga vocor." Literis transpositis: "by transposing the letters." -Ed.

[439] The language towght in Paradise.

[440] Eve. -Ed.

[441] The Tower of Babel. See Genesis 11. -Ed.

[442] Enoch.

Il:—I must distinguish with you. Before the flud, the spirit of God was not utterly obscured in man. Theyr <u>memories</u> were greater, theyr understanding more clere, and theyr <u>traditions</u>, most, unsearchable.[444] Nothing remayned of Enoch but (and if it pleas your mastership) mowght haue byn carryed in a cart. I can not bring you the brass, but I can shew you the bokes. <u>Slepe 28</u>[445] <u>dayes</u>, and you shall fynde them, under your pillow whan you do rise.

Δ: As concerning Esdras bokes,[446] which are missing, what say you?

Il: The prophets of the Jues[447] haue them. Δ: But we can hardely trust any thing in the Jues hands, concerning the pure veritie: They are a stiff necked people and dispersed all the world ouer.

Il:—I will shew you a trik. Δ: He lifted up his fote, and shewed the sole of his shoo: and there appeared the picture of a man, who seemed to haue a skorf or fowle skynne on his face: which one toke of: and then there appered on his forhed these <u>two figures, 88</u>.[448]

I will shew you more then that, to: and will speak to a man shortly, that shall bring Water to wash euery mans face.

Δ: What mean you, by euery man? Shall all men, be made cleane?

Il:—There is a difference in washing of faces.

EK: This creature seemeth to be a Woman[449] by his face: his appar-

---

[443] Jude 14–15: "Enoch also, the seventh from Adam, prophesied of these, saying, Behold, the Lord cometh with ten thousands of his saints, to execute judgement upon all, and to convince all that are ungodly among them of all their ungodly deeds which they have ungodly committed, and of all their hard speeches which ungodly sinners have spoken against him." This is quoted from 1 Enoch 1:9. See James H. Charlesworth, ed., *The Old Testament Pseudepigrapha*, vol. 1 (New York: Doubleday, 1983), pp. 12–13. -Ed.

[444] Note: excellent Memories, for Traditions contynuing and preseruing.

[445] Δ forte: <u>18</u>. Note, <u>28</u> dayes more do make iust the 40 dayes, before notified.

[446] Esdras bokes. -Δ. See II Esdras 14.37 ff. -Ed.

[447] The Jues.

[448] Δ this might seme to signifie the calling home of the Jues, A°. 1588 to come.

ell semeth to be like a Vice[450] in a play.

EK: Ar you not a Kinsman to Syngolla?

Il: I syr, and so are you a kinsman to Synfulla.

Δ: A man may finde corn in chaf.

Il:—So may you (perchaunce) finde me an honest man in my ragged clothes.

Δ: This other day, whan I was in dowt of the Grecian (the Macedonian) whether he had any good and profownd lerning or no, he was represented spiritually, and abowt his hat in great letters was written this greke word *Κατάριχτθ* : I pray you what doth it signifie? I axed the grecian and he sayd, *βέβαιθ* Il: Loke in your boke. Δ: I toke the common lexicon: and he sayd: No Not that: Then I axed if I shold take phauorinus his lexicon:[451] and he answered, Nor that. And I axed which then: and he sayd your boke covered with a white parchment: and I axed, that of Munsteris of Latine greke and hebrue? And he sayd, yea: and there you shall finde that Maculosus hath onely that one word *Μαβεριχτθ* longing to it. I loked & so fownd it: which satisfyed me very well.

Δ: I pray you what say you of Gariladrah;[452] do you know him? Who long sins[453] did deale with me?

---

449 Note, El semed to be woman.

450 Vice: "a character playing one of the vices in a morality play; jester." -Ed.

451 Varinus Phavorinus, *Lexicon græcum* (Rome, 1523). -Ed.

452 Gariladrah.

453 Since. -Ed.

Il:—Yf he were lesser then I, I durst speak to him: But bycause he is greater then I, I am not to speak to him. All under, and nothing above me, I deale.

Loke in your Tables and there you shall <u>finde an other **name of his**</u>.

Δ: I remember no such thing. Il:—Consider who hath set me here.[454] Yf the Truth thow hast allready, be of a greater then my self, then is it sufficient. Δ: What day was that name given me?

Il:—Immediately, sir, after your[455] Worships last coming.

Δ: That was Raphaël: And I remember that Gariladrah sayd that he must leave me and his better, (Raphael) shuld be my instructor, and that then the same Raphael was in my hed then. &c.

Δ: Sing a song to his prayse, who created us.

Il: I will sing a short song.

> Your doings are of GOD: your calling great:
> Go down and seke the Threasor,[456] and you shall obteyn it.
> Take no care: for, this Boke shall be done in <u>40 dayes</u>.[457]
> Begyn to practise in August.[458] <u>Serue god before.</u>
> You shall know <u>all thing, ictu oculi</u>.[459]
> And so, prayse, glory, and eternall singing
> with incessant humilitie be unto thee, Creator that
> hath framed, made and Created all things, for
> euer and euer, Now say you (yf you will).
> Amen. Δ: Amen Amen Amen.

---

[454] That was Uriel. Vide pag. precedent. -Δ. ("See the previous page." -Ed.)

[455] He pointed to EK.

[456] Thesaurus absconditus. -Δ. ("Hidden treasure." -Ed.)

[457] 40 dayes.

[458] August.

[459] Knowledge to be infused Ictu Oculi. -Δ. (Ictu Oculi: "with a stroke(or ray) of the eye." -Ed.)

Il: After the ende of 40 dayes, go down for the Threasor.[460] Whan those 40 dayes are done,[461] than this boke shall be finished. The rest of the time untyll August,[462] is for rest, labor, and prayer.

Δ: What labor? Il:—In digging up of those Threasors.

Δ: Must we nedes dig for them? Il:—Otherwise, yf thow willt.

Δ: How, I pray you? For to dig without lycence[463] of the Prince, is dangerous by reason of the lawes: and to ax licence, is half an odious sute.

Il:—Yf thow haue a parcell or part out of euery place of the erth, in any small quantitie, thow mayst work by the Creatures, whose powre it is to work in such causes: which **will bring** it (neuer trust me) before you can tell twenty.[464]

Δ: He meaneth, Neuer trust him, if it be not so, as he hath sayd.

Il:—No, neuer trust me, if it be not so:

Δ: You mean those ten places, marked in the Table, which, last day, I deciphred.[465]

Il:—I mary,[466] now you hit it. Yea sir, and your chest allso,[467] it wold do no hurt. Give me one: and I will make 40: and give you twenty and take twenty to my self: and whan you haue it, I pray you let me haue some little portion for my wife and children.

Δ: As concerning that Chest, I pray you how cam the Macedonian, or Mr Sanford to know of it, so particularly, as he did?

---

[460] Thesaurus abs.

[461] 40.

[462] Note: till August.

[463] Lycence, licence: "legal permission." -Ed.

[464] Without digging.

[465] Ten places.

[466] Mary: a mild oath. -Ed.

[467] The chest.

Il:—Husey told of it, openly, at the bord at braynford[468] in the hearing of diuerse. The Grecian will seke him oute. The Greke in grecia perhaps can finde out Threasor, but not in Anglia.[469] The Greke hath a Threasor in his hed, that will enriche him to be a fole. I was yesterday at London, I met with a blak dyer. He had a cupple of rings, that wold giue better instructions. Your Chymney <u>here</u> will speak <u>agaynst</u> you anon:[470] yet I am no brik layer.[471] I must be gone.

Δ: God, for his infinite mercyes be allwayes praysed, glorified, and extolled of all his Creatures. Amen.

He advised EK to comunicate to me the boke, and the <u>powder</u>, and so all the rest of the roll,[472] which was there fownd: saying, <u>True frends use not to hide any thing eche from other</u>.

Δ: An old proverb it is. Amicorum omnia comunia.

Unde, Deo soli omnis exhibeatur
Laus honor et gloria.[473]
Amen.

Note: There followeth Quinti Libri Mysteriorum Appendix.[474]

---

468 Braynford: "Brentford." -Ed.

469 Grecia:"Greece"; Anglia: "England." -Ed.

470 Anon: "soon." -Ed.

471 Δ True it is, I had hidden there, in a capcase the recordes of my doings with Saule & other &c.

472 The boke, The powder, the rest of the roll. -Δ. This is the so-called *Book of Saint Dunstan*. -Ed.

473 Amicorum . . . gloria: "Everything is shared between friends; therefore, to God alone are offered all praise, honor, and glory." -Ed.

474 Quinti Libri Mysteriorum Appendix: "Appendix to the Fifth Book of the Mysteries." -Ed.

Quinti libri Mysteriorum

Appendix

Aprilis 20.—Saterday

Δ: This satterday had byn great and eger pangs betwene EK and me: while he wold utterly discredit the whole process of our actions: <u>as, to be done by evill and illuding spirites</u>: seking his destruction: saying that he hath often here to fore byn told things true, but of illuding diuells: and Now, how can this be other, than a mockery, to haue a cornerd dark clowd to be shewed him in steade of the playn writing, which hitherto he had written out of? and that <u>whan they shold do good in dede that then they shrank from us</u>: and that he was not thus to leese[1] his time: But that he is to study, to lerne some knowledge, whereby he may liue: and that he was a cume[2] to my howse, and that he dwelled here as in a prison; that it wer better for him to be nere Cotsall playne where he might walk abroade, without danger or to be cumbred[3] or vexed with such sklaunderous fellows as yesterday he was, with one little Ned dwelling at the blak raven in Westminster: who rayled at[4] him for bearing witnes of a bargayn made betwene the same Ned (or Edward) and one Lush a Surgien, who was now falln in poverty, a very honest man &c: With a great deale of more matter; <u>melancholik, and cross</u> overthwartly to the <u>good and patient using of our selues to the accomplishing of this action</u>. I replyed, and sayd, that we might finde our selfs answered on thursday, as, That God wold clere when it pleased him: and that we were not to appoint God a time to performe his mysteries and mercies in; shorter then he hath spoken of: And that undowtedly, the occasion of this blak clowd, was some imperfection of oures, to be amended and that then, all wold be to our furder cumfort. And as concerning his dowting the goodnes of the Creatures, (dealing

---

1   Lease: "occupy." -Ed.

2   In Sloane 3677, EA reads "cumber." -Ed.

3   Cumbred: "obstructed." -Ed.

4   Railed at: "verbally abused." -Ed.

with us) he was to blame, to say or dowt the tree to be yll that bringeth furth good frute: for of these creatures, from the begynning of theyr dealing with us unto the last howre,

☞ we never hard other than the prayse of god, instructions and exhortations to humilitie, patience, constancy, fayth &c. The things they promise be such as god can performe, and is for his servyce and glory to performe: and such as haue byn imparted to man before: and therfore neyther impossible for man to enioye agayne, nor unmete for us to hope for: and thowgh his trubbled mynde did dowt, yet my quiet mynde, which god hath made ioyfull throwgh his mercyes, and which accuseth me not in this action of any ambition, hypocrisie, or disorderly longing, but onely is bent and settled in awayting the Lord his helping hand to make me wise for his servyce, (according as long tyme my daylie prayer to him hath byn): and seing I haue and do ax wisdome[5] at the lord his hands, and put my trust in him, he will not suffer me to be so confownded: nether will he offer a stone to his seely children, when in tyme of nede they ax bred at his hands: besides that, Voluntatem timentium se faciet deus:[6] and (by his graces) I feare him so, and am so carefull to do that shold pleas him, that I make no accownt of all this world possessing, unleast I might enioye his fauor, his mercies and graces. And whereas he complayned of want, I sayd my want is greater than his: for I was in det allmost 300 pownds,[7] had a greater charge than he; and yet for all my 40 yeres course of study, many hunderd pownds spending, many hundred myles travayling, many an incredible toyle and forcing of my will in study using to lerne or to bowlt out some good thing, &c. Yet for all this I wold be very

---

5   Sapientia. -Δ. ("Wisdom." -Ed.)

6   Voluntatem . . . deus: "He fulfils the desire of all who fear God" (misquoting Psalm 145:19). -Ed.

7   £s 300 det.

well pleased to be deferred yet longer, (a yere or more,) and to go up and down England clothed in a blanket, to beg my bred, so that I might, at the ende be assured to atteyn to <u>godly wisdome</u>, whereby to do God some service for his glory. And to be playne, that I was res-olued, eyther willingly to leave this world presently that, so, I might in spirit enioye the bottomles fowntayne of all wisdome, or els to pass furth my dayes on earth with gods favor and assurance of enioying here his mercifull mighty blessings, to understand his mysteries, mete for the performing of true actions, such as myght sett furth his glory, so, as it might be evident and confessed, that such things wer done Dextera Domini.[8] And many other discourses and answers I made unto his obiections and dowtes: Afterward [A meridie] I began to speak of the trubbles and misery foreshewed to be nere at hand, and by that tyme I had entred a little into the Consideration & talk of the matter, he appered that sayd he was called <u>El or Il</u>[9], <u>and sayd</u>,

--------- Now to the matter.

Δ: What matter?

Il:—I must have a Wallet to carry your witt and myne own in.

Δ: Benedictus qui venit in nomine domini.[10]

Il:—Then I perceyue that I shall haue a blessing. Blessed is the physitien that hath care of his patient, before the pangs of death doth viset him.

Δ: —What think you of that clowdy Heptagonum?

Il:—Dost thow consider, I go abowt it? I told thee, euery thing I did, was an Instruction. As I can not stand stedfastly uppon this, (it self one, and <u>one</u>, perfect:) so can not my mowth declare, much lesse speak, that you may comprehend it, what this is whereuppon I go.

---

8   Dextera Domini: "from the right hand of the Lord." -Ed.

9   Il: the first of the 7 sonns of sonns of light. -Δ (HM).

10   Benedictus . . . Domini: "Blessed is he who comes in the name of the Lord." -Ed.

EK: He went on the Heptagonon, as one might go on the top of a turning whele: (Δ: as some horses use to turne wheles as may appere in Georgius Agricola[11] de re metallica).

Il:—I know, what all your talk hath byn: But such myndes, such Infection, such Infection, such corruption: and must nedes haue a potion appliable for the cure. But how will you do? I haue forgotten all my droggs behinde me. But since I know that some of you are well stored with sufficient oyntments, I do entend to viset you onely with theyr help. You see, all my boxes ar empty?—EK: He sheweth, a great bundell of empty potichayre[12] boxes, and they seme to my hearing to rattle.

Δ: How commeth it, that you pretend to come from a favorable diuine powre to pleasure us, and your boxes ar empty.

Il:—You sayd euen now in your talk, Iovis omnia plena:[13] yf my empty boxes be vertuous, how much more shall any thing be, which I bring not empty?

Δ: Then I pray you, to say somwhat of the vertue of your empty boxes, bycause we may haue the better confidence of your fullnes.

Il: Will you haue my bill? Δ: Shall we go to the Apothecaries, with your Bill?

Il: I will shew it: Serve it, where you list.

    Iudra galgol astel.

Δ: You know we, understand it not: how can it be serued?

Il:—You must nedes haue an expositor. What boke of physik is that, that lyeth by you?

---

[11] 1494–1555 German mineralogist and author. -Ed.

[12] Potichayre: "apothecary (?)" -Ed.

[13] Iovis omnia plena: "Jove fills all," from Virgil's *Eclogues,* III., 60, repeated in Giovanni Pontano's astronomical poem *Urania siue de stellis,* Lib. I.628. Note that Pontano is cited by Philip Sidney in his *Defence of Poesia* (London: Dent 1595; Rutland, VT: Tuttle, 1997). -Ed.

[Δ: There lay by me on my desk, Marcus Heremita de Lege spiritu-ali[14] in greke and latine but the latine translation lay open before, on the left side of which, the sentence began: Non raro per negligentiam, quæ circa alicuius rei operationem comittitur, etiam Cognito obscu-ratur.[15] And on the right side, began: Corpus sine mente nihil pt perficere[16] &c.]

Il:—Mary here is good physik in dede. You fownd my name the other day. Go to my name [Δ: So I turned to the second boke and browght sigillum Æmeth: and there chose the Word Ilemese. He than axed me, which letter of this name I liked best, and I sayd, L: bycause it conteyned the name representing God: El, &c. Then he sayd somwhat farder of the letters, which I wrote not.

Il:—Go to great M, the second: for this is it that shall serue his turne. Yf this can not serue him, he shall haue a medicine, that a horse can not abyde. Use this, and I warrant you, your blindenes will be gone.[17]

Δ: It is here, greatly, to be Noted: that I turned in this boke of Marcus, 27 leaues furder: tyll I cam to the Quaternio of M, the second and there I fownd this sentence notified (by my lines drawn, and a Note in the margent Cor Contritum): Sine corde contrito impossibile est omnino liberari a malitia et vilijs. Conterit autem cor tripartita temper-antia somni dico et cibi, et corporalis licentiæ. Cæterum horum excessus et abundantia voluptatem generat. Voluptas autem prauas cogitationes ingerit repugnat verò præcationi et convenienti Cogitationi.[18]

---

14   De Lege Spirituali: "concerning the spiritual law." -Ed.

15   Non raro . . . obscuratur: "Furthermore, knowledge is obscured not rarely, through negligence, which is committed in the working of anything." -Ed.

16   Corpus . . . perficere: "Body without mind, achieves nothing . . ." -Ed.

17   A remedy for the blyndness of EK at this instant.

18   And so many dayes yet wanted of the 40, yf we accownt from the 6 day of Aprill: but if from the tyme of the begynning I wrote them, then there wanteth not so

Δ: This being considered by us, we ceased and this instant and thanked God of his mercies, that it wold pleas him to make us understand some iust cause whie clowdes now appeared in stede of brightnes &c.

Soli Deo omnis honor laus et gloria.[19] Amen.

Aprilis 23. Tuesday. mane hor. 8.

Δ: After our prayer iointly, and my long prayer, at my desk requesting God to deale with us, so, as might be most for his glory, in his mercies: not according to our deserts, and frowardnes: &c. At length appeared in the stone a white clowde, seven-cornered. And behinde the Clowde a Thunder seemed to yssue.

A Voyce: <u>Whan I gathered you, you were chosen of the myddest of Iniquitie:[20] Whome I haue clothed with garments made and fashioned with my owne hand.—I, AM, Therfore, Beleue:</u>

Δ: I prayed, and thanked the highest, that so mercifully regarded our miserie.

A Voyce: I, AM.

EK: Now standeth Uriel upon the clowde, and semeth to loke downward and kneled, saying,

Æternitie, Maiestie, Dominion and all powre, in heuen the earth,

---

much as 9 or 10 dayes. -Δ. Cor Contritum . . . Cogitationi: "Contrite heart): Without a contrite heart it is impossible to be completely freed of malice and inferiority. And so I say, the heart crushes the threefold temperance of sleep, food, and bodily license. An excess and abundance of these others creates pleasure, but pleasure brings on distorted thoughts and in fact hinders prayer and proper thought." -Ed.

19   Soli . . . gloria: "To God alone be all honor, praise, and glory." -Ed.

20   Nos. -Δ. ("We/Us." –Ed.)

and in the secret partes below, is thyne, thyne, yea thyne; and to none els due, but unto thee: whose mercies are infinite, which respectest the glorie of thy owne name, <u>above the frowardnes, and perversnes of mans nature</u>: which swarmeth with synnes, and is couered with Iniquitie: and in the which, there is fownde no place free from filthynes and abhomination. Glorie be to thee; ô, all powre: and magnified be thow, in the workmanship of thy own <u>hands</u>, from time to time, and with out ende of time, from generation to generation: and euen amidst and in the number of those, for whome thow hast prepared the flowres of thy æternall Garland.

Beare with them (ô lord) for thy mercyes sake. For, woldest thow seeke . . .[21] in the myddest of miserie? <u>Whom yf thow sholdest iudge according to thy iustice, How shold thy</u> Name be glorified so in thy <u>self, to</u> thy own determination, and writing, sealed before the Creation <u>of the Worldes?</u> The fire of thy Justice consumeth thyne own seat; and in thee, is no powre wanting, whan it pleaseth thee, to cast down, and gather them to gither, as the wynde doth the Snow, and in-hemme them with the mowntaynes, that they may not arrise to synne. But What thow art, thow art: and what thow willt, thow canst.

Amen.

Δ: Amen.

Ur:—I haue measured time (sayth the lord) and it is so: I haue appointed to the heauens theyr course, and they shall not pass it. The synnes of man shall decay, in despite of the enemy: But the fire of æternitie shall neuer be quenched, nor neuer fayle. More, then is, can not, nor may not be sayde. We can not be Wittnesses to him which wittnesseth of him self.

---

21 Δ Here I mist the hering of a word or more.

Nota et
Caue

But (**this sayeth the Lord**), Beholde yf you trubble me <u>ones more, or towche the wings of my excellency, before I shall move my self, I will raze you from the earth, as children of perdition and **will endue** those that are of quiet myndes, with the strength of my powre.</u>[22] You are not faithfull, sayeth the lorde whome you beleue not. Notwithstanding **I haue hardened the hart of One of you,** yea, <u>**I haue hardened him as the flynt, and burnt him to gither with the ashes of a Cedar: to the entent he may be proued iust in my work, and great in the strength of my Glory. Neyther shall his mynde consent to the wyckednes of Iniquitie. For, from Iniquitie I haue chosen him,**[23] **to be a first erthely witnes of my Dignitie.**</u>[24]

Your words are, yet, not offensiue unto God: Therfore, will not we, be offended at any thing that is spoken: For it must be done[25] and shall stand; yea and in the <u>**number**</u> which I haue allready chosen.

Note

But, this sayeth the Lord: Yf you use me like worldlings I will suerly stretch out my arme uppon you, and that heuily.[26] Lastly, I say,

---

22 Nota et Caue -Δ. ("Note this and beware." –Ed.)

23 Election confirmed.

24 One of us is by the Lord confirmed in constant purpose.

25 Δ I think "sayeth the Lord" is forgotten here.

26 Note.

$\left\{\begin{array}{l}\text{Be Faithfull,}\\\text{Honor God truely.}\\\text{Beleue him hartily.}\end{array}\right.$

EK: He kneleth down, and semeth to pray.—Now he standeth up.

Note

Ur: Lo, As a number increasing is allwayes bigger: so in this world decreasing, the Lord must be mightily glorified. <u>Striue not with God: But receyue, as he imparteth.</u>[27] The Mercy of my message, quencheth the obscuritie and dullnes of your sowles: I mean of the Infection, wherewithall they are poysoned. Lo, how the Earth cryeth vengeance.[28] Come, for thy Glory sake, it is tyme. Amen.

Δ: Seing it is sayd that in 40 dayes the boke shalbe finished and seing it is sayed that our former Instructers shall not come nor appeare to us tyll the boke be finished: And seing here to fore the boke used to appere to EK, that he might write, whan so euer he bent him self therto: and seing the same boke appeareth not so now: and seing we are desyrous to be fownd diligent in this work, and to omitt no Opportunitie wherein the writing therof might be furdred: We wold gladly know; What token, or warning shall be giuen us, henceforward, whan due tyme serueth for the same purpose.

Ur:—Dy in the folly: I haue sayde.

EK: It thundreth and lightneth abowt the clowde: and now all is vanished away.

Δ: EK sayd, that at the very begynning of this days action, when he

---

27 Note.

28 Vengeance cryed for.

expressed the first Voyce (this day), hard of him, his belly did seame to him, to be full of fyre: and that he thowght veryly, that his bowells did burne: And that he loked downward toward his leggs, to see if any thing appeared on fire: calling to his mynde, the late chance that befell to the Adulterous man and woman by Sainct Brydes church in London &c. Allso that whan he had made an ende, he thowght his belly to be wyder, and enlarged, muche more then it was before.

Δ: I sayde certayn prayers to the Almightie our God and most mercifull father, on my knees; and EK on his knees likewise, answered diuerse times, Amen.

After this, we made AG. to understand these the mercies of the Highest: and he reioyced greatly, and praysed the Lorde. And, so EK, was fully satisfyed of his Dowtes: And AG, and he, were reconciled of the great discorde which, yesterday, had byn betwene them, &c.

> Non nobis, Domine, Non nobis,
> sed nomini tuo Gloriam omnem
> Laudem et honorem damus, et
> dabimus in perpetuum.[29]
> Amen.

Aprilis 26. Fryday

Δ   **NOTE**

Δ: By the prouidence of god, and Mr Gilbert his meanes, and pacifying of EK his vehement passions and pangs, he cam agayn to my howse: and my wife very willing, and quietted in mynde, and very frendely to

---

[29] Non nobis . . . perpetuum: "Not for ourselves, O Lord, not for ourselves, but for the glory of your name, we give and we will give all praise and honor, forever" (Psalm 115:1). -Ed.

EK in Word, and cowntenance: and a new pacification on all partes confirmed: and all uppon the Confidence of God his servyce, to be faythfully and cherfly intended, and followed in and by our actions, throwgh the grace and mercy of the highest.

1583. Aprilis 28. Sonday. after Dynner abowt 4 of the clok.

Δ: As I and EK had diuerse talks and discourses of Transposition of letters: and I had declared him my rule for to know certaynly how many wayes, any number of letters (propownded,) might be transposed or altered in place or order: Behold, suddenly appered, the Spirituall Creature, Il, and sayd,

Il:—Here is a goodly disputation of transposition of letters. Chuse, whether you will dispute with me, of Transposition, or I shall lerne you.

Δ: I had rather lerne then dispute. And first I think, that those letters of our Adamicall Alphabet haue a due peculier unchangeable proportion of theyr formes,—and likewise that theyr order is allso Mysticall.

Il:—These letters[30] represent the Creation of man: and therfor they must be in proportion. They represent the Workmanship wherewithall the sowle of man was made like unto his Creator. But I understand you shall haue a paynter shortly.

Δ: —I pray you, what paynter may best serue for the purpose? Can master Lyne serue the turn well?

Il: Dost thow think that God can be glorifyed in hell, or can diuells dishonor him? Can Wickednes of a paynter, deface the mysteries of God? The truth is, I am come to aduertise you, least with a small error you be led, far, asyde.

---

30   The mysticall Alphabet.

Let me see the forme of your Table.[31]

Δ: —I shewed him the Characters and words which were to be paynted rownd abowt in the border of the Table.

Il:—How do you like those letters? Δ: I know not well what I may say. For, perhaps, that which I shuld like, wer not so to lyked: and contrarywise what I shold think well of, might be nothing worth.

Il:—Thow sayest wel.

Behold, great is the fauor and mercy of God toward those whome he fauoreth. All things are perfect but onely that: Neyther what that shewed or deliuered by any good and perfect messenger from God. A wicked powre did intrude him self;[32] not onely into your societie, but allso into the Workmanship of Gods mysteries. Sathan dare presume to speak of the Almighty. Those Characters are diuilish: and a secret band of the Diuell. But, this sayeth the lord, I will rayse them up, whom he hath ouerthrown: and blott oute his fotesteps where they resist my glorie. Neyther will I suffer the faithfull to be led utterly awry: nor finally permit darkness to enhemme them for euer. He sayth, I AM, and they[33] are most untrue. But behold. I haue browght thee the truth: that the Prince of reason, God of understanding may be apparent in euery part of his Cælestiall demonstration. Therfore, as thow saydst unto me ones,

So say I now to thee: Serue god.

Make a square,[34] of 6 ynches euery way. The border therof let it be (here) but, half an inche: but on the Table it self, let it be an inche broad.[35]

---

31 The Table of Practise.

32 Illuding spirits thrusting in themselues.

33 I understand that the characters are most untrue.

34 Δ The Inner square, of 6 ynches.

35 Δ vide post foliam, et etiam in Tabula cordis carnis et cutis, nam in lineis defendentibus, ibidem habes hanc tabula hic incipiendo sed in primo omittendo l et

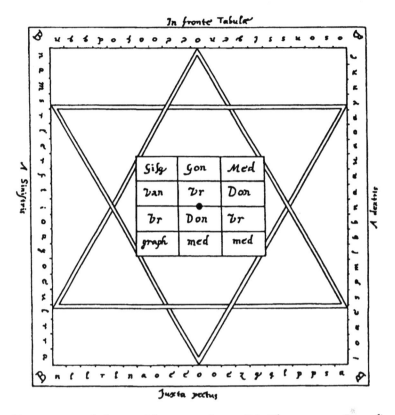

Euery one of those sides must haue 21 Characters: But, first, at euery corner make a great B.

Prayer is the key of all good things:

Δ: After our prayers made, EK had sight (in the stone) of innumerable letters and after a little while, they wer browght into a lesser square and fewer letters. First appered in the border opposite to our standing place, (which I haue used to call, in fronte Tabulæ) these letters following, beginning at the right hand, and proceding toward the left.

---

accipiendo o. ("See on the next sheet, and also in the table of the heart, flesh, and skin, for in the surrounding lines, you have this table here commencing the same, but omitting 'l' at the start, and gaining 'o'.") Note: This note is written inverted above the diagram in very small script. There is a hand pointing to the first "o" in the top border. In fronte tabulæ: "in front of the table"; a sinistris: "on the left"; a dextra: "on the right"; iuxta pectus: "next to the chest." -Ed.

1[36]	2[38]	3[39]	4[40]
Med	drux	drux	gon
fam	un	ur	med
med	tal	ur	un
drux	fam	don	graph
fam	don	ur	fam
fam	ur	drux	mals
ur	graph	un	tal
ged	don	med	ur
graph	or	graph	pa
drux	gisg	graph	pa
med	gon	med	drux
graph	med	med	un
graph	un	graph	un
tal[37]	ged	ceph	van
med	med	ged	un
or	graph	ged	med
med	van	ur	un
gal	ur	mals	gon - with a prik
ged	don	mals	drux
ged	don	fam	drux
drux	un	un	ur

----

36   In fronte Tabulae. ("In front of the table" -Ed.)

37   Fortè <u>med</u>. ("Perhaps 'med'" -Ed.)

38   A sinistris. ("To the left." -Ed.)

39   Juxta pectus. ("Next to the chest." -Ed.)

40   A dextris. ("To the right." -Ed.)

Il: What haue you in the myddle of your Tablet? Δ: Nothing.

Il: **Sigillum Emeth, is to be sett there.**

Il: The rest, after supper.

Δ: Soli Deo Omnipotenti sit laus perennis.[41]

    Amen.

After supper, retorning to our businesse, I first dowted of the heds of the letters in the border, to be written, which way they owght to be turned, to the center ward of the Table or from the Center ward.

    Il:—The heds of the letters must be next or toward the center of the square Table or Figure. Diuide that within, by 12 and 7.[42]

    Δ: I diuided it.

    Il:—**Grace, mercy and peace be unto the liuely branches of his flor-ishing kingdom: and strong art thow in thy glory, which dost unknytt the secret partes of thy liuely workmanship: and that, before the weak understanding of man. Herein is thy powre and Magnificence opened unto man: And why? bycause thy diuinitie and secret powre is here shut up in Numero Ternario et Quaternario: à quo principium et fun-damentum omne huius est tui sanctissimi operis.[43] For, yf thow (O God) be wunderfull and incomprehensible in thyne owne substance, it must nedes follow, that thy works are likewise incomprehensible. But, Lo, they shall now beleue, bycause they see, which heretofore could skarsly beleue. Strong is the <u>Influence of thy supercelestiall</u> powre, and mighty is the force of that arme, which overcommeth all things: Let all powre therfore rest in thee; Amen.**

---

41   Soli Deo . . . perennis: "To God alone be eternal praise." -Ed.

42   Note of the Square within.

43   Ternarius et Quaternarius. -Δ. Numero . . . operis: "In the numbers of the terna-ry and quaternary, from which is the beginning and the entire foundation of this, your most holy work." -Ed.

Δ: The Spirituall Creature seamed to eate fyre, like balls of fyre: hauing his face toward me, and his bak toward EK.

Il: Leave oute the Bees of the 7 names of the seven Kings, and 7 Princis: and place them in a table diuided by 12 and 7:[44] the 7 spaces being uppermost: and therein write, in the upper line, the letters of the king, with the letters of his Prince following next after his name: and so of the six other, and theyr Princis: And read them on the right hand from the upper part to the lowest, and thow shalt finde, then, the Composition of this Table. Therein they are all comprehended, sauing certayn letters, which are not to be put-in here: By reason that the Kings and Princis do spring from God; and not God from the Kings and Princis:[45] Which excellency is comprehended, and is allso manifest, in that Third and Fowrth member.

Rownd abowt the sides [of this square] is euery letter of the 14 names of the 7 kings and Princis.

Hereafter shall you perceyue that the Glorie of this Table surmownteth the glorie of the sonne.[46]

All things els appertayning unto it, are allready prescribed by your former instruction.

I haue no more to say, but God transpose your myndes, according to his own will and pleasure. You talked of Transposition.[47] Tomorrow I will be with you agayn. But Call not for me, least you incurre the danger of the former Curse.[48]

---

[44] 12, 7.

[45] Note of these kings and Princis.

[46] The dignity of the Table of practise.

[47] He alludeth to our talk had of Transposition of letters.

[48] Note, danger of violating precepts of doctrine.

l	o	n	e	g	a	n	o	g	i	l	a
o	g	o	n	r	o	l	e	g	o	b	o
s	e	f	a	f	e	l	e	l	a	b	a
o	n	o	m	t	u	r	o	p	e	n	y
n	o	d	s	i	l	l	o	p	s	a	n
s	e	g	r	o	r	n	e	s	p[49]	a	n
s	e	g	l	a	r	a	z	a	m	u	l

Aprilis 29. Monday, a meridie

Δ: As EK and I wer talking of my boke Soyga, or Aldaraia: and I at
length sayd that, (as far, as I did remember) Zadzaczadlin, was Adam[50]
by the Alphabet therof, suddenly appeared the spirituall creature,
which sayd yesterday that he wold come agayn, this day, uncalled: and
at his first comming he sayd:

Then, à primo.

Δ: Qui primus est et nouissimus, Alpha et Omega, misereatur nostri.[51]

Il:—Amen. Glorie be to thee, which art one, and comprehending

---

49 Fortè s p. -Δ. The manuscript originally had "p s," but these are crossed out and
    "s p" inserted. -Ed.

50 Adam.

51 A primo . . . nostri: "from the first. Δ: Which is the first and newest, Alpha and
    Omega, may he have mercy on us." -Ed.

all. Mervaylous is thy wisdome, in those, of whome, thow willt be comprehended.

A short prayer, but appliable to my purpose.

Euery prayse, with us, is a prayer.

Δ: He taketh-of, his pyed[52] coat, and threw it up on the corner of my desk and then he seemed clothed in an ancient doctorly apparayle: and on his hed he had a wrethe of white sylk of three braydes.[53]

Il:—Well I will give you my lesson, and so byd you farewell. First I am to perswade you to put away wavering myndes. Secondly, for your Instruction, in these necessarie occasions, thus it is:

> The owtsides or skyn must be the Centre.[54] There, is one fowndation.
> The Flesh must be the owtside.
> The Centre it self must be disseuered into 4 æquall partes:

There is your lesson.

Δ: We understand not, this dark lesson.

Il:—The hart must be the fowrth part of the body; and yet the body perfect and sownd. The Skynne must occupy the place of the hart and yet without deformitie. God is the begynning of all things: The fardest parte of all things is in the hands of God. The like shalbe fownd amongst the number of his One most holy name:[55] The Erth is a fowndation to euery thing: and differeth but only in forme. In the forme of his own application whereunto it is applied. **God is the begynning of all things, but not after one sorte, nor to euery one alike. But it is three manner of works, with his name:**[56]

---

[52] Pied: "spotted or patched." -Ed.

[53] Apparayle changed.

[54] An ænigmaticall lesson.

[55] Note.

[56] Three manner of works with God his Name.

The One, in respect of Dignification:
The second, in respect of Conciliation:
The third, in respect of <u>an ende and determined</u>
<u>Operation</u>.

Now syr, to what ende, wold you were your Character?

Δ: At our two first dealings to gither, it was answered by a spirituall
Creature, (whome we toke to be Uriel,) Sigillum hoc in auro sculpendum, ad defensionem Corporis omni loco, tempore et occasione, et in
pectus gestandum.[57]

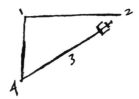

Il: But how do I teache? The Character is an Instrument, appliable
onely to <u>Dignification</u>. But there is no Dignification (Syr) but that
which doth procede, and hath his perfect Composition, <u>Centrally</u>, in
the square <u>number of 3 and 4</u>. The centre whereof shall be equall to the
greatest.

Δ: We understand not.   Il:—Hereby you may gather not onely to
what ende, <u>the blessed Character, (wherewith thow shalt be dignified)</u>
is prepared, but allso the nature of all other characters.[58] To the second.—Δ: Conciliation you meane.

Il:—The Table is an Instrument of Conciliation. And so are the
other 7 Characters: which you call by the name of Tables, squared out

---

57 Vide inscriptiones suo loco, An. 1582, Martij die 10. f. 6. -Δ. ("See the inscrip-
    tion in its own place, 10 March 1582, folio 6.") Sigillum ... gestandum: "Engrave
    this sigil in gold, for protecting the body in all places, times, and occasions: and
    to be worn on the chest." -Ed.

58 The Nature of all Characters.

into the forme of Armes: which are propre to euery king and Prince[59]
according to theyr order.[60]

Now to the last: Δ: As concerning the ende and determined
Operation.

Il: It onely consisteth in the mercy of God, and the Characters of
these bokes.[61] For, Behold, As there is nothing that commeth or
springeth from God, but it is as God, and hath secret Maiesticall and
inexplicable Operation in it: So euery letter here bringeth furth the
Names of God:[62] But, (in dede), they are but one Name; But according
to the locall and former being, do comprehend the universall generation corruptible and incorruptible[63] of euery thing. It followeth, then, it
must nedes comprehend the ende of all things.

Thus much, hitherto.

The Character is fals and diuilish.[64]

He that dwelleth in thee, hath told thee, so, long ago. The former
Diuel, did not onely insinuat him self, but these things.

Δ: I do mervayle, that we had no warning hereof ere now, and that
I was often tymes called on, to prepare those things, (character and
Table): and yet they were fals.

Il:—Yf it shold haue byn gon abowt to be made, it shuld not haue
byn suffred to pass under the forme of wyckednes.[65] The Truth is to be

---

[59] NOTE.

[60] Note here of the 7 Tables of Creation, how they apperteyn to the 7 kings and
Princes.

[61] This boke of 48 Tables.

[62] Note of the Names of God.

[63] Generation: corrup., incor. ("Generation: corruptible, incorruptible." -Ed.)

[64] The Character allso was a falls tradition.

[65] Note.

gathered uppon the first Demonstration (my demonstration and yours[66] are not all one: you will not be offended with me, syr.)

I gaue thee a certayn principle, which in it self is a sufficient demonstration: I told thee, the placing of the Centre, the forme of it, with a lineamentall placing and ordring of that which thow lookest[67] for. Δ: But truely I understand not.

Il:—I teache. Take cleane paper. It must be made 4 inches square.

Pray. Δ: We prayed.

Il: These letters, which I shall speak now, thow shalt, afterward, put them in theyr propre characters.[68]

Write: Neuer since the begynning of the world was this secret deliuered, nor this holy mysterie set open, before the Weaklings of this world. Write in the uppermost prik 'O', and 'b' on the right hand, and 'g' on the left &c. The two extreme pricks, one on the right hand, 'a' and the other, on the left 'o' &c.

There is the whole.

Δ: We prayed (unbidden) in respect of the mysterie revealed. EK, was skarse able to abide or endure the voyce of the spirituall Creature, when he spake of these things now: the sownd was so forcible to his hed that it made it ake vehemently.

---

66 Lepidè, mathematicas meas demonstrationes deuolat. -Δ ("Neat! He endorses my mathematical demonstrations." –Ed.)

67 He meaneth my propre Character truely made.

68 Note. These to be put in propre Characters.

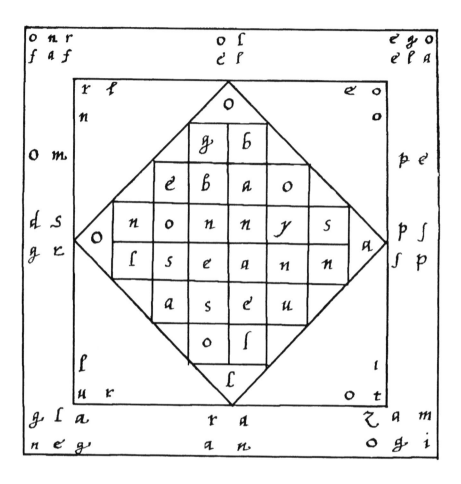

Il:—Set down the kings, and <u>theyr Princis</u> in a Table (as thow knowest them): with theyr letters bakward: excepting theyr Bees, from the right hand, to the left.[69] <u>Let Bobogel be first, and Bornogo is his prince.</u>[70]

Δ: Note here the three diuerse manners how the letters ar cumpassed. 1: The middel is called the Hart or centre, 2: those abowt, enclosing the hart, ar called the flesh, and 3: the two owtside pillers (of two letters in a row) is cownted the skyn.

o	g	o	n	r	o	l	e	g	o	b	o
s	e	f	a	f	e	l	e	l	a	b	a
o	n	o	m	t	u	r	o	p	e	n	y
n	o	d	s	i	l	l	o	p	s	a	n
s	e	g	r	o	r	n	e	s	p	a	n
s	e	g	l	a	r	a	z	a	m	u	l
l	o	n	e	g	a	n	o	g	i	l	a

Il:—Here, is the skynn turned into the Centre: and the Centre turned into 4 partes of the body.

Δ: I see now allso, how, the flesh, is become the owtside: o g e l o r n o &c. Il: I haue done tyll sone.

Δ: Deo nostro omnipotenti perennis laus sit et immensa gloria.[71] Amen.

---

69   So, on my Character or lamyne of dignification: are all the names of the 7 kings, and of the 7 Princis, perfectly: as in the great Table, (called often tymes Mensa Faederis) the Bees, onely, (being the first letter common to them all) kept bak, in memory. -Δ (HM).

70   Note, here, it may appere that Butmono is Prince to Bynepor, and Blisdon prince to King Bnaspol. -Δ (HM).

71   Deo nostro . . . gloria: "Perpetual praise and unlimited glory be to our almighty God." -Ed.

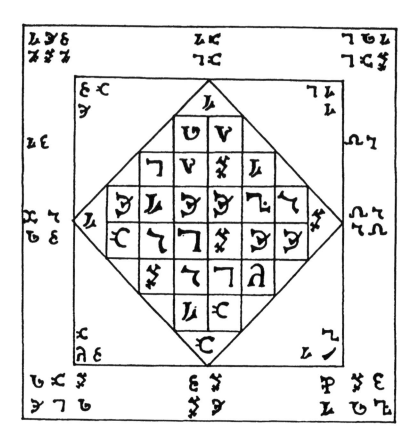

NOTE.

Δ: After that these things were finished, and EK rose up from the table and went to the west window, to read a letter which was, euen than, browght him from his wife: which being done, he toke a little prayer[72] boke (in english <u>meter</u> made by one William Hunnis which Mr Adrian Gilbert had here: and it lay on the Table by us all the while of this last action) and with this boke, he went into his bed chamber, intending to

_____

[72] The Title of the boke was *Seuen Sobs of a Sorrowfull Sowle for Synne.* -Δ. London: 1583. Hunnis' book consists of a translation of the *Seven Penitential Psalms* in rhyme.

pray on it, a certayn prayer, which he liked: and as he opened the boke, his ey espied strange writing in the spare white paper at the bokes ende: and beholding it, iudged it verily to be his own letters, and the thing of his own doing: but being assured that he never saw the like of this Character [for Conciliation], and that other, (notified by the hart or Center, skyn and flesh before this present howre, he becam astonied,[73] and in great wrath; and behold, suddenly, One appered to him and sayd, <u>Lo, this is as good as that other</u>: meaning that, which we had receyued, and is here before sett down on the former page. With this newes cam EK to me, as I was writing down fayre this last Action, and sayd, I haue strange matter to impart unto you: Then sayd I, What is that? And at the fyrst (being yet tossed in his mynde, with this great iniurie of the suttle supplanter of man, ambitiously intruding him self, to rob god of his glory) he sayd, you shall know, and at length shewed me this little paper, here, by, being the one of the white leafes in the ende of the forsayd little prayer boke. And I vewing it, fownd it to be ment to be the counterfeat of ours, but, with all, imperfect diuerse wayes, after the order of our method: yea thowgh the words, out of which it had sprong had bin good, and sufficient: and thereat laughed-at, and derided the Wicked enemy, for his envy, his ass-hedded folish ambition, and in dede mere blyndenes to do any thing well. To conclude, we fownd, that with an incredible spede this Diuilish figure was written down by some Wicked spirit, to bring our perfect doings in dowt with us: thereby eyther to provoke us to utter undue speaches of gods good creatures, or to wavering myndes of the Worthynes and goodnes of the same things receyuing, and so eyther to leaue of, or with fayntharted wavering to procede. But I by gods grace (contrary to such inconveniency) was armed with constancie, and confident good hope, that God wold not suffer me, (putting my trust in his goodnes and mercy, to receyue wisdome from him) to be so uniustly dealt withall or unkindely

---

73 Astonied: "bewildered." -Ed.

or unfatherly used at his hands &c: and entended after supper to make my ernest complaint to the diuine Maiestie against this wicked intrusion and temptation of the Illuding diuell and so we went to supper.

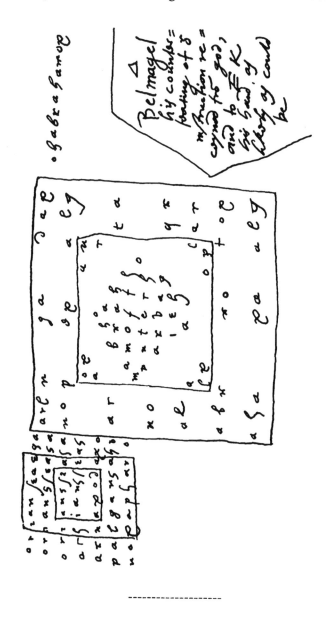

1583. Aprilis 29. Monday. <u>after supper</u>. hora 8 a.

Δ: I went into my oratorie, and made a <u>fervent prayer agaynst</u> the spirituall enemy: specially meaning the wicked one who had so suddenly so suttily and so liuely cownterfeted the hand and letters of EK: as is here before declared, and by the thing it self may appere here. <u>Likewise EK on his knees (at the greene chayre standing before my chymney)</u> did pray. After which prayers ended, I yea, rather, before they were ended, on my behalf, EK espyed a spirituall creature come to my Table: whome he toke to be IL, and so, a lowd, sayd, <u>He is here</u>. And thereuppon I cam to my desk, to write as occasion shold serue: And before I began to do any thing, I rehersed part of my intent, uttred to god by prayer and half turned my speche to god him self, as the cause did seme to require. Thereuppon that spirituall creature, who, as yet had sayd nothing, suddenly used these words:————————————I give place to my better.

EK: There semeth to me Uriel to be come, and IL to be gone away.
Δ: Then began that new-come Creature to say thus,

Most abundant and plentifull are the great mercies of God unto them which truely and unfaynedly feare, honor and beleue him. The Lord hath hard thy prayers, and I am URIEL,[74] and I haue browght the peace of God, <u>which shall from henceforth viset you</u>.

If I had not made this action perfect (sayeth the lord) and wrowght some perfection in you, to the ende you might performe: yea, if I had not had mercies (sayeth the lord) over the infinite number and multitude of <u>sowles, which are yet to put on the vilenes and corruption of the flesh,</u>[75] Or if it wer not time to loke down, and behold the sorrow of my Temple, Yet wold I, <u>for my promiss sake</u>, and the establishing of my kingdom, verifie my mercies uppon the sonns of men: Whereunto I

---

74 Uriel.

75 Note, sowles created before the bodies are begotten.

haue <u>Chosen three</u> of you,[76] as the mowthes and Instruments of my determined purpose. Therfore (sayeth the Lorde), Be of stowte and courragious mynde in me,[77] for me, and for my truth sake: And Fear not the assalts of temptation, For I haue sayd, <u>I am with you</u>. But as mercy is necessary for those that repent, and faithfully forget theyr offenses, So is Temptation requisite[78] and must ordinarilie follow those, whome it pleaseth him to illuminate with the beames of triumphant sanctification.

Yf Temptation wer not, how shold the sonnes of men (sayeth the lord) know me to be mercifull? But I am honored in hell; and wurshipped with the blasphemers: <u>Pugna erit, vobis autem victoria:</u>[79] yet, albeit, (thus sayeth my message) I will defend you from the <u>cruelltie of these dayes to come</u> and will make you perfect: <u>that perfectly you may begynne in the works of my perfection.</u>[80] But, what? and doost thow (Sathan) think to triumph? Behold (sayeth the God of Justice) I will banish thy servants from this place and region; and will set stumbling bloks before the feete of thy ministers:[81] Therfore, be it unto thee, as thow hast deserued: And be it to this people, and holie place, (as it is, the will of god; which I do pronownce) <u>light without darkness, Truth without falshode, righteousnes without the works</u> of wickednes. I haue pronownced it, and it is done.

But thow, o yongling,[82] (but, old synner,) why dost thow suffer thy

---

[76] Three elected.

[77] Fortitudo in deo et propter deum. -Δ. ("Strength in God and because of God." –Ed.)

[78] Temptation necessary.

[79] Pugna . . . victoria: "They will have fought, but victory will be yours." -Ed.

[80] A perfect begynning.

[81] Sententia contra istum Malignum spirituum qui nobis inpenere voluit. -Δ ("A judgment against this evil spirit who wished to use us." -Ed.)

[82] He spake to EK.

blyndeness thus to encrease: or why dost thow not yeld thy lymmes to the service and fullfilling of an æternall veritie? Pluck up thy hart: let it not be hardened. Follow the waye that leadeth to the knowledge of the ende; the open sight of god his word verified for his kingdoms sake.

You began in Tables, and that of small accownt. But be faithfull for you shalbe written within Tables of perfect and euerlasting remembrance. Considering the truth, which is the message of him which is the fowntayne and life of the true, perfect and most glorious life to come, Follow, loue, and diligently Contemplate the mysteries therein. He that hath done this euill, hath not onely synned against thee, but against God, and against his truth. Judgment is not of me, and therefore I cannot pronownce it: But what his Judgment is, he knoweth in him self. His name is BELMAGEL: and he is the fyrebrand, who hath followed thy sowle from the begynning;[83] yea seking his destruction. Who can better cownterfeat, than he, that in thy wickednes is chief lord and Master of thy spirites: or who hath byn acquaynted with the secrets of mans fingers, so much as he [that] hath byn a directer? My sayings are no accusation: neyther is it my propertie to be defyled with such profession.[84] But I cownsayle you generally; and aduertise you throwgh the grace and by the spirit of unspeakable mercy.

This night, yf your prayers had not byn; yea, if they had not perced into the seat of him which sitteth aboue: Thow, yea (I say) thow hadst byn carryed, and taken awaye, this night, into a willdernesse, so far distant hence Northward, that thy destruction had followed.[85] Therfore lay away thy works of youth; and fly from fleshly vanities. Yf not uppon Joye and pleasure of this presence, yet for the glorie of him that hath chosen you.

---

83 Angelus malus proprius ipius EK. ("The wicked angel belonging to EK himself." –Ed.)

84 Diuels are accusers proprely.

85 EK had byn carryed away in the wrath of God. If fervent prayer had not byn, as may appere in the begynning of this nights Action.

I say, be strong: Be Humble, with Obedience: For, <u>All the things, that haue byn spoken of, shall come to pass: And there shall not a letter of the boke of this prophesie perish.</u>[86] Finally, God hath blessed you, <u>and will kepe you from temptation</u>[87] and will be mercifull unto you: and perfect you, for the dignitie of your profession[88] sake: <u>Which,</u> world without ende for euer and euer, with us and all creatures, and in the light of his own cowntenance, be honored.

Amen. Amen. Amen.

Δ: Hereuppon I made most humble prayer with harty thanks to our God, for his help, cumfort, and Judgment against our enemie, in this case, (so greatly concerning his glorie.) And at my standing up I understode that Uriel was out of sight to EK. Yet I held-on my purpose to thank him; and to prayse god for Uriel that his so faithfull ministerie unto his diuine Maiestie, executed to our nedefull comfort in so vehement a temptation.

> Deo nostro Omnipotenti; sit omnis laus, honor,
> et gratiarum actio, nunc et in perpetuum,[89]
> Amen.

---

86 The boke of this Prophesie shall contynue.

87 = a malo Temptationis. -Δ. ("Against the evil of temptations." -Ed.)

88 Professio mea est Philosophia vera, vide Libro primo. -Δ. ("My profession is true philosophy. See Book 1." -Ed.)

89 Deo . . . perpetuum: "May all praise, honor, and thanksgiving be to our almighty God, now and forever." -Ed.

1583 Maij 5. Sonday. a meridie hor 4. vel circiter.

Δ: For as much as, on fryday last, while my frende EK was abowt writing of the Tables he was told that the same shuld be finished on monday next and that on sonday before, (it is to wete, this present sonday) at after none, all dowtes shold be answered; after, the after none had so far passed, as tyll somewhat past 4 of the clok: Then, we fell to prayer, and after a quarter of an howres invocation to god, and prayers made, EK sayd, here is one whome we toke to be Uriel, as he was, in dede. I had layd 28 questions or articles of dowtes in writing uppon my desk, open, ready for me to rede (uppon occasion) to our spirituall instructor, who, thus began his speche, after I had used a few wordes begynning with this sentence, Beati pedes, evangelizantium pacem &c.[90]

Uriel:—The very light and true wisdome (which is the Somme of my message, and will of him that sent me) make you perfect, and establish those things, which he hath sayd, and hath decreed: and likewise your myndes, that you may be apt vessells to receyve so abundant mercies. Amen. Δ: Amen, per te Jesu Christe:[91] Amen.

Ur:—This boke,[92] and holy key, which unlocketh the secrets of god his determination, as concerning the begynning, present being, and ende of this world, is so reuerent and holy: that I wonder (I speak in

---

90 Beati . . . pacem: "Blessed feet, gospel of peace" See Romans 10.15. Quomodo vero praedicabunt nisi mittantur? sicut scriptum est: Quam speciosi pedes evangelizantium pacem evangelizantium bona!: "And how shall they preach, except they be sent? As it is written: How beautiful are the feet of them that preach the gospel of peace, and bring glad tidings of good things!" This verse quotes from Isaiah 52:7. Quam pulchri super montes pedes annunciantis et praedicantis pacem: annunciantis bonum, praedicantis salutem, dicentis Sion: Regnabit Deus tuus!: "How beautiful upon the mountains are the feet of him who brings good tidings, who publishes peace, who brings good tidings of good, who publishes salvation, who says to Zion: 'Your God reigns.'" -Ed.

91 Per te Jesu Christe: "Through you, Jesus Christ." -Ed.

92 This Holy Book.

your sense) whie it is deliuered to those, that shall decay: So excellent
and great are the Mysteries therein conteyned, aboue the capacitie of
man: This boke (I say) shall, to morrow, be finished:[93] One thing
excepted: which is **the use thereof**. Unto the which the lord hath
appointed a day. But (bycause I will speak to you, <u>after the manner of</u>
<u>men</u>) See that all things be in a redynes <u>agaynst the first day of August</u>
<u>next</u>.[94] Humble your selues <u>nine dayes before</u>: yea, unrip (I say) the
cankers of your infected sowles: that you may be apt and meet to
understand the Secrets, that shalbe deliuered.[95] For why? The Lord
<u>hath sent his angels allready to viset the earth</u>,[96] <u>and to gather the</u>
<u>synnes thereof to gither, that they may be wayed before</u> him in the bal-
ance of Justice: and <u>Then</u> is the tyme that the promise of God, shalbe
fullfilled. <u>Dowt not, for we are good Angells.</u>[97]

The second of the greatest prophesie is this[98] (O ye mortall men)
For the first **was of him** self, that <u>He shold</u> come: And this, is <u>from him</u>:
in respect of <u>that he will come</u>. Neyther are you to speak the wordes of
this Testimonie, in one place, or in one people, <u>but, that the Nations of</u>
<u>the whole world may knowe</u> that there is a GOD which forgetteth not
the truth of his promise, nor the sauegarde of his chosen, for the
greatnes of his glory.[99]

---

[93] The boke to be finished to morrow.

[94] The day appointed for the use of this Book. Augusti 1.

[95] Our nine dayes contrition preparatiue. -Δ. Note the *Clavicula Salomonis* pre-
scribes a nine-day preparatory period before calling spirits that includes penitential prayers and abstaining from impurity. See S. L. Mathers, ed., *The Key of
Solomon the King* (York Beach: Samuel Weiser, 1972 repr. 1989), book 2, chapter 4. The magi (Zoroastrian priests) also undergo an elaborate nine-night purifi-
cation ceremony ("Barashnum") in order to prepare for higher religious ceremonies. –Ed.

[96] Angels sent to viset the heape of sinnes in the world abownding &c.

[97] Good Angels.

[98] The second of the greatest prophesie, is this.

[99] Our Testimony of this Prophesie, all the World ouer, to be (by us) published.

Therfore (I say) prepare your bodies, that they may be strong enowgh for armors of great profe.[100] Of your selfs, you cannot: <u>But desire and it shall be giuen unto you</u>. For Now, is euen that wicked childe grown up unto perfection: and <u>the fier tungs redy to open his Jaws.</u>[101] WO therfore shalbe to the Nations of the earth: And wo wo innumerable to those that say, we yelde: Wickednes (o lorde) is crept up, and hath filled the dores of thy holy sanctuarie: defyled the dwelling places of thy holy Angels: and poysonned the earth, as her own seat:

In 40 dayes more must this boke be perfyted in his own manner to the intent that you also may be perfyted in the workmanship of him, which hath sealed it.[102]

Oute of this, <u>shall be restored the holy bokes, which haue perished euen from the begynning, and from the first that liued</u> And herein shalbe deciphred perfect truth from imperfect falshode, <u>True religion from fals and damnable errors, With all Artes; which are propre to the use of man,</u> the first and sanctified perfection: Which when it hath spred a While, <u>THEN COMMETH THE ENDE.</u>[103]

Thy Character must haue the names of the fiue Angels (written in the myddst of Sigillum Emeth) graven uppon the other side in a circle.[104] In the myddst whereof, must <u>the stone</u> be which <u>was allso browght:</u>[105] Wherein, thow shallt, <u>at all times</u> behold, (priuately to thy self,) the state <u>of gods people throwgh the Whole earth.</u>

The fowre fete of the Table must haue 4 hollow things of swete

---

100 Our bodyes to be made strong.

101 Antichriste is allmost ready for his practise.

102 40 dayes more for the tables writing in their own Characters.

103 The frute of this boke.

104 The backside of my Character.

105 The use of the stone which a good Angel browght to me the last yere: remember it is half an inche thik.

wood,[106] whereuppon, they may[107] stand: <u>within the hollownes wherof thy seales may be kept unperished.</u>

<u>One</u> month is all, <u>for the use thereof.</u>[108]

Thus, sayeth the Lord, when I browght you up in likenes of birds, encreasing you, and suffring you to touche[109] the skyes, I opened unto you the ende of your reioysing: For, this Doctrine shall towche the skyes, and call the sterrs to testimonie therof: And your fotesteps shall viset (allmost) [all[110]] the partes of the whole world.

The sylk, must be of diuerse cullors, the most changeable that can be gotten:[111] For, who, is hable to behold the glory <u>of the</u> seat of God?

All these things must be used, as that day.[112]

<u>All errors and dowtes ells may be amended by the rules of reason: But Notwithstanding, Ask, and thow shalt be answered.</u>

Δ: As concerning Mals don Mals, what is the veritie to be placed in the middle of my practising Table?

Ur:—Write

---

106 The 4 hollow fete of the Table.

107 HM reads "must." -Ed.

108 The use of the Table of practise is onely for one Month.

109 Vide sup. A°. 1582 Maij 4.

110 Great long iornayes to be gon of us two.

111 The Cullor of the silk for the Table.

112 On the first of August next.

```
o o e        t i o
l r l  rather u l r
r l u  thus113 l r l
o i t        e o o
```

Δ: From whense, are these taken?

Ur: They owght to be gathered of those names, which are first gathered by thee, by ordre: (In the myddst of them:) the Kings and Princis being placed, as thow (of thy invention) diddst gather them: Not putting theyr own princis, next to the kings: but as they follow in Tabula, Collecta114 by thee: as thus,

a	l	i	g	o	n	o	r	n	o	g	o
o	b	o	g	e	l	e	f	a	f	e	s
a	b	a	l	e	l	u	t	m	o	n	o
y	n	e	p	o	r	l	i	s	d	o	n
n	a	s	p	o	l	r	o	r	g	e	s
n	a	p	s	e	n	r	a	l	g	e	s
l	u	m	a	z	a	a	g	e	n	o	l

Δ: Wherfore is the Table of Kings, and Princis set down in so diuerse manners?115 as, One, to haue Bobogel and Bornogo in the first row: and other to haue Baligon and Bagenol (his prince) in the first row: and here thirdly Baligon and Bornogo: and in the Heptagonon Blumaza semeth to be first, discoursed of, and his prince and Ministers: but very secretly:

---

113 Δ So they seeme to haue byn ment in the figure of the Table of practise before described.

114 The Princis here not put next to their kings.

115 Note. 4 diuerse Wayes.

Ur: Blumaza, is the first, in respect (<u>And so all the rest, are the first</u> <u>in respect) of theyr own being</u>. That secret is not to be deliuered but by the distinction of the boke: Notwithstanding, <u>thow hast truely consid-</u><u>ered of it</u> all ready.[116]

Δ: I required the perfect forme of the 21 letters, that I might imitate the same in the Table of practise, and in the holy boke writing &c.

Ur: They shall be deliuered to morrow.

Δ: Whether is the King his Name Bnaspen, or Bnapsen?

Ur: Bnapsen.

Δ: **The Character or Lamine for me was noted (Nouemb. 17. A⁰** **1582[117]) that it shold conteyne some token of my name: and now, in** **this, (accownted the true Character of Dignification) I perceyue no** **peculier mark, or letters of my name.**

Ur: **The forme in euery corner, <u>considereth thy name.</u>[118]**

Δ: **You meane there to be a certayn shaddow of Δelta? Ur: Well.**

Δ: Bycause many things do seeme to be taken from under the Table, as out of a stoare howse, shall there be any shelf framed under our square Table of Practise or handsome stole set in apt place to lay things on?

Ur: These things that were deliuered by shew, under an Imagined Table, were the members of God his secret Prouidence, <u>distributed unto</u> <u>his Angels as the Principals[119] of theyr Officis</u>. But under thy Table is nothing to be set.

Δ: What more uses are there of the great Circle or globe, wherein there are Capitall letters under the Kings names and Characters: and allso there are other letters with numbers: of which we haue receyued

---

[116] A Secret of preeminence due to the Kings &c: as in Astrology. I use to mak every planet a base or a grownd in his propre signification &c., & so every howse of the 12 &c. in respect of his proper and severall signification.

[117] P. 85. -E.A.

[118] The Symbolism of my name, in my character, how and where.

[119] Princeples.

no instruction: and more ouer of these letters, some are aversed som euersed, &c?

Ur:—The letters turned bak to bak, (being Capitall letters,) ar æqually to be diuided, according to theyr numbers, with a circle cumpassing the name and Character of the king under which they are placed.[120]

The other letters, <u>whose greatest number doth not excede 7</u>, are certayn By-notes of <u>wicked and euill powres</u>; which cannot, any way, but by the towche stone of truth be deciphred from the good. Wherof Notice shall be given at large, <u>by the boke</u>.

He that standeth in the myddst of the globe,[121] signifieth <u>Nature</u> whereuppon, <u>in the first point, is the use and practise</u> of this work that is to say, as concerning the <u>first part</u>. For it is sayde before The Boke conteyneth three kinde of Knowledges.

.3.   ⎰   1 The knowledge of GOD, truely.

.2.   ⎱   2 The number, and doing of his Angels, perfectly.

.1.   3 The begynning and ending of <u>Nature</u>, Substantially.

And this hath answered a great dowte.

Δ: What is the use of the 7 lamines,[122] (like armes,) and from what grownde are they framed or deriued?

Uriel:—They are the <u>ensignes of the Creation;</u>[123] <u>wherewithall they were created by God known onely by theyr acquayntance, and the manner of theyr doings</u>.

---

120 Δ perhaps somewhat like this:

121 The man in the myddest of the globe or circle.

122 Tables.

123 The 7 ensignes of creation.

Δ: Are they to be made in any metall?

Ur:—They are to be made in purified tynne: <u>And to be used at the time of theyr Call</u>.[124]

Δ: Ar the letters there to be altered into the <u>holy Alphabet letters</u> or characters?

Ur: <u>Into theyr propre Characters</u>. Δ: May I not use them as they ar, unaltered?

Ur:—...............

Δ: How to be used; hanged or layd?

Ur: To be layd before thee uppon the Table. Or thow mayst place them, (yf thow wilt,) <u>contynually at the 7 angles</u> of the Holy Seale: laying them besides, and against the points or Angles of the Holy Seale: <u>7 ynches from the utter border of the **holy Seale**, all **at ones**: Or els they may be paynted, On the Table</u>.[125]

Δ: What is the fowndation of the first 40 letters, in the principall, or holy Seale Emeth: and what other uses haue they, then yet hath byn spoken of: And what is the reason of suche theyr consequencie, or following eache other, Seing in our practise we cull them out by a peculier order?

Ur:—Thow hast nothing there, but what <u>hath byn sufficiently spoken of</u>.[126]

Δ: Yf 42 letters be 42 names, and 42 persons, how shall distinction be made betwene any two or three, of one name and in one row?

Ur:—How canst thow distinguish any thing with god?

Δ: Lord I know not.

Ur: Yet, **by the boke** it shall be perfectly known: but by skyll aboue nature.

---

[124] At the time of theyr call.

[125] The 7 ensignes to be paynted on the Table.

[126] Supra. -Δ. ("Above." -Ed.)

Δ: Haue I rightly applied the dayes to the Kings?

Ur:—The dayes are rightly applyed to the Kings.

Δ: How is this phrase The fifth of the seuenth understode, which Befafes[127] speaketh of him self?

Ur:—He speaketh so of him self, in respect <u>that **he shall be the fifth that shall be used**</u>. In consideration <u>of Nature</u> he is the <u>fifth</u>, allthowgh not consequently in the Order of Operation.

Δ: It was promised that we shold be instructed, whan the Day (in this practise) is to be accownted to begynne.

Ur:—It is not to be enquired, which is sufficiently towght, it is a thing most easy, and perfectly deliuered.

Δ: Adrian Gilbert[128] how far, or what points is he to be made priuie of our practise? Seing it was sayd,[129] that <u>none shall enter into the Knowledge of these mysteries with me, but onely this worker</u>. Truely the man is very Cumfortable to our societie.

Ur:—He may be made priuie of some things: such as shall be necessarie for the necessitie of the Necessities whereunto he shall be driuen.

Δ: The phrase of the last Ternarie,[130] which, Baligon (otherwise named Carmara, or Marmara) used, I understand not.

Ur:—He is the ende of the <u>Three last corruptible times:</u>[131] wherof, this is the last.

Δ: The one, at <u>Noes Flud</u> ended, the second at <u>Christ his first</u> comming and this is <u>the third</u>.

Ur:—It is so.

Δ: **The Characters and words annexed to the Kings names in the**

---

127 Befafes.

128 A.G.

129 Supra.

130 The last Ternarie.

131 Three times.

utter circumference of the great circle or Globe: How are they to be used?[132]

Ur: They[133] are to be <u>paynted uppon swete wood</u>: and so to be held <u>in thy hand,</u> as thow shallt haue <u>cause to use</u> them.

Δ: For the bringing of the erthes hither from the places of hidden Threasor, what is your order and direction?

Ur:—After you haue eaten, it shall be told you.

Δ: We prayed, and so went to supper.

1583

The same sonday. Maij .5. [after supper hora 8½]

Δ: After diuerse our eiaculations and pangs of prayer and thanks unto god, this was sayed.

Ur:—Be it thus unto you. [He prayeth in his own language.] After this holy boke is finished, then is it necessarie <u>with expedition</u>[134] that the foresayd commaundement, as concerning the fatching of the earth, be fullfilled and performed. And be it unto you as HE will. And HE sayeth thus.

My Angel shall be amongst you, and shall direct his iornay:[135] and <u>will bring his feete, euen into the place and places, where that erthly filth and Corruption lieth.</u> Behold I will deale mercifully with him: For, Error shall not deceyue him. Notwithstanding what I will haue done with it, or how it shall be bestowed, <u>is yet to be enquired of.</u>[136]

---

[132] Vide supra pagina precedente. -Δ. ("See above on the previous page." -Ed.)

[133] The 7 characters of the 7 kings as on the formar page is Babalel, Liba, &c.

[134] Expedition. -Δ. ("Expeditiousness." -Ed.)

[135] Journey. - Ed.

[136] How the Threasor is to be used.

Secret are the determinations, and unsearchable purposes, where-withall the most mightiest dealeth with worldlings, and loketh unto the use and necessarie application of worldly things. <u>Many temptations shall assayle him in following this commaundement.</u> But it is sayd, I Will be with him. God will deale mercifully with you. This is sufficient.

Yet ones more. Yf thow haue any dowte herein it shall be satisfyed.

Δ: What if he go first to Nubery, and with the erth being taken thence, to procede to the other places noted in the skroll and then with the erth of those ten places, the rest of the skroll, the <u>boke therewith fownd, and the red congeled thing in the hollow stone,</u>[137] <u>to come directly</u> hither: and then the rest of the peculier practise for enioying the premisses, to be lerned. Or how els will you haue him order his iornay?

Ur: **As thow wilt herein,** so shall it be browght to pas.

Δ: As concerning the Victorious Capitayn, The Lord Albert Laski the Polake who so much desyreth my acquayntance, and Conference, how shall I use my self, to God his best liking, my Cuntries honor, and my own good Credit?[138]

Ur:—Remember, it is sayde, that the Princis of the earth shall not dis-credit, much lesse work thy Confusion. <u>He that dwelleth in thee,</u>[139] <u>is above worldes: and shall giue thee sufficient discretion worldly, in worldly occasions.</u> For, Where the blessings of God are, euery thing is perfyted.

Δ: As concerning the Chamber for Practise, appointed by me, and the half-pace whereon the Table standeth, how is allowed of?

---

137 The Skroll, The Boke, The red powder.

138 Albertus Laski, Palatinus Siradiensis venit ex Polonia Londinum 1583 Maij ini-tio. -Δ. "Albert Laski, the Palatine of Sieradia (Sieradz), came from Poland to London in early May, 1583." The Polish prince Albertus Laski visited London on 1 May 1583. At the Queen's command, he was received with much honor. He visited Dee on 15 June along with Philip Sidney. The prince was so impressed with Dee and Kelley that they were invited to Lasco, the prince's seat near Krakow. They left with their wives and families on 21 September 1583. Laski plays a major role in Dee's subsequent actions. -Ed.

139 Δ My good Angel.

Ur:—The place can not Sanctifie the Action, but the Action the place. But I answer thee, **after the manner of men.**[140] It is sufficient.

Δ: The 4 hollow feete for comprehending the 4 lesser seales, how great owght they to be?

Ur: According to the <u>fete</u>, of the nearest proportion. And so, as the heith of the Table, be, as it, now, is.

EK: He semeth now to sit in the ayre: but I perceyue no chayre behynde him.

Δ: Are all these things of this dayes Action to be Noted with your name: as Uriel?

I am URIEL, which allwayes will answer <u>untill</u> this Action be finished.

I teache. Be Mercifull, Thankfull, and mery in him, and for him for whose name you shall susteyne <u>muche bodyly sadnes.</u>[141]

More then my message, I may not: And it is done.

Δ: As concerning the Vision which yester night was presented (unloked for,) to the sight of EK <u>as he sat at supper with me</u>, in my hall, I meane the <u>appering of the very sea</u>, and many ships thereon, and the Cutting-of <u>the hed of a woman</u>, by a tall blak man, What are we to imagin therof?

Ur:—The One, did signifie the <u>prouision of forrayn powres</u> against the Welfare of this land: which they shall shortly put in practise: The other, <u>the death of the Quene of Scotts. It is not long unto it.</u>[142] The

---

[140] Hereby may many other answers be considered.

[141] Multa nobis perpetienda propter Deum nostrum Omnipotentem. -Δ. ("Our great suffering near for our almighty God." -Ed.)

[142] Note The Quene of Scotts to be behedded. So she was Aᵒ. 1587 at Fodringam Castell. And allso the same yere a great preparation of ships against England by the King of Spayn, the Pope and other Princis called Catholik, &c.

Maiestie of his invisible powre, which overcommeth all things be
among you, uppon you, and rest with you for euer.

Δ: Amen.

EK: At his last words he flung fyre with his hands from him toward
us, and it spred it self in the manner of a Crosse.

> Δ: Gloria sit sempiterna Deo nostro
> Omnipotenti et Æeterno.[143]
> Amen.

May 6.

Monday, I went to London: and EK remayned attending the accomplishing of the promise, for the Tables ending and for the perfect forme
of the holy letters receyuing: Which two points (when I cam home that
after none), I fownd done. But it is to be Noted, that, When EK could
not aptly imitate the forme of the Characters, or letters, as they were
shewed: that then they appered drawn on his paper with a light yelow
cullor, which he drew the blak uppon, and so the yelow cullor disa-
pearing: there remayned onely the shape of the letter in blak: after this
manner and iust of this quantitie and proportion.

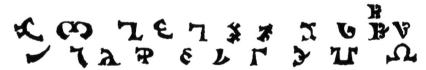

----

143 Gloria . . . Aeterno: "Everlasting glory be to our God, almighty and eternal." -
Ed.

Maij 8. Wensday, After dynner horam circiter 4 a

Δ: Being desyrous to furder all things on my part to be performed, and n . . . to lack the Cumpany of EK going for the Erthes,[144] (before spoken of) and to be away 10 or 12 dayes: and for as much as the boke was to be written in 40 dayes before August next: and uncertayn of those dayes whan they shold begynne: and allso for that I wold do all things (gladly) by warranty of cownsayle of our Instructor, I was desyrous to know whether the boke[145] were to be written in paper or parchment: in what cullor the lynes were to be ruled, grene or blew &c: and of diuerse other dowtes, necessary to be dissolued, I was carefull to haue had some advertisement. After long prayers of us both, Nothing was eyther seen in the ayre, or hard. Then it cam in my hed to set furth the stone.

EK sayd, that assone as he loked into the stone, he saw there the Table, Chayre, and three, com into the stone. Uriel sat down in the chayre: the other two, inclined theyr body to him reverently: and then, stode by; one on the one side of the chayre; the other on the other side.

The sides of the Table-cloth were turned up, and a thing like an yong shepe, bigger then a lamb, appered under the Table:[146] Then they two did knele before Uriel and sayd,

Verus et sanctus et sempiternus.[147]

Δ: Then they rose agayn: and they semed to haue talk, or conference togither and theruppon Uriel sayd,

Ur: Be it so, bycause powre is giuen unto him.

EK: The Table, Chayre and all the three do disapere: and thereup-

---

[144] The Erthes.

[145] The boke.

[146] The shepe under the Table.

[147] Verus . . . sempiternus: "True and holy and everlasting." -Ed.

pon immediately appered in the stone a fayr Pallace:[148] and out of the pallace cam a tall wellfauored man, very richely apparayled with a braue hat and a fether on his hed: and after him followed a great number, all like curteours: and this brave man sayd,

Man: How pitifull a thing is it, when the wise, are deluded?

Δ:—I smell the smoke; procede Syr, in your purpose.

Man: I come hither, for the desyre I haue to do thee good.

Δ:—Come you, or are you sent. Tell the Veritie I charge thee, in the name and by the powre of the æternall Veritie.

Δ: Note: After I perceyued euidently that it was a wicked tempter, who had powr permitted him at this instant, I began with some Zeale and egreness to rebuke, and to charge him. But he stiffly and stowtely did contemne me a good while, mock me, and at length thretten to destroy me, my wife, and children, &c.

Δ: I thereuppon made my ernest prayers to god agaynst this Spirituall enemy, but he in the myddle of my prayers, sayed thus,

Man:—As truely as the Lord liueth, all that is done, is lies.

Δ: That, thy sentence, will I record agaynst thee; to be layde to thy charge at the dredfull day.

Δ: After this great turmoyle past, was this voyce (following), hard of EK.

A voyce:—Pereant tenebræ, cum Principe Tenebrarum.[149]

Δ: All went suddenly out of sight, Prince and pallace and all. And the Chayre and Table and Uriel appeared againe.

Ur:—Arme your selues, for, great shall be the temptations following. You shall be hindred, in all, that may be.[150]

Nothing can hinder god his determined purposes.

---

[148] A Temptation permitted by God.

[149] Pereant . . . Tenebrarum: "May darkness perish with the Prince of Darkness." -Ed.

[150] Temptations & hinderances.

Δ: Man may hinder his owne saluation.

Ur:—Fullfill those things that are commaunded. Forme, and write the boke after thyne own Judgment. God his determination is iust; Therfore putto your hands.[151] More then hath byn sayd, and more plainely, cannot be uttred. His works are true, for, and to the ende.

Δ: Forasmuch as expedition is to be made for the erthes fatching and diuers other things: and we haue made assay to get an horse: But we could get none as we wold: And without somme better prouision of mony then we haue, we cannot redress the case. Therfore, if it might pleas god, that of the ten places Noted, we might haue but the possession of the smallest of them, deliuered here, unto us, at this pynche, it might greatly pleasure us.

Ur:—Will these worldlings hold on in theyr iniquitie?

EK: They pulle the leggs of the Table away, and seme to carry all away in a bundell like a clowde: and so disapered utterly.

Δ: Hereuppon I was exceding sorrowfull: and betoke my self to a lamentable pang of prayer.

Δ: After long prayer, appeared in the stone a thing like a Tunge, all on fyre thus hanging downward:

and from it cam this voyce:

Tung:—Thow hast deliuered thy self unto the desires of thy hart, and hast done that which is not Convenient. Thow hast spoken iniquitie, and therfore dothe the Veritie of Gods Doings by us, decay, in your Wickedness.

Δ: I dowt of the Veritie of that tung.

---

[151] The forme of the boke committed to my discretion.

Tung:—Man (o God) beleueth him self in his own Imagination. Therfore Wipe our holines from the face of the erth And Justifie owr doings, where we lawde and prayse thee.

Δ: I becam now abashed of my former speche, and perceyued my error: axed forgivenes bitterly at the Lord his hand: and at length it was sayde,

Tung:—Do that, which is commaunded, the Lord is Just.

Δ: O lord, forgiue me my trespaces, and deale not with me according to Justice: for, then I, and all mankinde shall utterly perish; Unleast thy mercy be our savegard, destruction is our desert.

Tung:—It <u>is forgiuen</u>: but it <u>shall be **punished**</u>.

EK: The Tung mownted up toward heven, and he saw it in the ayre out and above the stone aboue a hand bredth, mownting upward.

Δ: Thy Name be praysed in Æternitie, Ô God.

Amen.

Δ: Hereuppon, I was in an exceding great hevines, and sorrow of mynde: And sundry tymes, bewayled my case to God: and promised a greater care henceforeward, of Governing my Tung: and consenting to any unlawfull or unconvenient desire of my hert: yea, to forbeare to accumpany with my own wife, carnally: otherwise then by hevenly leave and permission, or if uppon my protestation making in the hardnes of the conflict <u>that unleast the lord order and redress my cause, I shall be overcome: That, if I shall, so deliberately call for help; and notwithstanding be entrapped,</u> That <u>then</u>, such trespace, shall not be imputed unto me, as gladly, gredyly or willingly committed of me &c.

May 9 Holly Thursday in the morning.

Δ: Being desyrous (before EK his going down into the Cuntrie,) to haue some Cumfort and token <u>of free forgiuenes</u> at Gods hands I browght furth the stone. Then I went into my Oratorie first requesting the Almightie God to respect the harty sorrowfull paines I had endured for my offenses; to regarde the Vows and intent of my better hede taking henceforth &c, and prayed the 22 Psalm in the conclusion of the pang.

EK:—One, all in white, appeareth in the stone, who sayde,[152]

————It is written: It is written: yea, it is written:

Euen as the father his compassion is great over his yonglings and Children: So, is the abundance of thy mercy (o Lord) great and unspeakable <u>to the **long offences** and sinnes of **thy servant**</u>. For, it is written, the light of thy eyes haue beheld those that feare thee: and those that trust in thy mercy, shall not be confownded. Be it, what it was: And be you, what you were: For, the Lord, is euen the same, that he was, before:

☛   <u>But be you **Warned.**</u>[153]

Behold, my armes ar longer then my body, and I haue eyes rownd abowt me: <u>I am that</u> which GOD <u>pronownceth</u> uppon you: Be it as I haue sayde.

Δ: Thereuppon he disapeared; and immediately, appered Uriel, who sayd,

Uri:—Actum est.[154] Δ: Then the other two, and the Table and Chayre, and the ancient furniture appeared, agayn <u>restored,</u>[155] <u>and more</u> bewtifull, then in foretyme.

---

[152] Δ Fortè Annaël.

[153] Misericordia Dei. -Δ. ("God's mercy." -Ed.)

[154] Actum est: "It has been done." -Ed.

[155] NOTE.

Uri:—Thus, sayeth the Lord: Euen as the Tabernacle <u>which I</u> <u>restore</u>, is ten times brighter then it was, So may your Worthynes deserue brightnes ten tymes clerer then this. The rising of synners doth greatly reioyce us [and] That, he hath sayde, Do good unto those that feare me: and defend them, bycause they know my name. For in Justice they shall finde me theyr God: & in mercy their great Comforter.[156] Therfore we say, In thy name (o thow most highest) fiat.

fiat.[157]

Justifie not your self:

Be Humble and diligent:

Continue to the ende. For great is the reward of them that fear the Lorde stedfastly.

Δ: Whereas the ordring of the boke[158] is referred to my Judgment: in my mynde it semeth requisite that as all the writing and reding of that holy language is from the right hand to the left, So the begynning of the boke must be, (as it were, in respect of our most usuall manner of bokes, in all languages of latin, greke, english &c) at the ende of the boke: and the ende, at the begynning, as in the hebru bible. Secondly the first leaf cannot be written in such little and æquall squares,[159] as all the rest of the 47 leaves are: bycause, the first leafe; excepting 9 lines (of the second page) therof: is all of words: some conteyning many letters, and some few, very diuersly: wherfore, I entend to make many leaves, serve to distinguish the 49 rowes of the first leafe: and at the ende of euery word to draw a line of partition, up and down, betwene the two next parallell lines &c. or as shall come in my mynde then.

---

[156] Justice.

[157] fiat: "Let it be so." -Ed.

[158] The boke.

[159] Note.

Ur:—He, that sayeth, Do this, directeth thy Judgment.

EK: Now is there a veale drawn before all: and all things appere far bewtifuller then euer they did.

Δ: I rendred thanks to the highest, and became in mynde Very Joyfull, that the Lord had pardoned my offences: whose name be praysed, extolled and magnifyed world with out ende. Amen.

I prayed after this the short psalme, Jubilate Deo quotquot in terra versamini[160] &c.

EK, immediately was to take bote and so to go to London: there to buy a saddell, brydle, and bote hose: for he had (here) yesterday, bowght a prety dun Mare, of goodman Pentecost: for iij £s, redy mony, in angels.

> God be his guyde, help, and defense.
> Amen.

Thursday. May 23. Circa 10½ mane

> Δ: EK being come yesterday agayne and hauing
> . . . the erthes of the eleuen places before speci-
> fyed:[161] we being desirous to . . . the furder
> pleasure of the highest therein, and in other
> matters perteyning to our Actions in hand: I
> made prayer to such intent, both in my oratory
> & at my desk, rendring thanks for EK his safe

---

[160] Jubilate . . . versamini: "Rejoice in God all ye dwelling on the Earth." This is reminiscent of several Psalms. -Ed.

[161] The Erthes.

retorne, and for the benefit receued of late of the <u>Governor and assistants for the Mines</u> Royall (which I perceyued, was the extraordinary working of god for theyr inward perswasion; they being els very unwilling so to let the lease, as I obteyned it.) And moving somwhat towching Albert Lasky At length, EK hard a Melody a far of, and the voyce of many, singing, these words,

The stone

Pinzu<u>a</u>[162] Lephe ganiúrax Kelpadman pacaph.

Δ: At length the curten was taken away, and there appered a clere whitish fume, but not fyre. After that, cam the three, which were want to come in.

Michael:—Grauida est terra, laborat inquitatibus inimicorum lucis. Maledicta igitur est, quia quod in utero perditionis et tenebrarum est.

Uriel:—Sordida est, et odiosa nobis.

Raphael:—Proprijs sese flagellat <u>tremulis.</u>[163]

EK: They loke abowt them, as thowgh they loked for somwhat or at somwhat.

Rap:—Veh dicit, sed non est qui audiat.

> Gementem vidimus: sed non est, qui misereat. Sanctificemur igitur, Sanctum eius, quia nos sanctificamur in illo.

---

162 This "a" was sownded to the ende of pinzu as we use in english balads, as with this word down is sownded as downa, down a down a, &c.

163 Michael: Gravida . . . tremulis: "Michael: The earth is pregnant and struggles with the iniquities of the enemies of light. It is therefore accursed, because it is in the womb of damnation and darkness. Uriel: It is filthy and offensive to us. Raphael: It scourges itself by its own shaking." -Ed.

Mich:—Fiat.[164]

EK: He plucketh all the usuall hangings down abowt the place and now they take the Table away, and the Chayre: And where the Chayre was, semeth a Canapy or cloth of stade to hang.

Michael:—Transeunt vetera, Incipiunt nova.[165]

EK: New seeme like clowdes to come abowt the Canapy being very beawtifull: and the bottom or flowr of the place, all couered with pretious stones: and in the middle therof, a rownd thing, like a carbuncle stone, bigger then ones fist.

Mi:	This.	
Uriel:	That.	} [They sayd, pointing abowt the howse.]
Rap:	We.	

EK: They bring in a Throne like a Judgis seat or Throne and set it up, with the bak of it to the Wall.

Mich: Be it couered for a season. For euer and euer and euer is thy Justice, O GOD. [all three sayd.] EK: And there came light fire flashing from the Throne]

Thre commeth a beame from the Throne, and throwgh Raphael his head, and semeth to come out at his mowth. The other two seeme to knele downe: Michael on his right hand, and Uriel on his left.

Raphael:—I will speak (o Lord) bycause it is iust[166] that thow hast commaunded:

Your rashnes (o worldlings) is trodden under fote: He sayeth, (I say not) your synns are forgiven.[167]

---

164 Rap: Veh dicit . . . Fiat: "Raphael: He says 'veh,' but it is not what he hears. We have seen lamentation, but he doesn't feel misery. May we be sanctified therefore, his holy one, because we are sanctified in that one. Michael: Let it be so." -Ed.

165 Nova. -Δ. Transeunt . . . nova: "The old ways cease, the new begin." -Ed.

166 Just.

167 Peccatorum remissio. -Δ. ("Remission of sins." -Ed.)

Δ: O blessed God; ô prayse we his mercyes for euer: ô Cumfortable newes.

Raph:—For, whome I will viset, those do I clense (sayeth the lord). Whan other things decay by reason of theyr age and filthynes (quæ nunc sunt in summo gradu,[168] and I will not suffer them to move one fote farder, sayth the lord,) Then shall your branches begyn to appere: And I will make you florish, for my gloryes sake. And my testimonies are true, and the wordes of my covenant iust: My pathes are thorny, but my dwelling place, is cumfortable.[169] My hand is heuy, but my help is great. Be ye cumforted in me: for from me, in my self, I am your Cumforter: and lift up your harts as from the strength of an other. But be you unto me a new people: bycause I am to you no new god. Dwell with me to the ende bycause I haue byn with you from the begynning: For Who soeuer shall arrise agaynst you (Behold) I am with you.

Your fathers liued in darknes; and yet were revived. Yea your fathers were in light, and yet they saw not Truth. But I will be known: yea the Nations uppon earth, shall say, Lo this is he, whome we haue risen agaynst. I AM: Therfore reioyce.

[All three sayd,] We perish (o lord) for our unrighteousnes sake [and therewith they fell down.] But in thee we were created and in thee We rise agayn:[170] Huseh Huseh Huseh garmal, Peleh Peleh Peleh pacáduasam.

Gyrd your gyrdles togither and pluck up your myndes: I say, open your eyes: and yf you haue eares, heare: for we tremble and quake. This mercy was neuer:[171] no not in Israël.

---

168 Quae . . . gradu: "which they are now in the highest degree." -Ed.

169 The Thorny path sup. 24 March.

170 Angeli iniusti, respectu Justiciae Divinae. -Δ. ("Unrighteous angels, with respect to Divine Righteousness." -Ed.)

171 Mercy.

Decedant mali, et pereant.[172]

Depart o ye blasphemers, and workers of Iniquitie: For Here is Glory, Justification, with Sanctification. I answere thee.

Δ: Note: he meaneth, now to such matters as I propownded first of my self, and this Polander prince &c to give answer. The Prince had left with me these questions:

1. De Vita stephani Regis Poloniæ quid dici possit?[173]

2. An successor eius erit Albertus Lasky, an ex domo Austriaca?[174]

3. An Albertus Lasky Palatinus siradiensis habebit regnum Moldauiæ?[175]

Behold you thanked God, and it is accepted. I say, Althowgh we require speede of thee and of you:[176] yet ....

....speede of us, you haue a Master, we are his mowth ....

are Schollars, without us, you could * not heare him: Neyther cowld we heare him of our selves.

Consider the first, respect the second: Measure your selues, as the third.

For what you were & shalbe is allready appointed. And What He Was, is and shalbe, it is not of our determination. His purposes are without ende: yet, to an ende; in you, to an ende. Therfor When you shall be called-uppon,[177] DO, that which is commaunded: But appoint no forme unto god his buylding. Many wyndes are to come: but theyr fury is in Vayne: It is sayd: **The Conquest shall be yours.**

---

[172] Decedant . . . pereant: "May the wicked depart and perish." -Ed.

[173] De Vita . . . possit?: "Regarding the life of Stephen, King of Poland, what can be said?" -Ed.

[174] An successor . . . Austriaca?: "Will his successor be Albertus Laski, or from the House of Austria?" -Ed.

[175] An Albertus . . . Moldauiæ?: "Will Albertus Laski, Palatine of Sieradia, have the kingdom of Moldavia?" -Ed.

[176] .... require none at Gods hands in this Case.

[177] Note, we shalbe called upon.

To the purpose. Who puft-up this princis father with <u>desire</u> to Viset these cuntries: or who hath prevented him? Euen he that hath prouided him **a sonne,**[178] **as an arme vnto his chosen.**

Truely the hills shalbe couered with blud: The Valleys shall take up the Cedar trees vnframed: **He seeth these places,** but knoweth not to what ende.

☞   He is dead,[179] in respect of his absence: <u>But honor them, whome God hath sanctified.</u> For, Behold the Lord hath sayd: Thow shalt gouern me a people: a time there is, which is prefixed: <u>and it is the course of the Sonne:</u> **Then** shall it be sayd vnto him, **O King.**[180]

When you semed to be carryed vnto mowntaynes, <u>you towched his</u> . . . Behold (sayeth He) Fornication[181] shall not prevayle: the <u>very stones</u> shall be taken away: and the Tables shalbe couered with blud: and theyr dayly bankett shall be Wo Wo.

Whatsoeuer **thow** takest in hand, First **loke up**: see if it <u>be Just.</u>[182] Yf it be, **put furth thy hand: For, it is graunted.**[183]

It is sayed, <u>I haue giuen thee powre, and thy perswasion</u>[184] <u>shall be like fire.</u> And for my names sake<u>, thow shalt triumphe against the mightiest.</u> But beware of Pride.

Many witches and enchanters, yea many diuels haue rosen up against **this stranger,**[185] and they haue sayd, We will preuayle against

---

178 Albertus Lasky.

179 The dead man. ☞

180 Prophetia de regno Alberti a Lasky, sed ipe noluit constanter se convertere ad Deum et adherere Deo, &c. ("A prophecy of the rule of Albertus Laski, but he himself has been constantly unwilling to convert himself to God and adhere to God." -Ed.)

181 Fornication.

182 Justa facienda. ("Just cause." -Ed.)

183 This phrase is heavily underlined in the manuscript. -Ed.

184 Perswasion, Δ.

185 Alb. Lasky ¶

him: for, why? There is one, <u>that aspireth and he it is, that seeketh his</u>
<u>confusion</u>. But I will graunt him <u>**his desire**</u>: He shall do good with
many: <u>your names</u> are <u>in one boke</u>.[186] Feare not, therfore, <u>Love</u>
<u>togither</u>.

    There shall arise, saying, let . . . .

talked with strangers: But I . . . .

I will driue them from theyr own . . . .

<u>the bones which are buryed a far of</u> . . . .[187]

They do spit vengeance agaynst . . . .

them in theyr own filthynes . . . .

All men loke upon the . . . bycause it is glorified . . . .

Happy are they, whose <u>faces are marked,</u>[188] and in w. . .

is a percing fyre of workmanship.

<u>I will move the Prince</u> (sayeth the Lord) Be . . . .

<u>shall shortly say,</u> Ô give me Cownsayle: for th. . . . .[189]

<u>cownsayled me, conspire agaynst me:</u>

Behold, <u>such</u>[190] as shewed thee, little frendship, are rather such . . .

dede (as thow <u>iustly</u> hast confessed,) as were forced to doe . . .

good: I say, <u>they,</u> begyn to repine at that, the haue . . .[191]

    Let those which are of tyme, yelde to time.[192] One euerlasting cum-
fort of grace, and perfect loue, be amongst you: to the honor and glory
of him that loueth you.

    Beleue, for the teacher his sake. All thow demaundest, is answered.

---

[186] Alb. Lasky his name, in one boke with our names.

[187] . . . rie bones . . . be . . . to.

[188] Faces marked.

[189] Forte: "They that." -E.A.

[190] The Cumpany for the mines royall, which had made A.G. and me a lease for
Deuonshire mynes, &c.

[191] Forte: "done." -E.A.

[192] Δ we were called to dynner often so he ended.

Of our selues, (we say,) We desire to be with you: And what is of us, the same be it unto you.

EK: They pluck the curten, affore the stone, all ouer. The curten is like beaten golde: [The other curtens did not cover all so wholy as this did.]

Δ: Semper sit benedictus Trinus et Unus.
Æternus et omnipotens Deus noster.
Amen.

Liber, sexti Mysteriorum (et sancti)
parallelus, Noualisque
sequitur.[193]

---

[193] Semper . . . sequiter: "May the Trinity in Unity, our eternal and almighty God, be ever blessed. Amen. Here follows the Sixth Book of the Mysteries (and holy), parallel, and of a new land." -Ed.

Appendix 1: Description of Sigillum Dei Aemeth from *Liber Juratus*

The following excerpt is from Sloane 3854, folio 114v, with variant readings from the Royal manuscript (abbreviated R) and from Sloane 3885 (abbreviated S). The diagram of the Sigillum Dei Aemeth is taken from Sloane 313. This is very close to the (although considerably corrupted) version shown by Athanasius Kircher in his monumental work *Oedipus Aegyptiacus* (1562). The drawing of the sigil does not occur in Royal, Sloane 3854 or Sl.3885. The version in Sloane 3853 (reproduced in C. J. S. Thompson, *The Mysteries and Secrets of Magic,* New York, 1973, p. 186, but without identifying the source) is somewhat different.

De compositione signi dei vivi[1]

Primo fac unum circulum cuius diameter sit trium digitorum propter tres clauos domini,[2] vel *5* propter *5* plagas, vel *7* propter *7* sacramenta, vel *9* propter *9* ordines angelorum, sed communiter *5* digitorum fieri solet. Deinde infra illum circulum fac alium circulum a primo distantem duobus granis ordei propter duas tabulas moysi, vel distantem a primo tribus granis propter trinitatem parsonarm. Deinde infra illos duos circulos in superiori parte quæ dicitur angulus meridiei fac unam crucem, cuius tibia aliquantulum intrat[3] circulum interiorem. Deinde a parte dextra crucis scribe .h. aspirationem deinde .t. deinde .o. deinde .e. x.[4] o. r. a. b. a.[5] l. a. y. q. c.[6] i. y. s. t. a. l.

[S 61v

[R9r]

---

1 R: "here folowithe the makinge off the seale off the trwe and lyuinge god."

2 Deest S.

3 S: "intret."

4 S: "y."

5 S adds: "e."

6 S: "t."

g. a. a. o. n.[7] o. s. v. l. a. r.[8] y. t. c.[9] e. k. s. s.[10] p. f. y. o. m. e. m. a. u.[11] a. r. e. l. a. c.[12] e. d.[13] a. t. o. n. o. n. a. o. y. l. e.[14] y. o. t. m. a[15] et iste[16] literæ sunt eque[17] distantes, et circu~dent circulum. eo ordine quo sunt prenominatæ[18] et sic magnum nomen domini semenphoras[19] *72* lit-erarum erit completum. hoc facto in medio circulorum scilicet in centro fac unum pentagonum talem, ✡ in cuius medio sit signum tau tale 𝐓· et super illud signum scribe[20] nomen dei el, et sub nomine aliud nomen dei .l.[21] ely. isto modo[22] Deinde infra angulum superi-orem[23] pentagoni[24] scribe istas duas litteras .lx.[25] Et infra alium

---

7   R has "w," but has "n" supra linea.

8   R (sup. lin.): "t."

9   Deest S.

10   R has "x," but has "s" supra linea.

11   R: "n," S: "x" (?).

12   R: "t."

13   R has "v," but has "t" supra linea.

14   R (sup. lin.) adds "p."

15   R ends "yleotsyma." Sloane 313: "htoexorahala/ yqciystalga∧ᵃ onosularitcksp-fyo/ mo (sup. lin: e)mau (sup.lin. x) aremlarclatcdaccnonaorleyot."

16   S: "istæ."

17   S: "æque."

18   Sloane 313: "nominate."

19   R: "schemhamphoras," S: "shemhamphorash," Sloane 313: "semamphoras."

20   R adds "hoc."

21   Deest R; S: "et sub nomen aliud dei sz."

22   Sloane 313 omits this diagram.

23   S: "inferiorem."

24   Sl. 313 adds "super nomine."

25   R: ".l.h.," Sloane 313 reads "l . et . x ."

angulum dextrum istas duas[26] .a.l. Et in alio [R 9v] post istum istas duas[27] n.m.[28] Deinde circa pentagonum fac unum eptagonum[29] cuius latus superius secundum sui medium contingat angulum superiorem pentagoni ubi .l.x.[30] scribebatur, et in eodem latere eptagoni[31] scribe hoc nome~ sancti[32] angeli quod est .casziel. Et in alio latere a dextris istud nomen alterius sancti angli quod est[33] .satquiel. Deinde in alio .samael. et in alio .raphael. postea .anael. postea .michael. postea .gabriel. et sic *7* latera eptagoni[34] erunt[35] adimpleta,[36] Deinde circa istum eptagonum[37] predictum fac alium eptagonum[38] non quoquo modo factum prius sed[39] taliter quod unum latus ipsius intercedet[40] latera alterius, Deinde fac alium eptagonum tale~[41] qualis prius[42] fuit

---

26 R omits "istas duas."

27 R omits "istas duas"; Sloane 3854 adds: ".l.a. et in alio post istum .l.c. Et in alio post istum."

28 S: ".v.m."; In Sloane 313 this phrase reads: "scribe illas 2. literas. l. et . x . et infra alium angulum dextrum istas 2. literas . a . l . et in alio post istum . l . a . et in alio post istum . l . c . et in alio post istum . n . m . ut hic post in figura deorsu~ in marg .. in ..."

29 S: "heptagonum."

30 R: ".l.h."

31 S: "heptagoni."

32 R: "scante."

33 R omits "casziel . . . quod est."

34 S: "heptagoni."

35 R: "sunt."

36 S: "adimpleti."

37 S: "heptagonu~."

38 S: "heptagonu~."

39 Sloane 313, S: "non q⁰ m⁰ primus factus est sed."

40 R: "incarceret."

41 Deest R.

42 S: "primus."

cuius anguli *7* contingant angulos *7* eptagoni secundi quibus esse
videtur. Hic tamen eptagonus infra perdictum secundum concludetur,
unu~[43] latus secundi eptagoni[44] supernudo et aliud subenudo, sed[45]
latus primo angulos[46] succedens subenudo ibit. et que[47] secuntur[48]
serie supereuntis et subeuntis alterutrum se habebunt, Deinde in quoli-

R 10r] bet angulo secundi eptagoni[49] una crux depingatur, Deinde in illo
latere secundi eptagoni[50] quod transit ab ultimo angulo eiusde~[51] ad

S62r] secundum angulum eiusde~ in eadem parte quæ est super[52] .casziel.
sillabe cuiusdam sancti[53] dei nominis scribatur,[54] Ita quod hac sillaba
.la. scribatur in illo loco lateris perdicti[55] qui est supra primam sillabam
de .casziel. et hec[56] sillaba .ya. in illo loco eiusdem[57] lateris qui est
supra ultimam sillabam eiusdem[58] .casziel. et hec[59] silliba .ly. in illo
loco eiusdem lateris qui est latus intersecans predictum latus et crucem

---

43 Deest R.

44 S: "hexagoni."

45 Deest R.

46 S: "angulo."

47 R, S: "quæ."

48 R, S: "sequntur."

49 S: "hexagoni."

50 S: "hexagoni."

51 Deest R.

52 S: "supra."

53 R: "scaneti."

54 S: "scribantur."

55 S: "prædicti."

56 R: "hac," S: "hæc."

57 Deest R.

58 R adds "de."

59 R, S: "hæc."

secundi anguli eiusdem, Deinde in[60] latere illo quod tendit ab angulo
primo eiusdem secundi eptagoni[61] ad tertium angulum eiusdem scribatur hoc nomen sanctum dei[62] .narath. ita quod hec[63] sillaba .na.
scribatur in illo loco eiusdeum lateris qui est supra primam sillabam de
.satquiel. et hec[64] sillaba .ra. in illo loco qui est supra ultimam eiusdem,
et hec[65] due[66] literae .t.h.[67] in illo loco qui est in eodem latere[68] inter
latus secans ipsum[69] et crucem tertiam,[70] Deinde in illo latere eiusdem
secundi eptagoni[71] quod tendit .a. tertio[72] angulo eiusdem ad quartum
eiusdem scribatur hoc creatoris nomen sanctum quod dicitur .libarre.   [10v]
ita quod hec[73] sillaba .ly. scribatur supra primam sillabam, de .raphael.
et hec[74] sillaba .bar. supra ultimam sillabam[75] * eiusdem, et hæc sillaba
.re. in illo loco *[76] eiusdem lateris qui est inter latus intersecans ipsum
et quintur angulum eiusdem secundi eptagoni,[77] Deinde in illo latere

---

60 S: "a."

61 S: "hexagoni."

62 S: "hoc sanctum nomen dei."

63 R, S: "hæc."

64 R, S: "hæc."

65 Deest R; S: "hæ."

66 R: "dua"; S: "duæ."

67 S: ".c.h."

68 Deest R.

69 S: "illud."

70 S: "terciā."

71 S: "hexagoni."

72 S reads simply: "tendit a 3°."

73 R, S: "hæc."

74 R, S: "hæc."

75 Sloane 3854 adds in margin: "i~ illo."

76 Text between * deest in Sl.3854.

77 S: "hexagoni."

eiusdem secundi eptagoni[78] quod est .a. quinta cruce[79] vsque ad ultimam scribatur hoc aliud sacrum creatoris nomen .libares. ita quod
hec[80] sillaba .ly. scribatur in illo loco lateris qui est supra primam sillabam ipsius .michael. et hec[81] sillaba .ba. in illo loco lateris qui est
supra ultimam sillabam eiusdem, et hec[82] sillaba .res. in illo loco eiusdem lateris qui est inter latus intersecans ipsum et ultimam crucem.
Deinde in illo latere eiusdem secundi iptagoni[83] quod vadit a secundo
angulo eiusdem secundi eptagoni[84] ad quintum[85] scribatur hoc[86] aliud
sacrum[87] nomen[88] .halg.[89] cum coniunctina ita quod coniuunctina in

[R11r]   illo loco eiusdem lateris scribatur qui[90] est supra primam sillabam de
.samael. et hæc litera .ly. in illo loco eiusdem lateris qui est supra ultimam eiusde~, et hæc sillaba .alg. in loco eiusdem lateris qui est inter
latus intersecans ipsum et quartam crucem, Sed caue quod ra[91] coniunctina sic debet scribi et[92] cum titulo intersecante propter timorem

[S3854   dei malum   nolitu~[93] diuideutem. Deinde in illo latere eiusdem
fol. 115r]
[S62v]   ─────────────

78   S: "hexagoni."

79   S reads simply: "quod est a 5ta cruce."

80   R, S: "hæc."

81   R, S: "hæc."

82   R, S: "hæc."

83   S: "exagoni."

84   S: "exagoni."

85   S: "quartum."

86   Deest R.

87   S: "sanctum."

88   R adds "dei."

89   Sloane 313: "lyalg"; S: "lialg."

90   R: "quid"; S: "q^i."

91   Deest S.

92   Deest S.

93   R: "volitum."

eptagoni[94] tendente a quarta cruce ad sextam scribatur hoc aliud
sacrum[95] dei[96] nomen .veham.[97] ita quod hæc sillaba .ve.[98] scribatur in
illo loco eiusdem lateris qui est supra primam sillabam de .anael. et hæc
litera .h. supra ultimam sillibam et hæc sillabam .am. in illo loco eiusdem lateris qui est latus secans ipsum et sextam crucem, Deinde in illo
latere quod tendit a sexto angulo[99] eiusdem secundi eptagoni[100] ad primum angulum scribatur hoc aliud sacrum[101] dei nomen .yalgal. ita
quod hec[102] litera .y. scribatur in illo loco[103] eiusde~ lateris[104] qui est
supra primam sillabam de .gabriel. et hæc sillaba .al. super[105] ultimam
et hæc sillaba .gal. in illo loco eiusdem lateris qui est inter latus intersecans ipsum et primam crucem, Deinde in medio lateris[106] primi et tertii   [R11v]
eptagoni[107] a dextris[108] scribatur .vos.[109] et in sequenti latere eiusdem
tertii eptagoni[110] a dextris[111] hoc Nomen .duymas.[112] et in alio

---

94   S: "hexagoni."

95   S: "sanctum."

96   Sloane 3854: "aliud dei sacrum"; Sloane 313: "a^d n^m dei sacru~."

97   Sloane 3854: "__ucham.__"

98   Sloane 3854: "__ue__"; S: "Ne" (?).

99   Deest R, S.

100 S: "hexagon."

101 S: "sanctum."

102 S: "hæc."

103 R: "in alla."

104 S: "lateris eiusdem."

105 S: "supra.,"

106 R: "latere."

107 S: "hexagoni."

108 S: "dexteris."

109 S: "Avs" (?).

110 S: "hexagoni."

111 S: "dexteris."

112 Sloane 313: "duynas"; S: "dvynas."

.Gyram. et in alio .Gram[113] et in alio .Aysaram. et in alio .Alpha. et ω.
in alio.[114] Deinde in alio spaciolo quod est sub secundi et tertii angulo
primo eptagonorum[115] scribatur hoc nomen dei .el. et in alio spaciolo
quod est a dextris sub angulis[116] secundi et tertii eptagonorum[117] sub
secunda cruce hoc nomen .ON. et in illo[118] alio spaciolo sub tertia
cruce. iteru~[119] hoc nomen .el. et in alio sub quarta cruce iterum .ON.
et in alio sub qinta[120] cruce iterum .el. et in alio sub sexu [121] cruce
iterum .ON. et in alio sub septima cruce .w. Deinde in illo[122] spacio[123]
quod clauditur[124] inter angulum primum[125] secundi eptagoni[126] et
secundum angulum eiusdem et primum latus tertii eptagoni[127] et por-
tionem circuli contingentem illos angulos depingatur una crux, in
medio .S.[128] spacii illius. Et in bucca superiori a leua crucis scribatur
hæc litera .a.[129] et super buccam crucis secundam a dextris hæc litera

---

[113] R: "Grani."

[114] Sloane 313, S: "et in alio .ω."

[115] S: "est sub angulo primo 2^i et 3^i hexagonoru~."

[116] S: "angulo."

[117] S: "hexagonorum."

[118] Deest R, Sl.313.

[119] R, S: "itarum."

[120] R: "sequenti"; S: "5ta."

[121] R: "sequenti"; S: "6ta."

[122] R: "alio."

[123] S: "spaciolo."

[124] S: "claditur."

[125] Deest R.

[126] S: "hexagoni."

[127] S: "hexagoni."

[128] R: "scilicet"; S: "si."

[129] S: "A."

.g. Et sub bucca inferiori a dextris[130] scribatur hæc alia[131] litera .a.[132]
Et sub quarta bucca hæc[133] litera .l. Deinde in alio spaciolo sequenti a [rR12r]
dextris in medio scribatur hoc nomen[134] .ely.[135] et in alio hoc nomen
.eloy.[136] et in alio .christos. et in alio .sother.[137] et in alio .Adonay.[138] et [S 3854
in alio .Saday. Deinde scias qd in exemplaribus communiter[139] pen- col 2]
tagonus fit de rubeo cum croceo in spaciis tincto. Et primus[140]
septagonus[141] de azurio, secundus de croceo, tertius de purpureo, et [S 63r]
circuli de nigro, et spacium inter circulos ubi est nomen de maximum.
ac venerabile[142] .schemhamphoras. tingitr croceo, omnia alia[143] spacia
viridi habent tingi, Sed in operationibus aliter fieri debet, quia de san-
guine aut. talpæ. aut .turturis. aut.[144]vpupæ. aut .vespertilionis. aut
omnium horum figuratur, et in pergameõ virgineo vitulino,[145] vel[146]

---

130 S: "dexte=/is."

131 Deest R.

132 S: "A."

133 S adds "alia."

134 R adds "dei."

135 S: "Ely."

136 S: "Eloy."

137 S: "Sother."

138 R: "ADONAI."

139 R: "quod communiter in exemplaribus."

140 R: "primu~."

141 S: "hexᵗagonus."

142 Sloane 313, Sl.3854 omit "de maximum ac venerabile."

143 R: "alio."

144 R, S: "at."

145 R: "vituluio."

146 Sloane 313: "aut."

equino, vel ceruino, et sic completur dei sigillum, Et per[147] hoc sanctum et sacrum sigillum quando erit sacratum poteris. facere operationes quæ postea dicentur[148] in hoc libro.[149] Modus autem sacrandi hoc sacrum sigillum talis[150] sicut sequitr[151] debet esse.

S 313
[R 6.r]

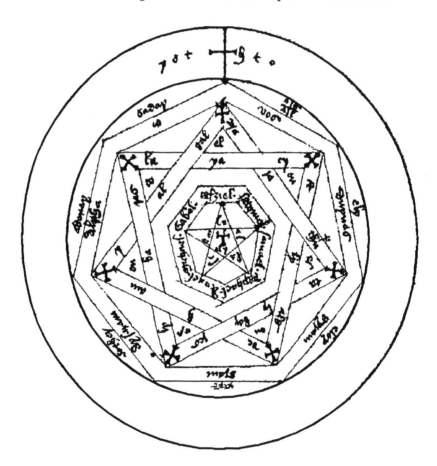

Figure 8. Sigillum Dei Aemeth from Liber Juratus.

---

147 R: "par."

148 S: "sequntur."

149 Sloane 3854: "libro sacro"; S: "sacº"; Sloane 313: "libello ∧ sacro."

150 S: "talitur."

151 S: "seqⁱtur."

Inspirante domino dixit Salomon unus est solus deus, sola fides,[R12v] sola virt~s, quã dominus hominibus voluit revelari et distribui tali[152] modo. Dixit[153] Angulus .Samael. Salomoni hic[154] dabis populo Israel qui et aliis similiter tribuent sic placuit creatori[155] et inbet ipsum Dominus[156] taliter consecrari.

Primo sit mundus operans non pollutus,[157] et cum deuocione faciat non astute, non commedat neque bibat, donec perfecerit opus, Et sanguis quo scriptu~[158] fuerit primo sit benedictus sicut postea dicetur, Deinde suffumigetur,[159] hoc sigillum ambra, musco, aloe, lapdano, albo, et rubeo, mastice, olibano, margaritis et thure. Invocando et orando dominum sicut postea de visione divina erudietur, Post[160] invocando angelos sicut etiam[161] infra[162] Dicetur, mutabitur tñ[163] peticio tali[164] modo,

S: Oratio   [S 3854
                                                                 fol. 115v

Ut tu domine per annunciationem concepcionem et citera. Hoc sacratissimum nomen ac sigillum tuum benedicere et consecrare

---

152   R: "hoc."

153   R: "Dexit."

154   R, S: "hoc."

155   R omits "sic placuit creatori."

156   S: "dominus ipsum."

157   S: "polutus."

158   R: "scriptus."

159   R: "suffumigetr."

160   S: "postea." In the margin of Sloane 313, there is a drawing of a hand pointing out the passage which is very similar to Dee's.

161   Deest S. In Sloane 313 it is written surpa linea.

162   Deest Sloane 3854.

163   R: "tamen"; S: "tantum."

164   R: "hoc."

digneris[165] ut per ipsum te[166] mediante possim vel possit talis[167] .N. celestes[168] coniuncere[169] potestates aereas et terreas[170] cum infernal- ibus subingare, [S 63v] invocare, transmutare[171] coniurare constringere,   [S 13r] excitare, gongregare,[172] dispergere, ligare ac ipsos innocuos reddere homines placare, et ab eis tuas[173] peticiones graciosius[174] habere, inimi- cos pacificare, pacificatos disimigere, sanos insanitate custodire vel infirmare. infirmos curare. homines bonos a malis custodire. et dis- tinguere, et cognoscere, omne corporale periculum euadere, Judices in placito placatos reddere, victoriam in omnibus obtinere, pecrata carnalia mortificare et spiritualia fugare vincere, et euitare, divitias in bonis aug- mentare et du~[175] in die indicii apparebit. a dextris tuis cum sanctis et electis tuis tuam possit cognoscere[176] maiestatem

   Et tunc illa nocte sub aere sereno[177] extra domum dimittat, Tunc habeas chirotecas[178] nouas sine creace factas inquas quis numquam manum posuerit[179] in quibus signum glutetur, et sic complebitur hoc sacrum[180] sigillum, Cuius primus eptagonus[181] .7. ordines, Secundus .7. Articulos Duplos tertius .7. sacramenta Designat[182]

---

[165] R: "digue ris."
[166] R: "et."
[167] S: "tali"; Sloane 3854: "tal."
[168] S: "cælestes."
[169] S: "convincere."
[170] R: "terreac."
[171] R: "transmittaere."
[172] S: "congregare."
[173] R, S: "suas"; Sloane 313: "meas vel suas."
[174] S: "graciosi."
[175] R: "dum"; S: "domine" (?); Sloane 313: "deuiu~." (?)
[176] Sloane 3854: "agnoscere."
[177] Deest R.
[178] S: "chirothechas"; Sloane 313: "cirothecas."
[179] R: "posuit."
[180] Sloane 3854: "sacrosct~m"; S: "sacosctmus." (?)
[181] S: "heptagonus."
[182] S: "designant."

Appendix 2: Athanasius Kircher: *Oedipus Aegyptiacus:* Sigillum Aemeth (Rome, 1652–4)

Amuleti alterius Cabalistici heptagoni Interpretatio

Hoc amuletum heptagonum circulo inclusum Veneri dicatum est, vti in Arithmetica hieroglyphica ostendimus. In circuitu signatae sunt 72 literae ex Cabala extractae, quarum vnaquaeque Angelum ex 72 indicat; de quibus vide Cabalam Hebraeorum fol. 275. Quis hic prima fronte non rideat maleferiatorum hominum stoliditatem, dum ineptijs huiusmodi Cabalisticis pessimé in Latinas literas transformatis, tantam tamen fidem habent, vt earum ope montes etiam se transferre posse, sibi persuadeant? Sed quoniam Diabolus humani generis hostis nihil agit, nisi quod in contumeliam Christi hominumque perniciem cedat; hinc ad Satanicam nequitiam tegendam, data opera, attributa Christi in cornibus heptagoni ponunt, id est, Angelus tenebrarum sub forma lucis sese exhibet; sunt autem sequentia attributa. Intra cornu AB, intra quadratum singulis Crucis angulis quatuor literae insertae spectantur a.g.l.a. quod Hebraicum nomen est, & in Cabala celeberrimum אגלא, quod expansé idem significat ac, אתה גבור לעולם אדני Tu fortis in aeternum Domine: Si enim capitalis singularum vocum literas in vnum iunxeris, prodibit nomen אגלא Agla, vti quadratum ostendit. Intra cornu BC ponitur אלי Eli, id est, Deus meus. Intra cornu CD ponitur אלהי Eloi, quod tametsi idem prorsus cum praecedente significet, tanquam diuersum tamen quidpiam posuerunt; vt vel hinc horum nebulonum supinam ignorantiam & inscitiam colligas. Intra DE Christus, deinde Sother, quod Graecé Saluatorem significat, né verminosum machinamentum Graeca voce carerer. Sequuntur postea Adonay & Sadai; illud Dominum, hoc Omnipotentem notat. Atque haec sunt septem attributa Christi, quibus subiungunt septem Veneris

Intelligentias, quae sunt Cafziel, Satquiel, Samael, Raphael, Mahel, Michael, Gabriel; quae vocabula Hebraica passim translata sunt; vt vel ex hoc ipso appareat, á Deo bonisque Angelis emanare minimé posse, quod tam turpiter, non nisi ab omnis turpitudinis Cacodaemone, transformatum est: talia sunt in heptagoni lateribus inscripta, verius ex culina Diaboli, quam ex Cabala translata vocabula. Inscribunt tandem huic heptagono pentagonum, in cuius centro litera T symbolum salutis; circa quod cum has literas ‏ע ‏ scribere debuissent, bestijs tamen inscitiores has supposuerunt e e e e y. Intra triangula vero ex Arabum amuletaria officina ponuntur yl, al, le, al, um, corruptissimé vti omnia alia; volebant enim illud Arabicum exprimere لا الله الا الله *la alla ella alla, non est Deus nisi Deus,* quod dum pronunciare nequirent, illorum loco dicta inconcinnissima verba posuerunt, yl, al, le, al, um: sed quid sibi velint duo verba, um, explico. In dicto Arabum pronunciato semper hae voces sequuntur, وصومد رسول الله *Mahumet rassulalla;* atque harum capitales literas referunt um. Vt vel ex hoc colligas, quantis modis illudat Daemon incautis hominibus, vt dum Christiani esse volunt, occulte Mahumetanismum profiteantur; in hoc enim vnico Amuleto quatuor sectarum, Iudaicae, Christianae, Mahumetanae, Paganae, ab ijs, qui illud portant, fit professio, id que occulto pacto Daemonis, ad Christianae religionis contumeliam ea de causa instituto. Sed quid pentagonum sibi velit, expono. Pentagonum Veteres, vti in Arithmetica docuimus, Marti, vti & heptagonum Veneri dedicarunt; quo quidem indicabant, neminem Venerem possidere, qui priús Martem non attraxisset; de quibus in Astrologia Aegyptiaca susiús; hoc enim pentagono victoriam in omnibus sibi spondebant. Porró finis huius Amuleti erat, amorem & beneuolentiam omnium, & consequenter carnalium desideriorum plenam fruitionem, victoriamque contra omnia aduersa eius gestatione obtinere; quod ex adiuratione quam pronunciare solent, qua & Deum, & Angelos, veriús Cacodaemones cum inuocatione Veneris aut Martis sacrilego & impio ritu sollicitare solent, patet, quam &, né Christianae aures vulnerentur, consultó omitto. Quicunque itaque huiusmodo possederit farinae Amuletum, illud non naturale, non Diuinum aut Angelicum, sed immediatum Diabolicae machinationis opus se possidere sibi persuadeat, non nisi cum aeterna animae ruina vsurpandum.

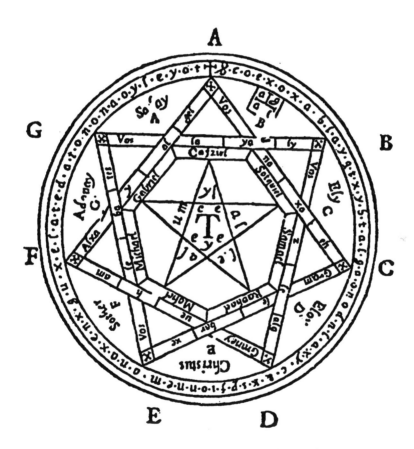

Figure 9. Sigillum Aemeth from Oedipus Aegyptiacus.

Appendix 3: *Theurgia Goetia.*[1]

It deals with aerial spirits, whose nature is neither entirely good nor evil:

To call forth any of the aforesaid aerial spirits or their servants, choose the uttermost private, secret and most tacit room in the house or in some certain island, wooded grove, or the most occult and hidden place, removed from all comers and goers, that no one chance (if possible) happen that way into your chamber or whatsoever place else you act your concerns in. Observe that it be very airy because these spirits are of that nature.

You may call these spirits into a crystal stone or glass receptacle, this being the ancient and usual way of receiving and binding spirits. This crystal stone must be four inches diameter set on a table of art, made according to the following figure, which is truly called the secret table of Solomon, having his seal on your breast and the girdle about your waist as is shewed in the book *Goetia* and you cannot err. The form of the table is this:

---

1   For a critical edition see Joseph Peterson, *The Lesser Key of Solomon* (York Beach, ME: Weiser Books, 2001), pp. 57–108.

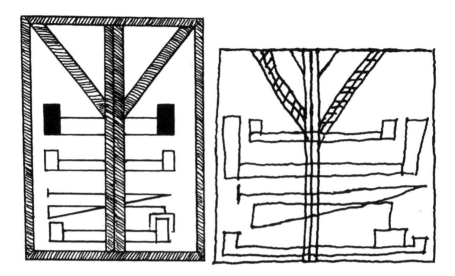

Figure 10. Seal of Solomon, from Harley 6483 (left); and from Sloane 3825 (right).

When you have thus got what is to be prepared, rehearse the conjuration following several times, that is, whilst the spirit comes, for without doubt he will come.

The Conjuration of the Aerial Spirits

I conjure thee O thou mighty and potent duke N. who ruleth under thy prince (or king) N. in the dominion of the East (or &c.) (Or, "I conjure thee o thou mighty and potent duke N. who wandereth here and there with thy prince N."[2])

I conjure thee N. that thou forthwith appear alone (or with thy servants) in this first (or second) hour of the day, here before me in this crystal stone (or here before this circle) in a fair and comely

---

2   This form of the introduction is thus to be varied depending on the office, place and number thou wishest to conjure.

shape, to do my will in all things that I shall desire or request of thee. I conjure and powerfully command of thee N. by him who said the word and it was done, and by all the holy and powerful names of God and by the name of the only Creator of Heaven, Earth, and Hell, and what is contained in them : ADONAY, EL ELOHIM, ELOHE, ELION, ESCERIE ZEBAOTH, JAH, TETRAGRAMMATON, SADAY, the only Lord of God of Hosts, that thou forthwith appear unto me here in this crystal stone (or here before this circle) in a fair and comely human shape, without doing any harm to me or any other creature that JEHOVAH created or made, but come thee peaceably, visibly, and affably, now without delay manifesting what I desire, being conjured by the name of the eternal living and true God: HELIOREN, TETRAGRAMMATON, ANEPHEXETON, and fulfill my commands and persist unto the end. I conjure, command and constrain thee spirit N. by ALPHA & OMEGA, by the name PRIMEUMATON, which commandeth the whole host of heaven, and by all those names which Moses named when he by the power of those names brought great plagues upon Pharoah, and all the people of Egypt: ZEBAOTH, ESCHERIE, ORISTON, ELION, ADONAY, PRIMEUMATON, and by the name of SCHEMES AMATHIA which Joshua called upon and the sun stayed his course, and by the name of Hagios, and by the SEAL OF ADONAY and by AGLA, ON, TETRA-GRAMMATON, to whom all creatures are obedient, and by the dreadful judgment of the high God and by the holy angels of heave and by the mighty wisdom of the great God of Hosts, that thou comest from all parts of the world and make rational answers unto all things I shall ask of thee, and come thou peaceably, visibly and affably, speaking unto me with a voice intelligible and to my under-standing. Therefore come, come thou in the name of ADONAY, ZEBAOTH, ADONAY, AMIORAM, come, why stayeth thou, has-ten: ADONAY SADAY, the King of kings commandeth thee!

When he is appeared show him his seal, and the pentacle of Salomon, saying as followeth:

The Address Unto the Spirit Upon His Coming

Behold the pentacle of Salomon which I have brought before thy presence. Behold the person of the Exorcist who is called OCTINOMOS, in the midst of the exorcism, who is armed by God and is without fear, who potently invocateth thee and called thee to appear. Therefore make rational answers to my demands and be obedient to me thy master in the name of the Lord: BATHAT rudhing upon ABRAC, ABEOR coming upon ABERER!

When thou hast had thy desire of the spirits, licence them to depart as is shewed in the first book *Goetia,* at the latter end of the conjurations.

Appendix 4: *Art Pauline.*[1]

The second example comes from *The Art Pauline*, which describes calling forth spirits governing the hours, and spirits governing the signs of the zodiac:

First draw two concentric circles whereupon thou wilt draw the seal. In the center circle draw the ascendant to the right, and the lord of the ascendant to the left, then in the outer circle draw the rest of the planets in the following order: Moon, Mercury, Venus, Sun, Mars, Jupiter, Saturn.

The seal being thus made, lay it on the table of practise whose form we now show, on that part which is noted with the same character as the lord of the ascendant.

---

1   For a critical edition see Joseph Peterson, *The Lesser Key of Solomon* (York Beach, ME: Weiser Books, 2001), pp. 109–45.

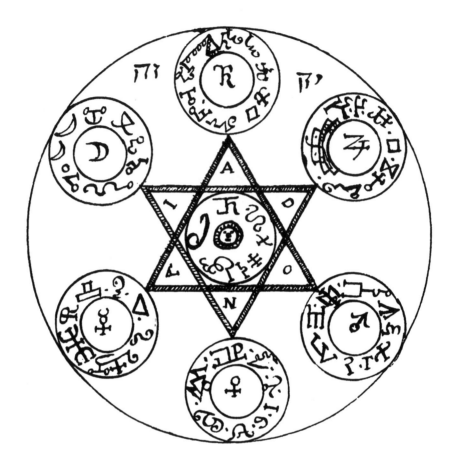

Figure 11. Table of Practice from the Art Pauline.

Perfume the seal with the thimmiamate proper to the planet, lay your hand upon it, and then say the following conjuration.

The Conjuration as Followeth:

O thou mighty, great and potent Angel N., who ruleth in the Nth. hour of the day, I the servant of the most high God do conjure and entreat thee in the name of the most omnipotent and immortal Lord God of

Hosts: JEHOVAH TETRAGRAMMATON, and by the name of that God which thou art obedient unto, and by the head of the hierarchy and by the seal or mark that thou art known in power by, and by the seven angels that stand before the throne of God and by the seven planets and their seals and characters, and by the angel that ruleth the sign of the twelfth house which now ascends in this Nth. hour, that thou wouldst be graciously pleased to gird up and gather thyself together and by divine permission to move and come from all parth of the world, wheresoever thou beest, and show thyself visibly and plainly in this crystal stone to the sight of my eyes, speaking with a voice intelligible and to my understanding and that thou wouldst be favorably pleased that I may have familiar friendship and constant society both now and at all tims when I shall call thee forth to visible appearance to inform and direct me in all things that I shall seem good and lawful uunto the creator and thee, O thou great and powerful angel N. I invocate, adjure, command and most powerfully call thee forth from thine orders and place of residence to visible appearance in and through these great and mighty signals and divine names of the great God, who was and is and ever shall be: ADONAY, ZEBAOTH, ADONAY AMIORAM, HAGIOS, AGLA, ON, TETRAGRAMMATON, and by and in the name PRIMEUMATON, which commandeth the whole host of heaven, whose power and virtue are most effectual for the calling and ordering of the creation, I do command thee to transmit thy rays visibly and perfectly unto my sight, and thy voice to my ears, in and through this crystal stone, that I may plainly see thee and perfectly hear thee speak unto me. Therefore move thee, O thou mighty and blessed Angel N., and in this potent name of the great God JEHOVAH, and by the imperial dignity thereof, descend and show thyself visibly and perfectly in a pleasant and comely form before me in this crystal stone to the sight of my eyes, speaking with a voice intelligible and to my apprehension, showing, declaring, and accomplishing all my desires that I shall ask or request of thee both herein and in whatsoever truths or things else that is just and lawful before the presence of Almighty God, the giver of all good gifts, unto whom I beg that he wuld be graciously pleased to bestow upon me. I thou servant of mercy N., be thou therefore unto me friendly, and do for me as for the servant of the most high God, so far as God shall give thee power in office to perform, whereunto I move thee in power and presence to appear, that I may sing with his holy Angels, OMAPPA-LA-MAN, HALLELUJAH, AMEN.

Appendix 5: *The Art Almadel*
(Ars Almadel Salomonis)[1]

[Editor's note: A text of this name is mentioned in Trithemius, and R. Scot.]

By this art Salomon obtained great wisdom from the chief angels that govern the four altitudes of the world, for you must observe that there be four altitudes, representing the four corners of the world, East, West, North and South. The which are divided into twelve parts, that is, evert altitude into three, and the angels of every of these altitudes have their particular vertues and powers as shall be shewed in this following matter.

The Making of the Almadel

Make the Almadel of pure white wax, but coloured suitable to the altitude as will be shown. It is to be four square, and six inches over every way, and in every corner a hole, and write betwixt every hole, with a new pen, these words or names of God following, But this is to be done in the day and hour of Sol. Write upon the first part towards the East, ADONAI, HELOMI, PINE, and upon the second towards the South, HELION, HELOI, HELI, and upon the West part: JOD, HOD, AGLA, and upon the fourt part which is the North write these names: TETRA-GRAMMATON, SHADAI, JAH, and betwixt the first and the other quarters make the pentacle of Salomon thus , and betwixt the forst and the other quarters write this word, ANABONA, and in the middle of the Almadel make a Six-angled figure, and in the midst of it a triangle

---

1   For a critical edition see Joseph Peterson, *The Lesser Key of Solomon* (York Beach, ME: Weiser Books, 2001), pp. 147–54.

wherein must be written these names of God, HEL, HELION, ADONAI, and this last name around the six-angled figure as well, as you may see in this figure, here made, it being for an example, &c.

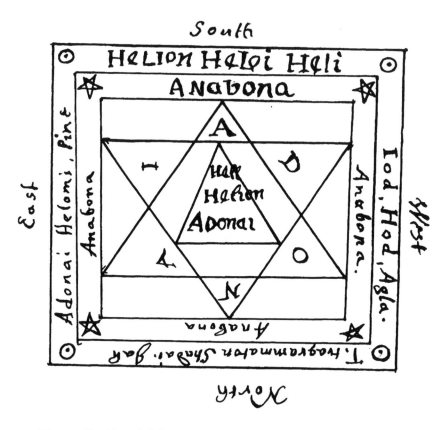

Figure 12. Almadel from Ars Almadel Salomonis.

And of the same wax there must be made four candles, and they must be of the same colour as the Almadel is of. You must divide the wax into three parts, one part for to make the Almadel of, and the other two parts for to make the candles of. And let there come forth from every one of them a foot made of the same wax, for to support the almadel wlth. This being done, in the next place you are to make a seal of pure gold or silver, but Gold is best, wherein must be engraven these three names: HELION, HELLUJON, ADONAY.

Note the first altitude is called Chora Orientis, or the East Altitude, and to make any experiment in this Chora, it is to be done in the day and hour of the Sun. The power and office of those angels is to make all things fruitful and increase, both animals and vegetables, in creation and generation, advancing the birth of the children, and making barren women fruitful, &c. Their names are these: Alimiel, Gabriel, Borachiel, Lebes and Hellison.

Note you must not pray for any angels but those that belong to the same altitude you have a desire to call forth. And when you operate, set the four candles upon four candle sticks, but be careful you do not light them before you begin to operate. Then lay the Almadel between the four candles upon the waxen feet that cometh from the candles, and lay the golden seal upon the Almadel. Then, having the invocation ready written on virgin parchment, light the candles and read the invocation as is set down at the latter end of this part.

And when he appeareth, he appeareth in the form of an angel carrying in his hand a fan or flag, having the picture of a white cross upon it. His body is wrapped round about with a fair cloud, and his face very fair and bright, and a crown of rose flowers is upon his head. He descends first upon the superscription of the Almadel, as if it were a mist or fog.

Then must the exorcist must have in readiness a vessel of earth, of the same colour that the Almadel is of, and the other of his furniture, it being in the form of a basin, and put therein a few hot ashes or coals, but not too much, lest it should melt the wax of the Almadel, and put therein three little grains of mastic in powder, so that it fumeth, and the smell may go upwards through the holes of the Almadel, when it is under it, and as soon as the angel smells it he beginneth to speak with a low voice, asking what your desire is and why you have called the princes and governers of his Altitude. Then you must answer him, saying, I desire that all my requests may be granted, and what I pray for may be accomplished, for your office maketh appear and declareth that such is to be fulfilled by you if it pleases God, &c, adding further the particulars of your requests, praying with sincerity and humility for what is lawful and just, and that you shalt indeed obtain from him.

But if he doth not appear presently, you must then take the golden seal, and make with it three or four marks upon the candles, by which means the angel will presently appear as aforesaid, and when the angel departeth he will fill the whole place with a sweet and pleasant smell, which will be smelt a long time.

Note the golden seal will serve, and is to be used in the operation of all the altitudes. The colour of the Almadel belonging to the first chora is lily white; to the second chora a perfect red rose colour; the third chora is to be a green mixt with a white silver colour; the fourth chora is to be a black mixt with a little green of a sad colour.

Of the Second Chora or Altitude

Note that all the other three altitudes, with their signs and princes have power over goods and riches, and can make any man rich or poor, and as the first Chora giveth increase and maketh fruitful, so to these giveth decrease and barrenness, &c.

And if any have a desire to operate in any of the other three Choras or Altitudes, they must do it on Sundays in the manner as above is shewed, but do not pray for anything that is contrary to the nature of their office, or against God and his laws, but what God giveth according to the course of nature, that you may desire and obtain.

All the furniture that is to be used is to be of the same colour as the

Almadel is of, and the princes of this Second Chora are named as followeth: Alphariza, Genon, Geror, Armon, Gereinin.

When you operate, kneel before the Almadel with clothes of the same colour in a closet hung with the same colours also, for the holy apparation will be of the same colour. And when he is appeared, put the earthen bason under the Almadel with fire and hot ashes and three grains of mastic in powder, to fume as above written, and when the angel smelleth the perfume, he turneth his face towards you, asking the exorcist with a low voice why he called the princes of this Chora or Altitude. Then you must answer as before, saying: I desire that my request may be granted, and the contents thereof may be accomplished, for your offices make appear and declare that such is to be done by you if it please God, &c. You must not be fearful but speak humbly, saying: I recommend myself wholly into your office, and I pray unto your princes of this Altitude that I may enjoy and obtain all things according to my wishes and desires, &c. You may further express your mind in all particulars in your prayers. Do the like in the two other Choras that follow.

The angel of this second Altitude appeareth in the form of a young child with clothes of satin and of a red rose colour, having a crown of red gilly flowers upon his head, his face looking upwards to heaven; and is of a red colour and is compassed round about with a bright splendour, as the beams of the Sun. And before he departeth he speaks to the exorcist saying: I am your friend and brother. And he illumineth the air round above with splendour, and he leaveth a pleasant smell, which lasteth a long time, &c.

Of the Third Chora or Altitude

In this Chora you are to do in all things as you are before directed in the other two. The angels of this Altitude are named as followeth:

Eliphamasai, Gelomiros, Gedobonal, Saranana, and Elomnia. They appear in the form of children or little women dressed in green and silver colours, very delightful to behold, and a crown of bay leaves, beset with flowers of white and green colours upon their heads. And they seem to look a little downwards with their faces, &c. They speak as the others do to the exorcist, and leave a mighty, sweet perfume behind them, &c.

Of the Fourth Chora or Altitude

In this Chora you must do as in the others, and the angels of this Chora are called Barchiel, Gediel, Gabiel, Deliel and Captiel. These appear in the form of little men or boys with clothes of a black colour, mixed with a dark green, and in their hands they hold a bird which is naked, and their heads are bear, only it is compassed round and beset with ivy and berries. They are all very beautiful and comely and are compassed round with a bright shining of divers colours. They leave a sweet smell behind them also, but it differeth from the others somewhat.

Of the Proper Times for Invoking These Angels

Note there are twelve princes ruling besides those in the four Altitudes, and they distribute their office amongst themselves, every one ruling thirty days, or thereabouts, every year. Now it will be in vain to call any of those angels unless it be those that then governeth, for every Chora or Altitude hath its limited time according to the twelve signs of the Zodiac, and in what sign the Sun is in, that angel or those angels that belong to that sign have the government. As, for example, suppose I would call the two first of those five that belong to the first Chora. Then choose the first Sunday on March, that is, after the Sun is entered Aries, and then I make my experiment. And so do the like if you will the next Sunday after again. But if you will call the two second that belong to the first Chora, then you must take the Sundays that are in April, after the Sun is entered Taurus.

But if you call the last of the five, then you must take those Sundays that are in May, after the Sun is entered Gemini, to make your experiment in: do the like in the other Altitudes, for they have all one way of working. But the Altitudes have a name formed severally in the substance of heaven even as a character, for when the angels hear the names of God that are attributed to them they hear it by the vertue of that character. Therefore it is in vain to call any spirit or angel unless you know what names of God to call them by. Therefore observe the form of this following conjuration or invocation.

The Invocation for to Call Forth Any of the Foresaid Angels

O thou great, mighty, and blessed angel of God N, who ruleth as the chief and first governing angel in the first Chora or Altitude in the East, under the great prince of the East whom you obey, and who is set over you as king by the divine power of God, ADONAI, HELOMI, PINE, who is the distributer and disposer of all things holy in Heaven, Earth, and Hell, I the servant of that God ADONAI, HELOMI, PINE, which you obey, do invocate, conjure and entreat thee N, that thou forthwith appeareth. And by the vertue and power of the same God, ADONAI, HELOMI, PINE, I do command thee forth by him whom you do obey and who is set over you as king by the divine power of God, that you forthwith descend from thy order or place of abode to come into me, and show thyself plainly and visibly here before me in this crystal stone, in thy own and proper shape and glory, speaking with a voice intelligible unto my understanding.

O thou mighty and blessed angel N, who art by the power of God ordained to govern all vegetables and animals, and causeth them and all other creatures of God to spring, increase and bring forth according to their kinds and natures, I the servant of the same your God, do entreat and humbly beseech thee to come and show unto me all things that I shall desire of thee, so far as in office you can, or be capable to perform, if God permit to the same.

O thou servant of mercy N, I entreat thee and humbly beseech thee, in and by these three names of your true God, ADONAI, HELOMI, PINE, and do constrain thee in and by this powerful name ANA-BONA, that thou forthwith appeareth visibly and plainly in thy own proper shape and glory, in and through this crystal stone, that I may visibly see thee, and audibly hear thee speak unto me, that I may have thy blessed and glorious angelic assistance, familiar friendship and con-stant society, communication and instruction, both now and at all other times, to inform and rightly instruct me in my ignorance and depraved intellect, judgement and understanding; and to assist me both herein, and in all other truths, else what the Almighty Adonai, the king of kings, the giver of all good gifts, shall in his bountiful and fatherly mercy be graceously pleased to bestow upon me, Therefore O thou blessed angel N. be friendly unto me, and do for me so far as God hath given you power in office to perform, whereunto I move you in power and presence to appear that I may sing with his holy angels: O Mappa-la-man! Hallelujah! Amen.

Note this invocation is to be altered according to the Altitude and angel you wish to call forth.

When he is appeared, give him or them a kind entertainment, and then ask what is just and lawful, and that which is proper and suitable to his office, and you shall obtain it.

SO ENDETH THE BOOK
ARS ALMADEL SALOMONIS

Appendix 6: Excerpt from Sloane 3849

Manner of Proceding in order to discover in the Crystall

Sic signum sancte Sanctis in fronte puery sic decendo In nomina pateris et filij et spiritus sancti amen dicat % paternoster / deinde istos spactanas o pater animary sequentes, viz t

Deus miserator[1] nostery et benedicat nobis illiminet vultum suum super nos et miseratas nostery ut Cognosamos in tarra viam tuam in omnibus gentibus salutarry tuum. Conficantur tibi populi deus Conficanter tibi populi omnes Litenter et exultent gentes quoniam iudicas populos iniquitate et gentes interra deriges Conficianter tibi populi deus Conficianter tibi populi omnes Terra dedit fractum suam

B
Benedicat nos deus deus noster
benedicat nos deua et metuante
eum omnes fines terra.
Gloria patri et fillio et Spiritu Sancto
Sicut erat in prinsipio et
secula seculorum amen
D
Deus[2] in nomine tuo salum me fac
et in vertute tua iudica me
D
Deus exoude orationem meum
auribus percipe verba oris mei

[f2v]

Quoniam aliena insurrexerunt aodversum me et fortes
que siderant animam meam et non proposuerunt deum ante

---

1   Psalm 67.

2   Psalm 54.

conspectum sum
Exe enim deus adiuuat me
et dominus susseptor est anime me
Avarta mala enemisis meis
et in veritate tua dispee illos
voluntary sacrificabo tibi et Confitebor
nomine tuo domine quoniam bonum est.
Quoniam Ex omni tribulatione eripaeisti me
et super enimicos meos dispecsit oculis meis
Glorie patrie

Misereri[3] mei deus et secundum
magnam miserecordiam tuam

Et secundum multitadinem meserationem
tuarum deld in equitatem meam
dE (?)
Amptus Sana me abiniquitate mea
et apeccato mea mandame
Quoniam iniquitatem meame ego cognosco
et pecatum meam contra me est semper
Tibibi soli pecam et malim corum te fesient nist
insermonibus tuis et vnitas cumim dicaris
Exe emam iniquitatibus conseptus suam
et in pecatis conceptis me mater mea

Exe (?) enimam veritatatem delexisti in terta   [f3r]
et occulta sapientia manistastati mighi
Asparges me domine isopo et mundaborir

---

3   Psalm 51.

haenabis me et semper muem dealdabor
Auditeiome dabis gouldinam et litia
et extutabunt essa humilitata
Cormandoem cre in me deus
et spiritum nona in viseribus meis
Me exrpissius mea sacie tua et
Scriptum sanctum tuamene anseris ame
Pedde mighi leticiam salataris tui
et speritum principialis confirma me
Docebo iniquos viuas tuas
et impije adte conuertantur
Libera mede sangunibus deus deus salutis
me et exultabit lingua me Iusticiam tuam
Domine labie me aparies
et os meum ani**abit landem tuam
Quoniam voluises sacri fissiam dedissem
vtique holo castis non delectabris
Sacrifitiam deo spritus contribulates
cor Contrat et humilitatem deus non dispities
Benin que sac domine in bona voluntate tua sion
vt edificanter mari Jeruselem

[f3v]   tunce acceptabis satis ficium iustisia obligationes
et holocasta tunck imponetsuper altera
tuim vertulos Amen. *******
O Dominee Jesu cristie rex gloria mitte mihie
trese angelos bono / ex parte tua dextra viz
ancor annasor anelose qui dicante et ofendantie
mihie veritatem sine falsetate et falatia de
omnibus rebus quas interagabo domine Jesue
cristi creator celie et tarra qui totam mundinum (?)

secistie exmihelo sac quod appariante isti angeli
boni prinsipialis palem puero / w: w: / exerdom (?)
nostrum Jesum cristium conceptus de spiritue
sancto vergine &c./
Sicat tues verus deus et homo mitte mihie
tres angelos bonos palem aparire ista cristalo
viz / Anser / annasor / Analos / admisu istris puerie
/ W: W: / per iste sacritissima nomina dei eloy tetera-
grammaton Saboth Alpha et omega principium
et finis expediatris vos angely deij per sanctam
mariam matrem domine nostri Jesu Cristy et per
nomen ordenes angelorum Cherubin Saraphin
tronos dominationes potestatis et principialis
et pervirtutem archangelius michalis gabrialis

qui non cestante clannary ante tronam dei semper   [f4r]
cantatis Sanctus Sanctus Sanctus dominus Deus
saboth quiest quierit et quiventurus / omnes reliquos qui
sunti? in est in decare mandum et pur puer celo et tarra
et parlac quod dominus noster Jesus cristus lactabit
ex manus beate maryu vergenis quanddo verus puer
erat elle in hac mundo et per vestem communam qua in dutus (?)
est Jesus et pervingen tam dequo sancta maria mageline
vnxit pedes Iesus et extarat eos calpilis cupitus suis
quando palem et sine mora comperiatis ad visma istius
puery : N: / N: / ista cristalo *******************
**(?) oher it will appeare as it weare a child in the Cristall
if hee doe not appeare begine againe and if hee had
apeared then spake to the first Angeli dei beni
venistie in nomini pateris et fillij et spiritus sanctus
pillam intentionem quam habuit dominus deus

noster Jesus Christus minente (?) quando deposuit
luisiseri mundecelom putrem serioris et eligit vos
probelantisiones angelis.
Then Cale for the second as you due for the first
so proside and begin againe vntill you haue them all
three and then say to the second Angell
Angeli dei beni venistris in nomine pateris et fillij et

[f4v]

Spiritus sancti per verginalem materis domine
nosteri Iesu Christie et per vergini tatem Johannes
baptisti et per capitutenis *
proceed to the theerd
Angeli dei beni venistris in nomine pateris et feillij et spiritis sancti
pre nerentiam passiones domine nostri Jesu Christi et per renerentiam
sacrimenti illiaris que dominus noster Jesus cristus fecit in send sua et
dedit desiputis suis dictus hoc est corpus meum hoc cessat * *

Then say this exortation ouer the cristall folowinge and mat this +
synd.

Quose Angeli + rogo vos presipio vobis vos exorsiso peromina prin-
cipialibe nomina qui noliset homin~ loqui nisi sp'us sancti + et per
reuerentiam sacrementy pasio dei nosteri Jesus Cristi et reuerentunam
sacromentie alteris q'd (?) deus noster Jesus cristus fecit cena sua et
dedid dicipulis suis dicence hoc este corpus meum q'd (?) mostratis
mihe sine salcitate vel fallatia petita et loquisita et petenta et reuerenda

Theise exortations you must repeate and let the child name them by
there names sainge ancor anasor anelos shew mee the persons and the
aparell of them that hath such a mans mony to this childe and the will
declare.

[f5r]

the pson or persons and the apparell of them that had such a mans
money [struck out: to this child] and if the Come not the first day folow

still to the Chilld untill you may haue a sight of them for the will apeare personalie as the to be knowne and the will declare how much of the mony is spent and how much is unspente.

And the feror day the better and let the child sit with his face to ward the sune lookinge in the cristal and euer aske him what hee seeth as you Reade

Trantiatis angeli dei et lenam vbi deus nostr Jesus Christus vos ordinauit et quoties cunque invocauero esto mihi parietis et ad measm interrogationem et mandatum est mihi quoties cunque sine mora veni- atis, In nomine patris et fillij et spiritus Sankti Amen +

Maim + fan + Abagarus +
Abrinon +

[5v, 6r are blank]

[6v]

Bibliography

Abano, Peter de. *Heptameron: or Magical Elements*. London, 1655.

Agrippa, Henry Cornelius. *De occulta philosophis Libri Tres*. Leiden: E. J. Brill, 1992, English translation by Robert Turner, published as *Three Books of Occult Philosophy*, London, 1651.

———. *The Fourth Book of Occult Philosophy*. Translated by Robert Turner. London, 1655.

Anon. *Lemegeton, or, the Lesser Key of Solomon,* manuscripts in the British Library: Harley 6483, Sloane 2731 (incomplete), Sloane 3825.

Anon. *Tractatus Varii Magici,* Sloane 3849.

Arbatel. *De Magia Veterum*. Basel, 1575. English translation by Robert Turner, published as Arbatel, *Of Magic,* London, 1655.

Barrett, Francis. *The Magus*. London, 1801. Reprint York Beach, ME: Samuel Weiser, 2000.

Brahe, Tycho. *The Magical Calendar,* 1582. Reprint *Magnum Opus Hermetic Sourceworks,* Edinburgh, 1979.

Bruno, Giordano. *De magia,* in *Jordani Bruni Nolani Opera latine conscripta*. Ed. Tocco. Neapoli, 1879–91. English translation in Robert De Lucca, Richard J. Blackwell, and Alfonso Ingegno, *Giordano Bruno, Cause, Principle and Unity: And Essays on Magic*. Cambridge: Cambridge University Press, 1998.

Calder, I. R. F. *John Dee Studied as an English Neoplatonist,* 2 vols. Ph. D. diss. The Warberg Institute, London University, 1952.

Charlesworth, James H. *The Old Testament Pseudepigrapha.* New York: Doubleday, 1983.

Clulee, Nicholas H. *John Dee's Natural Philosophy—between science and religion.* London and New York: Routledge, 1988.

Couliano, Ioan P. *Eros and Magic in the Renaissance.* Chicago: University of Chicago Press, 1987.

Davidson, Gustav. *A Dictionary of Angels Including the Fallen Angels.* New York: The Free Press, 1967.

Dee, Dr. John. *General and Rare Memorials pertayning to the Perfect Arte of Navigation.* London, 1577.

Dee, Dr. John and Edward Kelly. *Liber Mysteriorum Sextus et Sanctus.* 1583, manuscripts in the British Library: Sloane 3189 (original in Kelly's handwriting), Sloane 2599.

———. *Mysteriorum Libri Quinque,* 1581–1583. Sloane 3188 (original in Dee's handwriting), Sloane 3677 (copy by E. Ashmole).

———. *A True & Faithful Relation . . . between Dr. John Dee... and some Spirits,* Edited by Meric Casaubon. London, 1659.

———. *The Heptarchia Mystica of John Dee.* Introduced and annotated by Robert Turner. Edinburgh: Magnum Opus Hermetic Sourceworks, 1983.

French, Peter J. *John Dee: The World of an Elizabethan Magus.* London: Routledge and Kegan Paul, 1972.

Gollancz, Hermann. *Sepher Maphteah Shelomoh.* London: Oxford University Press, 1914.

Halliwell, James O., ed. *The Private Diary of Dr. John Dee.* London: Camden Society Publications, 1842. Reprint: New York: AMS Press, 1968.

Hay, George, ed. *The Necronomicon.* Jersey: Neville Spearman, 1978.

Honorius of Thebes. *Liber Juratus, or the Sworne Book of Honorius* (13th century?). Manuscripts in the British Library, Royal 17Axlii, Sloane 313, 3849 (excerpts), 3854, 3885.

Josten, C. H. *Elias Ashmole (1617–1692): His Autobiographical and Historical Notes, His Correspondence, and Other Contemporary Sources Relating to His Life and Work.* Oxford: Clarendon Press, 1966.

————, trans. *Monas Hieroglyphica.* AMBIX, XII, 1964, 84–221.

Katz, David S. *Philo-Semitism and the Readmission of the Jews to England.* Oxford: Clarendon Press, 1982.

Kieckhefer, Richard. *Forbidden Rites: A Necromancer's Manual of the Fifteenth Century.* University Park, PA: Pennsylvania State University Press, 1997.

Kircher, Athanasius. *Oedipus Aegyptiacus,* 4 vols. Rome, 1652–1654.

Laycock, Donald. *The Complete Enochian Dictionary, a Dictionary of the Angelical Language as Revealed to Dr. John Dee and Edward Kelley.* London: Askin Publishers, 1978.

Lilly, William. *Worlds Catastrophe.* London, 1647.

Moody, Raymond A. *Scrying—The Art of Female Divination.* Marietta: R. Bemis Publishing, Ltd., 1995.

Pickering, Chris. "The Scryers of John Dee," *Hermetic Journal* 32, 1986, pp. 9–14.

Postel, Guillaume. *De originibus.* Basel: Ioannem Oporinum, 1553.

Peterson, Joseph H., ed., *The Lesser Key of Solomon.* York Beach, ME: Weiser Books, 2001.

Reeds, Jim, "John Dee and the Magic Tables in the *Book of Soyga,*" www.research.att.com/~reeds/soyga.html; to appear in a forthcoming book, *John Dee: Interdisciplinary essays in English Renaissance Thought,* Kluwer of Amsterdam (due to publish 2002).

Regardie, Francis Israel, ed. *The Golden Dawn,* 4 vols., 1937–1940. St. Paul, MN: Llewellyn Publications, 1971.

Roberts, Julian, and Andrew G. Watson. *John Dee's Library Catalogue.* London: The Bibliographical Society, 1990.

Scot, Reginald. *The Discoverie of Witchcraft.* London, 1584.

Sherman, William H. *John Dee, the Politics of Reading and Writing in the English Renaissance.* Amherst: University of Massachusetts Press, 1995.

Tart, Charles. *Body Mind Spirit.* Charlottesville: Hampton Roads, 1997.

Trithemius, Johannes. *Book of Secret Things, and Doctrine of Spirits,* in Francis Barrett's *The Magus,* London, 1801, p. 135bis.

———. *De Septem Secundeis.* Translation in William Lilly, *Worlds Catastrophe.* London, 1647.

Turner, Robert, trans. *Ars Notoria,* London, 1657.

Whitby, C. L. *John Dee's Actions with Spirits.* 2 vols. New York: Garland, 1991.

Wilson, Colin. *Alien Dawn, An Investigation into the Contact Experience.* New York: Fromm International, 1998.

———. "Introduction to the Necronomicon," *Gnostica,* 48, Nov. 1978, p. 62.

Yates, Frances Amelia. *The Rosicrucian Enlightenment.* Boulder, CO: Shambhala, 1972.

———. *The Art of Memory.* Chicago: University of Chicago Press, 1966.

INDEX

Printed in the United States
124794LV00003B/40/P

Made in the USA
Middletown, DE
26 May 2021